ENGLISH LANGUAGE PROFICIENCY ASSESSMENTS FOR YOUNG LEARNERS

English Language Proficiency Assessments for Young Learners provides both theoretical and empirical information about assessing the English language proficiency of young learners. Using large-scale standardized English language proficiency assessments developed for international or U.S. contexts as concrete examples, this volume illustrates rigorous processes of developing and validating assessments with considerations of young learners' unique characteristics. In this volume, young learners are defined as school-age children from approximately 5 to 13 years old, learning English as a foreign language (EFL) or a second language (ESL). This volume also discusses innovative ways to assess young learners' English language abilities based on empirical studies, with each chapter offering stimulating ideas for future research and development work to improve English language assessment practices with young learners. *English Language Proficiency Assessments for Young Learners* is a useful resource for students, test developers, educators, and researchers in the area of language testing and assessment.

Mikyung Kim Wolf is Senior Research Scientist at the Center for English Language Learning and Assessment Research at Educational Testing Service.

Yuko Goto Butler is Associate Professor in the Educational Linguistics Division and Director of Teaching English to Speakers of Other Languages (TESOL) at the University of Pennsylvania Graduate School of Education, U.S.A.

Innovations in Language Learning and Assessment at ETS
Series Editors: John M. Norris, James E. Purpura, Steven John Ross, and Xiaoming Xi

The goal of the *Innovations in Language Learning and Assessment at ETS* series is to publish books that document the development and validation of language assessments and that explore broader innovations related to language teaching and learning. Compiled by leading researchers, then reviewed by the series editorial board, volumes in the series provide cutting-edge research and development related to language learning and assessment in a format that is easily accessible to language teachers and applied linguists as well as testing professionals and measurement specialists.

Volume 1: *Second Language Educational Experiences for Adult Learners*
John M. Norris, John McE. Davis, and Veronika Timpe-Laughlin

Volume 2: *English Language Proficiency Assessments for Young Learners*
Mikyung Kim Wolf and Yuko Goto Butler

ENGLISH LANGUAGE PROFICIENCY ASSESSMENTS FOR YOUNG LEARNERS

Edited by
Mikyung Kim Wolf
Yuko Goto Butler

First published 2017
by Routledge
711 Third Avenue, New York, NY 10017

and by Routledge
2 Park Square, Milton Park, Abingdon, Oxon, OX14 4RN

Routledge is an imprint of the Taylor & Francis Group, an informa business

© 2017 Taylor & Francis

The right of Mikyung Kim Wolf and Yuko Goto Butler to be identified as the authors of the editorial material, and of the authors for their individual chapters, has been asserted in accordance with sections 77 and 78 of the Copyright, Designs and Patents Act 1988.

All rights reserved. No part of this book may be reprinted or reproduced or utilised in any form or by any electronic, mechanical, or other means, now known or hereafter invented, including photocopying and recording, or in any information storage or retrieval system, without permission in writing from the publishers.

Chapters 3, 4 and 9 in this volume © 2016 by Educational Testing Service. Reprinted with permission of Educational Testing Service. All rights reserved.

Trademark notice: Product or corporate names may be trademarks or registered trademarks, and are used only for identification and explanation without intent to infringe.

Library of Congress Cataloging-in-Publication Data
Names: Wolf, Mikyung Kim, 1971– editor. | Butler, Yuko Goto, editor.
Title: English language proficiency assessments for young learners / edited by Mikyung Kim Wolf, Yuko Goto Butler.
Description: New York, NY : Routledge, [2017] | Series: Innovations in language learning and assessment at ETS | Includes bibliographical references and index.
Identifiers: LCCN 2016055246 | ISBN 9781138940352 (hardback) | ISBN 9781138940369 (pbk.) | ISBN 9781317379034 (epub) | ISBN 9781317379027 (mobipocket/kindle)
Subjects: LCSH: English language—Study and teaching—Ability testing. | English language—Age differences—Ability testing. | English language—Study and teaching—Ability testing. | English language—Study and teaching—Evaluation.
Classification: LCC PE1065 .E653 2017 | DDC 372.652/1076—dc23
LC record available at https://lccn.loc.gov/2016055246

ISBN: 978-1-138-94035-2 (hbk)
ISBN: 978-1-138-94036-9 (pbk)
ISBN: 978-1-315-67439-1 (ebk)

Typeset in ApexBembo
by Apex CoVantage, LLC

CONTENTS

Series Editors' Foreword   *viii*
Acknowledgements   *x*
List of Contributors   *xii*
List of Illustrations   *xiv*

Section 1
Introduction   1

1. An Overview of English Language Proficiency Assessments for Young Learners   3
   Mikyung Kim Wolf and Yuko Goto Butler

Section 2
Theoretical Basis and Assessment Frameworks   23

2. Theoretical and Developmental Issues to Consider in the Assessment of Young Learners' English Language Proficiency   25
   Alison L. Bailey

3. Designing the TOEFL® Primary™ Tests   41
   Yeonsuk Cho, Mitch Ginsburgh, Rick Morgan, Brad Moulder, Xiaoming Xi, and Maurice Cogan Hauck

4. TOEFL Junior® Design Framework   59
   Youngsoon So, Mikyung Kim Wolf, Maurice Cogan Hauck, Pamela Mollaun, Paul Rybinski, Daniel Tumposky, and Lin Wang

5 Designing Task Types for English Language Proficiency Assessments for K–12 English Learners in the U.S.   79
Maurice Cogan Hauck, Emilie Pooler, Mikyung Kim Wolf, Alexis A. Lopez, and David P. Anderson

Section 3
Empirical Studies for Validity Evidence   97

6 A Field Test Study for the TOEFL® Primary™ Reading and Listening Tests   99
Jiyun Zu, Bradley Moulder, and Rick Morgan

7 Strategies Used by Young English Learners in an Assessment Context   118
Lin Gu and Youngsoon So

8 Using the Common European Framework of Reference to Facilitate Score Interpretations for Young Learners' English Language Proficiency Assessments   136
Spiros Papageorgiou and Patricia Baron

9 Making a Validity Argument for Using the TOEFL Junior® Standard Test as a Measure of Progress for Young English Language Learners   153
Lin Gu, J. R. Lockwood, and Donald E. Powers

10 Comparing the Performance of Young English Language Learners and Native English Speakers on Speaking Assessment Tasks   171
Mikyung Kim Wolf, Alexis A. Lopez, Saerhim Oh, and Fred S. Tsutagawa

Section 4
Future Assessments and Innovations for Young Learners   191

11 Considering Young Learners' Characteristics in Developing a Diagnostic Assessment Intervention   193
Eunice Eunhee Jang, Megan Vincett, Edith H. van der Boom, Clarissa Lau, and Yehbeen Yang

12 Computerized Dynamic Assessments for
Young Language Learners 214
Matthew E. Poehner, Jie Zhang, and Xiaofei Lu

13 Measuring 21st-Century Reading Comprehension Through
Scenario-Based Assessments 234
*Jane R. Shore, Mikyung Kim Wolf, Tenaha O'Reilly, and
John P. Sabatini*

Section 5
Conclusion   253

14 Challenges and Future Directions for Young Learners' English
Language Assessments and Validity Research 255
Yuko Goto Butler

Subject Index   *275*

SERIES EDITORS' FOREWORD

The second volume in the *Innovations* series is an edited book by Mikyung Kim Wolf and Yuko Goto Butler titled *English Language Proficiency Assessments for Young Learners*. One of the first collections of its kind, this book provides a comprehensive overview of issues related to assessing the language proficiency of young English second and foreign language learners. This population of test takers differs in critical ways from adults, as do the purposes for assessing their language proficiency, and these differences have important implications for the design of meaningful, useful, and ethical language assessments. This volume therefore covers a host of issues that should be of central interest to the many stakeholders in young language learner assessment, including not only test developers, but also researchers, administrators, practitioners, and policy makers.

The chapters are divided into five sections related to designing, validating, and innovating young language learner assessments. Section one provides a comprehensive introduction to the volume, including a critical overview of and justification for assessing the English language proficiency of young learners. The next section then begins with an overview of key characteristics of young learners, providing an essential foundation for anyone interested in developing or using language assessments with this population. Subsequently, the conceptual and design frameworks for two recent ETS assessments—the *TOEFL® Primary*™ and *TOEFL Junior®* tests—are reported, offering readers unique insights into how constructs, test taker characteristics, and assessment purposes are built into the conceptual frameworks underlying these large-scale, standardized assessments. A final chapter of this section highlights design considerations for tasks to be used in U.S. assessments of K–12, or school-age, English language learners' proficiency development.

Section three shifts focus to a variety of empirical approaches utilized in validating young language learner assessments. These chapters summarize and illustrate some of the extensive research conducted at ETS for the *TOEFL Primary* and *TOEFL Junior* tests, including: field-testing of reading and listening items, exploration of young learners' test-taking strategies, comparisons with native speaker benchmarks, examining learning progress, and mapping of young learner assessments to the Common European Framework of Reference for enhancing score reporting and interpretation. Collectively, these chapters not only provide an indication of the substantial validity evidence supporting the use of ETS' young learner assessments, but they also serve as a guide for other test developers and researchers engaging in validation efforts for similar assessments.

A fourth major section of the book is devoted to research on innovative assessment design related to the promotion of learning among young learners, including chapters on diagnostic assessment, computerized dynamic assessment, and scenario-based assessment of reading comprehension. These chapters highlight and explore the critical inter-relationships between assessment, teaching, and learning—especially for assessments that are used with young learners—a point that is taken up as well in the concluding chapter by Butler. The final section offers important insights into future challenges and opportunities in assessing young learners' English proficiency, with an emphasis on guiding validity research into the future.

The publication of this volume marks an important milestone in the assessment of young language learners' proficiency. It demonstrates how rigorous procedures for conceptualizing, designing, and validating assessments—a hallmark of ETS language assessments—can be applied to emerging needs for assessment, primarily in educational sectors. It emphasizes the particular care that must be taken in using assessments with certain types of test takers. And it identifies critical challenges for assessment developers and others, as new demands for innovation arise and as tests are put into practice. *English Language Proficiency Assessments for Young Learners* is a most welcome addition to this book series, as it provides much-needed guidance and inevitably spurs much-needed attention to these and related issues.

ACKNOWLEDGEMENTS

We would like to acknowledge a number of people who have contributed to the publication of this volume. First of all, we wish to acknowledge and thank the series editors, John Norris, Jim Purpura, Steve Ross, and Xiaoming Xi, for providing us the opportunity to produce this volume on assessing young learners' English language proficiency. They also dedicated their time to offer invaluable feedback on earlier drafts of the individual chapters. Their constructive suggestions and encouragement were of great help to us. We also thank the publisher for its commitment and flexibility throughout the process of producing this volume.

Needless to say, we are tremendously grateful to the authors of the chapters for making it possible to create this volume. We were fortunate to collaborate with these authors who willingly agreed to contribute to this volume, bringing various perspectives from their extensive experience and knowledge around young language learners and assessment. We greatly appreciated the authors' collegial efforts to address all the feedback they received while undertaking multiple reviews and revisions of their chapters. Additionally, we thank other publishers and some authors for allowing us to reproduce their chapters with modifications to fit into this volume.

We also wish to acknowledge additional reviewers of the chapters. Besides the series editors' review and our own, the majority of the chapters received review and feedback through the ETS peer-review system. We express our deep gratitude to those reviewers and ETS technical review associate editors, Don Powers and Brent Bridgeman, for reviewing some of the chapters in this volume and providing their helpful comments and suggestions. We are also grateful to Ian Blood and Christopher Hamill for their editorial assistance with some chapters. Any errors in this volume remain ours.

Finally, I (Mikyung) would like to acknowledge my sons, Daniel and Ryan Wolf, who inspire me every day by showing how they differ in the ways they learn their first, heritage, and foreign languages as young language learners. We would also like to thank our spouses (Tom Wolf and Donald Butler) for their unyielding support of our work.

Mikyung Kim Wolf
Yuko Goto Butler

CONTRIBUTORS

David P. Anderson, Educational Testing Service, U.S.A.
Alison L. Bailey, University of California, Los Angeles (UCLA), U.S.A.
Patricia Baron, Educational Testing Service, U.S.A.
Yuko Goto Butler, University of Pennsylvania, U.S.A.
Yeonsuk Cho, Educational Testing Service, U.S.A.
Mitch Ginsburgh, Educational Testing Service, U.S.A.
Lin Gu, Educational Testing Service, U.S.A.
Maurice Cogan Hauck, Educational Testing Service, U.S.A.
Eunice Eunhee Jang, Ontario Institute for Studies in Education, University of Toronto, Canada
Clarissa Lau, Ontario Institute for Studies in Education, University of Toronto, Canada
J. R. Lockwood, Educational Testing Service, U.S.A.
Alexis A. Lopez, Educational Testing Service, U.S.A.
Xiaofei Lu, Pennsylvania State University, U.S.A.
Pamela Mollaun, Educational Testing Service, U.S.A.
Rick Morgan, Educational Testing Service, U.S.A.
Brad Moulder, Educational Testing Service, U.S.A.
Saerhim Oh, Teachers College, Columbia University, U.S.A.
Tenaha O'Reilly, Educational Testing Service, U.S.A.
Spiros Papageorgiou, Educational Testing Service, U.S.A.
Matthew E. Poehner, Pennsylvania State University, U.S.A.
Emilie Pooler, Educational Testing Service, U.S.A.
Donald E. Powers, Educational Testing Service, U.S.A.
Paul Rybinski, Educational Testing Service, U.S.A.

John P. Sabatini, Educational Testing Service, U.S.A.
Jane R. Shore, Educational Testing Service, U.S.A.
Youngsoon So, Seoul National University, South Korea
Fred S. Tsutagawa, Teachers College, Columbia University, U.S.A.
Daniel Tumposky, Educational Testing Service, U.S.A.
Edith H. van der Boom, Ontario Institute for Studies in Education, University of Toronto, Canada
Megan Vincett, Ontario Institute for Studies in Education, University of Toronto, Canada
Lin Wang, Educational Testing Service, U.S.A.
Mikyung Kim Wolf, Educational Testing Service, U.S.A.
Xiaoming Xi, Educational Testing Service, U.S.A.
Yehbeen Yang, Ontario Institute for Studies in Education, University of Toronto, Canada
Jie Zhang, University of Oklahoma, U.S.A.
Jiyun Zu, Educational Testing Service, U.S.A.

ILLUSTRATIONS

Figures

3.1	The Construct of Reading	46
3.2	The Construct of Listening	47
3.3	The Construct of Speaking	47
4.1	Defining the Target Language Use (TLU) Domain of the *TOEFL Junior* Test	64
4.2	An Example of Linking a Target Language Use (TLU) Task to an Assessment Task	66
6.1	Frequency Distributions of the Estimated Reading and Listening Abilities	109
6.2	Test Characteristic Curves for the Four Operational Base Forms	114
9.1	Average Total Scale Score by Test Administration for Students Who Took the Test Two, Three, Four, or Five Total Times	158
9.2	Histogram of Interval for the Analysis Sample	159
9.3	Smoothed Trends of Initial Score (Solid Line) and Second Administration Score (Dashed Line) as a Function of Interval, Separately for Each Skill Area and the Total	161
9.4	Scatterplot of Total Score Gain Versus Interval Where Both Are Centered Around Their Respective Country Means	164
10.1	Sample Screenshots of Scenario-based Prototype Tasks for Grades K–2	176
10.2	A Screenshot of the Playground Task for Grades K–2	176
10.3	Sample Screenshots From the Mixing Paint (Top) and Melting Ice (Bottom) Tasks	177
10.4	The Average Scores for the Holistic and Analytic Dimensions of the Playground and Mixing Paint Tasks, Grade K	181

10.5	The Average Scores for the Holistic and Analytic Dimensions of the Playground and Melting Ice Tasks, Grades 1–2	181
10.6	Visual Representation of the Common Error Types in Students' Responses	184
11.1	Young Learner Characteristics	196
12.1	Sample Reading Text and Item From Chinese C-DA Test	223
13.1	ELFA Subconstructs and Subskills	241
13.2	ELFA Example Item Directions	243
13.3	Task Sequencing in ELFA	244
13.4	Task Sample: Warm-up	244
13.5	Task Sample: Getting a Main Idea	245
13.6	Task Sample: Comparing and Integrating Multiple Sources of Information	246

Tables

3.1	Reading Test Structure	51
3.2	Listening Test Structure	52
3.3	Speaking Test Structure	54
4.1	Overall Structure of the *TOEFL Junior* tests	67
4.2	Scores on the *TOEFL Junior* Standard Score Report	71
4.3	Scores on the *TOEFL Junior* Comprehensive Score Report	72
5.1	Layers of Evidence-Centered Design and Key Features for Assessment Developers	83
5.2	Language on Scaffolding in ELPA21 ELP Standards and California ELD Standards	90
6.1	Reading Field Test Forms	102
6.2	Listening Field Test Forms	103
6.3	Sample Composition of the Field Test Sample by Region	105
6.4	Sample Size, Mean, and Standard Deviation of Raw Scores for Field Test Forms	106
6.5	Summary Statistics of the p^+ and r-biserial for Reading and Listening Items	107
6.6	Summary Statistics of the IRT Calibrated Item Pools for the Reading and Listening Tests	108
6.7	Means and Standard Deviations of the Latent Ability Estimates by Country	110
6.8	*TOEFL Primary* Reading Scale Score, Band Levels, and CEFR Levels	112
6.9	Summary of IRT Parameters for the Four Operational Base Forms	113
6.10	Reliability and Standard Error of Measurement of Operational Forms	115
7.1	Demographic Information of the Participants Sorted by Proficiency	122
7.2	Summary of the Listening and Reading Items	123

7.3	Strategies and Counts of Strategy Use	125
7.4	Frequency and Normalized Frequency of Reported Strategies	132
8.1	*TOEFL Junior* Section Scores at Different CEFR Levels	143
8.2	*TOEFL Junior* Comprehensive Overall Performance Levels and Descriptors With CEFR Profile Summary	144
8.3	*TOEFL Junior* Standard Overall Performance Levels and Descriptors With CEFR Profile Summary	145
8.4	*TOEFL Primary* Modified Descriptors and Original CEFR Descriptors	146
8.5	*TOEFL Primary* Score Ranges at Different CEFR Levels	147
9.1	Summary of Distribution of Number of Test Administrations in the Repeater Analysis Sample	156
9.2	Mean First and Second Scores and Mean Gain for Each Outcome by Interval	160
9.3	Summary of Results of Model 1 of the Effect of Interval on Gains	165
9.4	Summary of Results of Model 2 of the Effect of Interval on Gains	166
10.1	The Number of Study Participants	175
10.2	Analytic Scoring Rubric	178
10.3	Error Analysis Categories and Definitions	179
10.4	Performance on the School Day Items	180
10.5	Sample Responses on the Playground Task	183
11.1	Consolidated Diagnostic Profiles of Students in School B	200
11.2	Diagnostic Assessment Intervention Activities	201
14.1	Kane et al.'s (1999) and Chapelle et al.'s (2008) Interpretative Arguments	260

SECTION 1
Introduction

1
AN OVERVIEW OF ENGLISH LANGUAGE PROFICIENCY ASSESSMENTS FOR YOUNG LEARNERS

Mikyung Kim Wolf and Yuko Goto Butler

Learning English is vital for school-age children today given both the increasing globalization of academic, governmental, and economic affairs and the associated rise in the global profile of English as a lingua franca, as well as the potential for personal enrichment that comes with learning any foreign language. In countries where English is not an official language but a foreign language (EFL), English language classes have typically been included as a regular curriculum component in middle and high schools. Furthermore, some countries have begun to introduce an English course into elementary school curricula in consideration of the benefits of earlier language education (Rea-Dickins, 2000). In countries where English is a language of daily communication, formal instruction of English as a second language (ESL) in primary and secondary schools is commonly required to serve students whose first or home language is not English. Particularly in the ESL context, acquisition of English language proficiency (ELP) is essential for school-age children not only to achieve academic success but also to participate in social activities.

As the need for learning English among young learners increases, so does the need for appropriate measures for informing relevant stakeholders (e.g., learners, parents, and educators) of the learners' English proficiency levels. High-quality English language proficiency assessments (referred to as ELP assessments hereafter) can be instrumental at the institutional level in planning curriculum and instruction and placing students into appropriate programs. ELP assessments can also be useful at the individual level, supporting students, parents, and teachers to improve their English language learning and teaching. However, while there is a growing demand for standardized ELP assessments as an objective measure to gauge each student's level of English language development, extra care must be exercised in the development and use of standardized ELP assessments for young school-age children considering their unique characteristics compared to adult learners.

To address the increased need for appropriate assessment of English language proficiency in young students, this volume provides both theoretical and empirical information about the processes involved in the development of assessments targeting young school-age English language learners. For the purposes of this volume, we define the category of young English language learners as encompassing school-age children from the elementary to middle school grades (i.e., kindergarten to eighth grade in the U.S. system, ranging approximately from ages 5 to 13[1]). Certainly, there are very young children who learn English as a second language (L2, whether as ESL or EFL) before the beginning of their formal school education. However, we focus here on school-age children, as they are becoming increasingly exposed to standardized ELP assessments. Further, we include students at the upper elementary and middle school grade levels (around ages 9 to 13) as "young learners" in this volume because these students are still developing their cognitive abilities and gaining critical social/cultural experiences—a fact which needs to be carefully considered in the assessment of their English language proficiency.

This volume focuses primarily on the development and validation of large-scale, standardized ELP assessments for young students in both EFL and ESL contexts. A number of international standardized ELP assessments have been developed and are being used with young students (see Nikolov, 2016, for a discussion of global ELP assessments for young learners). In order to discuss the unique challenges and issues faced in developing ELP assessments for this population in real-world contexts, we consider research on ELP assessments developed for young students by ETS as concrete examples (e.g., the *TOEFL® Primary*™ tests, the *TOEFL Junior®* tests, and U.S. K–12 ELP assessments). Additionally, this volume includes chapters on nonstandardized assessments in order to facilitate the discussion of future research and development areas for innovative ELP assessments for young students. More details on the content and structure of this volume are provided later in this chapter.

We envision the main audience of this volume to be all those interested in the development and validation of ELP assessments for young students. Thus, this audience includes test developers, language testing researchers, and practitioners. We have compiled a collection of theoretical and empirical research papers that can serve as a useful resource to learn about the assessment development process as well as issues in need of further investigation in the assessment of young English language learners.

In this introductory chapter, we provide a brief description of young language learners' characteristics in relation to the development and use of ELP assessments. We also describe a few key aspects to consider in the development and use of standardized ELP assessments given young learners' characteristics. This background information is intended to provide context for the chapters to follow. In addition, we offer an overview of each chapter in order to help readers better understand the range of interrelated ELP assessment development and validation issues discussed throughout this volume.

Characteristics of Young Learners to Consider in the Development of English Language Proficiency Assessments

The characteristics of young learners that need to be considered in the development and use of ELP assessments may be described largely in terms of the following aspects: (1) English language learning contexts and language ability, (2) cognitive development, and (3) affective factors. We provide a brief account of each aspect to point out specific features and challenges in developing young learners' ELP assessments.

English Language Learning Contexts and Language Abilities of Young Learners

In developing an ELP assessment, the definition of the assessment construct is dependent upon the specific purposes for which the assessment will be used and target population who will take it (Bachman & Palmer, 1996, 2010). Suppose that the purpose of an ELP assessment is to measure young school-age learners' English language abilities for communication in school settings. The construct of young learners' English language abilities, then, needs to be defined with reasonable expectations about what young learners know and are able to do in English in the targeted contexts. Young learners' English language abilities and development are shaped not only by learners' personal attributes but also by the contexts in which their English language learning takes place (particularly by their formal school education) (McKay, 2006).

In both EFL and ESL contexts, national or local standards (and curricula) have been the major impetus that influences the ways in which young school-age students learn English (Butler, 2015; McKay, 2000; Nikolov, 2016). In many EFL countries, English curricula in schools place most emphasis on developing students' communicative language ability (Baldauf, Kaplan, Kamwangamalu, & Bryant, 2012; Enever, Moon, & Raman, 2009; McKay, 2000). On the other hand, studies have suggested that instruction and assessment with young students are not always carried out as intended in national curricula (e.g., Butler, 2015; Choi, 2008; Huang, 2011; Szpotowicz, 2012). For instance, in a four-year observational/interview study with EFL teachers from seven schools in Poland, Szpotowicz (2012) reported that the elementary grades (i.e., ages 7 to 10) contained very limited *interactive* oral language tasks as classroom activities. Thus, when students in the study were asked to perform interactive tasks in English during class, they were limited to using formulaic chunks or repeating memorized chunks of utterances. This finding is consistent with McKay's (2006) observation that young learners (especially in early elementary grades) tend to rely heavily on the formulaic language system and unanalyzed, memorized chunks to convey their intended meaning. In the discussion of her findings, Szpotowicz notes that teachers seemed to focus more on teaching foundational skills for students in the earlier grades. Campfield (2006) also notes that form-based instruction is prevalent in EFL contexts and that evaluating young students' oral production skills can be challenging partly due to young students' instructional settings.

In EFL contexts, young learners' target language use domains are largely bound to school contexts where major interactions take place with peers and teachers in English classrooms. These young learners' opportunities to engage in English are likely limited to textbook and instructional activities. This limited and unique exposure to the target language influences the way in which young learners develop both their proficiency as well as their background knowledge on social norms associated with the target language use.

In ESL contexts, young learners likely encounter more linguistically and cognitively complex language tasks as they are immersed in English-medium environments both inside and potentially outside of school. In K–12 school settings in the U.S., for example, ELP standards are rigorous, including the language skills that students need to meaningfully engage in various disciplinary areas (Bailey & Huang, 2011; Hakuta, Santos, & Fang, 2013; Wolf & Farnsworth, 2014). For instance, ELP standards for kindergarten contain "supporting own opinions and evaluating others' opinions in speaking and writing" (California Department of Education, 2012, p. 27).

Despite the enriched input that characterizes ESL contexts, it is important to note that young learners do not necessarily share common background knowledge and experiences (Lenski, Ehlers-Zavala, Daniel, & Sun-Irminger, 2006). In English-speaking countries, young ESL students are a highly heterogeneous group in terms of their linguistic, cultural, and educational background. When it comes to U.S. schools, recent statistics show that over 300 home languages are reported by K–12 English learners (National Clearinghouse for English Language Acquisition, 2011). The length of students' U.S. residence is varied. Some students are themselves immigrants, whereas others were born in the U.S. as children of immigrants. Students' formal schooling experience also varies; recently-arrived students may include both those with limited/interrupted formal education as well as those who have acquired academic literacy skills and content learning in their L1 (Wolf et al., 2014). Thus, even among middle schoolers, there are students who are still beginning to develop foundational English skills. The heterogeneous background of young English language learners implies that there are various contextual factors that affect these students' ELP attainment.

In both EFL and ESL contexts, younger students (i.e., in the early elementary grades) who also begin to acquire L1 literacy tend to develop comprehension skills (particularly listening skills) faster than productive skills in the L2 (Cameron, 2001; Molloy, 2015). Considering previous research findings on the transfer effect of L1 on L2 acquisition (e.g., Ellis, 2008; Gass & Selinker, 1994; Tessier, Duncan, & Paradis, 2013), young students' L1 development might influence their L2 development in oral language and literacy skills in different ways. Bialystok (2001) also illustrates that young learners at the early stages of L2 learning begin to acquire foundational skills such as phonological and decoding skills with simple vocabulary and sentences.

Considering the ways young students learn the target language, the construct of an ELP assessment for young learners should be defined differently from that of adult assessments, particularly with respect to the types and degree of ELP competence specified (Butler, 2016). Following the communicative language ability models that consist of language knowledge and strategic competence to use language communicatively to achieve specific purposes (Bachman & Palmer, 2010; Canale & Swain, 1980), young learners' language knowledge and strategic competence are continuously evolving as their cognitive maturity develops and as their range of instructional experiences expands. For instance, young learners' pragmatic and sociolinguistic knowledge (e.g., degree of formality and turn-taking conventions), as part of language knowledge, are likely different from that of adult learners (Butler & Zeng, 2014; Lenski, Ehlers-Zavala, Daniel, & Sun-Irminger, 2006; Szpotowicz, 2012). In the next section, we describe the cognitive characteristics of young learners that also have important implications for the development of ELP assessments.

Cognitive Development in Young Learners

Young learners' cognitive development is an important consideration in designing ELP assessments, as their cognitive abilities impact their L2 development as well as their performance on assessments. Cognitive domains encompass multiple areas such as visual-spatial processing, working memory, short-term memory, metalinguistic awareness, attention, abstract reasoning/concept formation, and executive functions (Barac, Bialystok, Castro, & Sanchez, 2014). One's cognitive ability develops along with the maturation of brain development. Thus, young learners' growing cognitive capacities must be carefully considered in the assessment of their ELP.

Research has shown that young learners' cognitive capacity is highly associated with their language development (e.g., Case, Kurland, & Goldberg, 1982; Garlock, Walley, & Metsala, 2001). For example, Garlock et al. (2001) found that the young learners in their study (ages 6 and 7) demonstrated a strong positive relationship between working memory and language abilities in phonological awareness, vocabulary size, and reading. Metalinguistic abilities also improved with the increased cognitive capacity. As described earlier, young learners have limitations in recognizing and extracting general structures across linguistic forms and meanings, with a tendency to use unanalyzed chunks (McKay, 2006). Thus, upper elementary or middle school students, whose cognitive and metalinguistic abilities are more developed, may acquire vocabulary and complex syntactic structures more efficiently than younger students (Bialystok, 2001; Hoff-Ginsberg, 1997).

In addition, younger students' cognitive abilities typically are not mature enough to formulate structured representations or abstract concepts (Craik &

Bialystok, 2006). Concrete objects with sensory supports are more readily accessible to younger students than abstract concepts in their L2 development and assessment. As an example of young learners' abstract conceptualization and reasoning, young learners have a "different concept of time and sequence" (Molloy, 2015, p. 4). Citing Orbach and Lamb (2007), who showed that children develop their ability to think flexibly (back and forth) about sequences of events at around 9 years old, Molloy argues that language learning or assessment activities for young children need to be designed in such a way that their development of abstract concepts is appropriately taken into account.

Young learners' cognitive development over attentional procedures needs special consideration in the development of ELP assessments. Young learners have relatively short attention spans (e.g., about 10–15 minutes on a given task), so they tend to get distracted easily, and their completion of a given task can also be strongly influenced by their interest levels (Bailey, Heritage, & Butler, 2014; Cameron, 2001; Hasselgreen, 2005; McKay, 2006). Furthermore, young students' use of various strategies to tackle given tasks, including completing assessments, is associated with their cognitive development. Tragant and Victori (2012), for instance, found that younger students (i.e., 12 and 13 years old) had more variability in the use of strategies (e.g., analysis and reduction strategies) compared to older students (i.e., 15 and 18 years old) who demonstrated similar use of the strategies examined in the study. In discussing the findings, the researchers note that younger students had a clear preference for a set of particular types of strategies, whereas older students used all the strategies in accordance with their higher level of cognitive maturity. This line of research indicates how young students' cognitive abilities influence their performance on assessments.

Given young learners' growing cognitive abilities (e.g., working memory, information processing speed, metalinguistic awareness, attention, and executive functions), a number of assessment design issues deserve consideration, including the length of assessments and assessment stimuli, clarity of task instructions, and appropriateness of the topics and content of tasks (Bailey, 2008; Bailey et al., 2014). We will revisit these considerations later in this chapter.

Affective Factors of Young Learners

Young learners' affective factors are also of critical importance for the development and use of ELP assessments. Bachman and Palmer (1996, 2010) explicitly mention affective schemata as one of the attributes that influence one's assessment performance. As far as young learners are concerned, the impact of their affective factors (e.g., motivation, attitudes, and self-esteem) can be even more influential on their assessment performance and L2 learning than for adult learners.

Generally, young learners' motivation toward L2 learning and assessment tends to be extrinsic, stemming from parents and schools. Previous research findings have indicated that there is a strong, positive relationship between young students' performance on assessments and their motivation in general (e.g., Brumen & Cagran, 2011). That is, when students are motivated, their assessment performance is increased. Hence, it is particularly crucial that young learners have positive experiences with ELP assessments and engage in L2 learning and assessment with high motivation.

Young learners' ability to control their emotions is not fully developed, and their emotions can have substantial impact on assessment performance (Aydin, 2012; Black, 2005; Molloy, 2015; and see Jang, Vincett, van der Boom, Lau, & Yang, 2017 in this volume). For instance, Aydin (2012) examined the relationship between test anxiety and performance in young EFL students ages 9 to 13 in Turkey. It was found that these students experienced test anxiety associated with testing time, challenges in comprehension of directions, and physical settings. Molloy (2015) notes that young learners may perform differently depending on the assessment environment. She asserts that young learners perform better when they are provided with clear instructions and purposes along with positive feedback and rewards. Previous research consistently argues that young learners' positive experience with assessments is critical in order for them to increase their motivation and self-esteem, which eventually leads to the promotion of L2 learning (Black & Wiliam, 1998; Brumen & Cagran, 2011; McKay, 2006; Moss, 2013).

The unique characteristics of young learners discussed in this section have important implications for the development and uses of standardized ELP assessments. In the next section, we describe some key features of item and test development for young learners.

Features to Consider in Standardized ELP Assessments for Young Learners

Assessing young learners' ELP can happen in many different ways depending on the purposes of assessment. Broadly speaking, like other educational assessments, ELP assessments can serve primarily as assessment *of* learning or as assessment *for* learning. Assessment *of* learning is intended to provide information about students' current levels and achievements after a certain period of instruction (i.e., for summative purposes), whereas assessment *for* learning is intended to provide information about students' strengths and weaknesses for improving learning during instruction (i.e., for formative purposes) (Black & Wiliam, 1998; Heritage, 2013; Purpura, 2016). While the primary purposes of summative and formative assessment differ, Bennett (2011) argues that all educational assessments ultimately share the underlying goal of advancing student learning. His argument may hold particularly true for young learners. That is, ELP assessments for young learners are generally intended to measure students' current ELP levels to help students improve their English skills, providing score reports or feedback of varying granularity for distinct users and uses.

The formats of ELP assessments that serve these purposes with young learners are wide-ranging, from standardized assessments to classroom-based assessments with varying degrees of formality (e.g., portfolio assessments, classroom tests and quizzes, observations, collaborative assessments, and self-assessments; see Bailey, 2017 in this volume for a discussion of various assessment types for young learners).

Standardized ELP assessments have been widely used in both EFL and ESL contexts. A standardized assessment is defined as an assessment that is "administered, scored, and interpreted in a standard manner" (Popham, 1999, p. 264). Distinguished from other assessment formats, standardized ELP assessments have the following major characteristics. Standardized ELP assessments usually undergo rigorous development processes including (1) careful target language use domain analyses to define the constructs to be measured, (2) item and task development with expert review of content appropriateness for the target population, (3) large-scale pilot and/or field testing with a representative sample of the target population, (4) various psychometric/statistical analyses to establish the technical qualities of items and test forms, and (5) scaling and standard-setting studies to create scaled scores and cut scores, as needed, for score reports. In addition to development procedures, administration settings are also an important factor in standardized assessment. Standardized ELP assessments are typically accompanied by administration manuals, and trained administrators work to ensure that the assessment settings are kept as consistent as possible. This is an important factor in supporting fair and adequate inferences about the abilities of test takers on the basis of standardized ELP test scores across administration settings.

Standardized ELP assessments for young learners can provide information about (1) individual students' achievements and levels of proficiency based on international, national, or local standards/curricula and (2) individual students' growth in their ELP attainment. The information provided by standardized ELP assessments can certainly be used for low-stakes purposes, for example when parents or schools simply wish to gauge students' ELP levels based on national or international yardsticks (e.g., Common European Framework of Reference). Even for young learners, however, results from standardized ELP assessments also can be used for relatively high-stakes purposes such as to inform placement decisions (i.e., to place students into appropriate instructional programs), exit decisions (i.e., to exit students out of certain programs), admission decisions for secondary or private schools, and for accountability purposes at the level of individual schools (i.e., to report students' proficiency and growth in ELP and to make funding/resource allocation decisions for schools). As an example, standardized ELP assessments in U.S. K–12 school settings are administered to very young students at the age of 5 (in kindergarten) for the purpose of identifying "English learners (ELs)"[2] who, once identified, will be eligible for appropriate ESL services (Hauck, Pooler, Wolf, Lopez, & Anderson, 2017; Wolf, Lopez, Oh, & Tsutagawa, 2017, both in this volume). This identification purpose of ELP assessments involves high-stakes decisions because students, once identified as

ELs, follow a certain academic path including taking ESL courses and taking summative ELP assessments annually until they meet the required proficiency level. Inaccurate identification based on ELP assessments entails substantial negative consequences impacting the provision of services for students in need, students' academic paths, funding/resource allocation, and program evaluation.

To ensure that standardized ELP assessments elicit young learners' abilities appropriately and, thus, provide adequate information to help with young learners' ELP development, below we highlight a few key aspects that need to be considered in the design and use of standardized ELP assessments for young learners:

- **Item/task design**: Items and tasks need to be developmentally appropriate for young learners in content and format (Hasselgreen, 2005; McKay, 2006; Muñoz, 2007). Items and tasks should also be reflective of activities to reinforce young learners' language learning (see Hauck et al., 2017 in this volume for a discussion on this point). Considering the importance of young learners' engagement and motivation in taking assessments to elicit sufficient evidence about their abilities, items and tasks should be designed in a way to increase students' interest in them. Finally, the number of items and tasks needs to be designed to balance the psychometric qualities of the assessment scores and young students' limited attention span. In the design of items and tasks, past research advocates for the benefits of including language teachers of young learners throughout the assessment development processes in order to take into account young learners' characteristics and instructional values of the items/tasks (e.g., Hasselgreen, 2005; Hurley & Blake, 2000).
- **Instructions**: Young learners do not necessarily understand why they take assessments, potentially resulting in limited engagement. In assessments employed in formal settings, very young learners may not be familiar with testing procedures and may not entirely understand the instructions given for each assessment and/or for each task. For young learners who are developing their comprehension of the language of assessments, standardized ELP assessments should have clear instructions about the assessments and tasks, accompanied by trained test administrators who can provide assistance for students. The language of instructions should be simple and accessible to young learners. Clear instructions are also important for young learners as they tend to perform differently depending on the clarity of purpose of the given activity (Cameron, 2001). Hence, it is important that sample tasks and practice tasks be available for young learners and their teachers.
- **Administration procedures and settings**: As described earlier, young learners' assessment results can be influenced by young learners' testing anxiety or lack of familiarity about testing, meaning the assessment results are not purely a reflection of their English language abilities. To prevent these construct-irrelevant factors from influencing assessment results, assessment procedures and settings are particularly important for young learners. For ELP assessments of young learners,

it is essential to have trained/qualified administrators and create comfortable testing environments where construct-irrelevant factors are controlled to the extent possible (National Association of the Education of Young Children, 2009).
- **Score reporting and feedback**: McKay (2006) stresses that assessments for young learners should be used in a manner by which assessment results provide information to help students succeed in their EFL/ESL learning and thereby increase their self-esteem. While it is important to consider positive and inspiring feedback or score reports for young learners, it is equally critical to provide descriptive information with students' strengths and weaknesses for teachers and parents, who are the major users of assessments for young learners. In a large-scale teacher survey, Breen et al. (1997) found that teachers highly valued assessments that inform them of students' ELP development processes and offer information to guide teaching strategies. Inarguably, the design of different levels of score reports for various stakeholders is a challenging—yet important—goal in standardized ELP assessments.
- **Empirical validation work**: Various uses and stakes involved in standardized ELP assessments for young learners point to the importance of empirical validation work. As large-scale standardized ELP assessments have a relatively short history compared to those for adult learners, it is important to garner empirical evidence to support the conceptual frameworks, including in particular the construct and test specifications, that have been used to build assessments for young learners. The interaction between young learners' characteristics and assessment characteristics (e.g., task types and feedback) needs to be examined empirically. Moreover, empirical investigation into the appropriateness of assessment uses (e.g., inferences about students' ELP and consequences of testing for students' ELP development and learning) are significant for improving standardized ELP assessment practices (Wolf, Farnsworth, & Herman, 2008; Wolf & Faulkner-Bond, 2016).

The features of standardized ELP assessments introduced here are certainly not a comprehensive list. Yet, we consider these to be highly important given the unique characteristics of young learners. A wide range of these and related issues pertaining to the assessment of ELP for young learners is discussed across the chapters in this volume.

Scope and Structure of This Volume

This volume is comprised of five sections: (1) introduction (current chapter), (2) theoretical basis and assessment frameworks, (3) empirical studies for validity evidence, (4) future assessments and innovations for young learners, and (5) conclusion.

The section on theoretical basis and assessment frameworks includes four chapters to illustrate theoretical underpinnings of the development of ELP assessments and concrete examples of the frameworks that were used to build a sample of standardized ELP assessments for young students (e.g., the *TOEFL®*

Primary™ tests, the *TOEFL Junior*® tests, and U.S. K–12 ELP assessments). The next section on empirical studies presents a few selected studies conducted during the development stages and operational uses of large-scale standardized ELP assessments. This section describes not only issues associated with the assessment development process but also validation efforts made during the development and operational stages. The section on future assessments and innovations includes three chapters showcasing innovative ways of assessing young learners' ELP in various contexts and for distinct purposes; the chapters in this section are not limited to standardized ELP assessments. The conclusion section contains a chapter summarizing the key validity issues that emerge across all chapters and suggests future research directions for ELP assessments for young learners.

By way of introduction, we provide here an overview and major areas discussed in each chapter. In Chapter 2, "Theoretical and Developmental Issues to Consider in the Assessment of Young Learners' English Language Proficiency," Bailey (2017) offers a comprehensive account of theory-based issues associated with developing and using ELP assessment for young learners. After addressing major points in children's cognitive and social development, which offer a substantial foundation for determining content and format of the assessment, Bailey reviews major theories in second language acquisition and their implications for assessment, including social interactionist theory, sociocultural theory, systematic functional linguistic theory, and complex adaptive systems theory. Drawing from different theoretical approaches, Bailey suggests three major ramifications for standardized ELP assessment for young learners: (a) incorporating language-learning elements such as scaffolding, (b) redefining ELP construct(s) in order to better reflect learners' actual language use, and (c) making better use of technology both for construct representation and delivery of assessment.

The next two chapters, "Designing the *TOEFL*® *Primary*™ Tests" (Chapter 3, Cho et al., 2017) and "*TOEFL Junior*® Design Framework" (Chapter 4, So et al., 2017), describe the theoretical underpinnings of the assessment construct and design framework for the *TOEFL Primary* and *TOEFL Junior* tests, respectively, both of which are primarily targeted at young EFL learners. Both chapters begin with a description of these tests' target populations, purpose, and intended uses, followed by the test development process, as well as overviews of task design including test contents and structure. The chapters also discuss challenges and solutions that emerged during the assessment development processes.

The last chapter in Section 2, "Designing Task Types for English Language Proficiency Assessments for K–12 English Learners in the U.S." (Chapter 5, Hauck et al., 2017), delves into the issues regarding the development of standardized ELP assessments in ESL contexts. Hauck et al. discuss the use of evidence-centered design to develop large-scale standardized ELP assessments in a principled way, drawing upon recent large-scale ELP assessment development work including the English Language Proficiency Assessment for the 21st century (ELPA21) and the English Language Proficiency Assessments for California (ELPAC). In these examples, the tests' development and use were tied directly to specific policy requirements; as a result, the test developers faced unique challenges such as how best to operationalize the expectations manifested in ELP standards for the development of state-regulated ELP assessment systems. The authors also explicate their approach to task design for assessing young learners' ELP based on the given standards.

Section 3, composed of five empirical studies, presents various types of research conducted to examine validity evidence for the *TOEFL Primary* tests, the *TOEFL Junior* tests, and U.S. K–12 ELP assessments. Some studies were conducted during assessment development stages, and others were conducted for examining intended assessment uses. The studies in this section employed different methodologies and offer a variety of evidence pertaining to the assessments' validity arguments. More importantly, they also report specific lessons that the authors have learned through developing and using ELP assessments targeted at young language learners. In Chapter 6, "A Field Test Study for the *TOEFL® Primary*™ Reading and Listening Tests," Zu, Moulder, and Morgan (2017) report the results of a large-scale field study as evidence for the validity of the *TOEFL Primary* tests as measurements of English reading and listening abilities among young learners. Of particular importance in this chapter are its descriptions of a range of statistical analyses (including classical item analysis, IRT calibration, scaling, and an evaluation performed on psychometric properties of the initial operational forms) conducted during the test's development, and a discussion on how such statistical analyses were utilized to ensure that items and tasks were designed to assess the target population of the *TOEFL Primary* tests.

Chapter 7, "Strategies Used by Young English Learners in an Assessment Context" by Gu and So (2017), centers on a small-scale exploratory study examining strategies that young learners used while taking the listening and reading tests of the *TOEFL Primary* tests. The study aimed to provide validity evidence to support the claim that the items were appropriate for the tests' target population. The study found that the young learners employed various types of strategies and that their strategy uses differed by proficiency level and by skill domain (i.e., listening and reading). The authors also discuss whether the strategies were construct-relevant or not, building a validity argument for the inferences made from the assessment results.

The Common European Framework of Reference (CEFR) is increasingly used as a scale of learning objectives not only in Europe but also in other parts of the world. In response to this trend, in Chapter 8, "Using the Common European Framework of Reference to Facilitate Score Interpretations for Young Learners' English Language Proficiency Assessments," Papageorgiou and Baron (2017) discuss challenges associated with using the CEFR in the context of young learners' ELP assessments. The authors conducted standard-setting studies during the development of the *TOEFL Primary* and *TOEFL Junior* tests. Based on the studies, the authors demonstrated how the CEFR was used to support inferences that one could make on the basis of scores of these ELP assessments for young learners. Reflecting their experience during this process, the authors also address challenges and concerns in using the CEFR in ELP assessments for young learners with various backgrounds.

Standardized ELP assessments can be instrumental in measuring young learners' ELP development. In Chapter 9, "Making a Validity Argument for Using the *TOEFL Junior*® Standard Test as a Measure of Progress for Young English Language Learners," Gu, Lockwood, and Powers (2017) examine the extent to which the *TOEFL Junior* Standard test can capture changes in learners' ELP development as a function of their learning. This study provides a critical piece of evidence for supporting a claim that the test can be used as a measurement for monitoring the students' developmental growth. The authors also address a number of issues that researchers commonly face when using nonexperimental longitudinal methods, as they did in their study, in order to investigate the developmental patterns and growth from learners in various learning contexts.

Chapter 10, "Comparing the Performance of Young English Language Learners and Native English Speakers on Speaking Assessment Tasks," focuses on the U.S. K–12 ESL context (Wolf et al., 2017). One of the important uses of ELP assessments in ESL contexts is to adequately identify which English learners are in need of ESL services. Considering that young English learners are still in the midst of cognitive, social-affective, and linguistic development, the authors stress the importance of including native English-speaking children (non-EL students) as a pilot or field-testing sample during the process of developing standardized ELP assessments. Based on a comparative study between EL and non-EL students, the authors argue that the examination of both groups' performance on assessments provides useful information to identify appropriate task types and scoring rubrics for the target age groups, as well as to enhance our understanding about second language development in general.

Section 4 addresses areas for future development and innovations in assessment for young learners. Acknowledging the importance of various methods and measures to assess young learners, we have included papers that are not limited to standardized assessments. The three studies in this section encompass various types of assessments and raise critical issues in the assessment of young learners; that is, how best to capture young learners' learning progress and to identify what kinds of pedagogical assistance should be offered to students and teachers through assessment, and how to accomplish this. The authors in all three chapters aim to situate their assessments in authentic learning experience, to make learning processes visible in order to provide pedagogically useful information, and to make test-taking itself a learning opportunity for young language learners.

In Chapter 11, "Considering Young Learners' Characteristics in Developing a Diagnostic Assessment Intervention," Jang et al. (2017) focus on an application of Cognitive Diagnostic Assessment (CDA) for young learners. Drawing examples from their intervention study on young struggling readers in Canada, the authors describe how individualized diagnostic feedback that young learners received during CDA can guide them to shift their focus from externally mediated learning to self-regulated learning. The authors lay out a number of specific young learner characteristics in cognition, metacognition, interest, and emotion that should be taken into account when designing and implementing CDA.

In Chapter 12, "Computerized Dynamic Assessments for Young Language Learners," Poehner, Zhang, and Lu (2017) discuss Dynamic Assessment (DA), an assessment approach grounded in Vygotsky's notion of the Zone of Proximal Development (ZPD). Particularly exciting in this chapter is their new development of a computerized form of DA to utilize in the role of standardized assessments. The chapter begins with the theoretical background of DA, followed by examples from two of the authors' recent projects to illustrate: (a) mediation process of young learners of Spanish and (b) implementation of computerized DA for college L2 learners of Chinese. Their computerized DA produces four types of scores: actual, mediational, transfer, and learning potential scores. Together with detailed breakdowns of each individual learner's performance and mediation records, the computerized DA can provide teachers with valuable pedagogical information. Although some of the data in this chapter did not come from young learners, the authors suggest potential merits and challenges of implementing the computerized DA to young learners, by combining their experience with both young learners and adult learners.

Chapter 13, "Measuring 21st-Century Reading Comprehension Through Scenario-Based Assessments," by Shore, Wolf, O'Reilly, and Sabatini (2017), also discusses the advancement of technology that allows improved assessment design and uses for young learners. This chapter focuses on a new assessment design technique called "scenario-based assessment (SBA)" and illustrates how technology-enhanced SBA can be used in standardized assessment settings as well as formative assessment settings to support young learners' reading assessment and development. One of the innovative features of SBA that the authors discuss is that assessments are designed to both measure and support ESL students' multi-layered thinking processes while students engage in carefully-sequenced reading tasks as the scenario of an assessment unfolds.

Finally, Section 5 serves to conclude this volume. In Chapter 14, "Challenges and Future Directions for Young Learners' English Language Assessments and Validity Research," Butler (2017) summarizes the major challenges when developing ELP assessments for young learners that have emerged from current research, including the studies contributing to the present volume. Using Kane's interpretation/use argument (Kane, 2013) as a framework, Butler also discusses key issues when building validity arguments for assessment development and score use for young learners. The chapter concludes with suggestions for future directions for young learners' ELP assessment and areas needing further research.

Closing Remarks

We close this introductory chapter with a few remarks for readers before proceeding to the rest of the chapters in this volume. The growing interest in and need for assessing young learners' ELP have generated much attention to the quality of sound ELP assessments and appropriate use of those assessments for young learners. We have attempted to address an array of issues to consider in the development and use of ELP assessments by a collection of theoretical and empirical perspectives on the assessment of young learners. Admittedly, this volume is not an exhaustive collection of the papers on young learners. However, each chapter in this volume offers a unique perspective on the assessment of young learners and provides stimulating ideas for conducting future research and development work to improve ELP assessment practices with young learners. The collected contributions in this volume also demonstrate the rigorous development processes that undergird quality ELP assessments and the importance of validation efforts to support appropriate uses of assessments for young learners. Furthermore, all chapters in this volume indicate that much empirical research needs to be done to better understand young learners' ELP development and the interaction between the unique characteristics of young learners and assessment features. We hope that this volume contributes to advancing our knowledge about the assessment of ELP in young learners, and to facilitating further discussions for the language testing and education fields in order to promote young learners' ELP development through sound assessment practices.

Notes

1 In previous literature, considering differences in child development and school systems across countries, young school-age learners have been divided into two (e.g., elementary vs. lower secondary grades and lower elementary vs. upper elementary) or three age/grade groups (e.g., 5–7 years old or early elementary grades; 8–10 years old or upper elementary; and 11–13 years old or lower secondary grades or middle grades). In this volume, we use the terms *young (language) learners*, *young school-age children*, and *young students* interchangeably to refer to this age group (5–13 years old) collectively. Wherever needed, we will describe specific ages or grade levels.
2 "English learners" is a term used in official documents in the U.S. to refer to K–12 students who are identified as students in need of official support to develop their English language proficiency in school settings.

References

Aydin, S. (2012). The effects of young EFL learners' perceptions of tests on test anxiety. *Education 3–13*, *40*(2), 189–204.

Bachman, L. F., & Palmer, A. S. (1996). *Language testing in practice*. Oxford: Oxford University Press.

Bachman, L. F., & Palmer, A. S. (2010). *Language assessment in practice*. Oxford: Oxford University Press.

Bailey, A. L. (2008). Assessing the language of young learners. In E. Shohamy & N. H. Hornberger (Eds.), *Encyclopedia of language and education, Vol. 7: Language testing and assessment* (pp. 379–398). New York, NY: Springer.

Bailey, A. L. (2017). Theoretical and developmental issues to consider in the assessment of young learners' English language proficiency. In M. K. Wolf & Y. G. Butler (Eds.), *English language proficiency assessments for young learners* (pp. 25–40). New York, NY: Routledge.

Bailey, A. L., Heritage, M., & Butler, F. A. (2014). Developmental considerations and curricular contexts in the assessment of young language learners. In A. J. Kunnan (Ed.), *The companion to language assessment* (pp. 423–439). Boston, MA: Wiley.

Bailey, A. L., & Huang, B. H. (2011). Do current English language development/proficiency standards reflect the English needed for success in school? *Language Testing, 28,* 343–365.

Baldauf, R. B., Kaplan, R. B., Kamwangamaly, K., & Bryant, P. (Eds.). (2012). *Language planning in primary schools in Asia.* London, UK: Routledge.

Barac, R., Bialystok, E., Castro, D. C., & Sanchez, M. (2014). The cognitive development of young dual language learners: A critical review. *Early Childhood Research Quarterly, 29,* 699–714.

Bennett, R. E. (2011). Formative assessment: A critical review. *Assessment in Education: Principles, Policy & Practice, 18*(1), 5–25.

Bialystok, E. (2001). *Bilingualism in development: Language, literacy, cognition.* Cambridge, UK: Cambridge University Press.

Black, P., & Wiliam, D. (1998). Assessment and classroom learning. *Assessment in Education: Principles, Policy & Practice, 5*(1), 7–74.

Black, S. (2005). Test anxiety. *American School Board Journal, 192*(6), 42–44.

Breen, M. P., Barratt-Pugh, C., Derewianka, B., House, H., Hudson, C., Lumley, T., & Rohl, M. (1997). *Profiling ESL children: How teachers interpret and use national and state assessment frameworks.* Canberra City, Australia: Department of Employment, Education, Training and Youth Affairs.

Brumen, M., & Cagran, B. (2011). Teachers' perspectives and practices in assessment young foreign language learners in three Eastern European countries. *Education 3–13, 39*(5), 541–559.

Butler, Y. G. (2015). English language education among young learners in East Asia: A review of current research (2004–2014). *Language Teaching, 48,* 303–342.

Butler, Y. G. (2016). Assessing young learners. In D. Tsagari (Ed.), *Handbook of second language assessment* (pp. 359–375). Berlin: Mouton de Gruyter.

Butler, Y. G. (2017). Challenges and future directions for young learners' English language assessments and validity research. In M. K. Wolf & Y. G. Butler (Eds.), *English language proficiency assessments for young learners* (pp. 255–273). New York, NY: Routledge.

Butler, Y. G., & Zeng, W. (2014). Young foreign language learners' interactions during task-based paired assessment. *Language Assessment Quarterly, 11,* 45–75.

California Department of Education. (2012). *The California English language development standards.* Sacramento, CA: Author.

Cameron, L. (2001). *Teaching languages to young learners.* Cambridge, UK: Cambridge University Press.

Campfield, D. E. (2006). *Assessing ESL (English as a second language) children's knowledge of word order.* Oxford: University of Oxford.

Canale, M., & Swain, K. (1980). Theoretical bases of communicative approaches to second language teaching and testing. *Applied Linguistics, 1*(1), 1–47.

Case, R., Kurland, D. M., & Goldberg, J. (1982). Operational efficiency and the growth of short-term memory span. *Journal of Experimental Child Psychology, 33*(3), 386–404.

Cho, Y., Ginsburgh, M., Morgan, R., Moulder, B., Xi, X., & Hauck, M. C. (2017). Designing *TOEFL® Primary™* tests. In M. K. Wolf & Y. G. Butler (Eds.), *English language proficiency assessments for young learners* (pp. 41–58). New York, NY: Routledge.

Choi, I.-C. (2008). The impact of EFL testing on EFL education in Korea. *Language Testing, 25*(1), 39–62.

Craik, F. I., & Bialystok, E. (2006). Cognition through the lifespan: Mechanisms of change. *Trends in Cognitive Sciences, 10*(3), 131–138.

Ellis, N. C. (2008). The dynamics of second language emergence: Cycles of language use, language change, and language acquisition. *The Modern Language Journal, 92,* 232–249.

Enever, J., Moon, J., & Raman, U. (Eds.). (2009). *Young learner English language policy and implementation: International perspectives.* Reading, UK: Garnet.

Garlock, V. M., Walley, A. C., & Metsala, J. L. (2001). Age-of-acquisition, word frequency, and neighborhood density effects on spoken word recognition by children and adults. *Journal of Memory and Language, 45,* 468–492.

Gass, S., & Selinker, L. (1994). *Second language acquisition: An introductory course.* Hillsdale, NJ: Lawrence Erlbaum Associates, Inc.

Gu, L., Lockwood, J. R., & Powers, D. (2017). Making a validity argument for using the *TOEFL Junior®* standard test as a measure of progress for young English language learners. In M. K. Wolf & Y. G. Butler (Eds.), *English language proficiency assessments for young learners* (pp. 153–170). New York, NY: Routledge.

Gu, L., & So, Y. (2017). Strategies used by young English learners in an assessment context. In M. K. Wolf & Y. G. Butler (Eds.), *English language proficiency assessments for young learners* (pp. 118–135). New York, NY: Routledge.

Hakuta, K., Santos, M., & Fang, Z. (2013). Challenges and opportunities for language learning in the context of the CCSS and the NGSS. *Journal of Adolescent and Adult Literacy, 56,* 451–454.

Hasselgreen, A. (2005). Assessing the language of young learners. *Language Testing, 22*(3), 337–354.

Hauck, M. C., Pooler, E., Wolf, M. K., Lopez, A., & Anderson, D. (2017). Designing task types for English language proficiency assessments for K–12 English learners in the U.S. In M. K. Wolf & Y. G. Butler (Eds.), *English language proficiency assessments for young learners* (pp. 79–95). New York, NY: Routledge.

Heritage, M. (2013). Gathering evidence of student understanding. In J. H. McMillan (Ed.), *SAGE handbook of research on classroom assessment* (pp. 179–195). Thousand Oaks, CA: SAGE Publications, Ltd.

Hoff-Ginsberg, E. (1997). *Language development.* Pacific Grove, CA: Brooks/Cole Publishing Company.

Huang, K.-M. (2011). Motivating lessons: A classroom-oriented investigation of the effects of content based instruction on EFL young learners' motivated behaviours and classroom verbal interaction. *System, 39,* 186–201.

Hurley, S. R., & Blake, S. (2000). Assessment in the content areas for students acquiring English. In S. R. Hurley & J. V. Tinajero (Eds.), *Literacy assessment of second language learners* (pp. 84–103). Boston, MA: Allyn & Bacon.

Jang, E. E., Vincett, M., van der Boom, E., Lau, C., & Yang, Y. (2017). Considering young learners' characteristics in developing a diagnostic assessment intervention. In M. K. Wolf & Y. G. Butler (Eds.), *English language proficiency assessments for young learners* (pp. 193–213). New York, NY: Routledge.

Kane, M. (2013). The argument-based approach to validation. *School Psychology Review, 42*(4), 448–457.

Lenski, S. D., Ehlers-Zavala, F., Daniel, M. C., & Sun-Irminger, X. (2006). Assessing English-language learners in mainstream classroom. *The Reading Teacher*, *60*(1), 24–34.

McKay, P. (2000). On ESL standards for school-age learners. *Language Testing*, *17*(2), 185–214.

McKay, P. (2006). *Assessing young language learners*. Cambridge, UK: Cambridge University Press.

Molloy, A. (2015). Seven essential considerations for assessing young learners. *Modern English Teacher*, *24*(1), 20–23.

Moss, C. M. (2013). Research on classroom summative assessment. In J. H. McMillan (Ed.), *SAGE handbook of research on classroom assessment* (pp. 235–255). Thousand Oaks, CA: SAGE Publications, Ltd.

Muñoz, C. (2007). Age-related differences and second language learning practice. In R. M. DeKeyser (Ed.), *Practice in a second language: Perspectives from applied linguistics and cognitive psychology* (pp. 229–255). New York, NY: Cambridge University Press.

National Association for the Education of Young Children. (2009). *Where we stand on assessing young English language learners*. Washington, DC: Author. Available from http://www.naeyc.org/files/naeyc/file/positions/WWSEnglishLanguageLearnersWeb.pdf

National Clearinghouse for English Language Acquisition. (2011). *What languages do English learners speak? NCELA fact sheet*. Washington, DC: Author. Available from www.gwu.edu/files/uploads/NCELAFactsheets/EL_Languages_2011.pdf

Nikolov, M. (Ed.). (2016). *Assessing young learners of English: Global and local perspectives*. New York, NY: Springer.

Orbach, Y., & Lamb, M. E. (2007). Young children's references to temporal attributes of allegedly experienced events in the course of forensic interviews. *Child Development*, *78*, 1100–1120.

Papageorgiou, S., & Baron, P. (2017). Using the Common European Framework of Reference to facilitate score interpretations for young learners' English language proficiency assessments. In M. K. Wolf & Y. G. Butler (Eds.), *English language proficiency assessments for young learners* (pp. 136–152). New York, NY: Routledge.

Poehner, M. E., Zhang, J., & Lu, X. (2017). Computerized dynamic assessments for young language learners. In M. K. Wolf & Y. G. Butler (Eds.), *English language proficiency assessments for young learners* (pp. 214–233). New York, NY: Routledge.

Popham, W. J. (1999). *Classroom assessment* (2nd ed.). Needham Heights, MA: Allyn and Bacon.

Purpura, J. (2016). Second and foreign language assessment. *The Modern Language Journal*, *100*(Supplement 2016), 190–208.

Rea-Dickins, P. (2000). Assessment in early years language learning contexts. *Language Testing*, *17*(2), 115–122.

Shore, J., Wolf, M. K., O'Reilly, T., & Sabatini, J. P. (2017). Measuring 21st century reading comprehension through scenario-based assessments. In M. K. Wolf & Y. G. Butler (Eds.), *English language proficiency assessments for young learners* (pp. 234–252). New York, NY: Routledge.

So, Y., Wolf, M. K., Hauck, M. C., Mollaun, P., Rybinski, P., Tumposky, D., & Wang, L. (2017). TOEFL Junior® design framework. In M. K. Wolf & Y. G. Butler (Eds.), *English language proficiency assessments for young learners* (pp. 59–78). New York, NY: Routledge.

Szpotowicz, M. (2012). Researching oral production skills of young learners. *Center for Educational Policy Studies (C.E.P.S) Journal*, *2*(3), 141–166.

Tessier, A., Duncan, T. S., & Paradis, J. (2013). Developmental trends and L1 effects in early L2 learners' onset cluster production. *Language and Cognition*, *16*(3), 663–681.

Tragant, E., & Victori, M. (2012). Language learning strategies, course grades, and age in EFL secondary school learners. *Language Awareness*, *21*(3), 293–308.

Wolf, M. K., Everson, P., Lopez, A., Hauck, M. C., Pooler, E., & Wang, J. (2014). *Building a framework for a next-generation English language proficiency assessment system* (ETS Research Report No. RR-14-34). Princeton, NJ: Educational Testing Service.

Wolf, M. K., & Farnsworth, T. (2014). English language proficiency assessments as an exit criterion for English learners. In A. Kunnan (Ed.), *The companion to language assessment* (pp. 303–317). New York, NY: John Wiley & Sons, Inc.

Wolf, M. K., Farnsworth, T., & Herman, J. L. (2008). Validity issues in assessing English language learners' language proficiency. *Educational Assessment*, *13*(2), 80–107.

Wolf, M. K., & Faulkner-Bond, M. (2016). Validating English language proficiency assessment uses for English learners: Academic language proficiency and content assessment performance. *Educational Measurement: Issues and Practice*, *35*(2), 6–18.

Wolf, M. K., Lopez, A., Oh, S., & Tsutagawa, F. S. (2017). Comparing the performance of young English language learners and native English speakers on speaking assessment tasks. In M. K. Wolf & Y. G. Butler (Eds.), *English language proficiency assessments for young learners* (pp. 171–190). New York, NY: Routledge.

Zu, J., Moulder, B., & Morgan, R. (2017). A field test study for the *TOEFL® Primary*™ Reading and Listening tests. In M. K. Wolf & Y. G. Butler (Eds.), *English language proficiency assessments for young learners* (pp. 99–117). New York, NY: Routledge.

SECTION 2
Theoretical Basis and Assessment Frameworks

2
THEORETICAL AND DEVELOPMENTAL ISSUES TO CONSIDER IN THE ASSESSMENT OF YOUNG LEARNERS' ENGLISH LANGUAGE PROFICIENCY

Alison L. Bailey

Knowing more than one language will increasingly put school-age students at an advantage in today's globalized societies. With more and younger children being taught English worldwide (Rich, 2014), assessment of their English proficiency will become increasingly widespread. Inevitably, the appropriate measurement of English proficiency will be critical if assessment is to play an effective role in children's English development and academic success. In devising English language proficiency (ELP) assessments for young school-age students, an array of issues needs to be carefully thought out in terms of young learners' characteristics and their language development (see Butler, 2017; Jang, Vincett, van der Boom, Lau, & Yang, 2017; Wolf & Butler, 2017 all in this volume for the description of young learners' characteristics). This chapter particularly provides an overview of developmental factors and second language acquisition (SLA) theory in order to provide direction for the successful creation and improved use of ELP assessments with young learners.

Theory of how language proficiency is acquired and progresses can help to identify and clarify the claims that are made in ELP tests and the validity of test interpretations. Such validity arguments are a critical feature of modern test development (Kane, 2013; see also Butler, 2017 for validity arguments in this volume), and, more specifically, play a key role in the interpretations and uses for which an assessment is designed (Bachman, 2005). Theory can also guide what content coverage to include in assessment. However, as important as articulating an underlying theory of language development is for guiding assessment development and use with young learners, theory also needs to be coupled with knowledge of child development.

In this chapter, I will first offer a brief account of crucial cognitive and social developments in young learners, which will help determine effective testing formats and administration choices, as well as developmentally appropriate content inclusion. Then, I will highlight some key theories of second language acquisition and discuss the implications of children's developmental factors and prior theories for the development of ELP assessments for young learners.

Role of Cognitive and Social Developments in the ELP Assessment of Young Learners

Considerations in the areas of young learners' cognitive and socio-emotional development need to be taken into account when designing and interpreting ELP assessments with this population. Among the differences in characteristics between young language learners and older children and adults are the following: greater limits to memory load, slower processing speeds, short-term motivation issues (young children's attention can wander more easily), greater risk of testing fatigue, greater likelihood of anxiety and/or wariness, and unfamiliar testing practices that may confuse or also add to the anxiety levels of young learners (see Bailey, Heritage, & Butler, 2014, for review).

As much as we may hear or read that young language learners are advantaged over adult learners due to greater brain plasticity (i.e., making and strengthening connections between neuronal cells as a result of recognizing auditory and visual input) in childhood (Gervain, 2015), young learners' abilities to process language information is limited compared to older children and adult language learners. One area of language development that brain plasticity may provide an advantage for is the acquisition of a native-like accent before the end of puberty; beyond this sensitive period, or biologically constrained timeframe, it becomes increasingly unlikely for a language learner to acquire a new language without retaining the accent of his or her L1 (Au, Oh, Knightly, Jun, & Romo, 2008).

The effects of working memory during English language assessment have been shown to impact younger children to a larger degree than adolescents. Gathercole, Pickering, Knight, and Stegmann (2004) have speculated that working memory for the kinds of English skills assessed with young learners (e.g., literacy fundamentals such as decoding words) is more critical than the kinds of higher-order thinking skills used in reading comprehension items on assessments with older students. Additionally, control of attention and processing speed are two areas that may also impact young learners' test performances. Young children are still developing the executive functioning abilities that enable them to control their attention and inhibit distractors. Research conducted across the age spans has found that processing speed, voluntary response suppression, and working memory do not mature until about 14 through 19 years of age (Luna, Garver, Urban, Lazar, & Sweeney, 2004).

Various socio-emotional developments are also still occurring in young learners with important implications for assessment of English proficiency. Young learners test performances may be affected by such aspects as testing fatigue, anxiety, and motivation. In terms of testing fatigue and anxiety, young learners will tire more easily and may be made anxious by the unfamiliar setting or testing administrator in ways that could affect their performances detrimentally (Bailey et al., 2014; McKay, 2006). Young learners may also not be as motivated to complete an assessment or perform optimally. This is also related to their abilities to sustain their attention on assessment, which is harder for them than it is for older students and adults. Assessment, therefore, must be made appealing to sustain the interests of young learners (Hasselgreen, 2005). Language assessment performance may also be negatively impacted by young learners' lack of opportunities to engage in social interactions with new or less familiar adults. Collectively, these cognitive and socio-emotional developments must be taken into consideration in ELP assessment development for use with young language learners. The youngest ESL and EFL learners (e.g., preschool-aged students) have their own special assessment needs related to cognitive and socio-emotional development—a topic outside the scope of the current chapter with its focus on school-age learners (see Bailey & Osipova, 2016; Espinosa, 2013 for reviews).

Language Acquisition Theories and Young Learners: Implications for ELP Assessment

SLA theories and learning theories more generally can offer ELP assessment much needed specificity about the nature of development across different aspects of language usage and form (e.g., Purpura, 2004). By taking account of SLA theories, test developers can help ensure that constructs and content coverage are included in assessments in meaningful ways (i.e., appropriate emphasis, predictable sequencing, expected rates of growth, etc.) (Bailey, 2010) and that chosen assessment formats are suited to the developmental needs and range of backgrounds presented by young language learners.

Informal or alternative assessment approaches (e.g., quizzes, peer and self-assessments, games, and teacher observations) are frequently created by the classroom teacher and used to ascertain student performance and progress. In contrast, formal or standardized assessments are by their very nature pre-formatted and likely normed on large samples of students. The advantages of informal assessments are in their sensitivity and suitability for use with school-age language learners. Spinelli (2008) argues that "These more authentic assessment procedures provide a means for ELLs to demonstrate what they know and can do in their own unique ways" (p. 113). The implication is that developers of standardized assessments may not anticipate all the ways in which young language learners may be able to demonstrate their English proficiency. However, there is no intrinsic reason that standardized assessments cannot attempt to measure the language proficiency of young learners in more authentic ways—considerations to which we return at the close of this chapter.

Cutting across the different theoretical positions is the basic question of *what do we think develops when we speak of growth in language abilities?* Past research has articulated the progression of language performance in different ways. For example, language growth of students may be judged by increases in the amount of language they produce, by how rapidly they acquire a new language, by improvements in accuracy and complexity of language forms or structures (e.g., tense markers and sentence types), as well as by expansions in repertoires for these forms or structures and in the repertoire of functions for which language is used (e.g., to explain, to describe, and to argue) (Bailey & Heritage, 2014). Theories that can capture some if not most of these dimensions of language progression would be the most likely candidates for enhancing the test development process.

A seminal SLA theory—the common underlying language proficiency—came out of the psycholinguistics tradition: "The uniqueness of psycholinguistics lies in providing theoretical models that offer a fundamental architecture for understanding how L2 acquisition works in the mind" (Dixon et al., 2012, p. 36). Common underlying language proficiency was posited to account for the interdependence (and transfer) between languages by L2 and bilingual speakers (Cummins, 2000; Genesee, Lindholm-Leary, Saunders, & Christian, 2006). The notion of transfer occurring between two languages, to which we later return, can be seen as a positive strategy when there is concordance between the two languages, or a negative one when the transfer of knowledge or skills leads to erroneous production and/or learning in the L2.

Most theories can be divided into those that offer models of language *usage* to account for language learning (e.g., knowledge of a language stems from exposure to authentic speech events) and those that offer *focus-on-forms* explanations (e.g., knowledge of a language stems from emphasizing "formal aspects of language ... by isolating them for practice through exercises"; Hummel, 2014, p. 259).[1]

The short review of SLA theories in this section is by no means exhaustive, and I highlight just a few of the most influential theories with implications for assessment of young learners.

Social Interactionist Theory and Dynamic Assessment

The social interactionist theory of language development follows the general learning principles of Vygotsky (1978) and posits "a dialectical relationship between language and thinking processes, with each process shaping and being shaped by the other in an internal mental system" (Mahn, 2013, p. 6151). Language, it is argued, is acquired through verbal exchanges with more expert others in students' everyday lives. Moreover, these interactions are tailored to the language level of the learner in ways that can support their acquisition of next-step skills (i.e., engaging children in dialogue in their *Zone of Proximal Development*, the zone between the levels at which children can succeed on a task independently and at which they can succeed with assistance). Under this model, young language learners construct their new language through routines, and with the aid of scaffolds (e.g., graduated assistance such as eliciting sentence fragments before moving on to short, simple sentence structures), and the modeling of target language uses by others (Bruner, 1985).

What begins as external and supported by more knowledgeable others becomes internal and controlled by the learner over time. Implications for language assessment development include creating tasks that include different levels of assistance for the test taker. Bailey (2016) describes how tasks may be designed to start out fully scaffolded and then slowly withdraw supports until the point that a student can no longer respond or responds incorrectly. Alternatively, a task may be designed to begin with no support and then, as necessary, the teacher or language tester can provide support in incremental amounts until the point that a student can perform the task competently and independently.

An assessment approach with close conceptual ties to social interactionist theories of learning includes *dynamic assessment* in which students may be taught relevant linguistic strategies to successfully complete a task (through mediated teaching that may use modeling and rehearsal) before being presented with a comparable task to solve alone. Rather than simply getting a static or "one-shot" response from a student completing a task, by using a pre- and post-test design, with observations of the task-solving stage, an assessor can not only compare across performances, but also use dynamic assessment to reveal information about the processes adopted by the student in completing the task. In a study of narrative language abilities in 7- and 8-year-old students with diverse language backgrounds, some with language impairment, Peña and colleagues (2006) found dynamic assessment could be a reliable way to distinguish between language impairment and differences due to a different L1 spoken by students.

Social interactionism also has implications for the use of paired-assessment techniques that require students to take each other's perspectives, take turns, and develop mutual topics (Butler & Zang, 2014). In the Butler and Zeng study of 4th and 6th grade students in an EFL context, the younger students were less able to succeed on these requirements than the older students leading the authors to conclude that developmental constraints on younger children make these dyadic assessment situations less effective.

Social Cultural Theory and Formative Assessment

Social cultural theory, with notions of situated learning, builds on the ideas of Vygotsky (e.g., learning embedded within the ongoing social world of the child) and explains learning as taking up a participation role within a community. Specifically, anthological and ethnographic approaches to the study of child development position children as "cultural apprentices" (Rogoff, 1990). These ideas extend to language acquisition that is achieved through the child seeking guided participation from more knowledgeable others such as older children, parents, and other caregivers. Such a theoretical approach informs assessment approaches that operationalize formative assessment as assessment *for* learning rather than as assessment *of* learning (Black & Wiliam, 1998). Formative assessment involves the careful observation of learning in situ and interactions with students to draw out student knowledge and skills. Educators and others who engage in contingent pedagogy (i.e., using evidence from formative assessment approaches to make next-steps instructional decisions and offer students feedback) build on students' current language to advance language learning (Bailey & Heritage, 2014). There have been few studies of formative assessment use in K–12 ESL and EFL situations to date, so large-scale and long-term effectiveness of teacher adoption of formative assessment approaches are wanting.

A central component of formative assessment is student self-assessment. Student self-assessment allows students to notice their own performances, reflect on what is effective and what is not, and incorporate teacher feedback. Student self-assessment fits within formative assessment approaches and social cultural theory with its emphasis on student agency in their own learning. Students can be involved in characterizing their own progress and in setting goals or objectives for their language learning which can also contribute to a personalized-learning approach to instruction. A study by Butler and Lee (2010) evaluated the effectiveness of 6th grade Korean students' self-assessment during EFL instruction for their language learning and confidence. Pre-constructed self-assessment items were given to students at regular intervals across the course of a semester. While there were modest but significant quantifiable improvements in language learning and confidence, the study revealed that the educational environment (e.g., emphasis on grading versus feedback) and attitude of teachers towards the use of self-assessment may make a difference in the impact of self-assessment for students.

Elsewhere, Butler and Lee (2006) found self-assessment to be less effective with younger EFL students: 4th graders were not as accurate as older students in terms of rating themselves consistent with their teacher's ratings and standardized test performance. However, more recently Bailey, Blackstock-Bernstein, Ryan, and Pitsoulakis (2016) reported that with appropriate scaffolds (e.g., guided to aurally notice different qualities of their oral explanations), 3rd and 4th grade ESL students rated their English performance comparable to the ratings of researchers. Second graders were not as accurate, but even these young students could still successfully participate in the self-assessment.

Systemic Functional Linguistic Theory and Portfolio Assessment

Other influential usage-based perspectives on language learning include systemic functional linguistics (SFL) and notions of SLA as a process of developing multi-competencies. Both have important implications for language assessment. SFL is an approach to explaining language focused on language functions or what language is used for within a social context (Halliday, 1994). Rather than focus on formal aspects of language, all levels, including the semantic and grammar levels, are characterized by their functions. More specifically, choice of certain words and sentence structures for example is made for conveying meaning in a register such as the language of K–12 schooling, where the genres may be, for example, science explanatory texts or personal narrative texts in language arts or social studies (Schleppegrell, 2002). The notions of genre and register have been influential in identifying the most meaningful content of ELP assessments that are aligned with school uses of language (e.g., Bailey, Butler, Stevens, & Lord, 2007). SFL can be influential in how ELP task design embeds word- and sentence-level language features within the language functions that may commonly predict their inclusion. For example, declarative utterances may be utilized to create an authoritative stance within explanatory texts (Schleppegrell, 2002).

SLA as a process of developing multi-competencies helps to reframe views of SLA that may position language learners as needing to *overcome* linguistic deficits (Cook, 2008). The theoretical viewpoint of multi-competencies posits students distribute linguistic resources across their range of developing languages, rather than focus the teacher, and by extension the language tester, on what students may more narrowly know and do within one language. Portfolio assessment is an alternative assessment approach that allows for a broad array of language skills to be represented. Student work samples can be collected across time and in various contexts to give a more comprehensive evaluation or profile of student performance (Puckett & Black, 2000). For example, the European Language Portfolio of the Common European Framework of Reference for Languages (CEFR, Council of Europe, 2001) uses the CEFR's language levels (performance level descriptors in common across all languages) so that students can directly judge their own language progress, functioning also as a form of self-assessment (Little, 2009).

Complex Adaptive Systems Theory and Learning Progression-Driven Assessment

Focus-on-forms accounts of language learning have their roots in the information processing and skill theories of cognitive psychology (R. Ellis, 2001), and even behaviorist models of learning. For example, the audio-lingual method postulates that SLA occurs (albeit often unsuccessfully) through repetitive drills to establish language patterns in the learner, such as sentence structure frames (Hummel, 2014). Nick Ellis (2008) argues that SLA requires both usage-based experiences and form-focused instruction (not as all-encompassing as focus-on-forms approaches, rather a complementary focus on formal features as they arise in meaningful communication). Usage-based components such as frequency of input, salience, contingency, and attending to competing cues for interpreting meaning may not be sufficient for SLA to result in proficiency. Usage-based accounts of language development that suffice for explaining L1 development do not account for SLA which often stops short of achieving full proficiency for many L2 learners. Other factors that do not occur in the context of L1 development are argued to impinge upon SLA success due to L1 "entrenchment" (e.g., such processes as interference from the L1 or over-shadowing by the L1). As a result, advancement in L2 may require complementary form-focused instruction to provide "a greater level of explicit awareness of L2 constructions" (N. Ellis, 2008, p. 373). ELP assessment might be best served to match these complementary theoretical approaches to SLA by including tasks that address the meaning-making purpose of language along with some attempt to assess student competencies in specific key skills that may impact communication if lacking from a student's core linguistic repertoire, such as personal pronoun control, verb agreement and tense, question formation, etc.

A recent theory of SLA has emerged from observations of the complementary nature of usage-based and focus-on-forms approaches that borrows from dynamic systems theory in the field of physics in its attempt to unite a number of disparate aspects. Complex adaptive systems (CAS) theory combines language experience (exposure), cognitive mechanisms, and social interaction (N. Ellis & Larsen-Freeman, 2009; Larsen-Freeman, 2011). Under this view, language "learning is dynamic, it takes place during processing" (N. Ellis, 2012, p. 202). Experience and cognition account for learners' processing and inferencing about language from the frequency of types (distinct items) and tokens (number of occurrences) in the input they receive. Ellis stresses, "[Learners] have to encounter useful exemplars and analyze them to identify their linguistic form, the meaning, and the mapping between these" (p. 202). Structures of language (e.g., phonological, morphological, and syntactic) emerge from these interrelated facets (N. Ellis & Larsen-Freeman, 2009). The social interaction is critical because learners respond to "affordances" (i.e., verbal supports from teachers, parents, and peers) emerging from authentic communicative situations (van Lier & Walqui, 2012). A major contribution of this viewpoint is the variability in development that it can account for, with no one single pathway for acquiring L2.

In the area of young learner assessment, CAS has recently influenced the design of the *Dynamic Language Learning Progressions* (DLLP) Project (Bailey & Heritage, 2014) that is creating empirically-based language progressions (i.e., generated from authentic student language samples), ostensibly for use in formative assessment to guide teachers in placing their students' language performances on developmental trajectories. DLLPs are informed by CAS in that they take account of diverse learner characteristics and contexts of learning that interact with development, can capture asynchronous or nonlinear progress in SLA, and simultaneously allow multiple pathways to development of English proficiency.

Such empirically-based progressions can also be used to align assessment systems in terms of common content and an underlying theory of learning (National Research Council, 2001) across formative, interim, and summative assessments, and have an advantage over typical grade-level English language development or proficiency standards (e.g., TESOL preK–12 *English Language*

Proficiency Standards, 2006) in this regard: students' progress can be normed relative to that of comparable students (e.g., same number of years of English exposure, same grade, and same reading level, etc.) in the DLLP database, "producing fairer and more precise expectations (i.e., grounded in real data)" (Bailey & Heritage, 2014, p. 487).

Broader Ramifications for ELP Assessment With Young Learners

This overview of developmental and theory-based issues has broad ramifications for the creation and use of ELP assessments in the areas of (1) language-learning approaches, (2) the ELP construct, and (3) technology use with young learners.

Language-Learning Approaches

A reconciliation of usage-based and focus-on-forms approaches to explaining how language is learned combines the basic tenets of both approaches (i.e., communicative purpose with appropriate attention to formal features) and can guide standardized assessment development in terms of task types and content. Tasks could mirror authentic activities that students encounter in their daily lives including school, home, and recreational language uses, and also embed the most predictable lexical, syntactic, and discourse/genre features that research suggests covary with these activities (e.g., Schleppegrell, 2002). For example, if tasks are designed to elicit personal storytelling, then students will need skills in the areas of key vocabulary for organizing the temporal and logical sequence of events (e.g., *first*, *then*, and *afterwards*, etc.), the past tense forms of verbs, and organization of extended discourse such as narrative macrostructures (e.g., orientation, complicating action, high-point, evaluation, and resolution, Labov, 1972). A standardized assessment can be designed to measure these formal subcomponents to complement the successful meaning-making aspects of the task that may be about sharing a personal story in order to, for example, comfort a friend who is afraid of going to the doctor, taking a final exam, or flying for the first time.

The notion of scaffolded assistance is another impactful ramification of articulating different language-learning approaches with respect to ELP assessment. Standardized assessment can create constructed response item types that vary the degree of assistance given to the test taker. Such variation can reveal what levels of support a student may require in order to respond accurately or completely, and assessments for English learners incorporating scaffolding are already underway (Wolf et al., 2016). Moreover, partial credit models of scoring already used in the standardized assessment field can be used to account for the different levels of assistance provided in such assessments.

The English Language Proficiency (ELP) Construct

In both ESL and EFL contexts, getting the ELP construct right will be paramount to both alternative and standardized forms of assessment. In the past, ELP assessment has placed far greater emphasis on social (or certainly less academic) contexts of language use (Butler, Stevens, & Castellon-Wellington, 2007). Yet young learners in both ESL and EFL contexts spend up to one third if not more of their day in school. The language construct or constructs that must be represented on ELP assessments need to be carefully considered and must reflect the comprehensive uses to which young language learners put their language (Frantz, Bailey, Starr, & Perea, 2014; Inbar-Lourie & Shohamy, 2009; Wolf et al., 2014). For example, young ESL learners are increasingly required to explain procedures in mathematics, argue from evidence in science, and analyze character motives in language arts both orally and in writing (e.g., *English Language Proficiency Development Framework*, Council of Chief State School Officers, 2012). In so much as international school curricula align with U.S. school reform efforts, this will also be true for the ELP construct in the EFL context, with increasing desire for English-medium instruction across the curriculum in Asia, for example (Kirkpatrick, 2011).

Technology Use With Young Learners

With the innovations offered by digital technology, standardized assessment can also approach the dialogic nature of paired-assessment and the reflective and reflexive nature of self-assessment discussed above as forms of alternative assessment. Computer- and apps-based scholastic tests and out-of-school uses of digital devices are cumulative experiences with technology that prepare young learners well for innovative language assessments that mimic the electronic game world (Butler, Someya, & Fukuhara, 2014) and utilize virtual interlocutors or avatars to evaluate conversational skills (Evanini et al., 2014). Young language learners' scores in such computer-based assessments are generated by Automated Speech Recognition and Natural Language Processing software and are found to correlate highly with human ratings of their speech (e.g., Evanini, Heilman, Wang, & Blanchard, 2015). While this technology has yet to be put into school settings and made readily accessible to teachers and students, the findings are encouraging for the future of assessment with young learners: Children respond as if the digital contexts are authentic contexts for generating evidence of communicative competence, and virtual interlocutors may be more appealing not simply for their game-like or visual appeal but because young children may be less anxious when tested by a nonhuman (avatar) interlocutor.

Electronic gaming as a fully immersive learning experience has been found promising with young EFL language learners (Butler et al., 2014). The next step of embedding assessment within electronic games promises to provide information on both processes and outcomes of learning, as well as provide a high degree of adaptability to individual learning styles (Bellotti, Kapralos, Lee, Moreno-Ger, & Berta, 2013). This would seem particularly suited to the inherent heterogeneity found in young learners. While there are studies of the effectiveness of game-based assessment used with young students in content areas such as science (Wang, 2008) and mathematics (Zapata-Rivera, 2009), application of games to language assessment of young learners is relatively scarce. It has been tried only within some limited areas (e.g., vocabulary assessment, Zapata-Rivera, 2009).

Clearly, more research and development is needed at the intersection of language, game-based assessment and technology. This is despite the design of language assessment as games (electronic or otherwise) long being touted as a desirable trait in order to gain and hold the attention of young learners and motivate their interest in responding optimally (Hasselgreen, 2005). Moreover, if assessment no longer resembles the testing that has traditionally stopped instruction, required separate episodes of review and preparation and, when administered, may have caused undue anxiety, games that embed assessments as a form of "stealth assessment" (Shute & Kim, 2014) avoid all of the above and seem ideally positioned for use with young learners.

Concluding Remarks

There are, of course, many remaining challenges for both alternative and standardized assessments of ELP in young learners. A key challenge has been alluded to throughout this chapter—the homogeneity assumption that standardized assessments depend on for the validity of their interpretation is, in fact, violated by their use with young language learners. In other words, standardized assessments assume that each test taker shares much the same testing experience, but young learners, as a group, are wildly disparate in terms of their cognitive and socio-emotional maturity. Where they fall along these developmental trajectories can alter the assessment experience for them and affect how certain we can be in our interpretations of their assessment results. There are several ways the field of language assessment can address this challenge, including the use of multiple measures, varied item types, and/or assessing at multiple time-points to build up a more comprehensive profile of student language performances (Bailey et al., 2014). Whether these techniques alone or in combination can mitigate the effects of the homogeneity assumption are questions that need immediate attention by assessment developers working with young learners.

Another challenge that faces standardized ELP assessment developers is the selection of a meaningful comparison group by which to judge the learner's performance. To whom are young ESL and EFL students to be compared—native speakers of English? And if so, are these to be monolingual native speakers of English,[2] or might proficient bilingual speakers be the model by which to hold aspiring bilingual students (Garcia & Menken, 2006; see also Wolf, Lopez, Oh, &

Tsutagawa, 2017 in this volume for this issue). Cook (2007) reminds us that native-like proficiency in English as L2 is a largely unrealistic goal. Moreover, the standards that exist (many K–12 ESL standards created by U.S. states and other English-speaking countries, as well as language-general standards such as the CEFR) outline the expectations we hold for language proficiency, and these are currently largely aspirational, based as they most often are on best guesses, not data, for the course and duration of language development in young learners.

Finally, innovations in technology, especially those that conceptualize language assessment (both standardized and alternative) as an extension of gaming formats and practices, still need considerable research and development efforts in order to bring them to fruition with young language learners. However, we conclude on a strong note of optimism: Innovations with the most adaptable of human minds—those of young children—as the target of new assessments of language stand to make the most gains if they are not only appealing but also relevant for the scholastic and personal lives of young learners of English everywhere.

Notes

1 Not to be confused with *form-focused* approaches that draw "students' attention to aspects of linguistic form in classrooms characterized by a meaning- or communication-based approach" (Hummel, 2014, p. 259).
2 Which of the many varieties of English to choose poses an additional question, of course.

References

Au, T. K. F., Oh, J. S., Knightly, L. M., Jun, S. A., & Romo, L. F. (2008). Salvaging a childhood language. *Journal of Memory and Language*, 58(4), 998–1011.

Bachman, L. F. (2005). Building and supporting a case for test use. *Language Assessment Quarterly*, 2(1), 1–34.

Bailey, A. L. (2010). Assessment in schools: Oracy. In M. James (Section Ed.), *International Encyclopedia of Education* (3rd ed.) (pp. 285–292). Amsterdam: Elsevier.

Bailey, A. L. (2016). Assessing the language of young learners. In E. Shohamy & I. Or (Eds.), *Encyclopedia of language and education, Vol. 7: Language testing and assessment* (3rd ed.) (pp. 1–20). Berlin: Springer.

Bailey, A. L., Blackstock-Bernstein, A., Ryan, E., & Pitsoulakis, D. (2016). Data mining with natural language processing and corpus linguistics: Unlocking access to school-children's language in diverse contexts to improve instructional and assessment practices. In S. El Atia, O. Zaiane, & D. Ipperciel (Eds.), *Data mining and learning analytics in educational research* (pp. 255–275). Malden, MA: Wiley-Blackwell.

Bailey, A. L., Butler, F. A., Stevens, R., & Lord, C. (2007). Further specifying the language demands of school. In A. L. Bailey (Ed.), *The language demands of school: Putting academic language to the test* (pp. 103–156). New Haven, CT: Yale University Press.

Bailey, A. L., & Heritage, M. (2014). The role of language learning progressions in improved instruction and assessment of English language learners. *TESOL Quarterly*, 48(3), 480–506.

Bailey, A. L., Heritage, M., & Butler, F. A. (2014). Developmental considerations and curricular contexts in the assessment of young language learners. In A. J. Kunnan (Ed.), *The companion to language assessment* (pp. 423–439). Boston, MA: Wiley.

Bailey, A. L., & Osipova, A. (2016). *Multilingual development and education: Home and school contexts for creating and sustaining the linguistic resources of children.* Cambridge, UK: Cambridge University Press.

Bellotti, F., Kapralos, B., Lee, K., Moreno Ger, P., & Berta, R. (2013). Assessment in and of serious games: An overview. *Advances in Human-Computer Interaction*, *1*, 1–11.

Black, P. J., & Wiliam, D. (1998). Assessment and classroom learning. *Assessment in Education: Principles Policy and Practice*, *5*, 7–73.

Bruner, J. (1985). *Child's talk: Learning to use language*. Oxford, England: Oxford University Press.

Butler, F. A., Stevens, R., & Castellon-Wellington, M. (2007). ELLs and standardized assessments: The interaction between language proficiency and performance on standardized tests. In A. L. Bailey (Ed.), *Language demands of school: Putting academic language to the test* (pp. 27–49). New Haven, CT: Yale University Press.

Butler, Y. G. (2017). Challenges and future directions for young learners' English language assessments and validity research. In M. K. Wolf & Y. G. Butler (Eds.), *English language proficiency assessments for young learners* (pp. 255–273). New York, NY: Routledge.

Butler, Y. G., & Lee, J. (2006). On-task versus off-task self-assessment among Korean elementary school students studying English. *The Modern Language Journal*, *90*(4), 506–518.

Butler, Y. G., & Lee, J. (2010). The effects of self-assessment among young learners of English. *Language Testing*, *27*(1), 5–31.

Butler, Y. G., Someya, Y., & Fukuhara, E. (2014). Online games for young learners' foreign language learning. *ELT Journal*, *68*(3), 265–275.

Butler, Y. G., & Zang, W. (2014). Young foreign language learners' interactions during task-based paired assessments. *Language Assessment Quarterly*, *11*(1), 45–75.

Cook, V. (2007). The goals of ELT: Reproducing native-speakers or promoting multi-competence among second language users? In J. Cummins & C. Davison (Eds.), *International handbook on English language teaching* (pp. 237–248). New York, NY: Springer.

Cook, V. (2008). Multi-competence: Black hole or wormhole for second language acquisition research. In Z. Han (Ed.), *Understanding second language process* (pp. 16–26). Clevedon, UK: Multilingual Matters.

Council of Chief State School Officers. (2012). *Framework for English language proficiency development standards corresponding to the Common Core State Standards and the Next Generation Science Standards*. Washington, DC: Author.

Council of Europe. (2001). *Common European Framework of Reference for languages: Learning, teaching, assessment*. Cambridge, UK: Cambridge University Press.

Cummins, J. (2000). *Language, power, and pedagogy: Bilingual children in the crossfire*. Clevedon, UK: Multilingual Matters.

Dixon, Q. L., Zhao, J., Shin, J.-Y., Wu, S., Su, J.-H., Burgess-Brigham, R., Unal Gezar, M., & Snow, C. (2012). What we know about second language acquisition: A synthesis from four perspectives. *Review of Educational Research*, *82*(5), 5–60.

Ellis, N. C. (2008). Usage-based and form-focused language acquisition: The associative learning of constructions, learned attention, and the limited L2 endstate. In P. Robinson & N. C. Ellis (Eds.), *Handbook of cognitive linguistics and second language acquisition* (pp. 372–405). New York, NY: Routledge.

Ellis, N. C. (2012). Second language acquisition. In S. M. Gass & A. Mackey (Eds.), *Handbook of second language acquisition* (pp. 193–210). New York, NY: Routledge.

Ellis, N. C., & Larsen-Freeman, D. (2009). *Language as a complex adaptive system.* Malden, MA: Wiley-Blackwell.

Ellis, R. (2001). Introduction: Investigating form-focused instruction. *Language Learning, 51*(1), 1–46.

Espinosa, L. (2013). Assessment of young English-language learners. In C. A. Chapelle (Ed.), *The encyclopedia of applied linguistics* (pp. 1-7). Oxford, UK: Blackwell Publishing.

Evanini, K., Heilman, M., Wang, X., & Blanchard, D. (2015). *Automated scoring for the TOEFL Junior® comprehensive writing and speaking test* (ETS Research Report No. RR-15–09). Princeton, NJ: Educational Testing Service.

Evanini, K., So, Y., Tao, J., Zapata-Rivera, D., Luce, C., Battistini, L., & Wang, X. (2014). *Performance of a trialogue-based prototype system for English language assessment for young learners.* Proceedings of the Interspeech Workshop on Child Computer Interaction, Singapore. Available from http://www.wocci.org/2014/files/submissions/Evanini14-POA.pdf

Frantz, R. S., Bailey, A. L., Starr, L., & Perea, L. (2014). Measuring academic language proficiency in school-age English language proficiency assessments under new college and career readiness standards in the United States. *Language Assessment Quarterly, 11*(4), 432–457.

Garcia, O., & Menken, K. (2006). The English of Latinos from a plurilingual transcultural angle: Implications for assessment and schools. In S. J. Nero (Ed.), *Dialects, Englishes, creoles, and education* (pp. 167–183). Mahwah, NJ: Lawrence Erlbaum.

Gathercole, S. E., Pickering, S. J., Knight, C., & Stegmann, Z. (2004). Working memory skills and educational attainment: Evidence from national curriculum assessments at 7 and 14 years of age. *Applied Cognitive Psychology, 18*(1), 1–16.

Genesee, F., Lindholm-Leary, K. J., Saunders, W., & Christian, D. (2006). *Educating English language learners: A synthesis of empirical evidence.* New York, NY: Cambridge University Press.

Gervain, J. (2015). Plasticity in early language acquisition: The effects of prenatal and early childhood experience. *Current Opinion in Neurobiology, 35,* 13–20.

Halliday, M. A. K. (1994). *Introduction to functional grammar* (2nd ed.). London, UK: Edward Arnold.

Hasselgreen, A. (2005). Assessing the language of young learners. *Language Testing, 22*(3), 337–354.

Hummel, K. M. (2014). *Introducing second language acquisition: Perspectives and practices.* Malden, MA: Wiley Blackwell.

Inbar-Lourie, O., & Shohamy, E. (2009). Assessing young language learners: What is the construct? In M. Nikolov (Ed.), *The age factor and early language learning* (pp. 83–96). Berlin, Germany: Mouton de Gruyter.

Jang, E. E., Vincett, M., van der Boom, E., Lau, C., & Yang, Y. (2017). Considering young learners' characteristics in developing a diagnostic assessment intervention. In M. K. Wolf & Y. G. Butler (Eds.), *English language proficiency assessments for young learners* (pp. 193–213). New York, NY: Routledge.

Kane, M. (2013). Validating the interpretations and uses of test scores. *Journal of Educational Measurement, 50*(1), 1–73.

Kirkpatrick, A. (2011). English as a medium of instruction in Asian education (from primary to tertiary): Implications for local languages and local scholarship. *Applied Linguistics Review, 2,* 99–120.

Labov, W. (1972). *Language in the inner city: Studies in the Black English vernacular* (Vol. 3). Philadelphia, PA: University of Pennsylvania Press.
Larsen-Freeman, D. (2011). A complexity theory approach to second language development/acquisition. In D. Atkinson (Ed.), *Alternative approaches to second language acquisition* (pp. 48–72). London: Routledge.
Little, D. (2009). *European language portfolio: Where pedagogy and assessment meet.* Proceedings of the International Seminar on the European Language Portfolio, Graz, Austria.
Luna, B., Garver, K. E., Urban, T. A., Lazar, N. A., & Sweeney, J. A. (2004). Maturation of cognitive processes from late childhood to adulthood. *Child Development, 75*(5), 1357–1372.
Mahn, H. (2013). Vygotsky and second language acquisition. In C. A. Chapelle (Ed.), *The encyclopedia of applied linguistics* (pp. 6150–6157). Oxford, UK: Blackwell Publishing.
McKay, P. (2006). *Assessing young language learners*. Cambridge, UK: Cambridge University Press.
National Research Council. (2001). *Knowing what students know: The science of design and educational assessment*. Washington, DC: National Academy Press.
Peña, E. D., Gillam, R. B., Malek, M., Ruiz-Felter, R., Resendiz, M., Fiestas, C., & Sabel, T. (2006). Dynamic assessment of school-age children's narrative ability: An experimental investigation of classification accuracy. *Journal of Speech, Language, and Hearing Research, 49*(5), 1037–1057.
Puckett, M. B., & Black, J. K. (2000). *Authentic assessment of the young child*. Upper Saddle River, NJ: Prentice Hall.
Purpura, J. E. (2004). *Assessing grammar*. Cambridge, UK: Cambridge University Press.
Rich, S. (2014). Taking stock; where are we now with TEYL? In R. S. Rich (Ed.), *International perspectives on teaching English to young learners* (pp. 1–22). Basingstoke, UK: Palgrave Macmillan.
Rogoff, B. (1990). *Apprenticeship in thinking: Cognitive development in social context*. Oxford, UK: Oxford University Press.
Schleppegrell, M. J. (2002). Linguistic features of the language of schooling. *Linguistics and Education, 12*(4), 431–459.
Shute, V. J., & Kim, Y. J. (2014). Formative and stealth assessment. In J. M. Spector, M. D. Merrill, J. Elen, & M. J. Bishop (Eds.), *Handbook of research on educational communications and technology* (pp. 311–321). New York, NY: Springer.
Spinelli, C. G. (2008). Addressing the issue of cultural and linguistic diversity and assessment: Informal evaluation measures for English language learners. *Reading & Writing Quarterly, 24*(1), 101–118.
TESOL. (2006). *PreK–12 English language proficiency standards*. Washington, DC: Author.
van Lier, L., & Walqui, A. (2012). Language and the common core standards. In K. Hakuta & M. Santos (Eds.), *Understanding language: Commissioned papers on language and literacy issues in the Common Core State Standards and Next Generation Science Standards* (pp. 44–51). Palo Alto, CA: Stanford University.
Vygotsky, L. S. (1978). *Mind and society: The development of higher mental processes*. Cambridge, MA: Harvard University Press.
Wang, T. H. (2008). Web-based quiz-game-like formative assessment: Development and evaluation. *Computers & Education, 51*(3), 1247–1263.
Wolf, M. K., & Butler, Y. G. (2017). Overview of English language proficiency assessments for young learners. In M. K. Wolf & Y. G. Butler (Eds.), *English language proficiency assessments for young learners* (pp. 3–21). New York, NY: Routledge.

Wolf, M. K., Everson, P., Lopez, A., Hauck, M., Pooler, E., & Wang, J. (2014). *Building a framework for a next-generation English language proficiency assessment system* (ETS Research Report No. RR-14-34). Princeton, NJ: Educational Testing Service.

Wolf, M. K., Guzman-Orth, D., Lopez, A., Castellano, K., Himelfarb, I., & Tsutagawa, F. (2016). Integrating scaffolding strategies into technology-enhanced assessments of English learners: Task types and measurement models. *Educational Assessment*, *21*(3), 157–175.

Wolf, M. K., Lopez, A., Oh, S., & Tsutagawa, F. S. (2017). Comparing the performance of young English language learners and native English speakers on speaking assessment tasks. In M. K. Wolf & Y. G. Butler (Eds.), *English language proficiency assessments for young learners* (pp. 171–190). New York, NY: Routledge.

Zapata-Rivera, D. (2009, April). *Assessment-based gaming environments*. Paper presented at the Annual Meeting of the American Educational Research Association, San Diego, CA. Available from http://www.ets.org/Media/Conferences_and_Events/AERA_2009_pdfs/AERA_NCME_2009_Zapata_Rivera1.pdf

3

DESIGNING THE *TOEFL®* *PRIMARY*™ TESTS

Yeonsuk Cho, Mitch Ginsburgh, Rick Morgan, Brad Moulder, Xiaoming Xi, and Maurice Cogan Hauck

The *TOEFL® Primary*™ tests were introduced in 2013 to meet the assessment needs of young learners between approximately 8 and 11 years of age who are learning English in countries where English is a foreign language (EFL) and have limited opportunities to use English either inside or outside the classroom.[1] As independent measures of English language proficiency, the *TOEFL Primary* tests provide users a snapshot of English ability in listening, reading, and speaking. The purpose of this chapter[2] is to give an overview of the development process of the *TOEFL Primary* tests. To that end, we first explain the intent of the *TOEFL Primary* tests and present a conceptual foundation that helped define what the tests should measure. Then we describe how the final design of the *TOEFL Primary* tests was made throughout the test development process. We conclude with a discussion of the research that is needed to build validity arguments for the *TOEFL Primary* tests.

TOEFL Primary Tests' Intended Population, Purposes, and Uses

The *TOEFL Primary* tests are designed to accommodate a broad range of English proficiency levels represented in the intended population. The Council of Europe (n.d.) suggested that the proficiency levels A1, A2, and B1 on the Common European Framework of Reference (CEFR) be expected for most elementary or low secondary students learning a foreign language in the formal school environment. This recommendation was supported by the results of Rixon's (2013) worldwide survey of policy and teaching practice of teaching English in primary or elementary schools; about a third of respondents reported that the target proficiency levels at the end of primary or elementary school were in the range of

A1 to B1. However, these three levels may not reflect the "real" proficiency levels of young EFL learners because of extra opportunities to learn English beyond the formal school curricula. Young EFL learners, for example, may attend private English language enrichment classes or have tutors for additional support. Such an opportunity helps students acquire more advanced English knowledge and skills than is expected of students whose English learning occurs mainly in regular school-based English classes at the primary and elementary school levels, (e.g., Chien, 2012; Garton, Copland, & Burns, 2011). Considering such variability in young EFL learners' experiences in learning English, *TOEFL Primary* tests are therefore developed to cover a wider range of levels of English proficiency.

The intended purpose of the *TOEFL Primary* tests is primarily to support teaching and learning by providing meaningful feedback that educators can incorporate into their instruction. We expect that educators and parents use test scores to determine what their students and children have accomplished and to identify areas for improvement. As the *TOEFL Primary* tests measure core communication skills derived from EFL curricula and provide detailed and meaningful feedback, teachers and parents may find the test results relevant in providing instructional support appropriate to students' ability levels. In addition, some schools may use *TOEFL Primary* scores to place students into levels of instruction, if appropriate. These actions are expected to enhance young EFL students' learning experience and ultimately lead to improved English proficiency. It is not desirable to use *TOEFL Primary* test scores for high-stakes decisions, such as admitting students, evaluating teachers, or comparing or ranking individual students.

Conceptual and Practical Bases for Defining the English Ability of Young EFL Learners

To understand how young EFL students learn English and subsequently to define a construct of English ability for *TOEFL Primary*, we considered (a) general insights from the literature and (b) the content of EFL curricula and textbooks. In this section, we discuss the key points related to the language learning of young EFL students. Further, we describe how information from EFL curricula and textbooks informed the construct definition of English ability for the *TOEFL Primary* tests.

Insights From Research: What Characteristics Are Associated With the English Language Proficiency of Young EFL Learners?

The Meaning-Based Approach in Learning English as a Foreign Language

According to MacNamara (1972), children possess an innate desire to make sense of the world, and this desire also applies in learning a language. As MacNamara described, language spoken to young learners in their first language usually contains concrete information that they can understand without knowing grammatical rules. During the first few years of language learning, children focus mainly on meaning for communication. Throughout this process, they acquire language rules implicitly, almost as a byproduct of recognizing meaning. The acquisition of language rules is, thus, incidental for the first several years of first-language learning. MacNamara supported this position with examples of children's language performance. He stated that children attend mainly to meaning, disregarding function words such as prepositions while still conveying the substance of their messages.

MacNamara's explanation has an intuitive appeal, and it may be relevant to the experience of elementary school EFL students who often learn English without receiving explicit instruction on language rules. Others, including Cameron (2001, 2003) and McKay (2006), have also concluded on the basis of both theoretical and empirical evidence that children seek meaning first. On this basis, Cameron recommended that in order to optimize children's language learning, language tasks used in classrooms should be meaning-focused. Thus, decontextualized tasks that require metalinguistic knowledge or explicit knowledge of language rules should be avoided with young learners (Pinter, 2006). McKay (2006) also advised against teaching explicit grammar rules to young learners, emphasizing the meaning-based approach to language learning for young learners.

Linguistic Knowledge as an "Enabling Tool" for Communication

With regard to assessing young learners, therefore, the component elements of linguistic knowledge, such as grammar, vocabulary, and pronunciation, should be viewed as ancillary rather than central to the definition of language ability. Some evidence indicates that it is unrealistic to expect a steady, predictable increase in either grammatical accuracy or vocabulary knowledge for young EFL learners. Zangl (2000) explained that the language development of young EFL learners is an uneven progression consisting of "peaks and troughs." Students make progress through "seemingly regressive periods" in which they produce errors that they did not produce before. This is partly due to a shift from relying on memorized language chunks to manipulating language structures based on their understanding of rules. Zangl advocated the importance of considering the different stages of foreign language development when evaluating young EFL learners and interpreting their test results.

Related to Zangl's (2000) point, Johnstone (2000) expressed doubt about the validity of language proficiency levels defined by existing scales and standards because of a lack of empirical evidence regarding the development of foreign language ability among young students. Although increasing grammatical accuracy and vocabulary are often viewed as indicators of higher proficiency, empirical evidence suggests otherwise. For example, Johnstone (2000) described interview data from students between 5 and 12 years of age who were learning a foreign language. Although older students produced more language, their language showed little improvement over their young counterparts in terms of grammatical accuracy and size of vocabulary (Johnstone, 2000). Johnstone also described the students' language as consisting largely of memorized expressions, suggesting little ability to manipulate language structures. This observation is consistent with a study by Traphagan (1997), who observed elementary school children learning Japanese as a foreign language. Traphagan noted that young learners' use of a certain grammatical particle in Japanese exhibited fewer errors and pauses compared to adult learners of Japanese as a foreign language. She posited that this difference between adults and children may be due to children's tendency to learn a foreign language through memorized chunks, whereas adult and proficient foreign language learners are more likely to go beyond the regurgitation of formulaic chunks and show ability to manipulate language structures. Traphagan (1997) also observed that more proficient learners tended to produce more words in the target language, similar to Johnstone's (2000) finding. Moreover, Traphagan (1997) found that the language produced by less proficient students generally consisted of short and simple responses.

Oral Language Central to the Language Ability of Young EFL Learners

Previous research also supports the notion that oral language, rather than written language, is central to the language ability of young EFL learners. This is reflected in the EFL curricula of many countries (Butler, 2009; Hasselgren, 2000; Pinter, 2006; Zangl, 2000), in which more emphasis is placed on oral skills during early foreign language education. McKay (2006) noted that the content of most EFL instruction in the first two years focuses on listening and speaking, with reading and writing being taught later. She emphasized the importance of oral language work for foreign language development, arguing that oral language should be a key component of a language assessment designed for young learners.

A similar viewpoint was expressed earlier by Cameron (2001, 2003), who suggested that classroom activities for young EFL learners should center on fostering oral language skills. She further argued that the development of oral language skills supports learning about language use contexts and discourse features in English, that is, how ideas are connected in various types of text (e.g., a conversation or a story) associated with different types of discourse (e.g., description or narration).

In summary, although the literature on young EFL learners is limited, it provides insight into how young students learn a foreign language and suggests important implications for the design of an EFL assessment for children. Examples of such implications include the desirability of using meaning-focused assessment tasks and avoiding overemphasis on grammatical accuracy and vocabulary size. If measures of grammatical accuracy and lexical knowledge are included as part of the language construct for young learners, expectations should be lower than they would be for older learners. Finally, any assessment for learners should reflect that oral language is a core component of young EFL learners' language ability.

Insights From Practice: What Do Young EFL Learners Learn, and What Are They Expected To Do With English?

Many EFL education policies for young learners emphasize the development of the ability to communicate in English (Gorsuch, 2000; Li, 1998; Mikio, 2008; Wu, 2001). To gain a concrete understanding of how communication in English is defined for young EFL learners and how it is fostered during the early years of EFL instruction, curricula and textbooks from Brazil, Chile, China, Egypt, Japan, Korea, the Philippines, Qatar, and Singapore were analyzed (Turkan & Adler, 2011). European Language Portfolios (ELPs) from various European countries were also consulted to capture language standards for primary students. Primary ELPs include age-appropriate language performance descriptors associated with proficiency levels of the CEFR.

EFL curricula delineate what young EFL learners should learn and be able to do in terms of language objectives. Language objectives are written with varying levels of specificity and granularity. They address many aspects of language use including linguistic resources (e.g., grammar and vocabulary), language functions (e.g., comprehend, infer, and explain), text type (e.g., description and narrative), and topics (e.g., people, animals, and weather). The results of the curriculum analysis indicated a great deal of commonality in EFL education across countries in terms of expected language objectives; in general, EFL education focuses on the development of oral language (i.e., listening and speaking), reading skills, and occasionally on the most rudimentary elements of writing. There is minimal explicit attention given to language rules.

EFL textbooks are a useful resource that illustrates how language objectives are taught and relate to language use activities. Classroom language tasks or activities (e.g., information gap and role-play) are designed to provide young EFL learners with opportunities to learn and use the language knowledge and skills specified in the language objectives. Given the emphasis on communication in English, such classroom language activities are generally meaning-focused and intended to replicate a variety of real-life communication contexts. Language activities are typically organized around a theme (e.g., my weekend) to allow learners to use learned expressions in a variety of settings relevant to young learners (e.g., plan a weekend with a classmate or survey the class on favorite weekend activities). The language use contexts replicated in the EFL classroom are largely *social*, meaning that students primarily use language to communicate with people around them (e.g., family, friends, classmates, and teachers) on familiar topics (e.g., myself, animals, and people) and to obtain basic information from familiar sources (e.g., stories, announcements, and directions).

Informed by the above results, we developed a construct definition of English communication for young EFL learners between 8 and 11 years of age for three language skills: reading, listening, and speaking (see Figures 3.1–3.3). The writing construct was not considered for *TOEFL Primary* tests, given that little emphasis is placed on this skill during the early years of EFL education.

For each skill, the *TOEFL Primary* construct definition first provides an overall, high-level definition of what it means for young EFL learners to use English for communication in each skill. Each overall definition is articulated in terms of communication goals and underlying language resources. Communication goals refer to types of communication that young EFL learners attempt in settings specified in the overall definition. However, for young EFL learners, the communication goals are likely to be achieved in the classroom with their peers who are also EFL learners and share the same language background. The communication goals provide a basis for developing language test task types, which are shown later in the discussion of the test design. Figures 3.1–3.3 also present the language knowledge (e.g., vocabulary and grammar) and skills (e.g., identify characters) that young EFL learners need to achieve communication goals. These linguistic resources are specified as enabling knowledge and skills, which are called on to accomplish communication goals.

Overall

The Reading test measures young EFL learners' abilities to read a variety of written English texts in familiar contexts (e.g., school, home, playgrounds, and museums).

Communication Goal

The Reading test measures young EFL learners' abilities to achieve the following communication goals:

- identify people, objects, and actions
- understand commonly occurring nonlinear written texts (e.g., signs, schedules)
- understand written directions and procedures
- understand short personal correspondence (e.g., letters)
- understand simple, written narratives (e.g., stories)
- understand written expository or informational texts about familiar people, objects, animals, and places

Enabling Knowledge and Skills

To achieve these goals, young EFL learners need the ability to:

- recognize the written English alphabet and sounds associated with each letter
- identify words based on sounds
- recognize the mechanical conventions of written English
- recognize basic vocabulary
- process basic grammar
- identify the meaning of written words through context
- recognize the organizational features of various text types

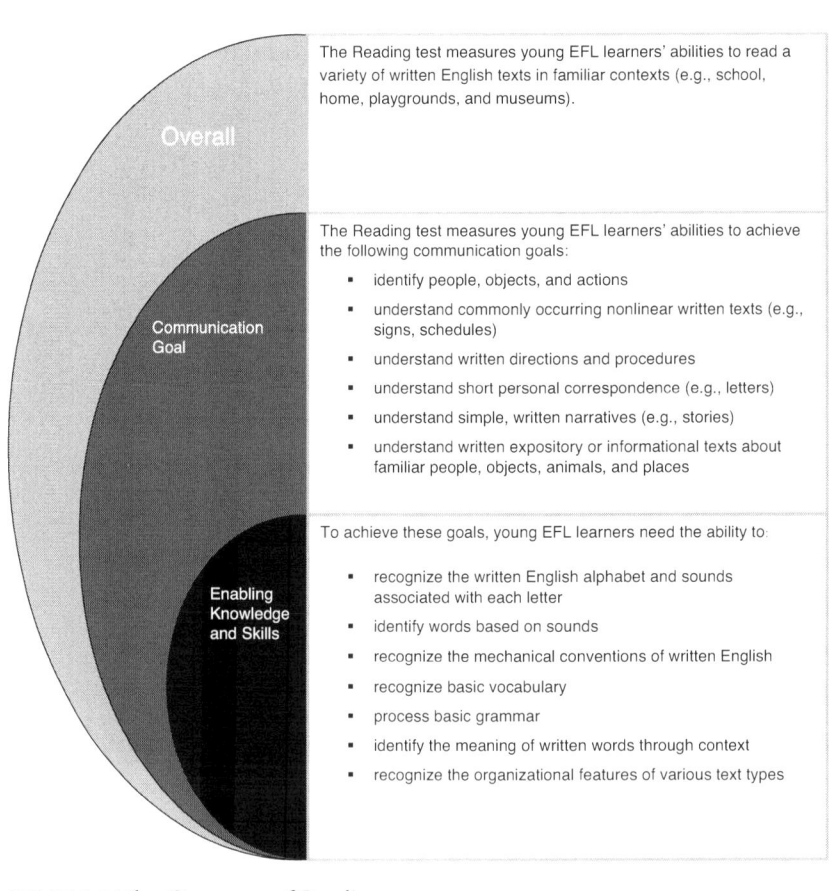

FIGURE 3.1 The Construct of Reading

Overall

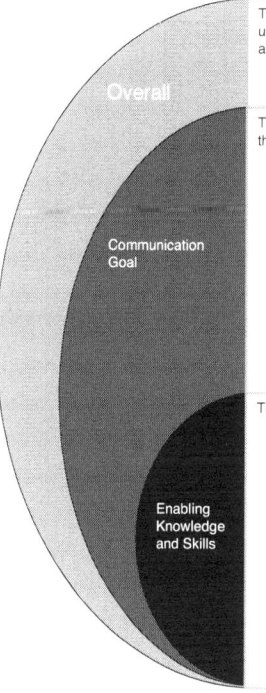

The Listening test measures young EFL learners' abilities to understand conversations related to their daily lives, spoken stories, and talks on familiar topics (e.g., animals).

Communication Goal

The Listening test measures young EFL learners' abilities to achieve the following listening communication goals:

- understand simple descriptions of familiar people and objects
- understand spoken directions and procedures
- understand dialogues or conversations
- understand spoken stories
- understand short informational texts related to daily life (e.g., phone messages, announcements)
- understand simple teacher talks on academic topics

Enabling Knowledge and Skills

To achieve these goals, young EFL learners need the ability to:

- recognize and distinguish English phonemes
- comprehend commonly used expressions and phrases
- understand very common vocabulary and function words
- identify the meaning of spoken words through context
- understand basic sentence structure and grammar
- understand the use of intonation, stress, and pauses to convey meaning
- recognize organizational features of conversations, spoken stories, and teacher talks

FIGURE 3.2 The Construct of Listening

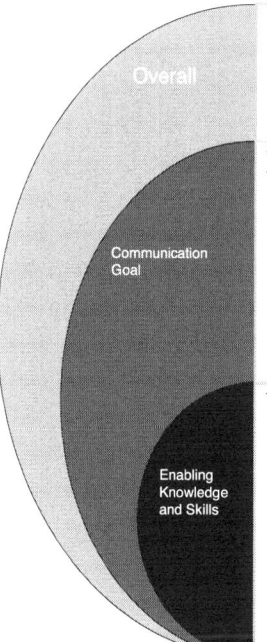

Overall

The Speaking test measures young EFL learners' abilities to communicate orally in routine social situations related to their daily lives to fulfill various communication goals.

Communication Goal

The Speaking test measures young EFL learners' abilities to achieve the following speaking communication goals:

- express basic emotions and feelings
- describe people, objects, animals, places, and activities
- explain and sequence simple events
- make simple requests
- give short commands and directions
- ask and answer questions

Enabling Knowledge and Skills

To achieve these goals, young EFL learners need the ability to:

- pronounce words clearly
- use intonation, stress, and pauses to pace speech and convey meaning
- use basic vocabulary and common and courteous expressions
- use simple connectors (e.g., *and, then*)

FIGURE 3.3 The Construct of Speaking

These enabling knowledge and skills are part of the task design and may be measured directly if deemed appropriate in the context of assessing different levels of complexity within the communication goals. In particular, the use of matching pictures and words is justifiable with EFL learners with less developed English abilities. These students are likely to rely on content words or phrases to communicate in English. Similarly, it is reasonable to use questions asking about how a particular word is used in the context of a reading passage in order to assess the reading abilities of advanced EFL learners.

Design of the *TOEFL Primary* Tests

The content and structure of the *TOEFL Primary* tests are the result of a multistage test development effort: three rounds of prototyping followed by pilot testing and field testing. We provide high-level descriptions of each stage below to explain how information from various test development stages, as well as practical considerations, influenced the final test design.

Test Development Process and Key Design Considerations

A variety of assessment task types were proposed, based on the aforementioned construct definition, to measure EFL learners' English ability. To evaluate the appropriateness of new item types and assessment procedures and to collect detailed feedback, prototyping studies were conducted with small groups of young English learners in four countries (China, Korea, Mexico, and the U.S.A.) as well as with native English-speaking students in the U.S.A. In these studies, students were interviewed after trying the prototype test items. Concurrently, EFL teachers' evaluations of the new task types were gathered in China, Korea, and Mexico.

Results of the prototyping studies contributed to three main changes in our understanding of the construct and our approach to task design. One important change was to emphasize tasks measuring the ability to achieve communication goals over tasks measuring discrete language skills. Initially, a wide range of tasks types— from a measure of phonemic awareness to a measure of story comprehension— were prototyped to approximate language activities familiar to young EFL learners. For example, one set of prototype language tasks included a phonemic awareness task, which was designed to measure the ability to match sounds to letters. According to our analysis of curricula and textbooks, this ability appeared to be a common language objective across countries. Feedback from teachers, however, indicated that even though language tasks focusing on discrete knowledge and skills are relevant, they are not as valuable as communication-oriented tasks that focus directly on students' ability to use English to accomplish communication goals. This was also supported by data from cognitive interviews with students (for more details, see Cho & So, 2014). As a result, tasks directly measuring enabling knowledge and skills have minimal inclusion on the *TOEFL Primary* tests.

Another major change that arose from findings of the prototyping studies concerned the administration format of Speaking test items. Various administration formats were considered. Speaking administration formats can be broadly divided into two categories: computer-administered (defined herein as a format in which test takers speak to a computer that records their responses), and direct face-to-face assessment (in which test takers speak to a human interlocutor). The face-to-face format can be divided further into individual and group (or pair) assessment, both being administered by an interviewer. With young students, face-to-face administration is generally thought to make speaking tasks more interactive and engaging. Thus, face-to-face individual and group administrations were initially attempted. These two administration models assumed that certified local teachers, not test takers' own teachers, would administer the test and score the responses. During the prototyping study, however, limitations of the face-to-face speaking assessment format became apparent. Some children felt uncomfortable talking to an adult they had never met. Other limitations included a lack of qualified teachers who could administer the test and evaluate the spoken responses and, in the group or pair administration model, unequal assessment opportunities among test takers. Given these findings, a computer-administered assessment format was chosen. This decision, in turn, allowed test developers to explore a wider range of engaging contexts and innovative assessment types using technology. Further information about the design of the speaking tasks is presented later.

Finally, through prototyping studies, a number of design issues, both general and specific, were identified for some of the reading and listening tasks, leading to the revision of test and item-writing specifications. Examples of general issues included unclear task descriptions, memory load, and the linguistic complexity of questions and response options. Based on feedback gathered in the prototyping studies, many task types underwent several iterations to mitigate potential sources of construct-irrelevant score variance (for further information, see Cho & So, 2014).

Pilot studies followed the prototyping studies to explore the influence of task features on item difficulty and to inform test form composition (see Zu, Moulder, & Morgan, 2017 in this volume for the details of the pilot studies). Data from the pilot test administrations were collected from more than 1,300 students across eight countries for the Reading and Listening tests and from more than 400 students across 11 countries for the Speaking test. The pilot data were analyzed to (1) obtain item parameters (i.e., item difficulty and discrimination) and reliabilities, (2) evaluate the relationship among item types and test sections, (3) determine optimal form composition to maximize reliability while minimizing the number of test items, and (4) decide a Reading test length appropriate for test takers. On the basis of this analysis, item and test specifications were revised again. The analysis of pilot study results also led to two major test design decisions regarding the Reading test length and the distribution of content on the Reading and Listening tests.

First, the length of the current Reading test was informed by an analysis of speededness in performance data. Because children generally have shorter attention spans than adults (e.g., Robert, Borella, Fagot, Lecerf, & de Ribaupierre, 2009), it was decided during the conceptualization stage that the maximum testing time for each skill must not exceed 30 minutes. Given this constraint, two Reading test forms with different numbers of items and with common questions positioned early, middle, and late in the test forms were piloted to determine an appropriate test length. The results indicated that students' performance declined on the longer test form, therefore supporting the use of fewer items.

The other important decision that emerged from the pilot study results was to offer the Reading and Listening tests at two difficulty levels, Step 1 and Step 2, while keeping the Speaking test as a single-level test. Pilot testing showed performance differences in the reading and listening skills of learners among participating countries, suggesting a single-level test could not effectively address the assessment needs of young EFL learners from different backgrounds. These results might be explainable by differences in foreign language education policy and curriculum among the participating countries. Two additional possible explanations for the performance differences among the countries in the pilot study were offered: (1) that the difficulty of reading and listening items reflects the intrinsic difficulty of a particular communication goal and (2) that a multiple-choice format, in which reading and listening skills are measured, limits a range of responses. The pilot-phase analysis indicated that some task types were either too easy or too challenging for test takers in some countries, thereby having little utility from a measurement perspective. For example, a task in which test takers match a single word to a picture is inherently simpler than one in which test takers answer comprehension questions after reading a long text. The picture matching task provides little opportunity for proficient EFL learners to demonstrate what they are able to do, while the reading comprehension task suffers from the same limitation for test takers with lower levels of proficiency. Given the results of the pilot study, and to make efficient use of testing time while maintaining sufficient test reliability, the test design was modified to include two levels of Reading and Listening tests, with one level designed for students in the lower and middle range of proficiency assessed and one level designed for students in the middle and upper range. The item types used in each test level reflect concerns for both construct coverage and statistical characteristics.

Subsequent to the pilot study, large-scale field testing was conducted to obtain a sufficient number of items for test assembly and to develop a scale for score reporting. Data were obtained from more than 3,700 students across 14 countries for the Reading and Listening tests, and from more than 500 students across 12 countries for the Speaking test. Additional information about the design of the *TOEFL Primary* scoring system is described in the discussion of score reporting.

Test Content and Structure of the TOEFL Primary Tests

On the basis of the pilot and field testing results, the final versions of the *TOEFL Primary* tests were assembled. Per the final test specifications, the Reading and Listening tests are paper-based and consist of single-selection multiple-choice items. Task directions and items are presented in a color test book, and students mark their answers on a separate answer sheet. Listening test stimuli are played on audio CDs. The Speaking test is computer-based and consists of constructed-response items. Students view and listen to test prompts on computer and respond through microphones. Each test can be taken independently of the others, depending on the child's English learning experience and assessment needs. The Reading and Listening tests are offered at two test levels, Step 1 and Step 2, whereas the Speaking test is a single-level test.

Tables 3.1 and 3.2 show the blueprints of the two test levels for the *TOEFL Primary* Reading and Listening tests. Each test includes 30 multiple-choice questions that contribute to scores and a few pretesting questions that do not contribute to scores. The allotted time for a single test is 30 minutes.

TABLE 3.1 Reading Test Structure

Item type	Task description	Communication goal	Number of items*	
			Step 1*	Step 2**
Match Picture to Word	Match a picture to one of three words.	Identify people, objects and actions.	6	
Match Picture to Sentence	Match a picture to one of three sentences.	Identify people, objects and actions.	7	
Sentence Clue	Read a 4-sentence description and identify what is being described.	Understand written expository or informational texts.	5	7
Telegraphic	Answer questions about a poster, a schedule, etc.	Understand nonlinear texts.	8	4
Correspondence	Read a letter or email and answer comprehension questions.	Understand personal correspondence.	4	4
Instructional	Read directions and answer comprehension questions.	Understand written directions and procedures.		3
Narrative	Read a story and answer comprehension questions.	Understand narratives or stories.		8
Short Expository	Read an expository text and answer comprehension questions.	Understand written expository or informational texts.		4
Total			**30**	**30**

* The number of items represents items that contribute to a test score. An operational test is longer because it includes pre-testing items.
** Shaded cells indicate that item types do not appear in the test level.

52 Yeonsuk Cho et al.

TABLE 3.2 Listening Test Structure

Item type	Task description	Communication goal	Number of items* Step 1**	Step 2**
Listen and Match	Listen to a sentence and select a corresponding picture.	Understand spoken descriptions.	7	
Follow Directions	Listen to directions and select a corresponding picture.	Understand spoken directions and procedures.	7	6
Question-Response	Listen to three versions of a 2-turn conversation and choose a conversation that makes sense.	Understand dialogues or conversations.	6	
Dialogue	Listen to a dialogue and answer a comprehension question.	Understand dialogues or conversations.	5	5
Social-Navigational Monologue	Listen to a phone message/announcement and answer a comprehension question.	Understand short spoken informational texts.	5	5
Narrative	Listen to a story and answer comprehension questions.	Understand spoken stories.		8
Academic Monologue	Listen to an academic monologue and answer comprehension questions.	Understand simple teacher talks.		6
Total			30	30

* The number of items represents items that contribute to a test score. An operational test is longer because it includes pre-testing items.
** Shaded cells indicate that item types do not appear in the test level.

Each task type in the *TOEFL Primary* tests is designed to assess young EFL learners' ability to achieve one of the communication goals outlined in the test construct. In determining the composition of each test, input from experienced EFL teachers, in addition to performance data on each item type, was taken into consideration. During the pilot testing stage, 29 experienced EFL teachers from five countries were surveyed (Hsieh, 2013), and these teachers evaluated the degree of importance of individual communication goals measured by the *TOEFL Primary* tests and the effectiveness of the assessment task types.

In both the Reading and Listening tests, the majority of the communication goals are assessed at both Step 1 and Step 2, which explains the overlap in task types between the two steps (Tables 3.1 and 3.2). It should be noted, however, that although the same task types are shared for both steps, the level of linguistic complexity of stimuli in Step 1 is simpler than in Step 2. In addition, topics in Step 1 do not go beyond personal experiences and common, everyday surroundings. Step 1 is suitable for EFL learners who can comprehend:

- basic formulaic expressions;
- basic vocabulary and phrases related to common objects and people;
- short and simple utterances related to survival needs (e.g., simple requests or directions); and
- short and simple texts relevant to students' daily lives (e.g., schedules or phone messages).

Step 2 is recommended for EFL learners who have the same skills listed above and can also comprehend:

- simple and short stories and conversations on topics beyond personal experiences;
- simple explanations of objects related to content learning; and
- unfamiliar words, given a sufficient amount of contextual clues.

The Speaking test is a single-level test consisting of seven constructed-response items. The test is computer-administered and lasts about 20 minutes. Individual test takers wear headsets to listen to prompts and to record their responses. Because of the use of open-ended item types, the Speaking test can be taken by both Step 1 and Step 2 test takers. Similar to the Reading and Listening task types, the Speaking task types are associated with the communication goals outlined in the test construct (see Table 3.3).

A unique design feature of the Speaking test is the use of a context and fictional characters. For example, one of the Speaking test forms uses a trip to the zoo as a context, consisting of a series of events upon which the Speaking tasks are based. Throughout the test, virtual characters (e.g., a zookeeper and children) appear at different times, functioning as interlocutors.[3] This contextualization is intended to create an authentic communication purpose for each Speaking task so that test takers feel engaged and motivated to respond to the speaking prompts.

A second unique design feature is the inclusion of fun elements and scaffolding to enhance children's test taking experience. The fun elements, consisting of animations, playful characters, and whimsical content, are used to keep test takers engaged and to elicit more spontaneous and natural responses. The speaking test also incorporates the concept of scaffolding into task design by providing relevant key words to test takers in advance or directing their attention to a particular aspect of a stimulus that test takers need to describe.

TABLE 3.3 Speaking Test Structure

Item type	Task description	Communication goal	Maximum score points
Warm-Up	Answer a question with one word.	Warm-up.	Not scored
Expression	Express emotion or opinion in response to a question.	Express basic emotions, feelings, and opinions.	3
Description	Describe a picture.	Give simple descriptions.	3
Directions	Explain a procedure based on sequenced pictures or animations.	Give directions.	5 (or 10)★
Narration	Explain a sequence of events shown in pictures or animations.	Explain and sequence simple events.	5 (or 10)★
Questions	Ask three questions.	Ask questions.	3
Requests	Make requests.	Make requests.	3
Total			27

★ Each Speaking test form includes one additional direction or narration task.

Development of the Score Reporting System for the *TOEFL Primary* Tests

Following the field test administrations, we analyzed the Reading and Listening score data using a two-parameter (2PL) logistic item response theory (IRT). The field test yielded a usable sample size of at least 1,200 for each multiple-choice item. The 2PL model relates the probability of responding correctly, given a person's ability level, to the difficulty of a test item.

Items from the overlapping field test forms were calibrated concurrently using Educational Testing Service (ETS) proprietary software, which uses a marginal maximum likelihood estimation method to estimate item parameters including item difficulty and item discrimination. Item parameters for reading and listening were estimated and evaluated separately. Following the field test administrations, items with extreme difficulty or low discrimination were removed from the item pool. Tests were assembled that met both content and statistical specifications for each of the two test levels. Some overlap in test items between the two levels was allowed. Raw-to-ability scale conversions were created to report test performance on a single continuous scale across Step 1 and Step 2. Both the Reading and Listening tests have a separate scaled scores range of 100 to 115, with a scaled score of 100 indicating the lowest performance on both Step 1 and Step 2. Scaled scores range from 101 to 109 for Step 1 and from 104 to 115 for Step 2.

Unlike Reading and Listening test results, Speaking test results are not converted to another scale prior to reporting. Instead, Speaking results are reported as the sum of individual task ratings resulting from use of the tasks' rating scales. Total Speaking scores range from 0 to 27. To ensure the consistency of Speaking test scores, operational speaking forms with similar score means and standard deviations of scores were created. The average reliability of the test forms was .90, as computed from field test data.

In addition to the aforementioned numeric scores, TOEFL Primary score reports also provide a performance description with a band score. As discussed earlier, one of the main intended effects of TOEFL Primary is to encourage continued language learning efforts by individual students. As Roberts and Gierl (2010) note, a score report "serves a critical function as the interface between the test developer and a diverse audience of test users" (p. 25). Ideally, score reports explain what is expected on the test and how test results should be interpreted. A numeric score by itself does not provide meaningful information that can be used to support teaching and learning.

To aid the interpretation of test results, score bands were derived to characterize a typical performance at a particular band or score range. Both the score bands and performance descriptions were developed through an item mapping procedure. Item mapping is one approach to relating content information to test scores so that scores convey meaningful information about test taker performance (Tong & Kolen, 2010). In an item mapping procedure, both item performance data and expert judgments are utilized to articulate the performance of typical test takers at a given performance level, thus classifying test takers into different levels of ability. For an optimal level of classification accuracy and consistency, based on analysis of the field test data, it was recommended that test performances be categorized into six bands for Reading and Listening (across Step 1 and Step 2) and five bands for Speaking. According to Livingston and Lewis (1993), classification accuracy is the extent to which the classification of a test taker based on observed test scores corresponds to the classification of the test taker based on estimates of "true" score—the hypothetical score that test taker would receive if a test had no measurement error. Classification consistency measures the extent to which the classification of a test taker based on test scores is consistent across different test administrations.

ETS test developers who created the TOEFL Primary items reviewed the multiple-choice items, arranged in order of difficulty, to characterize performance levels. They analyzed the content of the items representing score bands and articulated the characteristics of the items in each band. For the Speaking test, average score profiles were created based on total raw scores. Test developers reviewed typical speech samples corresponding to average score profiles and articulated typical characteristics of performance for each score band. During the content review, test developers observed that performance patterns across score bands reflected both (a) the difficulty levels of various communication goals and (b) the complexity of language and topics. For example, the item mapping data indicated that, among the target population, the ability to understand spoken narratives is more difficult to acquire than the ability to understand spoken directions. Performance descriptors capture these patterns and explain linguistic characteristics of individual items and types of language tasks represented at a given score range. The performance descriptors also include suggestions for improving students' English abilities, which are based on the characteristics of performance at the next higher score band. Performance descriptors were refined in an iterative process to present them in plain and descriptive language (without linguistic jargon) that parents and teachers can easily understand.

In addition to reporting *TOEFL Primary* scores, score reports also show how *TOEFL Primary* scores relate to scores or levels of other frameworks or references for language learning. For example, *TOEFL Primary* scores are linked to the Lexile framework so that test users can use Lexile scores to identify reading materials that match their current reading levels (Metametrics, 2013). *TOEFL Primary* scores are also linked to the CEFR to help test users interpret scores in terms of a widely recognized proficiency scale. The linkage between *TOEFL Primary* scores and these frameworks was established using the field testing data. Further information about the methodology or results of these linking studies can be found in Cline, Sanford, and Aguirre (2011), and Baron and Papageorgiou (2014).

Research for the *TOEFL Primary* Tests and Young EFL Learners

Following ETS's long tradition of backing test-related claims with empirical evidence, ongoing research is in place to monitor the quality of the *TOEFL Primary* tests and to evaluate the validity of score uses and claims about the tests. At the beginning of test development, we proposed a research agenda to support test design decisions at each stage of test development and to identify areas of future research with the aim of building a validity argument for the *TOEFL Primary* tests, as has been done for *TOEFL iBT®* (Chapelle, 2008). During test development, because our efforts were largely intended to guide and support test design, research findings produced evidence related to limited types of inferences in the validity argument, mostly the domain description, evaluation, and generalization inferences.

Now that the *TOEFL Primary* tests are in operational use, research has expanded to gather evidence across all six types of inference: domain description, evaluation, generalization, explanation, extrapolation, and utility. For example, research is being conducted to evaluate the impact of the *TOEFL Primary* tests on teaching and learning for young EFL learners by analyzing educators' and parents' perceptions of English teaching and learning practices before and after the introduction of the *TOEFL Primary* tests. This type of research addresses a utility-related validity inference by evaluating our claim that *TOEFL Primary* supports teaching and learning. Another study being conducted as part of ongoing research seeks to improve our current 'domain description' by addressing young EFL learners' writing ability, which is currently excluded from *TOEFL Primary*'s construct.

These are just a few examples of an array of research studies that are in progress to evaluate the validity of the *TOEFL Primary* tests, according to the current ETS research agenda. The current research agenda focuses mainly on test validation against potential issues that we have identified based on knowledge of the *TOEFL Primary* tests and target population. However, as the tests become widely used by young test takers, we expect new issues to emerge and more empirical data to become available. Both new areas of topics and enriched data will influence the direction of future research for the *TOEFL Primary* tests. Continued empirical research will help strengthen the validity arguments of the tests and result in improved understanding of young EFL learners whose performance and behaviors in large-scale testing contexts are yet to be understood.

Notes

1 The *TOEFL Primary* tests can, however, be used with older students in certain educational contexts if appropriate.
2 This chapter is a shortened version of a previously published report: Cho, Y., Ginsburgh, M., Morgan, R., Moulder, B., Xi, X., & Hauck, M. C. (2016). *Designing the TOEFL Primary Tests* (Research Memorandum, RM-16-02). Princeton, NJ: Educational Testing Service.
3 For a sample speaking test, see https://toeflprimary.caltesting.org/sampleQuestions/TOEFLPrimary/index.html.

References

Baron, P. A., & Papageorgiou, S. (2014). *Mapping the TOEFL® Primary™ test onto the Common European Framework of Reference* (TOEFL Research Memorandum ETS RM 14-05). Princeton, NJ: Educational Testing Service.

Butler, Y. G. (2009). How do teachers observe and evaluate elementary school students' foreign language performance? A case study from South Korea. *TESOL Quarterly, 43*, 417-444.

Cameron, L. (2001). *Teaching languages to young learners*. Cambridge: Cambridge University Press.

Cameron, L. (2003). Challenges for ELT from the expansion in teaching children. *ELT Journal, 57*, 105-112.

Chapelle, C. A. (2008). The TOEFL validity argument. In C. Chapelle, M. Enright, & J. Jamieson (Eds.), *Building a validity argument for the test of English as a foreign language* (pp. 319-352). London: Routledge.

Chien, C. (2012). Differentiated instruction in an elementary school EFL classroom. *TESOL Journal, 3*, 280-291.

Cho, Y., & So, Y. (2014). *Construct-irrelevant factors influencing young EFL learners' perceptions of test task difficulty* (TOEFL Research Memorandum ETS RM 14-04). Princeton, NJ: Educational Testing Service.

Cline, F., Sanford, E., & Aguirre, A. (2011, June). *Linking TOEFL junior reading scores to the Lexile measure*. Poster presented at the 33rd Language Testing Research Colloquium (LTRC), Ann Arbor, MI.

Council of Europe. (n.d.). *ELP checklists for young learners: Some principles and proposals.* Available from http://www.coe.int/t/DG4/Education/ELP/ELP-REG/Source/Templates/ELP_Language_Biography_Checklists_for_young learners_EN.pdf

Garton, S., Copland, F., & Burns, A. (2011). *Investigating global practices in teaching English to young learners.* (ELT Research Papers 11–01). London, UK: The British Council.

Gorsuch, G. (2000). EFL education policies and educational cultures: Influences on teachers' approval of communicative activities. *TESOL Quarterly, 34,* 675–710.

Hasselgren, A. (2000). The assessment of the English ability of young learners in Norwegian schools: An innovative approach. *Language Testing, 17,* 261–277.

Hsieh, C. (2013, September). *Establishing domain representations for a large-scale language assessment for young EFL learners.* Paper presented at the 15th Midwest Association of Language Testers (MwALT) Annual Conference, East Lansing, MI.

Johnstone, R. (2000). Context-sensitive assessment of modern languages in primary (elementary) and early secondary education: Scotland and the European experience. *Language Testing, 17,* 123–143.

Li, D. (1998). It's always more difficult than you plan and imagine. *TESOL Quarterly, 32,* 677–703.

Livingston, S. A., & Lewis, C. (1993). *Estimating the consistency and accuracy of classifications based on test scores* (Research Report No. RR-93–48). Princeton, NJ: Educational Testing Service.

MacNamara, J. (1972). Cognitive basis of language learning in infants. *Psychological Review, 79,* 1–13.

McKay, P. (2006). *Assessing young language learners.* Cambridge: Cambridge University Press.

Metametrics. (2013). *Linking the TOEFL primary with the Lexile framework.* Unpublished manuscript. Durham, NC: Metametrics.

Mikio, S. (2008). Development of primary English education and teacher training in Korea. *Journal of Education for Teaching, 34,* 383–396.

Pinter, A. (2006). *Teaching young language Learners.* Oxford: Oxford University Press.

Rixon, S. (2013). *Survey of policy and practice in primary English language teaching worldwide.* London: British Council.

Robert, C., Borella, E., Fagot, D., Lecerf, T., & de Ribaupierre, A. (2009). Working memory and inhibitory control across life span: Intrusion errors in the reading span test. *Memory and Cognition, 37*(3), 336–345.

Roberts, M. R., & Gierl, M. J. (2010). Developing score presorts for cognitive diagnostic assessments. *Educational Measurement: Issues and Practice, 29*(3), 25–38.

Tong, Y., & Kolen, M. (2010). Scaling: An ITEMS module. *Educational Measurement: Issues and Practice, 29*(4), 39–48.

Traphagan, T. W. (1997). Interviews with Japanese FLES students: Descriptive analysis. *Foreign Language Annals, 30*(1), 98–110.

Turkan, S., & Adler, R. (2011). *Conceptual framework for the assessment of young learners of English as a foreign language.* Unpublished manuscript.

Wu, Y. (2001). English language teaching in China: Trends and challenges. *TESOL Quarterly, 35*(1), 191–194.

Zangl, R. (2000). Monitoring language skills in Austrian primary (elementary) schools: A case study. *Language Testing, 17*(2), 250–260.

Zu, J., Moulder, B., & Morgan, R. (2017). A field test study for the *TOEFL® Primary*™ Reading and Listening tests. In M. K. Wolf & Y. G. Butler (Eds.), *English language proficiency assessments for young learners.* New York, NY: Routledge.

4

TOEFL JUNIOR® DESIGN FRAMEWORK

Youngsoon So, Mikyung Kim Wolf, Maurice Cogan Hauck, Pamela Mollaun, Paul Rybinski, Daniel Tumposky, and Lin Wang

This chapter[1] describes a framework of the *TOEFL Junior*® tests, which were introduced recently by Educational Testing Service (ETS) for young English language learners worldwide. Specifically, this chapter includes the key elements of the *TOEFL Junior* test design framework and its development process. By documenting a design framework, we wish to demonstrate that our test design and development processes meet high professional standards in order to produce a quality assessment. The framework document is also intended to serve as a reference point during investigations of validity evidence to support the intended test uses over time.

Two different versions of the *TOEFL Junior* tests were developed so as to reach a wider potential population of test takers and to provide stakeholders with the option to select a version that best meets their needs and serves their purposes. The generic name, *TOEFL Junior*, will be used in our framework document inclusively to refer to the two *TOEFL Junior* tests—the paper-based *TOEFL Junior* Standard test and the computer-delivered *TOEFL Junior* Comprehensive test—when the discussion applies equally to both tests. However, the specific name will be used when the discussion is only pertinent to that test. Further information about how specifically the two versions of the test differ is presented in later sections of this chapter.

This chapter is organized into the following sections. First, the background and motivations for developing a new English proficiency test are discussed, followed by a description of the target population and intended uses of the new test. Next, the characteristics of language use in the target language use domains are discussed as guidelines for the development of test specifications. In the next section, the constructs that are to be measured in the test are defined. Then there is a brief discussion of what information is provided in the score report of the test. Finally, this chapter concludes with reflections on the lessons learned through the development of the *TOEFL Junior* test and the subsequent efforts to validate uses of the test results.

Background to Create *TOEFL Junior*

English proficiency is an increasingly important competence to develop for students worldwide. Mastery of English expands access to a range of personal, educational, and professional opportunities. As a result, in many education systems around the globe, English is a regular part of public school curricula. Whereas some countries introduce English into the curriculum in secondary school, other public systems (and private ones as well) start English instruction at much lower grades (e.g., third grade in Korea and first grade in China). Further, English as a foreign language (EFL) instructional programs worldwide have been placing a growing emphasis on communicative language ability (Bailey, Heritage, & Butler, 2014). This educational context increases the need for well-designed, objective measures of proficiency in English for young learners.

TOEFL Junior has been developed to address this need by providing much-needed information on the English language proficiency (ELP) attainment of young adolescent English learners worldwide. *TOEFL Junior* focuses on English learners' communicative language ability to participate in English-medium instructional contexts.

English-medium instructional contexts can take a range of forms, including (a) schools in English-dominant countries, (b) international schools in non-English-dominant countries in which content instruction is delivered in English, and (c) schools in any country in which some content instruction is delivered in English. Although these instructional models are different in several respects, they commonly call for students to use English to learn new information in content areas. We also maintain that the traditional distinction between English as a second language (ESL) and EFL is of little importance in the aforementioned instructional models; the most relevant feature of all models is that English is used as an instructional language regardless of whether English is the language of communication outside of school. To differing degrees, these models also call for the use of English for nonacademic purposes, such as for social interactions, service encounters, and classroom management.

Given the wide range of English-language learning contexts with varied standards and curricula, an international English proficiency assessment would be instrumental in providing some degree of standardized information about learners' proficiency levels. *TOEFL Junior* can serve as an international benchmark for English learning, providing students, parents, teachers, and schools with an objective measure of students' ELP.

Target Population and Intended Uses

TOEFL Junior is designed for students ages 11 and older whose first language is not English and who are in the process of developing the proficiency required to participate in an English-medium instructional environment. Their native languages, educational backgrounds, and real-world experiences will vary, but they are typically expected to have at least five full years of educational experience at the elementary and/or middle school level.

TOEFL Junior is designed to measure the ability to use English for communicative purposes in situations and tasks representative of English-medium school contexts. The test scores can provide information for the following uses: (a) to determine students' ELP levels to perform tasks representative of English-medium middle school settings, (b) to support decisions regarding placement of students into different programs, and (c) to monitor student progress in developing ELP over time.

Identifying the Test Domains of Language Use

Identifying the characteristics of target language use (TLU) domains or situations is a key step towards supporting the claim that test takers' performance on test tasks relates to their expected performance in real-life communicative situations. Normally, the closer the correspondence between TLU tasks and test tasks, the greater the validity of interpretations about a test taker's language proficiency based on his or her test performance (Bachman & Palmer, 1996, 2010). TLU descriptions thus provide useful guidelines for the development of item and task specifications.

In the process of designing *TOEFL Junior*, a team of ETS researchers, test developers, and consultants (e.g., university faculty in the field of language assessment) identified TLU tasks that middle school students are expected to perform in English-medium secondary school contexts by analyzing two main sources of data. First, the literature on language used in academic contexts was reviewed. Second, English language standards/curricula and textbooks from EFL countries (i.e., Chile, China, France, Korea, and Japan) were reviewed along with ELP standards for English learners in U.S. middle schools (i.e., California, Colorado, Florida, New York, and Texas state standards and the WIDA/TESOL K–12 standards).[2] Research from the two aforementioned sources has identified important real-world tasks at the middle school level as well as skills needed to complete those tasks. It has also indicated that TLU tasks in an academic context can be categorized into three domains related to the purpose of language use: (a) social and interpersonal, (b) navigational, and (c) academic. In the following section, a brief summary of literature is provided that supports our rationale for categorizing the three language use domains. Next, the three domains are defined and illustrated with real-life language use examples.

Literature on the Language Demands of Academic Contexts

As mentioned earlier, the construct targeted by the *TOEFL Junior* test is the communicative English language ability needed to study in an English-medium middle school. Efforts to describe the language that students use in school can be traced back to Cummins's (1980, 1981) seminal work. Cummins differentiated social language ability, labeled as *basic interpersonal communication skills* (BICS), from more cognitively demanding, decontextualized language ability, which he labeled as *cognitive academic language proficiency* (CALP). The BICS-CALP categorization has spawned research that has sought evidence that academic language proficiency is distinguishable from the language proficiency needed for social and interpersonal purposes. In turn, this research has led to the definition and identification of the characteristics of academic language proficiency.

The research findings support the conclusion that the general language proficiency tests do not necessarily capture language skills needed for academic study. First, students do not necessarily perform equally well on standardized content assessments (e.g., math and science) given in English and English language development (ELD) assessments mandated for all English learners attending U.S. schools (Butler & Castellon-Wellington, 2005; Stevens, Butler, & Castellon-Wellington, 2000). Second, the language measured in ELD assessments does not adequately represent the language used in standardized content assessments. In other words, existing ELD assessments have been found to be limited with respect to measuring the range of language ability required to take content assessments (Butler, Stevens, & Castellon-Wellington, 2007). Third, the language assessed in ELD assessments does not always accurately represent the language actually used in classes (Schleppegrell, 2001). These findings indicate that many widely used ELD assessments do not accurately measure 'academic English' required for students' participation in English-medium academic settings.

Academic English can be broadly defined as the language used "for the purpose of acquiring new knowledge and skills [. . .] imparting new information, describing abstract ideas, and developing students' conceptual understanding" (Chamot & O'Malley, 1994, p. 40). More specific characteristics of academic English have been identified by analyzing linguistic features such as nominalizations that are encountered in school-based texts (Schleppegrell, 2001). Scarcella (2003) further listed various features of academic English, from discrete linguistic features (phonological, lexical, and grammatical features) and language functions (sociolinguistic features) to stylistic register (discourse features). However, a fully comprehensive characterization of academic English remains to be developed. Nonetheless, the evidence collected thus far shows that the difference between language used for general purposes and that used for academic purposes is relative, with complex sentence structures and specialized vocabulary being used relatively more frequently in academic language (Bailey, 2007; Cummins, 2000).

It should be noted that the literature on academic language proficiency does not undermine the importance of English for social and interpersonal purposes. Social language remains an important, foundational element of the language proficiency needed in school settings. Therefore, the *TOEFL Junior* test aims to measure the full range of language uses that students encounter in English-medium school settings to reflect the complex and multifaceted nature of the language that students need to learn in school contexts.

Based on the arguments provided above and Bailey and colleagues' research on *school language* (Bailey, 2007; Bailey, Butler, LaFramenta, & Ong, 2004; Bailey & Heritage, 2008), three domains of language use are identified and considered in the *TOEFL Junior* test design: social and interpersonal, navigational, and academic. The distinction between navigational and academic domains is analogous to Bailey and Heritage's (2008) division of academic English into school navigational language (SNL) and curriculum content language (CCL). More detailed discussion of how the three domains are defined and operationalized in the test is provided in the next section.

Target Language Use (TLU) Domains for TOEFL Junior

The three domains discussed above (i.e., social and interpersonal, navigational, and academic language use domains) are fluid and cannot be clearly differentiated in all language use situations. Figure 4.1 illustrates some examples of three TLU subdomains. The fuzzy boundaries among the subdomains are symbolized with dotted lines in the figure. The distinctions among the three domains may be treated as an oversimplification of the complex process of language use. However, for the purpose of operationalizing the TLU domains into the test design, this classification is effective for describing the wide range of language use activities in English-medium instructional contexts. For example, the test item developers can be mindful of the differences in the main purposes of language activities as well as the characteristics of language (e.g., word choice and sentence structures) across the subdomains.

The social and interpersonal subdomain encompasses uses of language for establishing and maintaining personal relationships. For example, students participate in casual conversations with their friends where they have to both understand other speaker(s) and respond appropriately. Students sometimes exchange personal correspondence with friends or teachers. The topics may include familiar ones, such as family, daily activities, or personal experiences. The tasks in this subdomain tend to involve informal registers of language use.

The navigational subdomain captures the need for students to communicate to 'navigate' school or course information. In school contexts, students communicate with peers, teachers, and other school staff about school- and course-related materials and activities but not about academic content. For example, students communicate about homework assignments to obtain and/or clarify details. In some cases, they need to extract key information from school-related announcements.

64 Youngsoon So et al.

The academic subdomain entails language activities performed to learn academic content in English. Language functions such as summarizing, describing, analyzing, and evaluating are typically needed to learn academic content. The topics may be discipline related, including science, math, and social studies. Examples include comprehending ideas in lectures or class discussions, participating in short conversations about academic content in a class, comprehending written academic texts, and summarizing oral or written academic texts. Language used for this purpose typically involves more formal and technical registers with increased syntactic complexity.

Of the three subdomains, the academic subdomain is believed to play a more significant role in students' success in academic settings; this is why the area representing the academic subdomain is larger than those representing the other subdomains in Figure 4.1. The language in the academic subdomain has also

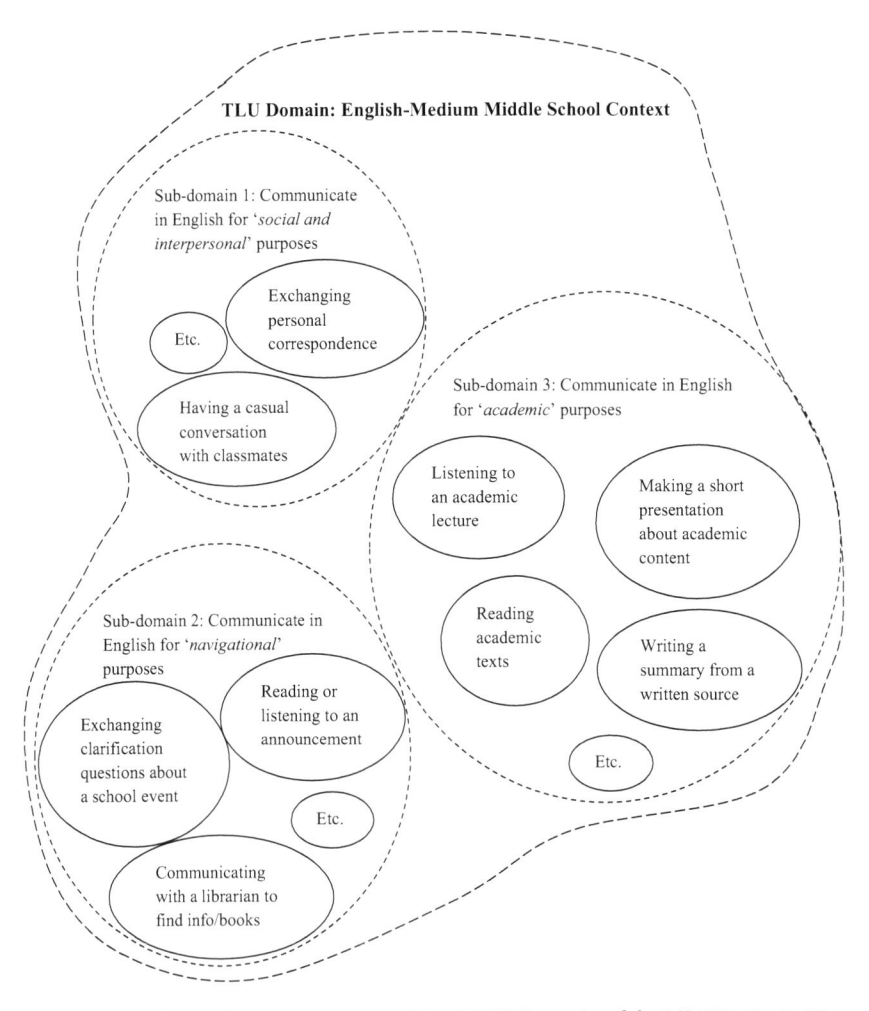

FIGURE 4.1 Defining the Target Language Use (TLU) Domain of the *TOEFL Junior* Test

been found to be more difficult to master (Bailey, 2007; Cummins, 2000). For these reasons, the academic subdomain is emphasized more than the other two subdomains in *TOEFL Junior*, with more items tapping this subdomain.

Construct Definition

A Model of Language Knowledge

Bachman and Palmer's (2010) model of language knowledge has been adapted as a framework of reference for designing test tasks and organizing the test. The breadth of the model makes it possible to (a) recognize the complex nature of the target construct, (b) identify specific component(s) of language knowledge that test tasks are designed to measure, (c) describe the specific features of reading/listening passages, and (d) specify the expected characteristics of the test takers' responses to speaking and writing test tasks.

Bachman and Palmer's (2010) model of language knowledge consists of two broad categories: organizational knowledge and pragmatic knowledge. *Organizational knowledge* refers to knowledge about the formal structure of a language at the sentence level (i.e., grammatical knowledge) or discourse level (i.e., textual knowledge). The second category, *pragmatic knowledge*, is the knowledge needed for a language user to produce and/or process language appropriately in relation to other variables such as the language users' intentions and situational factors.

It should be pointed out that not all of the areas of language knowledge in Bachman and Palmer's (2010) framework are considered appropriate or equally important for inclusion and measurement for the *TOEFL Junior* intended population. For example, knowledge of cultural references, part of pragmatic knowledge, is inappropriate to be measured the *TOEFL Junior* test because it can be a source of between-group test bias. In addition, some areas of language knowledge form a fundamental basis for language users to perform communicative tasks using language, whereas other areas require a certain level of mastery of the first type of knowledge to be appropriately used in context. The grammatical knowledge is an example of the former type of knowledge, whereas the functional knowledge is an example of the latter type of knowledge; the latter requires a foundation in the former. In designing the *TOEFL Junior* test, the former type of language knowledge is categorized as *enabling skills* and is considered to be fundamental to any communicative language use. Both types of knowledge are needed for students to perform successfully *TOEFL Junior* tasks as well as TLU tasks.

Linking Test Tasks to Target Language Use (TLU) Tasks

A set of communicative tasks was identified that represents the TLU domain of the *TOEFL Junior* test, and these identified TLU tasks served as the basis for designing test tasks. In operationalizing each TLU task, the linguistic characteristics of a task stimulus (e.g., a listening passage) and its expected response (e.g., a spoken constructed-response) were designed to be as similar as possible to the language knowledge required to perform a similar task in a nonassessment situation in the TLU domain, as represented in Figure 4.2. Figure 4.2 demonstrates how Bachman and Palmer's (2010) language knowledge model was utilized in test design in order to match the linguistics characteristics of a test task with those of a corresponding real-life language use task. Efforts were made to reproduce the linguistic characteristics of the TLU tasks in the test tasks to the highest possible extent.

TLU task characteristics

Follow and recount basic/routine oral instructions, procedures, or assignments

Situational characteristics

Setting: classroom, library, field trip location, administrator's office, etc.

Participant: student and teacher/administrator/peer/parent

Content: school trip, homework, school announcement, sports practice/game, school club activity, etc.

Linguistic characteristics of input

Grammatical knowledge: Knowledge about general academic language (less formal than content-specific academic language, but more formal than everyday language)

Textual knowledge: Knowledge about the conventions for marking inter-sentential relationships and for organizing units of information into a coherent text; mostly monologic with sporadic interruptions

Functional knowledge: Knowledge of using language for ideational functions

Sociolinguistic knowledge: Register in the middle of the formality continuum

Linguistic characteristics of expected output

Grammatical knowledge: Knowledge about general academic language

Textual knowledge: a monologue or dialogue depending on whether the discourse triggers follow-up questions

Functional knowledge: Knowledge of using language for ideational functions in order to deliver information

Sociolinguistic knowledge: Register in the middle of the formality continuum

Test task characteristics

Nonacademic Listen-Speak

Situational characteristics

Setting: imaginary school-related setting with contextual information provided

Participant: test taker (speaking to an imaginary friend/teacher/parent)

Content: school trip, homework, school announcement, sports practice/game, school club activity, etc.

Linguistic characteristics of input

Grammatical knowledge: Knowledge about general academic language (less formal than content-specific academic language, but more formal than everyday language)

Textual knowledge: Knowledge about the conventions for marking inter-sentential relationships and for organizing units of information into a coherent text; mostly monologic with sporadic interruptions

Functional knowledge: Knowledge of using language for ideational functions

Sociolinguistic knowledge: Register in the middle of the formality continuum

Linguistic characteristics of expected output

Grammatical knowledge: Knowledge about general academic language

Textual knowledge: a monologue

Functional knowledge: Knowledge of using language for ideational functions in order to deliver information

Sociolinguistic knowledge: Register in the middle of the formality continuum

FIGURE 4.2 An Example of Linking a Target Language Use (TLU) Task to an Assessment Task

Overall Structure of the Test

The two versions of the *TOEFL Junior* test (i.e., *TOEFL Junior* Standard and *TOEFL Junior* Comprehensive) were developed to have different sections, as summarized in Table 4.1. The Language Form and Meaning section is only present in *TOEFL Junior* Standard, whereas the Speaking and Writing sections are included only in *TOEFL Junior* Comprehensive. The Language Form and Meaning section in *TOEFL Junior* Standard assesses enabling skills in order to *indirectly* measure students' ability to use their knowledge of English grammar and vocabulary for communicative tasks in speaking and writing.

TOEFL Junior Standard consists of all selected-response questions and is delivered in paper-and-pencil format. On the other hand, *TOEFL Junior* Comprehensive is administered on a computer and consists of both selected-response and constructed-response questions. The receptive skills (i.e., listening and reading) are measured through selected-response questions, and the productive skills (i.e., speaking and writing) are measured through constructed-response questions.

Organization of the test by modality (i.e., reading, listening, speaking, and writing) reflects the structures of most curricula and textbooks currently in use. However, the design team also acknowledged that, in real life, multiple language modalities are often required to complete a single language use task. Hence, integrated tasks, which require multiple modalities (e.g., listening and speaking), are also included in the Speaking and Writing sections of the *TOEFL Junior* Comprehensive test.

Construct Definition by Section

This section presents detailed information about the definitions of the constructs for each of the test sections. In each section of *TOEFL Junior*, with the exception of the Language Form and Meaning section in *TOEFL Junior* Standard, items are selected to tap into the target construct in each of the three TLU subdomains:

TABLE 4.1 Overall Structure of the *TOEFL Junior* tests

Section	*TOEFL Junior* Standard		*TOEFL Junior* Comprehensive	
	No. of items	Testing time	No. of items	Testing time
Listening	42	40 min	36	35 min
Language Form and Meaning	42	25 min	n/a	
Reading	42	50 min	36	40 min
Speaking	n/a		4	25 min
Writing	n/a		4	40 min
Total	126	115 min	80	140 min

social and interpersonal, navigational, and academic. The two sections that appear in both tests (i.e., Listening and Reading) target the same constructs in the two tests and therefore are discussed only once in this section.

Language Form and Meaning

The Language Form and Meaning section is differentiated from other sections in *TOEFL Junior* in that test items in the section aim to measure enabling skills (i.e., grammar and vocabulary knowledge) required for communication, whereas items and tasks in the other sections measure the ability to apply such enabling skills in actual communicative tasks. The items are presented as gap-filling questions within the context of a cohesive paragraph. Therefore, students are required to take into account the context of an entire passage to identify the structure of English and choose appropriate lexical units.

The items are divided into two categories and the constructs are defined as follows:

- *The ability to recognize a proper grammatical structure within context.* Students must be able to identify a proper structure needed to complete a grammatically accurate sentence in English.
- *The ability to identify an appropriate lexical item within context.* Students must be able to identify a word that semantically completes a sentence within the context of a paragraph.

Listening

TOEFL Junior assesses the degree to which students have the listening skills required to function in English-medium instructional environments. In such contexts, students are exposed to a wide range of aural input, for example, from personal conversations to short lectures on academic content. Therefore, it is essential for successful participation in school that students attain listening proficiency sufficient to comprehend different genres of spoken discourse. Moreover, in listening to a wide range of aural input, students need to understand main ideas, find important details, make inferences based on what is not explicitly stated, make predictions based on what the speaker says, understand a speaker's purpose, and correctly interpret such features of prosody as intonation and contrastive stress. These listening abilities are operationalized in the test for the three subdomains as follows:

- *The ability to listen for social and interpersonal purposes.* Students must be able to comprehend conversations on familiar topics about day-to-day matters that take place in a school setting.
- *The ability to listen for navigational purposes.* Students must be able to comprehend the language that teachers and other school staff (e.g., librarian and

school nurse) produce for a range of purposes other than presenting academic content. This includes language that fulfills a range of speech functions (e.g., providing directions, making announcements, and giving reminders).
- *The ability to listen for academic purposes.* Students need to comprehend ideas presented in a lecture or discussion based on academic material. Listening passages in the Listening section of *TOEFL Junior* do not require subject-specific background knowledge in any given content area. Such content-related concepts are presented, explained, and reinforced in the assessment so that a proficient listener can learn their meanings in the stimulus.

It should be noted that Bachman and Palmer's (2010) framework (discussed in the 'A Model of Language Knowledge' section) was referenced in characterizing linguistic features of listening materials in the three TLU subdomains and reflecting them in listening passages. This process was also applied in developing reading passages.

Reading

TOEFL Junior assesses the degree to which students have mastered the reading skills required for English-medium instructional environments. A wide range of reading subskills, including understanding main ideas, identifying important details, and making inferences, are expected of students in schools. In addition, different types of text are required for successful participation in English-medium instructional environments, and there is a relationship between text types and the three TLU subdomains. The reading abilities measured in *TOEFL Junior* are defined as follows, according to TLU subdomain:

- *The ability to read and comprehend texts for social and interpersonal purposes.* Students should be able to read and comprehend written texts on familiar topics in order to establish or maintain social relationships. Text types for this purpose may include correspondence (e.g., email and letters).
- *The ability to read and comprehend texts for navigational purposes.* Students need to be able to read and comprehend texts in order to identify key information from informational texts. Such texts include those containing school-related information, occasionally in less linear formats (e.g., directions, schedules, announcements, and brochures).
- *The ability to read and comprehend academic texts.* Students need to be able to read and comprehend academic texts in a range of genres (e.g., expository, biographical, persuasive, and literary) across a range of subject areas (e.g., arts/humanities, science, and social studies). As with listening, reading texts will not require any specific background or prior knowledge but will sometimes require students to read in order to learn new information in an academic context.

Speaking

TOEFL Junior Comprehensive assesses the degree to which students have the speaking skills required by English-medium instructional environments. This includes the abilities for the three TLU subdomains:

- *The ability to use spoken English for social and interpersonal purposes.* Students must be able to communicate orally in routine tasks and situations encountered in the school environment. For example, this includes the ability to communicate personal information, needs, and opinions on a wide range of familiar topics such as hobbies or weather.
- *The ability to use spoken English for navigational purposes.* Students must be able to engage in discussions and interactions on topics related to learning activities. This includes the ability to make requests, ask for assistance or information, and convey simple instructions.
- *The ability to use spoken English for academic purposes to communicate about and demonstrate knowledge of academic course content.* Students must be able to participate in classroom activities to convey academic knowledge. This includes the ability to respond to oral questions about academic content and to convey information heard or read in an academic context.

As discussed in the 'Linking Test Tasks to Target Language Use (TLU) Tasks' section, efforts were made to design test tasks similar to language use tasks that students are expected to perform in the TLU domain. Figure 4.2 illustrates that the linguistic characteristics of input (e.g., a listening stimulus to be summarized) were matched between a test task and a corresponding TLU task by referring to Bachman and Palmer's (2010) model. The figure also shows that the linguistic characteristics of an expected response to the speaking task were specified in terms of types of language knowledge in Bachman and Palmer's (2010) model. This design process was applied to both speaking and writing tasks.

Writing

TOEFL Junior Comprehensive assesses the degree to which test takers have the writing abilities required by English-medium instructional environments at the middle school level:

- *The ability to write in English for social and interpersonal purposes.* In English-medium instructional environments, students must be able to engage in written communication for the purposes of establishing and maintaining social and interpersonal relationships. This includes the ability to write informal correspondence to peers or teachers.
- *The ability to write in English for navigational purposes.* In school settings, students must be able to extract key school-related information from a variety

of spoken or written stimuli and keep written records for future reference. For instance, students may need to write simple, short summaries of school-related information (e.g., a field trip, announcements, or procedures).
- *The ability to write in English for academic purposes.* In English-medium instructional environments, students must be able to communicate in writing using appropriate written language on subject matters representing a range of content areas. This includes the ability to produce connected text, to describe a process in an academic context, and to understand and be able to summarize important information from spoken and written stimuli.

Score Report

A score report for both the *TOEFL Junior* Standard and the *TOEFL Junior* Comprehensive tests contains the following information: overall score level, scores for each of the sections, a Common European Framework of Reference (CEFR; Council of Europe, 2009) level for each test section, and can-do statements that describe what students can typically do at the scored CEFR level. The can-do statements included in the score reports are adapted from the CEFR can-do statements (Council of Europe, 2009), modified to make them more appropriate for the language use required for the target age group of the test. Tables 4.2 and 4.3 summarize the scores that are provided on the score reports for *TOEFL Junior* Standard and *TOEFL Junior* Comprehensive, respectively.

As summarized in Tables 4.2 and 4.3, CEFR levels reported for each test section represent four levels: below A2 (the lowest performance level measured by the test), A2, B1, and B2 (the highest performance level measured by the test). These levels were established through standard-setting studies that ETS conducted separately for the two *TOEFL Junior* tests.[3] Chapter 8 of this volume, by Papageorgiou and Baron (2017), describes the standard-setting procedures for the *TOEFL Junior* tests.

TABLE 4.2 Scores on the *TOEFL Junior* Standard Score Report

Section/overall	Reported score range(increments of 5 for the section scale scores)	CEFR level and can-do statements	Additional information
Listening	200–300	Below A2, A2, B1, B2	n/a
Language Form and Meaning	200–300	Below A2, A2, B1, B2	n/a
Reading	200–300	Below A2, A2, B1, B2	Lexile scores
Overall score level	1–5	n/a	Overall performance descriptor and CEFR profile for the three sections

Note. CEFR = Common European Framework of Reference.

TABLE 4.3 Scores on the *TOEFL Junior* Comprehensive Score Report

Section/overall	Reported score range (increments of 1)	CEFR level and can-do statements	Additional information
Reading	140–160	Below A2, A2, B1, B2	Lexile scores
Listening	140–160	Below A2, A2, B1, B2	n/a
Speaking	0–16	Below A2, A2, B1, B2	n/a
Writing	0–16	Below A2, A2, B1, B2	n/a
Overall score level	1–6	n/a	Overall performance descriptor and CEFR profile for the four skills

Note. CEFR = Common European Framework of Reference.

In the next three sections, more detailed explanations are provided for the following three test development procedures: (a) section scores, (b) overall score levels and performance descriptors, and (c) scoring rubrics for the speaking and writing tasks.

Section Scores

Scaled Score Development for Selected-Responses Sections (Listening, Reading, and Language Form and Meaning)

The raw scores (i.e., the number of items answered correctly) in each section of *TOEFL Junior* are converted to scaled scores in order to ensure that scores are comparable across test forms that may not have the same difficulty level (Kolen, 2006). As a result of appropriate statistical adjustments for form difficulty, scaled scores hold their meaning over time and across different test forms. Specifically, the following guidelines were considered in particular when creating scaled scores for *TOEFL Junior*:

- Use distinctive scales that do not overlap with other scales, either between the two *TOEFL Junior* tests or with any other ETS tests, to avoid confusion and misuses.
- Make every item or raw score point in the meaningful raw score range count toward a scaled score point, if possible, to avoid loss of information that results from converting multiple raw score points to a single score point on the scale.
- Ensure that for every scaled score point there is at least one item or one raw score point to avoid the unjustified differentiation of test takers.

It is worth emphasizing that the first point was considered particularly important in the score scale development for the two *TOEFL Junior* tests. As discussed in the previous sections of this chapter, the two versions were developed to provide stakeholders with options from which to choose as suited their needs and purposes. However, we did not want the test scores from one version to be misinterpreted or misused in contexts where the use of the other version seemed more appropriate. This consideration provided the main rationale for developing different score scales for the two *TOEFL Junior* tests. The resulting scaled scores for the *TOEFL Junior* Standard test and the *TOEFL Junior* Comprehensive test can be found in Table 4.2 and 4.3, respectively.

Determining the Speaking and Writing Scales

For the speaking and writing sections that consist of four constructed-response tasks each, each response is scored by two human raters on a holistic rubric scale of 0 to 4. The scoring rubrics for the speaking and writing items are provided on the website of the test.[4] Therefore, a raw score for an individual test taker ranges from 0 to 16 in each section, with the number of items being 4 in each section (see Table 4.1). Unlike in the selected-response sections discussed above, raw scores in the speaking and writing sections were decided not to be converted into scaled scores because of the following two reasons.

First, the meanings of raw scores in the speaking and writing sections can be more easily interpreted than can the meanings of raw scores on the selected-response items, particularly with reference to the performance levels that the scoring rubrics describe. A test taker may be assisted in understanding the typical characteristics of his or her performance on each item, by calculating an 'average item score' (i.e., by dividing a total section score by 4, the number of items) and then referring to the description of the performance associated with the score in the scoring rubric.

Second, being few in number, these items are susceptible to memorization. This means that pretesting the constructed-response items would pose a test security risk. Consequently, conventional score equating that requires pretesting of items is not feasible for constructed-response items. Instead of conventional score equating, quality control is maintained by other measures such as rigorous test development processes utilizing the evidence-centered design approach (Mislevy, Steinberg, & Almond, 2002), trying out new items in small-scale sessions before they are used in the test,[5] as well as through rigorous training of human raters and monitoring of their performance. These quality control methods ensure quality and stability in the meaning of scores for the speaking and writing sections of the *TOEFL Junior* Comprehensive test.

Overall Score Levels and Performance Descriptors

Based on the section scores explained earlier, total scaled scores were calculated for each *TOEFL Junior* test. However, there is a limit to the amount of information that a numeric score can provide about a test taker's language performance across different sections of a test, especially in light of the fact that there are many possible combinations of section scores that could arrive at the same total scaled score. To overcome this limitation of total scaled scores, it was decided that overall score levels would be reported instead. The overall score levels are band scores, as discussed in the next subsection. They are intended to help test users better understand the test results and better interpret their meanings. The following two steps were followed in developing the overall score levels and level descriptors: (a) developing band levels and (b) developing performance descriptors. More details about the procedures can be found in Papageorgiou, Morgan, and Becker (2015) for the *TOEFL Junior* Standard test and in Papageorgiou, Xi, Morgan, and So (2015) for the *TOEFL Junior* Comprehensive test.

Developing Overall Score Levels

The main goal of this step was to determine the number of overall score levels and to set cut scores to classify test takers into levels both meaningfully and reliably. Despite differences in the specific data considered for the two tests primarily because of the difference in structure between the two tests, the general procedures for the development of band levels were the same across the two tests.

On the basis of test taker performance data collected from either operational test forms (for *TOEFL Junior* Standard) or pilot administrations (for *TOEFL Junior* Comprehensive), three proposals for each of the tests were developed to set the number of overall score levels and cut scores. The reliability of each proposal was estimated using RELCLASS (Livingston & Lewis, 1995) in order to calculate the chances of misclassifying test takers into the incorrect levels. In addition, the CEFR profiles of the band levels for each solution were examined to provide an initial understanding of how proficiency progresses from lower to higher levels. A five-score-level solution for *TOEFL Junior* Standard and a six-score-level solution for *TOEFL Junior* Comprehensive were finally selected. Note that the numbers of overall score levels for the two *TOEFL Junior* tests differ so as to prevent any misuse of the results, such as making direct comparisons between the score levels of the two tests.

Developing Overall Score-Level Performance Descriptors

After final decisions were made about the overall score levels for each of the *TOEFL Junior* tests, assessment specialists and researchers collaborated to develop performance descriptors that capture a typical student's language proficiency within each overall score level. Following is the information that was taken into account in developing the performance descriptors: (a) the means and standard deviations of each of the test sections by overall score level; (b) the characteristics of reading and listening items answered correctly by students at different levels; (c) the test performance of U.S. middle school students (both English learners and native English speakers), reported in Wolf and Steinberg (2011); (d) descriptors of the proficiency scales of the CEFR to which the test scores are mapped;

(e) typical profiles of students across sections; and (f) the rubrics used to score the writing and speaking tasks (*TOEFL Junior* Comprehensive only). The results of the procedures used to define overall score levels to develop performance descriptors for each of the overall score levels are found at the following websites: http://www.ets.org/toefl_junior/scores_research/standard/overall/ for *TOEFL Junior* Standard and http://www.ets.org/toefl_junior/scores_research/comprehensive/overall/ for *TOEFL Junior* Comprehensive.

The Relationship of Overall Score Levels Between the Two TOEFL Junior Tests

Despite the potential usefulness—relative to numeric scores—of reporting overall score levels and accompanying descriptors, there exists a potential for misuse of the score levels. One of these potential misuses is to claim that results from the two *TOEFL Junior* tests are equivalent. To prevent this unjustified use, different numbers of overall score levels were developed for the two tests, as discussed earlier. In addition, empirical evidence was collected to illustrate why the aforementioned misuse is not warranted.

In the investigation of the relationship of the overall score levels between the two *TOEFL Junior* tests, Papageorgiou et al. (2014) found that there is not a one-to-one correspondence in the overall score levels between the two tests. Instead, there is a probabilistic relationship between the overall score levels. For example, students who received the highest overall score level on the *TOEFL Junior* Standard are not always projected to receive the highest level on *TOEFL Junior* Comprehensive. Furthermore, as explained in previous sections, the two *TOEFL Junior* tests are composed of different sections, thereby measuring different constructs.

Hence, overall score levels should not be compared directly between the two tests. Rather, stakeholders should choose the test that best fits their needs and interests.

Scoring Rubrics of the Speaking and Writing Tasks

The speaking and writing scoring rubrics were developed in a multistage process. A small-scale prototype study was conducted with English learners in the United States to try prototype items and gather indicators of different levels of performance on the items. Experts experienced in evaluating the speaking and writing abilities of nonnative English speakers (e.g., *TOEFL iBT®* test-certified raters) analyzed responses to the prototype items, and the results were used to formulate descriptors for the initial sets of scoring rubrics. Test-taker responses from pilot administrations were then used to further refine the scoring rubrics. The final version of the speaking scoring rubrics is found at http://www.ets.org/s/toefl_junior/pdf/toefl_junior_comprehensive_speaking_scoring_guides.pdf and that of the writing scoring rubrics is at http://www.ets.org/s/toefl_junior/pdf/toefl_junior_comprehensive_writing_scoring_guides.pdf. A more detailed explanation about the rubric development is provided in So et al. (2015).

Conclusion

This chapter presents both theoretical and practical considerations that guided decisions through the *TOEFL Junior* development process. These considerations have formed the basis for determining validity research areas needed at various stages of test development and use. For example, the test design team referred to the information discussed in this chapter to collect validity evidence at different stages of test development. The information has also served as a frame of reference, subsequent to the introduction of the test, to validate assessment-based interpretations and uses of *TOEFL Junior* test results. The comprehensive list of research topics that have been addressed to validate the claims associated with the *TOEFL Junior* test scores is presented in So et al. (2015).

As a final note, we would like to highlight the fact that collaboration was essential among a team of experts each with expertise in different areas (i.e., researchers in language assessment, item developers, and psychometricians) in the test design and development process. As illustrated in this chapter, multiple considerations were taken into account from the very early stage of test development (e.g., identifying the target language use domain), to operationalization of the constructs appropriate to the intended test-taker population, and to the design and organization of the score report to make it informative and useful for the intended uses. At each of these stages, the collective intelligence gained by the diverse expertise of the test development team was important to ensure that the resulting assessment is technically sound and that it will bring beneficial consequences for English language learning and teaching for the target test-taker population.

Notes

1. This chapter is a shortened version of a previously published report: So, Y., Wolf, M. K., Hauck, M. C., Mollaun, P., Rybinski, P., Tumposky, D., & Wang, L. (2015). *TOEFL Junior*® Design Framework (*TOEFL Junior* Research Report No. 02, ETS Research Report No. RR-15-13). Princeton, NJ: Educational Testing Service.
2. Due to space constraints, the results of the curricula and standards reviews are not included in this chapter. They are summarized in Appendices A–D in So et al. (2015) for each of the four language skills (listening, reading, speaking, and writing).
3. Details about the relationship between *TOEFL Junior* scores and the CEFR levels in each of the *TOEFL Junior* tests can be found on the *TOEFL Junior* website at https://www.ets.org/toefl_junior/scores_research/standard/cefr (for *TOEFL Junior* Standard) and at http://www.ets.org/toefl_junior/scores_research/comprehensive/cefr/ (for *TOEFL Junior* Comprehensive).
4. The speaking scoring rubrics are found at http://www.ets.org/s/toefl_junior/pdf/toefl_junior_comprehensive_speaking_scoring_guides.pdf, and the writing scoring rubrics are at http://www.ets.org/s/toefl_junior/pdf/toefl_junior_comprehensive_writing_scoring_guides.pdf.
5. This trialing process is different from pretesting because trial items are administered to students who are believed to represent the target test-taker population. Conversely, pretest items are administered to actual test takers at the time when they are taking an operational test.

References

Bachman, L., & Palmer, A. (1996). *Language testing in practice*. Oxford, UK: Oxford University Press.

Bachman, L., & Palmer, A. (2010). *Language assessment in practice: Developing language assessments and justifying their use in the real world*. Oxford, UK: Oxford University Press.

Bailey, A. L. (2007). Introduction: Teaching and assessing students learning English in school. In A. L. Bailey (Ed.), *The language demands of school: Putting academic English to the test* (pp. 1–26). New Haven, CT: Yale University Press.

Bailey, A. L., Butler, F. A., LaFramenta, C., & Ong, C. (2004). *Towards the characterization of academic English in upper elementary science classrooms* (Final Deliverable to OERI Contract No. R305B960002; CSE Technical Report No. 621). Los Angeles, CA: University of California, National Center for Research on Evaluation, Standards, and Student Testing.

Bailey, A. L., & Heritage, H. M. (2008). *Formative assessment for literacy, Grades K–6: Building reading and academic language skills across the curriculum*. Thousand Oaks, CA: Corwin Press.

Bailey, A. L., Heritage, H. M., & Butler, F. A. (2014). Developmental considerations and curricular contexts in the assessment of young language learners. In A. J. Kunnan (Ed.), *The companion to language assessment* (pp. 423–439). Malden, MA: Wiley-Blackwell.

Butler, F. A., & Castellon-Wellington, M. (2005). Students' concurrent performance on tests of English language proficiency and academic achievement. In J. Abedi, A. Bailey, F. Butler, M. Castellon-Wellington, S. Leon, & J. Mirocha (Eds.), *Validity of administering large-scale content assessments to English language learners: An investigation from three perspectives* (CSE Technical Report No. 663). Los Angeles, CA: University of California, National Center for Research on Evaluation, Standards, and Student Testing.

Butler, F. A., Stevens, R., & Castellon-Wellington, M. (2007). ELLs and standardized assessments: The interaction between language proficiency and performance on standardized tests. In A. L. Bailey (Ed.), *The language demands of school: Putting academic English to the test* (pp. 27–49). New Haven, CT: Yale University Press.

Chamot, A. U., & O'Malley, J. (1994). *The CALLA handbook: Implementing the cognitive academic language learning approach*. Reading, MA: Addison-Wesley.

Council of Europe. (2009). *Common European Framework of Reference for Languages: Learning, teaching, assessment (CEFR)*. Available from http://www.coe.int/t/dg4/linguistic/Source/ManualRevision-proofread-FINAL_en.pdf

Cummins, J. (1980). The construct of proficiency in bilingual education. In J. E. Alatis (Ed.), *Georgetown University round table on languages and linguistics: Current issues in bilingual education* (pp. 81–103). Washington, DC: Georgetown University.

Cummins, J. (1981). The role of primary language development in promoting educational success for language minority students. In California State Department of Education (Ed.), *Schooling and language minority students: A theoretical framework* (pp. 3–49). Los Angeles, CA: National Dissemination and Assessment Center.

Cummins, J. (2000). *Language, power and pedagogy: Bilingual children in the crossfire*. Clevedon, UK: Multilingual Matters.

Kolen, M. J. (2006). Scaling and norming. In R. L. Brennan (Ed.), *Educational measurement* (4th ed., pp. 155–186). Westport, CT: Praeger.

Livingston, S. A., & Lewis, C. (1995). Estimating the consistency and accuracy of classifications based on test scores. *Journal of Educational Measurement, 32*, 179–197.

Mislevy, R. J., Steinberg, L. S., & Almond, R. G. (2002). Design and analysis in task-based language assessment. *Language Testing, 19*(4), 477–496.

Papageorgiou, S., & Baron, P. (2017). Using the Common European Framework of Reference to facilitate score interpretations for young learners' English language proficiency assessments. In M. K. Wolf, & Y. G. Butler (Eds.), *English language proficiency assessments for young learners* (pp. 136–152). New York, NY: Routledge.

Papageorgiou, S., Morgan, R., & Becker, V. (2014). *Development of overall score levels and performance descriptors for the TOEFL Junior Standard test.* Unpublished Manuscript. Princeton, NJ: Educational Testing Service.

Papageorgiou, S., Xi, X., Morgan, R., & So, Y. (2015). Developing and validating band levels and descriptors for reporting overall examinee performance. *Language Assessment Quarterly*, *15*(2), 153–177.

Scarcella, R. (2003). *Academic English: A conceptual framework* (Technical Report No. 2003–1). Santa Barbara, CA: University of California, Linguistic Minority Research Institute.

Schleppegrell, M. J. (2001). *The language of schooling.* Mahwah, NJ: Lawrence Erlbaum.

So, Y., Wolf, M. K., Hauck, M. C., Mollaun, P., Rybinski, P., Tumposky, D., & Wang, L. (2015). *TOEFL Junior design framework* (TOEFL Junior® Research Report TOEFL JR–02; ETS Research Report No. RR–15–13). Princeton, NJ: Educational Testing Service.

Stevens, R., Butler, F. A., & Castellon-Wellington, M. (2000). *Academic language and content assessment: Measuring the progress of ELLs* (CSE Technical Report No. 552). Los Angeles, CA: University of California, National Center for Research on Evaluation, Standards, and Student Testing.

Wolf, M. K., & Steinberg, J. (2011). *An examination of United States middle school students' performance on TOEFL Junior* (ETS Research Memorandum No. RM-11–15). Princeton, NJ: Educational Testing Service.

5
DESIGNING TASK TYPES FOR ENGLISH LANGUAGE PROFICIENCY ASSESSMENTS FOR K–12 ENGLISH LEARNERS IN THE U.S.

Maurice Cogan Hauck, Emilie Pooler, Mikyung Kim Wolf, Alexis A. Lopez, and David P. Anderson

English learners (ELs) make up nearly 10% of the U.S. school population. In school year 2012–13, approximately 4.85 million students in grades prekindergarten through 12 were officially classified as ELs (Soto, Hooker, & Batalova, 2015). In addition to being a large population, U.S. K–12 EL students are a complex and heterogeneous one. They fit a range of different profiles, including: early arrivals, who receive all of their formal schooling in the U.S. (and a sizable proportion of whom are U.S.-born citizens, Office of English Language Acquisition, 2015); recent arrivals, comprising both students who have acquired significant literacy skills and content knowledge in their first language as well as students with interrupted formal education; and long-term EL students, who have been designated as ELs for over six years, and who often possess relatively strong oral skills but limited literacy skills (Abedi, 2008; Wolf et al., 2014). A considerable majority of these students are, in keeping with the theme of this volume, young learners (i.e., those that are in kindergarten through Grade 8).

Providing high quality assessments of English language proficiency (hereafter, U.S. K–12 ELP assessments) for K–12 English learners is of tremendous importance. Assessments that provide valid, meaningful, and useful information about the developing English language proficiency of these students can play an important role in supporting the English language development for their overall academic success and life opportunities.

The purposes of this chapter are two-fold: first, we aim to provide a general overview of Educational Testing Service (ETS)'s development work for U.S. K–12 ELP assessments, focusing on how the Evidence Centered Design (ECD) framework is operationalized in the development of U.S. K–12 ELP assessments. The second purpose is to describe in some detail the design of task types[1] and test items to assess young language learners' ELP in the current context of EL education in the U.S. (e.g., new challenging academic standards, new ELP standards, and next-generation ELP assessments). Through this focus on task types and test items, we hope to provide some useful insight into challenges we have encountered and approaches we have explored in developing ELP assessments for young EL students.

In this chapter, we first provide an overview of the educational context for U.S. K–12 ELP assessments, and then briefly describe the new standards and the need these standards have created for new ELP assessments, which constitute a significant part of educational reform efforts impacting the field of ELP testing for K–12 ELs in the U.S. This contextual background is provided to help readers understand key issues in the design and development of new U.S. K–12 ELP assessments. Then, we delineate how Evidence Centered Design (ECD) has been employed in ETS's K–12 ELP assessment development work, followed by a discussion of the construct for these assessments. Following this background, we provide a fairly detailed discussion of the design of task types, drawing examples from two U.S. K–12 ELP assessment systems: the English Language Proficiency Assessment for the 21st Century (ELPA21) and the English Language Proficiency Assessments for California (ELPAC). In doing so, we hope to illustrate some principles that are broadly applicable to the theme of this volume, the design of assessments for young EL students. We conclude the chapter by acknowledging some important topics related to next-generation U.S. K–12 ELP assessments which we are not able to discuss in this chapter, but which offer useful avenues of future documentation and research.

Educational Context for and ETS Role in U.S. K–12 ELP Assessments

The educational context for U.S. K–12 ELP assessments, and indeed the design requirements of the assessments themselves, have been deeply influenced by federal legislation. Ever since the 2002 reauthorization of the Elementary and Secondary Educational Act as the No Child Left Behind (NCLB) Act, federal law has required all U.S. states to develop ELP standards and to administer standards-based ELP assessments annually to all EL students, from kindergarten through Grade 12 (NCLB, 2002). The Elementary and Secondary Educational Act was recently reauthorized as the Every Student Succeeds Act (ESSA, 2015). ESSA similarly stresses the importance of schools being accountable for EL students' attainment of ELP.

For purposes of federal accountability reporting, these K–12 ELP assessments are used to report on EL students' level of ELP and progress in developing ELP. In addition, states use summative K–12 ELP assessments as one of the major criteria in making decisions about students' exit from EL status (Cook & Linquanti, 2015; National Research Council, 2011; Wolf et al., 2008). This exit decision, or reclassification, use means that U.S. K–12 ELP assessments have significant stakes for individuals, as EL status has a marked effect on students' academic paths (e.g., the types of courses and assessments taken and graduation requirements).

State departments of education (individually or in consortia of states) play a substantial role in governing and designing U.S. K–12 ELP assessments, which are part of their accountability systems. Such agencies typically issue a request for proposals, which establishes a number of goals and constraints for the design effort, ranging from the population, standards, test purposes, and scores to be reported (all of which, as described above, are largely influenced by federal legislation) to logistical requirements such as the timelines for administration, the estimated numbers of students participating, and the available budget. The role of test developers such as ETS is to propose a solution that will produce the highest quality assessment possible given the objectives and constraints.

ETS has had broad involvement in U.S. K–12 ELP assessment design and development activities for a range of states since 2002. In the years directly after the passage of NCLB, ETS was involved in the design and/or ongoing development of assessments including the New York English as a Second Language Achievement Test (NYSESLAT), the California English Language Development Test (CELDT), and the Comprehensive English Language Assessment (CELLA) for a consortium of states.

More recently, ETS's work in this area has focused on two assessment systems, English Language Proficiency Assessments for the 21st Century (ELPA21) and the English Language Proficiency Assessments for California (ELPAC). The ELPA21 consortium, organized by the Council of Chief State School Officers (CCSSO), has been developing a new ELP assessment system to serve its 10 member states: Arkansas, Iowa, Kansas, Louisiana, Nebraska, Ohio, Oregon, South Carolina, Washington, and West Virginia. ETS was responsible for the design and development of a sizable pool of test items to support field testing and initial operational forms. At the time of this writing, California (which serves nearly 1.4 million EL students) is well along in the process of creating its next-generation ELP assessment system, called the ELPAC. The ELPAC summative assessment is scheduled to have its first operational administration in the spring of 2018, and ETS is the test developer responsible for all aspects of assessment design, development, and implementation.

Challenging New Standards and the need for Next-Generation ELP Assessments

Since 2012, most states in the U.S. have begun to implement new academic content standards designed to ensure that all students receive a K–12 education that positions them to succeed in either entering college or beginning a career (e.g., Common Core State Standards [CCSS] and Next Generation Science Standards [NGSS]). These college and career readiness (CCR) standards are characterized by increased academic rigor and high language demands (Bunch,

Kibler, & Pimental, 2012; Hakuta, Santos, & Fang, 2013; Wolf, Wang, Blood, & Huang, 2014). For example, the CCSS for English language arts call upon students to demonstrate academic abilities such as (1) close reading and analysis of complex informational texts, (2) analytic and logical writing of information and arguments, (3) research skills, and (4) effective presentation and academic discussion to build knowledge, evaluate information, and express opinions. The CCSS for mathematics also feature explicit language demands, specifying key practices that involve mathematical communication such as (1) constructing viable arguments and critiquing the reasoning of others and (2) expressing regularity in repeated reasoning (National Governors Association Center for Best Practices, Council of Chief State School Officers, 2010). Similarly, the NGSS feature explicit language demands associated with the science practices (Lee, Quinn, & Valdés, 2013), such as (1) asking questions, (2) constructing explanations, (3) engaging in argument from evidence, and (4) obtaining, evaluating, and communicating information.

These increased language use expectations for all students have far-reaching implications for EL students, as new ELP standards have been established to correspond to the language demands in the CCR content standards. For example, the ELPA21 consortium and the state of California have each developed new ELP standards, written to correspond to CCR standards and reflecting a strong interconnection between language and content. These new ELP standards are also organized in a manner that emphasizes the integrated use of language skills (i.e., collaborative/interactive, interpretive/receptive, and productive), unlike earlier ELP standards that are arranged following the traditional structure of four discrete language skills (i.e., listening, reading, speaking, and writing).

The rigorous academic standards and ELP standards created a need for next-generation U.S. K–12 ELP assessments. In the next section, we will describe the ECD model that ETS has utilized for ELPA21 and the ELPAC.

Applying Evidence-Centered Design to the Development of U.S. K–12 ELP Assessments

ETS's work on the design and development of U.S. K–12 ELP assessments is grounded in Evidence Centered Design (ECD), which approaches educational assessment as "an evidentiary argument for reasoning about what students say, do, or make in particular task situations as well as to generally claim what they can know, do, or have accomplished" (Mislevy, 2011, p. 6). ECD provides a framework for constructing and documenting such an evidentiary argument through the process of conceptualizing, designing, developing, implementing, and operating an assessment system (Mislevy, Steinberg, & Almond, 2003). This section provides a brief overview of ECD and its application to U.S. K–12 ELP assessments, drawing on examples from ELPA21 and the ELPAC to illustrate points as appropriate.[2]

Although the ECD approach is inherently iterative, it is commonly conceptualized as a series of five layers that constitute a progression from more abstract conceptualization to more specific and concrete instantiation. In Table 5.1, adapted from Mislevy (2011)'s work, we present the five layers of ECD and, for each layer, the key features on which ETS assessment developers focused in developing K–12 ELP assessments. Following the table, the application of each of these layers to U.S. K–12 ELP assessments is briefly discussed.

Domain Analysis

Because U.S. K–12 ELP assessments are focused on the ELP of students in schools within the U.S., the real-world domain of interest consists of the English language skills students need in order to gain the academic content knowledge necessary to be college- and career-ready. The functional domain analysis—the documentation of these real-world domains in terms that can support assessment design and development (as well as other purposes such as development of curricula and instruction)—is contained in the ELP standards adopted by the state or consortium of states. As the key overall guiding document for subsequent test design work, the applicable ELP standards are the basis for the conceptualization of language proficiency, the conceptualization of student progress (or sequence of language development), and, at the most general level, the organizational

TABLE 5.1 Layers of Evidence-Centered Design and Key Features for Assessment Developers

ECD layer	Key features
Domain analysis	Documents the following information: • the important and salient aspects of the domain • the work and situations that are central to the domain • the knowledge representations central to the domain
Domain modeling	Provides a model for articulating the assessment argument based on the domain analysis
Conceptual assessment framework	Asks the questions: • What claims do we want to be able to support about student knowledge, skills, and abilities (KSAs) based on assessment scores? • How do we coordinate the substantive, statistical, and operational aspects of the assessment to gather evidence in support of these claims? Contains the following elements: student model, evidence model, task model
Assessment implementation	Contains production aspects of assessment development: authoring tasks, scoring details, statistical models
Assessment delivery	Contains the following elements: student interaction with tasks, evaluation of performances, creation of feedback

structure of the assessments (e.g., the organization into specific grades or grade bands). In this respect, a key aspect of ECD—the domain analysis—is in place before ETS's work as a test developer begins.

Domain Modeling

As noted in Table 5.1, in order to articulate the assessment argument based on the domain analysis, it is necessary to create an operational model of the domain to be measured. In the context of U.S. K–12 ELP assessments, this requires analyzing the ELP standards to define the operational construct of the assessments. While analyzing the ELP standards, it is important to identify which knowledge, skills, and abilities (KSAs) from the standards can be assessed effectively within the limitations of a standardized assessment. The analysis of ELP standards also involves interpreting the standards appropriately and sampling KSAs in order to make an operational definition of the construct and, later, to formulate the claims and blueprint. Given the central role of domain modeling and construct definition in the design and development of the current generation of U.S. K–12 ELP assessments, we discuss the ELP construct based on ELP standards in more detail in a subsequent section.

Conceptual Assessment Framework

The three elements of the Conceptual Assessment Framework together capture the key conceptual decisions underlying the assessment. The *student model* consists of a representation of the KSAs of the students who will be taking the assessment with regard to their English language proficiency. At this point, specific claims are articulated about inferences we can make based on the assessment scores. The *task model* consists of two documents: the item specifications (or item writing guidelines), which provide the "recipe" for developing each of the task types to be contained on the assessment; and the test blueprints, which, as the metaphor of their name implies, provide information about how the task types defined in the item specifications will be assembled into test forms.

The *evidence model* documents ways to collect empirical evidence and relate it to claims made about the test takers. The evidence model involves determining important characteristics of student performance (i.e., scoring specific tasks) and analyzing the way performance across several tasks can be combined to support specific claims (i.e., various statistical models and data analyses). As noted above, U.S. K–12 ELP assessments must produce scores that can be used to satisfy a range of accountability requirements. Under current federal requirements, for example, states need to report on EL students' performance and progress in attaining listening, speaking, reading, and writing skills. This requires a summative assessment system on a common vertical scale so that individual student performance can be tracked over time.

Assessment Implementation and Assessment Delivery

Because of our focus on designing task types, the final two layers of ECD, Assessment Implementation and Assessment Delivery, will not be discussed in any depth in this chapter. These layers involve the practical steps that are needed to progress from the relatively abstract conceptual plan captured in the Conceptual Assessment Framework to an assessment system that can be administered, scored, and reported. Such steps include: production and banking of an item pool; assembly, scoring, and analysis of test forms (iteratively for such events as prototypes, pilots, and/or field tests before operational launch); standard setting; and score reporting. In U.S. K–12 ELP assessments, these steps are often largely determined by the request for proposals and the contract.

Defining the Construct of U.S. K–12 ELP Assessments

As noted above, the ECD process for designing U.S. K–12 ELP assessments begins with the de facto domain analysis provided by the state or consortium's ELP standards. Establishing a construct definition based on this domain analysis, however, is made challenging by the fact that educational standards are designed to structure activities and learning in the classroom rather than for assessment development.

The conceptualization of ELP constructs has been influenced by the explicit demand for more sophisticated, academic language use for all students in the U.S. K–12 educational system, including ELs, and by the accompanying strong interconnection between language and content areas.

The ELPA21 consortium conceptualizes the ELP construct as the academic language used across different academic areas (e.g., English language arts, mathematics, and science). The ELP Standards adopted by the ELPA21 consortium (Council of Chief State School Officers [CCSSO], 2014; henceforth, ELPA21 ELP Standards), are centered around a set of language functions and language forms that EL students need in order to develop competence in the practices associated with different academic areas. While proficiency in the four language skills of listening, speaking, reading, and writing is still required, the focus on language functions and forms enables the ELPA21 ELP Standards to correspond closely to the rigorous language demands of the CCR standards.

Similarly, the ELP construct as based upon the *California English Language Development Standards: Kindergarten through Grade 12* (California Department of Education, 2014; California ELD Standards, henceforth) is conceptualized as the key KSAs that EL students need in order to access, engage with, and achieve in grade-level academic content. The California ELD Standards, similar to the ELPA21 ELP Standards, are not structured around the separate language domains of listening, speaking, reading, and writing. Rather, the California ELD Standards are organized around higher-level communicative modes that are necessary to access the more rigorous language demands embodied in the CCR standards. For example, the first of the California ELD Standards calls for, "Exchanging information and ideas with others through oral collaborative discussions on a range of social and academic topics" (California Department of Education, 2014, p. 26). To meet this standard, ELs must apply both receptive and productive language skills in joint communication with peers, teachers, or others.

This focus on communicative meaning-making through the use of higher-order linguistic modes requiring integrated use of language skills has important implications for the design of task types. In the next section, we describe how ETS has operationalized the assessment of such standards by defining specific claims about student performance to be made based on test scores and by subsequently designing task types to gather evidence to measure the construct and support the claim.

Designing Task Types and Test Items

Developing the task model for the assessment (i.e., designing and documenting the task types which will be used in the development of the item pool) is a crucial step in moving from an abstract plan for an assessment towards creation of the actual test materials. The task types used on the assessment must capture appropriate evidence about students' KSAs as described in the standards and must sample the domain as effectively as is possible within practical constraints.

In this section, we first discuss how assessment claims for U.S. K–12 ELP assessments can be articulated in order to sample the domain in a principled manner. We then draw on examples from ELPA21 and the ELPAC to consider four topics central to task types for assessing EL students' ELP: (a) integrated language skills, (b) pedagogically sound task types, (c) scaffolding, and (d) considerations for K–2 students. We have chosen these four topics as they are specifically pertinent to new K–12 ELP assessments and young EL students.

Developing Assessment Claims

A pressing constraint on the design of task types is the need to sample the domain in a manner that is consistent with the construct definition. For U.S. K–12 ELP assessments, a particular challenge is posed by the tension between the standards (with their emphasis on integrated skills) and the federal reporting requirements (which call for separate scores for listening, speaking, reading, and writing).

Drafting assessment claims is a key activity in the process of determining how the domain will be sampled, and particularly how scores from integrated tasks will be mapped to the four domains for reporting. For both ELPA21 and the ELPAC, assessment claims consist of two parts: (1) a set of high-level, general statements about one of the four language domains and (2) more detailed claims that state explicitly how each standard maps onto each of the four domains for purposes of assessment.[3]

The two levels of claims are a useful means of explicitly documenting the manner in which each of the specific standards maps onto the four language domains of listening, speaking, reading, and writing. For example, ELPA21 contains the following high-level claim for the Writing domain (Oregon Department of Education, 2016):

> The English language learner can write comprehensible texts that are the result of grade-appropriate activities.

For the purposes of assessing specific standards within the domain of writing, several more specific claims were developed, including the following (Oregon Department of Education, 2016):

> **Standard 2: Writing claim**: The English language learner participates in written exchanges of information, ideas, and analyses, responding to peer, audience, or reader comments and questions.

During the process of task design and item development, each item is developed and reviewed for its alignment to a specific claim, ensuring in turn its alignment to the targeted standard. As the item pool is being developed, detailed assessment claims also support clear formal analysis about what claims are being assessed, in which domains, and by how many items.

This two-part structure of high-level claims and detailed claims underlies the development of the item pool. We now turn to some specific considerations in designing item and task types.

Assessing Integrated Language Skills

The integrated use of language skills—using two or more of the four skills (listening, speaking, reading, and writing) in order to accomplish a communicative goal—is a clear emphasis throughout in the standards for ELPA21 and California. Each of the 10 ELPA21 ELP Standards involves the use of two or more language skills, often in an integrated manner. Similarly, the California ELD Standards foreground the importance of using language in an interactive, often integrated manner by organizing the first four Part I standards (1. Exchanging information and ideas; 2. Interacting via written English; 3. Supporting opinions and persuading others; and 4. Adapting language choices [California Department of Education, 2014]) under the general category of "Collaborative Mode." The standards categorized under "Productive Mode" also call for integrated skills as students are expected to produce speech or text based on topics they have learned about through reading, listening, and/or viewing.

We will describe two task types[4] in order to illustrate how ETS has designed test items to address the integrated nature of the standards. We will begin with a task type designed to assess ELPA21 ELP Standard 2, "Participate in grade-appropriate oral and written exchanges of information."

As noted above, the high-level claim and the more specific claim served to narrow the focus of this relatively broad standard. A parallel process of disaggregation of the proficiency level descriptors by domain included in the ELPA21 ELP Standards enabled the task type design to also target specific student proficiency levels.

The ELPA21 "Writing Questions" task type was designed to assess this claim at proficiency levels 2 and 3 (out of 5). In "Writing Questions" tasks, students are presented with information in the form of an announcement (e.g., one explaining the visit of a famous journalist to the students' school) and are asked to write questions based on the announcement (e.g., three questions they would like to ask the journalist). Although not particularly elaborate, this task type reflects a key shift from an "independent" writing task to an integrated task. This task type is integrated in that the student writing takes place in a clear communicative context, the student writing requires comprehension of specific input, and performance on the task can be used to support inferences about the student's ability to participate in a short written exchange by asking questions.

The ELPAC integrated skills task type "Summarize an Academic Presentation" is designed to assess a student's ability to express "information and ideas in formal oral presentations on academic topics" (California ELD Standard P1.C.9.). This is, in many ways, a paradigmatic example of an academically focused integrated skills task as it calls on the student to comprehend grade-appropriate academic content and then demonstrate comprehension by summarizing that content orally.

The stimulus for this task type takes the form of a brief scripted academic presentation from the science content area, which is read aloud by the examiner.[5] To ensure that language, rather than content, is being measured, the presentation is self-contained (i.e., does not presume any prior knowledge), and the science topics are selected from the Next Generation Science Standards at grades *lower* than the grade being assessed. Visual support is provided to aid comprehension; for example, if the presentation describes a scientific process, an image of each step of that process is provided.

After listening to the presentation, the student is prompted to retell the main points, with the visual support (and any key terms provided) available as an aid to memory. The criteria for evaluating responses place primary emphasis on the student's language proficiency, with content accuracy as a secondary consideration.

Pedagogically Sound Task Types

Given that U.S. K–12 ELP assessments take place within a standards-based educational system, it is of particular importance that the task types used on these assessments be pedagogically sound. Pedagogically sound task types should call on students to perform engaging activities that realistically represent contexts in which they would use English to accomplish meaningful tasks in classrooms where English is the medium of instruction. The more the assessment tasks look and feel like classroom tasks, the more valid the evidence gathered by the tasks will be. Additionally, pedagogically sound task types help to ensure that any "washback" (i.e., influence of the assessment on teaching and learning) will be positive, so that preparation for the test will promote instruction of the same skills called for by the standards.

Test developers can help ensure that tasks are pedagogically sound by asking themselves throughout the task design process, "What would preparation for this task look like in the classroom?" Additionally, pedagogical appropriateness of task types can be greatly enhanced by directly involving educators in key stages of the item development process, as educators have unique knowledge about the classroom context in which the students will be taking the assessment and how the standards are being implemented in daily classroom life.

Educators can provide valuable input during the task design phase if the development process allows for educator review of tasks before large-scale item production begins (e.g., at the stage of prototyping or informal piloting). For example, in the ELPAC item development process, educator input during a small-scale pilot enabled ETS to revise task types to align to a classroom practice of assessing collaborative writing standards in relatively formal registers. Even after draft items have been produced, educator input can have a substantial positive impact. For example, the educators on the ELPA21 kindergarten content review panel gave key input that helped to ensure that the demands of the kindergarten reading tasks did not exceed those of the corresponding kindergarten English language arts (ELA) standards.

Scaffolding

One additional hallmark of the current generation of ELP standards is the degree to which they emphasize scaffolding (i.e., various types of support for student to complete given tasks) as an important indicator of student proficiency in English (Wolf et al., 2016). Table 5.2 shows some of the wording of the ELPA21 Standards and the California ELD Standards, respectively, with regard to scaffolding.

On U.S. K–12 ELP assessments, scaffolding has the potential to improve measurement by giving students at relatively low proficiency levels an opportunity to meaningfully demonstrate what they can do, even on relatively challenging tasks. This is particularly beneficial for young EL students who are commonly provided with scaffolding in their daily instruction. Scaffolding can both make the test taking experience much more positive for such students and provide better measurement of student language skills at relatively low proficiency levels.

TABLE 5.2 Language on Scaffolding in ELPA21 ELP Standards and California ELD Standards

ELPA21 ELP Standards (CCSSO, 2014, p. 2)	California ELD Standards (California Department of Education, 2014, p. 150)
ELLs at all levels of ELP should be provided with scaffolding in order to reach the next reasonable proficiency level as they develop grade-appropriate language capacities, particularly those that involve content-specific vocabulary and registers. The type and intensity of the scaffolding provided will depend on each student's ability to undertake the particular task independently while continuing to uphold appropriate complexity for the student.	The California ELD Standards establish three overall levels of scaffolding that teachers can provide to ELs during instruction: *substantial*, *moderate*, and *light*. ELs at the emerging level of English language proficiency will generally require more substantial support to develop capacity for many academic tasks than will students at the bridging level.

Scaffolding is typically thought of as most at home in instructional settings or small-scale formative assessments. Using scaffolding in large scale assessments requires some modifications to ensure standardization. Although not all classroom-based scaffolding techniques can be operationalized effectively in a large-scale standardized assessment, some forms of scaffolding that can be applied include:

- modeling how to respond to a question;
- breaking down a task into steps or parts;
- providing key words needed to answer;
- providing a sentence frame, sentence starter, or graphic organizer; and
- allowing for re-prompting if a student does not give a complete or expected answer on speaking tasks (and other individually-administered tasks).

In the course of work on ELPA21 and the ELPAC, ETS has developed a number of task types that include some of the scaffolds listed above. For example, "Read-Along Word with Scaffolding" is an ELPAC reading task type designed for the kindergarten level. In this task type, the student, with involvement and support available from the examiner, provides the individual letter names and the initial letter sound for a decodable, grade-appropriate word. The student is also prompted to read the word independently, and if the student cannot decode the word, the examiner reads the word aloud to the student. The student is then asked which of three pictures represents the word. The examiner repeats the word in the prompt, both for students who have read the word on their own and those who were not able to.

In sum, rather than starting off by asking students to read and identify the meaning of a word, the work of reading the word is broken down into smaller steps, a process that gathers more robust information about students at differing levels of proficiency. California educators who administered this task type during pilot testing reported that the scaffolding had a positive effect on the young learners, providing a feeling of success even for students who were not able to complete the final task.

Considerations for K–2 Students

A distinguishing feature of U.S. K–12 ELP assessments is their inclusion of students in kindergarten, Grade 1, and Grade 2 (i.e., K–2 students). K–2 students[6] are not included in the international K–12 ELP assessments described in other chapters in this volume, and they are not included in other federally mandated U.S. state content assessments. In the current U.S. federal accountability system, states are required to provide information about EL students' ELP at all grades, whereas information about students' knowledge of content areas such as math and English language arts must be reported only at Grade 3 and above.

As discussed by Bailey (2017, in this volume), there are a range of complex issues involved in assessing young learners—cognitive, social, and literacy development; the importance of effective testing formats and administration models; and inclusion of appropriate content. Each of these factors tends to be more pronounced for K–2 students than for young learners at Grade 3 and above. For many K–2 students, U.S. K–12 ELP assessments will be the first standardized assessment they have ever encountered. These very young learners, particularly those with limited formal schooling, are less likely to understand what is expected of them in a testing situation and may not be familiar with the concept of "known answer" questions (Lopez, Pooler, & Linquanti, 2016).

There are significant differences in test formats between U.S. K–12 ELP assessments for K–2 students and those for older students. For example, ELPA21 and the ELPAC use separate test forms (with distinct blueprints, task types, and items) for kindergarten, Grade 1, and Grade 2, rather than using a single form for a grade span such as K–1 or even K–2. Within the test materials, there are also differences for K–2 assessments in presentation and response modes. Most significantly, kindergarten and Grade 1 assessments are typically individually administered. For Grade 2, a small-group administration model is typically used.

The rapid rate of social and cognitive development among K–2 students means that there are significant developmental differences from year to year, or even from the beginning of the year to the end of the same year (Bailey, Heritage, & Butler, 2014). As a result, many of the practices that are appropriate for all students—ensuring that tasks are meaningful, contextualized, engaging, accessible, and not overly long or tiring—have specific and distinct applications for K–2 students. For example, what constitutes an engaging and accessible topic is likely to be substantially different for K–2 students as these students are likely to have smaller realms of experience. Given that little commonality can be assumed about students' home experiences, especially given the heterogeneity of EL populations, it often helps to limit contexts to the world of school and the classroom (Martiniello, 2008). School or classroom contexts are likely to be familiar to most (though not all) K–2 students, and performance on these tasks is very likely to be construct-relevant. Similarly, while graphics and visual cues are important in ELP assessments for all learners, they are particularly crucial in making tasks engaging, accessible, and appropriately scaffolded for K–2 students.

The conceptual goals of task types for K–2 student can be similar to those for older students, though the operationalization of task types for K–2 should have some key differences. For example, the ELPAC "Summarize an Academic Presentation" task type described above is used from kindergarten through Grade 12. However, the content and presentation are significantly different between kindergarten and in higher grade spans. At kindergarten, the word count is much shorter, visual support is considerably simpler, written labels are not provided as scaffolding, and scoring materials emphasize the need to consider what constitutes an "age appropriate" summary of the main points.

Most significantly (for this task type and others), the individual administration model used at kindergarten and Grade 1 allows for flexible scaffolding and multiple opportunities for students to demonstrate what they know and can do. Again using "Summarize an Academic Presentation" as an example, the examiner points to parts of the graphic while providing the directions and presentation to the student; the student has an opportunity to interact with the graphic by pointing to key elements as they give their response; and prompting guidelines are provided to enable the examiner to offer additional clarification and scaffolding as appropriate to the needs of the individual student in a standardized manner.

For K–2 students, who are in the relatively early stages of developing literacy in any language, there are distinct challenges in creating task types to assess students' reading and writing skills in English. In these domains, it is crucial to consider how "grade appropriate" is operationalized in the ELA standards, as the ELP task types must not expect EL students to do more than what is expected in the general ELA classroom.

A useful approach for EL assessments of reading is to design task types that provide a cline of difficulty starting with foundational literacy skills (e.g., directionality of print and phonemic awareness) and increasing in challenge up to (but not exceeding) tasks that assess higher level reading comprehension skills that are called for by the ELP and ELA standards. The ELPAC "Read-Along Word with Scaffolding" task type described earlier represents one operationalization of this approach.

Conclusion

This chapter has provided a relatively high-level overview of some central issues involved in the design and development of U.S. K–12 ELP assessments, with a focus on how the emphases in recently developed state content standards and

ELP standards have influenced the conceptualization of the ELP construct and the design of appropriate task types. Given the theme of this volume, we have focused primarily on the aspects of developing task types and items appropriate to assessing young learners.

Because of the space limitations of this chapter, our discussion of U.S. K–12 ELP assessments certainly has not been exhaustive; some of the additional important issues concerning these assessments which we have not touched on include: the development of proficiency-level descriptors; standard-setting; score reporting; appropriate measurement models (including the implications of integrated-skills task types for measurement models); implications of mode of administration for these assessments (i.e., paper-delivery vs. computer-delivery); the design and use of initial identification assessments as compared to annual summative assessments; and appropriate practices to ensure accessibility for all students. As the new generation of U.S. K–12 ELP assessments are currently under development or relatively early in their implementation process, we hope that these topics and more will be investigated in the near future.

This is a time of considerable change, challenge, and opportunity for K–12 EL students in the U.S. and those who are responsible for educating them. Effective U.S. K–12 ELP assessments are an essential tool in helping to ensure that EL students are gaining the English-language skills needed to fully engage in the varieties of academic discourse they need to meet the challenge of the standards and take advantage of educational opportunities (Hauck, Wolf, & Mislevy, 2016). We hope that this chapter may contribute in some manner by sharing information about approaches to the design and development of effective U.S. K–12 ELP assessments.

Notes

1 In this chapter, we use the term "task type" to describe a unit of item design that foregrounds construct-related aspects of test items. While the term "item type" is sometimes also used for this purpose, we prefer task type given that item type is also widely used for descriptions that foreground format and response mode (e.g., selected response items types, constructed response item types, and technology-enhanced item types).
2 Note that some of this discussion appears in similar form in Hauck, Pooler, and Anderson (2015).
3 In ELPA21 documentation, these specific claims are referred to as "sub-claims." For ease of reference in this chapter, we are using the ELPAC terminology of "high-level claims" and "claims."
4 The task types described in this chapter are based on the ELPA21 test specification document (Oregon Department of Education, 2016) and the ELPAC task types document (California Department of Education, 2015).
5 Note that this task type occurs in the Speaking domain, which is individually administered to students in all grades.
6 Note that in some states Kindergarten assessments are commonly given to "Transitional K" students, who may be as young as 4 years old.

References

Abedi, J. (2008). Classification system for English language learners: Issues and recommendations. *Educational Measurement: Issues and Practice, 27*(3), 17–31.

Bailey, A. L. (2017). Issues to consider in the assessment of young learners' English language proficiency. In M. K. Wolf & Y. G. Bulter (Eds.), *English language proficiency assessments for young learners* (pp. 25–40). New York, NY: Routledge.

Bailey, A. L., Heritage, M., & Butler, F. A. (2014). Developmental considerations and curricular contexts in the assessment of young language learners. In A. J. Kunnan (Ed.), *The companion to language assessment* (pp. 1–17). Boston, MA: Wiley. doi:10.1002/9781118411360.wbcla079

Bunch, G. C., Kibler, A., & Pimental, S. (2012). *Realizing opportunities for English learners in the Common Core English Language Arts and disciplinary Literacy Standards.* Commissioned paper by the Understanding Language Initiative. Stanford, CA: Stanford University. Available from http://ell.stanford.edu/papers/practice

California Department of Education. (2014). *The California English language development standards.* Sacramento, CA: Author.

California Department of Education. (2015). *Definitions of proposed task types for the English Language Proficiency Assessments for California.* Sacramento, CA: Author. Available from http://www.cde.ca.gov/ta/tg/ep/documents/elpactasktypes.pdf

Cook, H. G., & Linquanti, R. (2015). *Strengthening policies and practices for the initial classification of English learners: Insights from a national working session.* Washington, DC: Council of Chief State School Officers.

Council of Chief State School Officers. (2014). *English language proficiency standards with correspondences to K–12 English language arts (ELA), mathematics, and science practices, K–12 ELA standards, and 6–12 literacy standards.* Washington, DC: Author.

Every Student Succeeds Act. (2015). Public Law No. 114–354.

Hakuta, K., Santos, M., & Fang, Z. (2013). Challenges and opportunities for language learning in the context of the CCSS and the NGSS. *Journal of Adolescent & Adult Literacy, 56*(6), 451–454.

Hauck, M. C., Pooler, E., & Anderson, D. P. (2015). *ELPA21 item development process report* (Final Deliverable to the CCSSO ELPA21 Project Contract). Princeton, NJ: Educational Testing Service.

Hauck, M. C., Wolf, M. K., & Mislevy, R. (2016). *Creating a next-generation system of K–12 English learner language proficiency assessments* (Research Report No. RR-16–06). Princeton, NJ: Educational Testing Service.

Lee, O., Quinn, H., & Valdés, G. (2013). Science and language for English language learners in relation to Next Generation Science Standards and with implications for Common Core State Standards for English language arts and mathematics. *Educational Researcher, 42*(4), 223–233.

Lopez, A., Pooler, E., & Linquanti, R. (2016). *Key issues and opportunities in the initial identification and classification of English learners* (ETS Research Report No. RR-16–09). Princeton, NJ: Educational Testing Service.

Martiniello, M. (2008). Language and the performance of English language learners in math word problems. *Harvard Educational Review, 78*, 333–368.

Mislevy, R. J. (2011). *Evidence-centered design for simulation-based assessment* (CRESST Report 800). Los Angeles, CA: National Center for Research on Evaluation, Standards, and Student Testing (CRESST).

Mislevy, R. J., Steinberg, L. S., & Almond, R. A. (2003). On the structure of educational assessments. *Measurement: Interdisciplinary Research and Perspectives, 1,* 3–67.

National Governors Association Center for Best Practices, Council of Chief State School Officers. (2010). *Common core state standards.* Washington DC: Author.

National Research Council. (2011). *Allocating federal funds for state programs for English language learners.* Washington, DC: National Academies Press.

No Child Left Behind Act of 2001. (2002). Public Law No. 107–110, 115 Stat. 1425.

Office of English Language Acquisition, U.S. Department of Education. (2015). *Fast facts: Profiles of English learners.* Washington, DC: Author.

Oregon Department of Education. (2016). *ELPA21 test specifications.* Salem, OR: Author. Available from http://www.ode.state.or.us/wma/teachlearn/testing/dev/testspecs/elpa21testspecsg6-8_1516.pdf

Soto, R., Hooker, A. G., & Batalova, J. (2015). *States and districts with the highest number and share of English language learners.* Washington, DC: Migration Policy Institute.

Wolf, M. K., Everson, P., Lopez, A., Hauck, M., Pooler, E., & Wang, J. (2014). *Building a framework for a next-generation English language proficiency assessment system* (ETS Research Report No. RR-14-34). Princeton, NJ: Educational Testing Service. doi:10.1002/ets2.12034

Wolf, M. K., Guzman-Orth, D. A., Lopez, A., Castellano, K., Himelfarb, I., & Tsutagawa, F. S. (2016). Integrating scaffolding strategies into technology-enhanced assessments of English learners: Task types and measurement models. *Educational Assessment, 21*(3), 157-175.

Wolf, M. K., Kao, J., Griffin, N., Herman, J., Bachman, P., Chang, S., & Farnsworth, F. (2008). *Issues in assessing English language learners: English language proficiency measures and accommodation uses: Practice review* (CRESST Report 732). Los Angeles, CA: University of California, National Center for Research on Evaluation, Standards and Student Testing (CRESST).

Wolf, M. K., Wang, Y., Blood, I., & Huang, B. H. (2014). Investigating the language demands in the Common Core State Standards for English language learners: A comparison study of standards. *Middle Grades Research Journal, 9*(1), 35–52.

SECTION 3

Empirical Studies for Validity Evidence

6

A FIELD TEST STUDY FOR THE *TOEFL® PRIMARY*™ READING AND LISTENING TESTS

Jiyun Zu, Bradley Moulder, and Rick Morgan

The *TOEFL® Primary*™ tests were developed to measure the English language proficiency of young learners between the ages of approximately 8 and 11 who are learning English as a foreign language (EFL). The tests measure reading, listening, and speaking skills. During the development of the *TOEFL Primary* tests, there were three stages of empirical studies: item prototyping, pilot testing, and field testing (see Chapter 3 for the development process of the *TOEFL Primary* tests). The focus of this chapter is to describe the field test study performed for the *TOEFL Primary* Reading and Listening tests.

One purpose of the field test study was to provide evidence for the validity of the *TOEFL Primary* tests as measures of English language reading and listening proficiency of young learners. It did so by (a) identifying items from a wide variety of item types (or item sets) that measured a common skill (either reading or listening), (b) discarding items that were poor indicators of that skill, and (c) identifying items at various difficulty levels so that they could serve as good measures of language proficiency for the full range of ability that is observed in young learners who are learning English as a foreign language. Another purpose of the field test was to enable the assembly of parallel operational test forms. This served both a practical purpose of preparing interchangeable test forms and a construct validation purpose of testing whether parallel forms could be developed; doing so demonstrates a consistency of the construct across test forms, whereas failing to be able to do so potentially indicates a problem with identifying or measuring the construct. This constitutes validity evidence regarding the internal structure of the test items, a form of validity evidence (American Educational Research Association, American Psychological Association, & National Council on Measurement in Education, 2014).

The chapter includes a description of the field test study design, statistical analyses conducted, estimation of psychometric properties of the tests, and how the empirical findings informed the final test design for the *TOEFL Primary* tests. In this chapter, we aim to provide various statistical techniques that can be used during the test development stage. We also describe types of evidence that will be needed when making validity arguments for the tests particularly as they pertain to young learners from various language and cultural backgrounds learning English as a foreign language.

Decisions Made Prior to the Field Test Study

As mentioned at the beginning of this chapter, the *TOEFL Primary* field test study was conducted after item prototyping and pilot testing. Prior to the field test study, many decisions regarding the *TOEFL Primary* tests design have been made by the test design and development team at Educational Testing Service (ETS). The following five test design considerations were particularly important for shaping the field test design.

First, the *TOEFL Primary* Reading and Listening tests were to consist of three-option multiple-choice items, for a paper-and-pencil test administered in classrooms. The Speaking test was to be a separately administered computer-based test. The field test study described in this chapter was for the Reading and Listening tests.

Second, the Reading and Listening tests' scores would be reported separately within an item response theory (IRT) framework. A two-parameter logistic IRT model (2PL; Birnbaum, 1968) is used for item calibration (the details of the 2PL IRT model are included in the Method section).

Third, for standardized testing that involves multiple test forms, test equating is usually conducted to provide interchangeable scores on different test forms. For the *TOEFL Primary* tests, a pre-equating design is adopted. Pre-equating is a process of obtaining the equating conversion of a test form before the test form is administered operationally (Kolen & Brennan, 2004, p. 205). Pre-equated test forms allow test takers to receive scores immediately because the score conversion is available before the operational administration of the test form. To make pre-equating possible, all operational items in a new form must have been previously pretested, i.e., administered to a sample of examinees but without the item score contributing to the total score. Item statistics (e.g., IRT parameter estimates) from pretesting are used to derive the equating conversion of the new form that consists of these pretested items. For *TOEFL Primary* Reading and Listening tests, pretest items are embedded within test forms with operational items.

Fourth, considering the shorter attention span of young children, each test (Reading and Listening) was designed to have a 30-minute time limit. Speededness results from the pilot testing suggested that approximately 36 items was an appropriate length for each test. Of these, it was decided to report scores based on 30 items and use the other six items for pretesting.

Fifth, the Reading and Listening tests were further separated into a Step 1 test and a Step 2 test. These two Steps shared a certain degree of common content (see Chapter 3 for the *TOEFL Primary* test structure), but the difficulty level of the Step 1 test was less than that of the Step 2 test. This decision was made in response to pilot testing results, which suggested that test takers at this age range differed substantially in terms of reading and listening proficiencies. For some countries, participating students' scores on the pilot test forms clustered near chance level. For countries whose participating students had strong English proficiency, scores on the same form were too high for good measurement (e.g., if all test takers answer an item correctly, this item does not contribute in differentiating low and high ability students). Given that only 30 items are operationally scored, it was not feasible to include enough items with a wide range of difficulties in one test to serve this young and diverse testing population. By offering the tests in two Steps, young EFL learners across the world could take a test that is more tailored to their proficiency level. A test that better matches test takers' ability requires a smaller number of items to achieve the same amount of precision.

Main Goals of the Field Test Study

With an improved test design after the pilot testing, a field test study was conducted to accomplish the following objectives with consideration of the specific purposes and design features of the *TOEFL Primary* tests:

- pretest a sufficient number of items for assembling operational forms for each Step of the test;
- obtain a sufficient number of valid responses to each item to calibrate the items using the 2PL IRT model;
- based on IRT parameter estimates from the field test data, assemble an operational form for each Step of the test and examine the psychometric properties of these operational forms;
- establish meaningful band levels and scale scores based on the field test data; and
- provide data to support standard setting studies for alignment with the Common European Framework of Reference (CEFR).

Method

Field Test Forms

A total of 123 Reading items and 120 Listening items were assembled into six field test forms. Each form consisted of 41 Reading items and 40 Listening items. The design of the six forms for Reading and Listening are provided in Tables 6.1 and 6.2, respectively. For example, the first row in Table 6.1

TABLE 6.1 Reading Field Test Forms

Item sequence	Item set	Number of items	Form 1	Form 2	Form 3	Form 4	Form 5	Form 6
1–5	Match Picture to Word 1	5	x	x				
	Match Picture to Word 2	5			x			x
	Match Picture to Word 3	5				x	x	
6–10	Match Picture to Sentence 1	5	x	x				
	Match Picture to Sentence 2	5			x			x
	Match Picture to Sentence 3	5				x	x	
11–18	Sentence Clue 1	8	x				x	
	Sentence Clue 2	8		x	x			
	Sentence Clue 3	8				x		x
19–22	Telegraphic 1	4	x				x	
	Telegraphic 2	4		x	x			
	Telegraphic 3	4				x		x
23–25	Instructional 1	3	x					x
	Instructional 2	3		x			x	
	Instructional 3	3			x	x		
26–27	Correspondence 1	2	x					x
	Correspondence 2	2		x			x	
	Correspondence 3	2			x	x		
28–35	Narrative 1	8	x			x		
36–37	Correspondence 4	2	x			x		
38–41	Short Expository 1	4	x			x		
28–35	Narrative 2	8		x			x	
36–41	Short Expository 2	6		x			x	
28–31	Narrative 3	4			x			x
32–41	Research Items	10			x			x

shows that a set of five "Match Picture to Word" items were items 1 to 5 in Form 1 and Form 2 (see Chapter 3 for the item types). The second row in Table 6.1 shows that another five "Match Picture to Word" items were items 1 to 5 in Form 3 and Form 6. As shown in Tables 6.1 and 6.2, the six test forms had the following characteristics: Each form shared common

TABLE 6.2 Listening Field Test Forms

Item sequence	Item set	Number of items	Form 1	Form 2	Form 3	Form 4	Form 5	Form 6
1–4	Listen and Match 1	4	x	x				
	Listen and Match 2	4			x		x	
	Listen and Match 3	4				x		x
5–10	Follow Directions 1	6	x	x				
	Follow Directions 2	6			x		x	
	Follow Directions 3	6				x		x
11–16	Question-Response 1	6	x					x
	Question-Response 2	6		x	x			
	Question-Response 3	6				x	x	
17–22	Dialogue 1	6	x					x
	Dialogue 2	6		x	x			
	Dialogue 3	6				x	x	
23–27	Social-Navigational Monologue 1	5	x				x	
	Social-Navigational Monologue 2	5		x				x
	Social-Navigational Monologue 3	5			x	x		
28–30	Academic Monologue 1	3	x				x	
	Academic Monologue 2	3		x				x
	Academic Monologue 3	3			x	x		
31–40	Narrative 1	10	x			x		
	Narrative 2	10		x			x	
	Research Items	10			x			x

items with three other forms, and each item appeared in two forms. Having items appear in multiple forms rather than in only one form is generally preferred because it prevents the item parameter estimates from being determined by the specific group that takes that form. Moreover, with each item appearing in two forms, the sample size per form can be only half of the sample size needed per item.

Sampling and Administration

We aimed to conduct the field study under conditions that would best resemble future operational conditions with regard to population representativeness and test administration characteristics. The target sample size was $n = 500$ per form, $N = 3,000$ total for the field study. With each item appearing in two forms, this would achieve $n = 1,000$ per item. The sample size needed for achieving accurate IRT item parameter estimates depends on many factors, such as the model, the number of items, how discriminating the items are, and how well the prior distribution of the ability matches the real distribution. For a 2PL IRT model, which was the model employed and described in more detail later in this chapter, previous research suggested a sample size of 1,000 tends to produce accurate item parameter estimates (De Ayala, 2009, p. 105). The sampling design targeted representation from countries in proportion to their likelihood of adopting the *TOEFL Primary* tests, as determined by their participation rates for other *TOEFL* products (e.g., *TOEFL iBT*® and *TOEFL Junior*® tests) and responses from partner organizations at the time of the field test study. Participating countries included countries from Asia, Europe, the Middle East, and South and Central America. Test forms were spiraled across test centers within each country whenever possible. This helped balance form distribution within a country and improved the comparability of the overall demographics of students who were administered each test form. Spiraling test forms within a classroom would have been ideal but impractical because the Listening tests required playing the same audio to all students within a classroom.

The Reading and Listening tests were administered in classrooms. Each student was administered both a Reading and a Listening test form, with the Reading test preceding the Listening test. A total of 3,739 valid responses on the field test forms were received. A slight majority (52%) of the test takers were female and 48% were male. Most (95%) were between ages 8 and 12. Test takers were from 36 countries. Table 6.3 summarizes the sample composition by region. The majority of the sample was from Asia and South and Central America. The sample composition was consistent with the estimated rates of use for the *TOEFL Primary* tests at the initial launching stage. Thus, results based on this sample are likely to be reflective of the initial tests takers of the *TOEFL Primary* tests.

TABLE 6.3 Sample Composition of the Field Test Sample by Region

Region	Percentage
Asia	70
South and Central America	19
Europe	7
The Middle East	4

Classical Item Analysis

Classical item analysis, typically used for the preliminary screening of items, was conducted using GENASYS (Educational Testing Service, 2007), an Educational Testing Service proprietary data analysis system. Classical item analysis results included statistics such as p⁺, biserial correlation, as well as plots of option characteristic curves for each item. The statistic p⁺, which is the proportion of students in a sample who answered an item correctly, is a measure of item difficulty. The biserial correlation, which ranges from −1 to 1, reflects the item score and total score relationship. It was used as an item discrimination measure. Option characteristic curves plot the probability of picking each option of an item conditional on the total raw score (Livingston & Dorans, 2004). These plots are especially useful for identifying popular wrong options.

Items with poor classical item statistics were flagged and were reviewed by content experts to judge whether they were flawed or inappropriate for the testing population. These items included those with p⁺ values smaller than the chance level (.33) or larger than .95, or with biserial correlation smaller than .2, or with salient distractors (proportionally more high ability examinees selecting an incorrect option than the correct one). Content experts and psychometricians jointly determined whether an item should be removed from further analysis.

Item Response Models and Concurrent Calibration

All field test items were dichotomously scored. The Reading and Listening items were each modeled separately by a 2PL IRT model. The 2PL IRT model presents the probability of answering the i th item correctly given the latent ability θ, as follows:

$$p(x_i = 1 \mid \theta) = \frac{e^{1.702 a_i (\theta - b_i)}}{1 + e^{1.702 a_i (\theta - b_i)}} \quad (1)$$

where

x_i is the response to item i, 1 if correct and 0 if incorrect; a_i is the discrimination parameter for item i, a higher a_i means the item better differentiates higher and

106 Jiyun Zu et al.

lower ability examinees; b_i is the difficulty parameter for item i, a higher value means the item is more difficult; and 1.702 is a constant so that the logistic item response curve and the normal ogive differ by no more than .01 for all values of θ.

For each skill, Reading and Listening, data from all six field test forms were concurrently calibrated using GENASYS. Item parameters were estimated through an expectation/maximization algorithm for marginal maximum likelihood (Bock & Aitkin, 1981). The expected a posteriori (EAP; Bock & Mislevy, 1982) estimates of test takers' latent abilities were also obtained. A sparse matrix of all examinees by all items across all forms is created: 1 is given if a test taker answers an item correctly, 0 for an incorrect response, and a "not reached" code is assigned for items in forms that the student does not take. With one concurrent calibration run, all item parameters across all forms of the skill can be put on the same IRT scale.

Results

Raw Scores of the Field Test Forms

Test takers who answered fewer than six items per test (i.e., Reading or Listening) were considered as not motivated, and were eliminated from the analysis. Of the 3,739 test takers, only 15 answered fewer than six Reading items, and only 31 answered fewer than six Listening items. The sample size, mean, and standard deviation of raw scores for the six field test forms are presented in Table 6.4. Students were distributed across the six field test forms fairly evenly. Some inconsistency was unavoidable due to the need to administer the same form to all students within each classroom. The smallest sample size per item

TABLE 6.4 Sample Size, Mean, and Standard Deviation of Raw Scores for Field Test Forms

	Reading			*Listening*		
	Sample size	Mean	SD	Sample size	Mean	SD
Overall	3724	28.24	8.37	3708	28.04	8.29
Form 1	585	28.27	8.36	582	28.31	8.34
Form 2	550	28.79	7.35	549	28.83	7.31
Form 3	487	28.72	8.31	487	28.69	8.39
Form 4	737	27.54	8.78	735	27.57	8.75
Form 5	729	29.84	8.29	719	30.01	8.18
Form 6	636	26.33	8.46	636	26.30	8.51

was 1,036, which was for the Listening items that appeared in Forms 2 and 3. All sample sizes satisfied the rule of thumb for 2PL item calibrations.

As seen in Table 6.4, the mean raw scores for the Reading forms ranged from 26.33 (Form 6; which means on average students who took Form 6 answered 64% of the items correctly) to 29.84 (Form 5; which means on average students who took Form 5 answered 73% of the items correctly). The mean raw scores for the Listening forms ranged from 26.30 (Form 6; 66%) to 30.01 (Form 5; 75%). Note that it is not appropriate to compare raw scores across forms because they are affected by the difficulty level of the form as well as the ability level of the sample for each form.

Results From Classical Item Analysis

The p+ and r-biserial values for the field test items are summarized in Table 6.5. For both Reading and Listening items, the average p^+ was .73. The average biserial correlation (r-biserial) values were approximately .57 for both Reading and Listening. After the review of item content by the content experts, only one Reading item with r-biserial = −0.06 was removed from further analysis.

Summary of IRT Calibrated Item Pool

2PL IRT-calibrated item pools were created by concurrent calibration of all field test items for each skill. Summary statistics of the IRT item parameters for Reading and Listening items are presented in Table 6.6. The average *a* value (i.e., item discrimination estimates) for the Reading items was 0.97 and that for the Listening items was 0.92. This indicates that most of the items discriminate the test takers' abilities well. There was only one Reading item and one Listening item with $a < 0.2$. Both items were removed from consideration for operational use because of their poor discriminating power.

The IRT *b* parameters reflect the difficulty of the items, with smaller *b* values indicating easier items. The average *b* value for the Reading items was −0.83 and

TABLE 6.5 Summary Statistics of the p^+ and r-biserial for Reading and Listening Items

	Reading		Listening	
	p+	r-biserial	p+	r-biserial
Mean	0.73	0.58	0.73	0.57
SD	0.15	0.12	0.14	0.09
Median	0.74	0.60	0.76	0.58
Min	0.32	−0.06	0.31	0.21
Max	0.98	0.79	0.97	0.75

TABLE 6.6 Summary Statistics of the IRT Calibrated Item Pools for the Reading and Listening Tests

	Reading (122 items)		Listening (120 items)	
	IRT a	IRT b	IRT a	IRT b
Mean	0.97	−0.83	0.92	−0.84
SD	0.38	0.73	0.37	0.66
Median	0.93	−0.85	0.88	−0.94
Min	0.22	−2.59	0.06	−2.47
Max	2.31	1.99	2.47	2.19

that for the Listening items was −0.84. Given that the test takers' latent ability θ is assumed to follow a normal distribution with mean 0 and standard deviation 1, these average b values indicated that an average item in the pool was relatively easy for an average person in the field test sample.

Summary of Estimated Abilities

Each test taker's Reading and Listening abilities (θ) were estimated using the expected a posteriori estimation method (Bock & Mislevy, 1982). The average Reading ability of the field test sample was 0.16, and the standard deviation was 1.27. For the Listening ability, the mean was also 0.16, and the standard deviation was 1.26. Histograms of the ability estimates are provided in Figure 6.1. As shown in Figure 6.1, for both Reading and Listening tests, there were only a small number of test takers with low abilities (e.g., $\theta < -2$) and there were relatively more high ability examinees (e.g., $\theta > 3$).

These ability estimates were also used to evaluate test takers' performance by native country. The means and standard deviations of the Reading and Listening estimated latent abilities by country are summarized in Table 6.7. Note that it is not appropriate to rank the countries based on these data, because the field test takers are not representative of all young English learners in each country. To prevent the ranking of countries by test scores, country names are not reported here. Instead, country results are displayed anonymously from lowest to highest average ability in Table 6.7.

As shown in Table 6.7, there were substantial differences between students' abilities across countries. The top performing country had average latent abilities 1.27 and 1.12 respectively for Reading and Listening, whereas the lowest performing county had average latent abilities −1.01 and −1.09. Consistent with the findings from the pilot test, these results further confirmed the benefits of providing *TOEFL Primary* Reading and Listening tests in two Step tests.

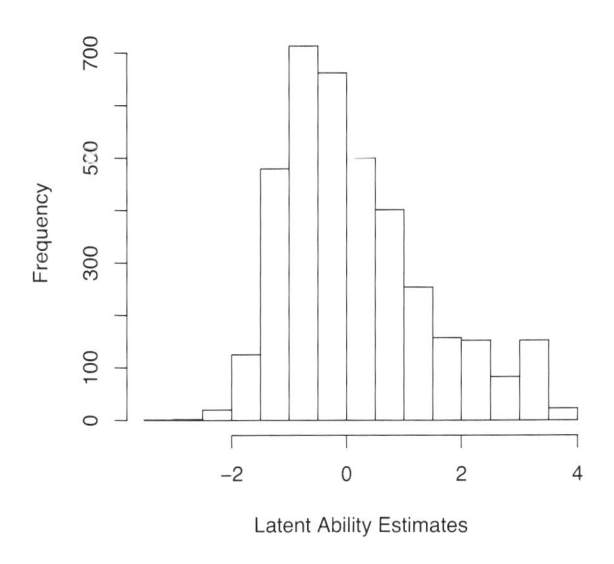

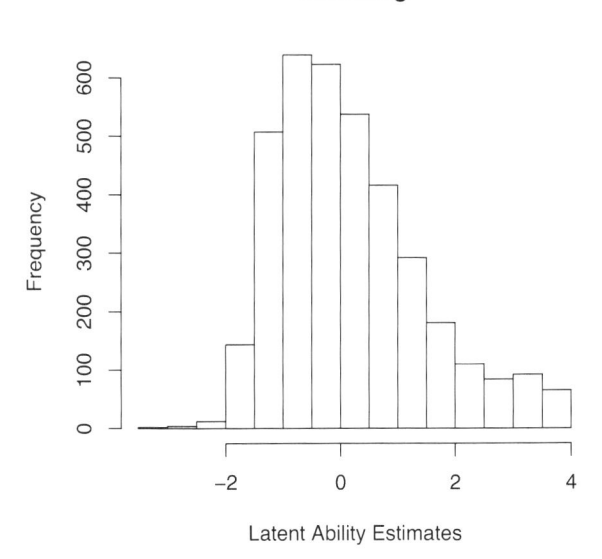

FIGURE 6.1 Frequency Distributions of the Estimated Reading and Listening Abilities

TABLE 6.7 Means and Standard Deviations of the Latent Ability Estimates by Country

Country	Reading		Listening	
	Mean	SD	Mean	SD
1	−1.01	0.66	−1.09	0.62
2	−0.75	0.91	−0.89	0.72
3	−0.73	0.58	−0.81	0.75
4	−0.24	1.04	−0.02	1.11
5	0.20	1.12	0.26	1.11
6	0.26	1.29	0.24	1.16
7	0.41	1.11	0.42	1.05
8	0.44	1.27	0.38	1.25
9	0.75	1.45	0.89	1.37
10	1.27	1.24	1.12	1.16

Establishing Band Levels and Scale Scores

TOEFL Primary reports band levels with performance descriptors, scale scores, and the Common European Framework of Reference for Languages (CEFR) levels. Here, we focus on describing the establishment of band levels and scale scores. Cut scores for the CEFR levels were determined by a separate standard setting study (see Baron & Papageorgiou, 2014, and Chapter 8 of this volume for details).

TOEFL Primary band levels and scale scores were created by taking several factors into consideration. First, the scores from the two Steps of the *TOEFL Primary* tests needed to be on the same scale, so that scores are comparable as to the level of English language proficiency regardless of the Step of the test. For example, a scale score of 105 from a Step 1 test form should be associated with the same proficiency level of a scale score of 105 from a Step 2 test form. The latent ability θ in the IRT model is on the same scale for both Steps. Therefore, we relied on θ to establish band levels and scale scores. Second, the two Steps share certain common content; thus, it was appropriate for the two Steps to have overlapping band levels and scale scores. Third, scores needed to reflect real differences among students with respect to their proficiency rather than small, apparent differences that may not be supported by the test reliability. Fourth, the band levels, scale scores, and CEFR levels needed to be consistent with but not redundant with each other.

Band Levels

As mentioned above, establishing band levels relied on the latent ability θ. We considered the latent ability θ corresponding to the 70% chance of answering an item correctly, denoted as $\theta_{70\%}$, as the ability needed to consistently answer an item correctly. Computationally, $\theta_{70\%}$ was found by taking the inverse of the item characteristic curve obtained based on the field test item parameter estimates. After the $\theta_{70\%}$'s for all items in the item pool were obtained, items were sorted by $\theta_{70\%}$. Five cuts were placed on $\theta_{70\%}$'s to create six band levels considering both content and statistical factors. The items grouped in each band level should enable meaningful and informative performance feedback; the band levels ought to provide reliable classification; the number of examinees in each band should not be too many or too few; the band level cuts needed to be consistent with CEFR cuts whenever possible. After the six band levels were established, ETS test developers reviewed the items grouped in each band according to the ordered $\theta_{70\%}$ to develop performance descriptors for that band.

Scale Scores

Scale scores, rather than number-correct raw scores, are usually reported to test takers as an indicator of their performance on a standardized test. Scale scores are reported because test forms will vary slightly in difficulty. If raw scores are reported, those students taking more difficult forms would be unfairly disadvantaged. For a newly developed test such as *TOEFL Primary* tests, a scale for the scale scores needed to be determined. Once the scale has been established, test equating is conducted to make sure the same scale score indicates the same level of proficiency across different test forms.

The scaling process for the *TOEFL Primary* tests involved the following steps. First, a 16-point scale was chosen, which balanced the need of providing scores that are sensitive to actual student proficiency differences, while not reporting small differences between test results and among students that may not be supported based on the test reliability and standard error of measurement. Three scale scores were assigned within each of the five highest band levels, and the lowest scale score was reserved for the lowest band level. The scales were determined to be from 100 to 115, with Step 1 scores ranging from 100 to 109, and Step 2 scores from 104 to 115 (the lowest scale score of 100 was also possible on Step 2). This decision was made considering the standard error of measurement of the raw scores and allowed the two Steps to have overlapping scale scores.

Second, within the bands that had three scale scores, whenever possible, equal interval of the latent ability θ's was determined to correspond to each scale score point. The relationship between integer scale scores, band levels, and CEFR levels for the Reading tests is summarized in Table 6.8 as an example. The band levels in the Step 1 tests are indicated by the number of stars, whereas the band levels in the Step 2 tests are indicated by the number of badges.

Third, based on the test blueprint and IRT parameter estimates from the field test, an initial operational form was assembled respectively for the *TOEFL*

TABLE 6.8 *TOEFL Primary* Reading Scale Score, Band Levels, and CEFR Levels

Scale score	Band	Step 1	Step 2	CEFR level
100	1	1 star	1 badge	Below A1
101	2	2 stars	Not	Below A1
102	2	2 stars	Assessed	A1
103	2	2 stars	By Step 2	A1
104	3	3 stars	2 badges	A1
105	3	3 stars	2 badges	A1
106	3	3 stars	2 badges	A1
107	4	4 stars	3 badges	A2
108	4	4 stars	3 badges	A2
109	4	4 stars	3 badges	A2
110	5	Not	4 badges	A2
111	5	Assessed	4 badges	A2
112	5	by Step 1	4 badges	A2
113	6	Not	5 badges	A2
114	6	Assessed	5 badges	B1
115	6	by Step 1	5 badges	B1

Primary Reading test—Step 1, Reading test—Step 2, Listening test—Step 1, and Listening test—Step 2. We refer to these four forms as base forms. For each base form, the relationship between raw score to θ is found by the inverse of the test characteristics curves (TCCs) calculated based on the field test IRT parameter estimates for the items in each form. Inversing a TCC is one Step of the IRT true-score equating procedure. The algorithm described in Kolen and Brennan (2004, p. 177) was used. Then the θ to scale score relationship obtained in the second step was used to derive the base form raw-to-scale score conversion. Future new forms are then equated to the base forms by IRT true-score equating to ensure that the same scale score on each new form indicates the same proficiency level.

Statistical Properties of Operational Base Forms

As mentioned briefly above, based upon the IRT item statistics from the field-testing, test developers assembled the first operational forms for the *TOEFL Primary* Reading and Listening tests for Step 1 and Step 2, respectively. All items in these forms were from the IRT calibrated item pool where their IRT parameters were available on the same scale. Forms were assembled to follow the test specifications as defined in the test blueprints (see Tables 3.1 and 3.2 in Chapter 3 for the blueprints). Within the test specifications, items were selected to ensure the maximum difficulty separation between the Step 1 and Step 2 tests. This was designed to allow the base forms to serve test takers of a wider range of proficiency levels. The psychometric properties of the resulting four base forms (TOEFL Primary Reading test—Step 1, Reading test—Step 2, Listening test—Step 1, and Listening test—Step 2) were examined.

Item Parameters and Test Characteristic Curves

Summary statistics of the IRT a and b parameters of the four base forms are provided in Table 6.9. The average a parameters for the Step 1 forms were around 1.2 and those for the Step 2 forms were approximately 0.8. The larger average a parameters for the Step 1 forms indicate that the Step 1 forms were more discriminating than the Step 2 forms. In terms of form difficulty, for the Reading test, the Step 1 form had average b values of −1.47 and the Step 2 form had average b values of −.51. For the Listening test, the Step 1 form had average b values of −1.32 and the Step 2 form had average b values of −.56. The average difficulty difference between the two Reading forms was 0.96, and average difficulty between the two Listening forms was 0.76. Given that the latent ability θ follows a normal distribution of standard deviation 1, the average difficulty between the two Steps was 0.96 and 0.76 standard deviation of the test takers' latent abilities for Reading and Listening tests, respectively.

Test characteristic curves (TCCs) describe the relationship between the latent ability (θ) and the expected raw score on a test form. The expected raw score at each θ value was calculated from the item parameter estimates (a's and b's) of the operational items in the form using the 2PL IRT model (Equation 1). TCCs for the two Reading base forms and the two Listening base forms are presented in Figure 6.2. The gaps between the TCCs of the Step 1 and the Step 2 forms revealed the difficulty difference between the two Steps in terms of expected raw scores. For example, in Figure 6.2 we can see that a student with ability level $\theta = 0$ was expected to answer 28 items correctly on the

TABLE 6.9 Summary of IRT Parameters for the Four Operational Base Forms

Form	IRT a				IRT b			
	Mean	SD	Min	Max	Mean	SD	Min	Max
Reading—Step 1	1.26	0.35	0.66	2.31	−1.47	0.55	−2.59	−0.47
Reading—Step 2	0.86	0.34	0.24	1.57	−0.51	0.56	−1.56	0.71
Listening—Step 1	1.20	0.35	0.77	2.47	−1.32	0.32	−2.21	−0.65
Listening—Step 2	0.77	0.30	0.24	1.79	−0.56	0.67	−2.47	0.78

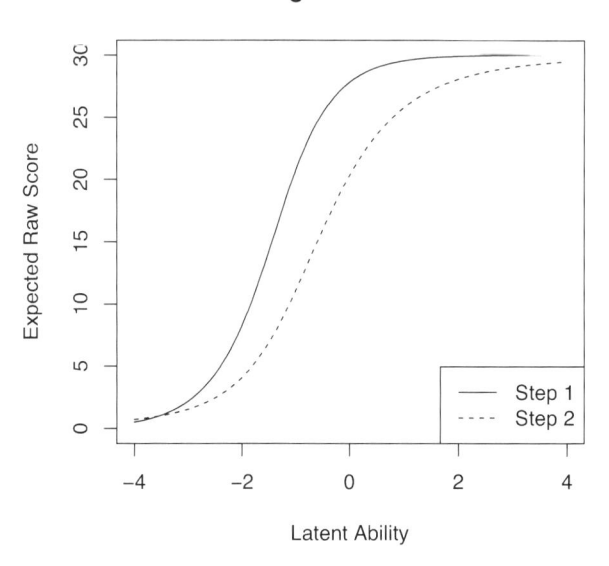

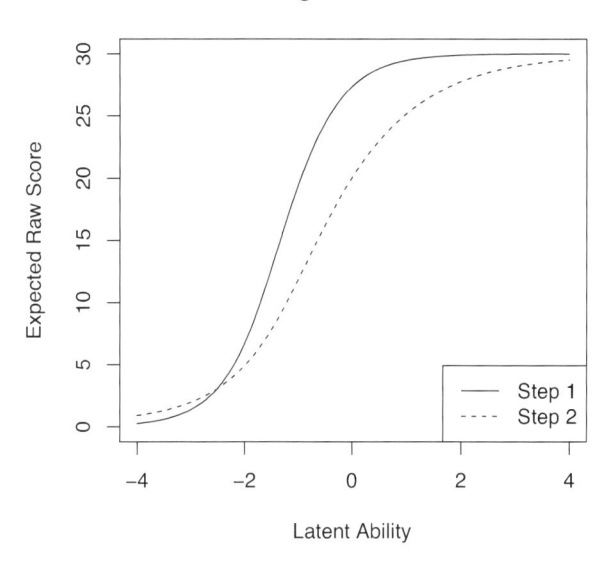

FIGURE 6.2 Test Characteristic Curves for the Four Operational Base Forms

Reading—Step 1 test and answer 20 items correctly on the Reading—Step 2 test. The difference was larger for middle-ability students, but was smaller for low- or high-ability students. This is expected because a student with very good English language skills would answer virtually every item correctly regardless of whether the test was Step 1 or Step 2. Similarly, a student with a low level of English language skills would be expected to score near chance level on both the Step 1 and Step 2 tests.

Reliability and Standard Error of Measurement

Reliability is the degree to which a test form produces consistent scores. The standard error of measurement (SEM) indicates the extent to which test takers' scores differ from their "true scores." A test taker's "true score" is the average of the scores that test taker would earn on all possible forms of the test. Both reliability and SEM reflect important statistical properties of a test form.

The reliability and standard error of measurement of the raw scores and scale scores of the four operational base forms were calculated using the software POLYCSEM (Kolen, Zeng, & Hanson, 1996). The calculation involves IRT parameters of items in a form and a frequency distribution of θ as inputs. The θ distributions of operational samples for the Step 1 and Step 2 tests would not be available until the operational forms have been administered. We used the empirical distribution of the bottom 75% of the estimated θ in the field test sample as an approximation to the proficiencies of those who might take a future Step 1 test, and used the upper 75% of the estimated θ in the field test sample to approximate the proficiencies of those who might take a future Step 2 test. There were four approximated distributions of θ's, respectively, for the Reading test—Step 1, Reading test—Step 2, Listening test—Step 1, and Listening test—Step 2. The resulting reliability and SEM estimates of the raw scores and scale scores of the four operational base forms are reported in Table 6.10. The estimated scale score reliabilities were .86 (Reading) and .87 (Listening) for the Step 1 tests and .83 (Reading) and .82 (Listening) for the Step 2 tests. The *TOEFL Primary* tests are quite reliable for 30-item, low-stakes tests. Note that

TABLE 6.10 Reliability and Standard Error of Measurement of Operational Forms

	Raw score		Scale score	
	Reliability	SEM	Reliability	SEM
Reading—Step 1	.88	1.84	.86	0.90
Reading—Step 2	.84	2.11	.83	1.25
Listening—Step 1	.89	1.98	.87	0.85
Listening—Step 2	.82	2.13	.82	1.30

results reported here are approximations of the reliabilities of operational forms to be administered. The reliability and SEM should be continuously examined as new test takers take operational forms.

Discussion

This chapter described a field test study performed on the *TOEFL Primary* Reading and Listening tests. It reviewed the process from field-test form construction to test forms administration to data collection to statistical analyses. The latter included classical item analysis, IRT calibration, scaling, and an evaluation of psychometric properties of the initial operational forms. By demonstrating each step taken from conducting the field testing to assembling an operational test, we attempted to illustrate how and why various statistical analyses were undertaken during the test development stage. While the underlying principles and major analysis procedures in this chapter may be similar to those used to develop any tests, some notable lessons emerged for developing an assessment for young students with such a variety of learning backgrounds across countries.

During the process, many challenges and issues in developing English language proficiency assessments for young learners became apparent. Due to the young age of the test takers, the test could not be too long. For the *TOEFL Primary* tests to achieve a high reliability, given that it was constrained to 30 items per skill, high-quality items were required. Substantial differences in English Reading and Listening proficiencies across countries were observed in the pilot and field testing results. Because most young learners are just beginning their English study, the age at which they start to learn English has a large effect on their proficiency. Many factors such as country/region, education policy, and the social-economic status of the family may affect the way a child starts learning English. To develop reasonably short *TOEFL Primary* tests that produce reliable scores and are useful for children globally, it was decided to design the Reading and Listening tests as two Steps. The psychometric properties of the first operational forms for two Steps showed that splitting the tests into two Steps allows the base forms to reliably measure test takers of a wider range of proficiency levels.

The field test study for the *TOEFL Primary* Reading and Listening tests yielded valuable information in a number of respects for the development of technically sound test forms as well as preliminary validity evidence for the intended uses of the tests. Based on the evidence collected from the study, the *TOEFL Primary* tests were demonstrated to provide useful information about the English language skills of young students learning English as a foreign language, which may be used to determine students' accomplishment, identify areas for improvement, or track progress. A research program is in place to support the maintenance and continuous improvement of the tests. The research program includes using operational data to evaluate validity evidence, gathering information on the impact of the *TOEFL Primary* tests on teaching and learning, and monitoring and maintaining the score scales (see Chapter 3 for the current *TOEFL Primary* research agenda). Continuous research will be needed to ensure that the validity of the assessment for the intended purpose is adequately supported.

References

American Educational Research Association, American Psychological Association, & National Council on Measurement in Education. (2014). *Standards for educational and psychological testing*. Washington, DC: American Educational Research Association.

Baron, P. A., & Papageorgiou, S. (2014). *Mapping the TOEFL® Primary™ test onto the common European Framework of Reference*. (Research Memorandum 14–05). Princeton, NJ: Educational Testing Service.

Birnbaum, A. (1968). Some latent trait models and their use in inferring an examinee's ability. In F. M. Lord & M. R. Novick (Eds.), *Statistical theories of mental scores* (pp. 395–479). Reading, MA: Addison-Wesley.

Bock, R. D., & Aitkin, M. (1981). Marginal maximum likelihood estimation of item parameters: Application of an EM algorithm. *Psychometrika, 46*, 443–459.

Bock, R. D., & Mislevy, R. J. (1982). Adaptive EAP estimation of ability in a microcomputer environment. *Applied Psychological Measurement, 6*, 431–444.

De Ayala, R. J. (2009). *The theory and practice of item response theory*. New York, NY: The Guilford Press.

Educational Testing Service. (2007). *GENASYS [Computer software]*. Princeton, NJ: Educational Testing Service.

Kolen, M. J., & Brennan, R. L. (2004). *Test equating, scaling, and linking: Methods and practices* (2nd ed.). New York, NY: Springer.

Kolen, M. J., Zeng, L., & Hanson, B. A. (1996). Conditional standard errors of measurement for scale scores using IRT. *Journal of Educational Measurement, 33*, 129–140.

Livingston, S. A., & Dorans, N. J. (2004). *A graphical approach to item analysis* (Research Report 04–10). Princeton, NJ: Educational Testing Service.

7
STRATEGIES USED BY YOUNG ENGLISH LEARNERS IN AN ASSESSMENT CONTEXT

Lin Gu and Youngsoon So

Recent years have witnessed an increased interest in assessing young learners' English proficiency. To meet the growing need for research-driven language proficiency assessments for young learners, Educational Testing Service (ETS) recently expanded its repertoire of English language assessments to serve test takers of a wide age range. In addition to the tests targeted at adult learners, such as the *TOEFL iBT*® and the *TOEIC*® tests, ETS has launched two new tests that target English language learners of younger ages: the *TOEFL*® *Primary*™ tests, designed for young students who are 8 years old or older, and the *TOEFL Junior*® tests, designed for adolescents older than 11. For more detailed information about these tests, see Chapters 3 and 4.

This chapter reports on a small-scale, exploratory study that examined strategies used by young learners of different proficiency levels when taking the *TOEFL Primary* listening and reading comprehension items. The impetus behind this endeavor, implemented at the prototyping stage of the *TOEFL Primary* development, was to ensure that the design of item types was appropriate for the targeted test-taking population. The underlying focus was to examine the extent to which the items measure the construct that the test intends to measure by investigating the strategies used by test takers while taking the test. The importance of collecting evidence based on response processes was highlighted in Purpura (2014), as such evidence not only provides support for proposed score interpretation and use, but may also inform construct definition and influence test design.

Cohen and his associates (e.g., Cohen, 2012; Cohen & Upton, 2006) particularly advocated that understanding the strategies test takers use when interacting with test items illustrates whether or not the processes elicited by test items are construct-relevant, and therefore would allow us to evaluate the appropriateness of the inferences made based on the test performance. This line of investigation becomes especially crucial when designing tests for populations whose assessment behaviors are not well understood. Little empirical research is available to examine the strategies young English language learners use in an assessment context. As a result, knowledge of the response processes engaged in by young learners is limited. Therefore, in order to address this lack of information, we conducted this study in the context of the prototyping study of the *TOEFL Primary* tests. The outcome of this study permitted an opportunity to evaluate the extent to which test performance based on the prototype items provides meaningful information about young learners' English language proficiency. We hope that the results can not only provide useful suggestions for designing assessments for young English language learners, but also offer insight into further areas of research on the strategies used by young English language learners.

Strategies Used by Language Learners

Many researchers have studied the strategies employed by second language (L2) learners when they read or listen to L2 texts. Most of the previous studies focused on adult language learners (e.g., Block, 1986; Cohen & Upton, 2006; Kern, 1994, for reading strategies; Chang, 2009; James, 1986; Murphy, 1987, for listening strategies). Although some other studies have investigated strategies adolescent L2 learners use (e.g., Hosenfeld, 1984; Nevo, 1989, Nikolov, 2006, for reading strategies; O'Malley, Chamot, & Kupper, 1989; Vandergrift, 2003, for listening strategies), those studies targeted learners who were older than the learner population intended for the *TOEFL Primary* tests. Because of the age difference, findings from previous studies may not be directly applicable or generalizable to the *TOEFL Primary* test-taking population. For example, in a study focusing on the same age group as the one in the current study, Cho and So (2014) found that presenting questions and options in both aural and written formats in a listening comprehension test distracted students' attention from listening and thus hindered their performance. This finding contradicted the test developers' intent to reduce the burden of memorizing the listening input by providing the same information in two modalities. This unexpected result highlights the importance of collecting data on how test takers from the intended population interact with test tasks. Hence, the results from the previous studies must be interpreted with discretion because they involved learners who differed in age from our intended population. With this caveat in mind, in the next section we will review selected studies whose results have direct implications on assessment development and validation.

By examining reading and test-taking strategies, Cohen and Upton (2006) investigated whether a new type of reading task actually measured what it purposed to measure during the development stage of the *TOEFL iBT* test. The new task, the Reading to Learn task, was designed to simulate the academic task of forming a comprehensive and coherent representation of the whole text rather than focusing on discrete points in the text. Strategic behaviors collected through verbal reports were organized into three categories: reading, test management, and test-wiseness. The results revealed that the new task did not require different academic reading skills from those elicited by traditional reading tasks. This finding failed to demonstrate that the new task constituted an improvement over existing academic reading tasks that the designers envisioned. The authors attributed this misalignment between test developers' intention and the actual thought processes employed by test takers to certain design features of the test (e.g., order of the tasks). The authors, therefore, highlighted the importance of studying strategies test takers use, especially for those tests with innovative item types.

In the context of *TOEFL iBT* testing, Swain, Huang, Barkaoui, Brooks, and Lapkin (2009) also examined test taker strategy use in responding to the speaking section of the test. The coding scheme of strategic behaviors consisted of five main categories: approach, communication, cognitive, metacognitive, and affective. Using simulated recall, the study found that test takers employed a variety of strategies, and strategy use varied across different task types. The authors interpreted strategy use as integral to performing different *TOEFL iBT* speaking tasks. Therefore, strategy use should be considered as part of the construct the test intends to measure. Although the findings supported the inclusion of strategy use in the definition of the test construct, the authors also recognized the challenges of incorporating strategy use in the construction of the scoring rubrics due to the varied relationship between examinees' reported strategy use and their proficiency level, as well as the fact that some strategies are unobservable due to limitations of the data collection method. In sum, these studies demonstrate the importance of understanding strategies test takers use to inform item design during test development processes.

It is worth noting that researchers have adopted different approaches to gain an understanding of the interplay between cognition and L2 assessment performance. For example, Purpura (2014) identified five main approaches, including the factorial approach, the learner strategies approach, the strategic competence approach, the cognitive processing approach, and the social approach. In this study, we adopted the conceptual framework proposed by Cohen (2006, 2011, 2012; Cohen & Upton, 2006). This decision was driven by the purpose of the study, that is, to investigate the alignment between test construct and the actual response processes engaged in by young L2 learners in an assessment context. In this framework, strategies are classified into two broad categories: language learner strategies and test-taking strategies. Language learner strategies resemble the processes that language learners employ to assist them in learning and using language in real-world nontesting contexts, whereas test-taking strategies refer to the types of processes that are elicited due to the assessment context. The latter category is further divided into test-management strategies and test-wiseness strategies. Test-management strategies enable test takers to utilize their experience and knowledge of the test (e.g., item format and response time) to facilitate productive use of the language knowledge needed for responding to test items. Conversely, test-wiseness strategies are characterized as those entailing minimal or no engagement with the necessary language knowledge in test takers' efforts to answer test items. This distinction between the two test-taking strategies, test-management and test-wiseness, is vital because the former, along with the language learner strategies, are considered to be largely construct-relevant, whereas the latter are largely construct-irrelevant. As argued by Cohen and Upton (2006), test-management strategies are actually construct-relevant strategies in which students engage in the processes that are purported in a test. In contrast, Cohen (2012) suggests that revisions should be considered when an item is found to mainly trigger test-wiseness strategies.

We believe that because strategies that threaten the validity of inferences are explicitly specified in this framework, adopting this approach enables us to evaluate construct-relevance of the reported strategies, and therefore to examine the impact of strategy use on the interpretation and use of test results.

Research Questions

The current study investigated the strategies that young L2 learners employ when they are responding to the prototype reading and listening items of the *TOEFL Primary* tests. In particular, we wanted to understand whether their reported strategies are relevant to the assessment construct, that is, the reading and listening abilities of English language learners. Considering that the targeted test-taking population consists of learners from a wide age range who have different English language learning experiences, we decided to examine strategy use by proficiency level to inform the appropriateness of the test items for test takers at different levels of English language ability. We addressed the following questions:

1. What strategies do young *TOEFL Primary* test takers report using when answering reading and listening comprehension questions?
2. To what extent are these strategies construct-relevant or construct-irrelevant?
3. To what extent does the use of construct-relevant and construct-irrelevant strategies relate to learner proficiency level?

Method

Participants

Participants were recruited from an after-school English language learning program in China. Because the *TOEFL Primary* tests are designed for learners 8 years old and older, we tried to include learners who were within or close to this age range. We also tried to include students of different levels of English ability within each age, based on their teachers' evaluation. As the result of this identification process, 16 Chinese native speakers participated in the study. The

TABLE 7.1 Demographic Information of the Participants Sorted by Proficiency

ID	Proficiency	Age	Grade	Gender	Section Completed
1	Low	6	1	M	Listening
2	Low	6	1	F	Listening
3	Low	7	1	M	Listening
4	Low	7	1	F	Reading
5	Low	7	2	M	Reading
6	Medium	6	1	M	Reading
7	Medium	7	2	F	Listening
8	Medium	8	2	F	Listening
9	Medium	9	3	M	Listening
10	Medium	9	4	F	Reading
11	Medium	10	5	F	Reading
12	Medium	11	5	M	Listening
13	High	9	3	M	Reading
14	High	10	4	M	Listening
15	High	10	5	F	Reading
16	High	11	5	F	Listening & Reading

participants' demographic information is summarized in Table 7.1. Note that the students were classified into different ability groups on the basis of their test performance on the *TOEFL Primary* prototype items during this study. More information on this classification process is included in the analysis section. Each participant completed only one of the listening or reading sections of the test, with the exception of one student.

We also collected background information regarding their English language learning experiences. No participant had lived in an English-speaking country. We found that almost half of the learners had experiences in taking various standardized English language tests designed for young English learners. All participants started learning English in school from the first grade, except for one who started learning English in the third grade. Fifteen participants reported that they learned English before school age, starting as early as age 3.

Instruments

The prototype *TOEFL Primary* listening and reading test items were used for data collection. The listening and reading sections had four and three parts, respectively. Table 7.2 presents a brief description of the item types used in each part along with the number of items associated with each item type.

TABLE 7.2 Summary of the Listening and Reading Items

Section	Description	# of Items
Listening Section		
Part 1: Word-picture matching	Listen to words and find the picture that matches the word.	3
Part 2: Conversation	Listen to a conversation between two speakers and answer a question.	1
Part 3: Narrative	Listen to a narrative passage and answer questions based on the passage. There are three narrative listening stimuli, each with two to four questions.	9
Part 4: Expository	Listen to an expository passage and answer questions based on the passage. There are three expository passages, each followed by two questions.	6
Reading Section		
Part 1: Word-picture matching	Match words to parts of a picture	3
Part 2: Description-word matching	Read a short description about either a person or an object and choose a word that fits the description.	4
Part 3: Reading comprehension	Read a passage and answer questions based on the passage. There are four passages, each with three to four questions.	14

Data Collection

A retrospective interview was employed as the method of data collection. Considering the relatively young age of the participants, we decided not to use verbal reports, which would require the participants to verbalize the thought processes they engaged in when responding to the test, either while they were performing the test (introspectively) or immediately after (retrospectively). We believed that for our target age learners, the task of verbalizing one's thoughts would be mentally taxing, and therefore would make them uncomfortable with participating in the study.

We allotted one hour to interview each student. As a result, most of the participants were asked to work on either the listening or the reading items with one exception, in which one 11-year-old high-proficiency participant completed both listening and reading items. Therefore, nine students took the listening items and eight students took the reading items. The information on the section(s) completed by each participant is summarized in Table 7.1.

Individual interviews were carried out in Chinese by one of the authors who is a native Chinese speaker. Those given the reading items were asked to complete all parts before the interview. We decided not to interview the students after each part because we wanted to minimize the degree of interruption so that the students would answer the questions as they would during a real test-taking situation. The protocol for the listening sections was different. The participants were interviewed immediately after they had completed each listening part. This decision was made because, unlike in the reading section where the test takers would have access to the input during the interview, the listening input was given aurally. We, therefore, decided to break the interview session into manageable intervals so that the students would not forget important thought processes that they had deployed.

During the interviews, the participants were asked why they thought the selected option was the correct one, why they rejected the alternatives, and whether they wanted to change their original answers. Probing questions were aimed to elicit not only the strategies they used when processing the input and responding to the test items, but also information on what they do when their limited understanding of the input prohibited them from answering the test items. All interviews were translated into English and then transcribed for analysis.

Analysis

Adopting Cohen's framework (Cohen, 2006, 2011, 2012; Cohen & Upton, 2006), we classified the reported strategies into three categories: language learner strategies, test management strategies, and test-wiseness strategies. Both language learner strategies and test management strategies were considered to be construct-relevant, whereas test-wiseness strategies were considered to be construct-irrelevant.

To answer RQ 1 and 2, each interview transcript was double-coded by using a list of strategies adapted from the previous literature on strategy use. Any discrepancies were resolved through discussion. These codes were constantly reviewed and modified throughout the coding process to improve clarity. Coded strategies were then classified into language learner, test-management, and test-wiseness strategies.

In responding to RQ 3, participants were grouped into three performance levels based on the total number of correct responses achieved upon the first attempt. For both listening and reading, participants were classified as low, medium, and high, respectively, if they had answered correctly less than 50% of the items, more than 50% but less than 75% of the items, and more than 75% of the items. Due to the small sample size, we decided not to perform significance testing. Instead, the frequencies of strategies learners used were compared across performance levels.

Results

Strategy Used by Young Learners

We coded a total of 308 instances of strategy use across listening and reading items that were reported to be used in responding to the test items. The coding results showed that language learner strategies were the most frequently used strategies, accounting for close to 40% of all strategy use, followed by test-wiseness strategies (37%) and test-management strategies (23%). Table 7.3 includes the list of all strategies and counts of strategy use.

TABLE 7.3 Strategies and Counts of Strategy Use

		Total	Listening	Reading
Language learner strategy				
1	Make use of morphosyntactic meaning of words	23	6	17
2	Translate	23	10	13
3	Recognize proper nouns	16	15	1
4	Figure out the meaning of a word based on the context	12	5	7
5	Relate personal experience	10	2	8
6	Not being distracted by unknown words	10	3	7
7	Make inferences	9	4	5
8	Relate bits of information together	7	2	5
9	Identify associated words	5	0	5
10	Guess the meaning of a word based on words that are associated	5	4	1
11	Use prior knowledge	2	2	0
12	Use knowledge of punctuation marks	1	0	1
	Total: language learner strategies	123	53	70
Test-management strategies				
1	Eliminate an option that is deemed to be incorrect/unreasonable/implausible	28	10	18
2	Determine where the relevant information to an item can be found	16	3	13
3	Pay attention to the instructions	5	3	2
4	Focus on parts of the stimulus input that are related to the test questions	5	4	1
5	Compare multiple-choice options	4	4	0
6	Choose an option that contains a word that is correctly identified as a key word from the stimulus input	3	3	0

(*Continued*)

TABLE 7.3 (Continued)

		Total	Listening	Reading
7	Review questions while receiving the stimulus input	3	3	0
8	Stop processing the stimulus input once the information needed is believed to have been found	3	3	0
9	Ignore parts of the stimulus input that seem irrelevant to answer the questions	2	2	0
10	Keep track of the time	1	1	0
11	Make use of knowledge of item format/type	1	1	0
	Total: test-management strategies	71	37	34
Test-wiseness strategy				
1	Match words between the options and the stimulus input	69	37	32
2	Make a random guess	28	18	10
3	Match words between the options and the question	5	3	2
4	Eliminate an option that cannot be understood	5	3	2
5	Eliminate an option that contains a word not heard	3	3	0
6	Eliminate an option that does not contain a word/phrase from the stimulus input	2	2	0
7	Use clues in the questions (e.g., options or other items) to answer an item under consideration	1	1	0
8	Choose an option that only contains known words	1	1	0
	Total: test-wiseness strategies	114	68	46
	Total of all strategies	308	158	150

Language Learner Strategy

We observed 123 reported instances of language learner strategy use across listening and reading items. A total of 12 language learner strategies were identified. Below, these strategies are listed in descending order of frequency and are illustrated with excerpts from the interviews.[1]

Make Use of Grammatical Knowledge of Words

Learners utilized their knowledge of morphosyntactic meaning (e.g., part of speech, tense, and plural) of words to respond to test items.

Example: The student (ID 10) was asked to match words with pictures. She used her knowledge of part of speech of the targeted word to answer the item.

R: Why did you choose this option? [Pointing at the option 'Pulling']
S: There should be a verb here. The other two are not verbs so I think it should be this one.

Translate

Learners translated parts of the input from English into Chinese. This strategy was often used when a learner was trying to figure out or confirm the meaning of the input.

Example: The student (ID 12) translated the word 'colorful' into Chinese when trying to figure out the meaning of one of the options to the question 'What is a scrapbook?'

R: Why did you choose this? [Pointing at the option 'A colorful book of photos']
S: *Colorful* is colorful, so it means a colorful photo book.

Recognize Proper Nouns

Proper nouns were recognized by learners to help focus on and retrieve key information in the input.

Example: The student (ID 9) recalled the names of the main characters when responding to the question, 'Which of the following comes first in the story?'

R: Can you tell me why you chose this option? [Pointing at the option 'Katie and Jack play']
S: I heard *Katie* and *Jack*. They were two people in the story. They went out to play.

Figure Out the Meaning of a Word Based on the Context

When an unfamiliar word was encountered, one strategy used was to make an educated guess based on the context.

Example: The student (ID 12) successfully guessed the meaning of an unknown word.

R: How did you respond to this question? [Pointing at the question 'What is a scrapbook?']
S: I don't know the word [Pointing at the word 'scrapbook'] at the beginning. But it explained that you can put pictures in it so maybe it is an album. So I chose B ('A color book of photos').

Relate Personal Experience

Personal experience was used as a tool to respond to test items.

Example: The student (ID 9) made an inference based on his personal experience in responding to the question 'Where is Jerry?'

R: You chose C ('At home'). Why did you think that he was at home?
S: It says he heard his mother talking. Only at home could he hear his mother talking.

Not Being Distracted by Unknown Words

When encountering an unknown word, instead of trying to figure out the meaning, learners simply ignored the word when the understanding of the global message did not depend on the word.

Example: The student (ID 13) comprehended the major proposition of the question and provided the answer without being distracted by 'suit' which was confirmed as an unknown word in an earlier part of the interview.

R: Why did you choose C ('Because his parents said he must wear it') to this question? [Pointing at the question 'Why does Jerry wear a suit?']
S: Why does Jerry wear that? Because his parents told him to wear it.

Make Inferences

Learners were able to use explicitly stated information to figure out the parts that were not told.

Example: The student (ID 10) made the inference in responding to the question 'Why is Jerry excited about the store?'

R: Why did you choose this option? [Pointing at the option 'Because he likes every kind of candy']
S: Because the passage says that he visits the store every day so he must like candy very much.

Relate Bits of Information Together

Learners connected different pieces of information from the stimulus input.

Example: The student (ID 11) related two pieces of information, eating the ice cream and finishing the story, when answering the question.

R: Your answer shows that you think Mary will eat the ice cream. How do you know that she hasn't had the ice cream?
S: Because it says she will eat it after she has finished her story. It also says that she is going to finish the story, which means she has not finished the story yet. Therefore, Mary has not had the ice cream yet.

Identify Associated Words

Use of this strategy was observed when learners worked on the description-word matching tasks, in which they were asked to read a short description about either a person or an object and choose an option that fits the description.

Example: The student (ID 6) associated two related words, 'teeth' and 'mouth'.

R: Why did you choose 'Teeth' for this question?
S: Because it says they are in your mouth, and teeth are in your mouth.

Guess the Meaning of a Word Based on Words That Are Associated

Learners made an educated guess of an unfamiliar word based on their knowledge of words that share similar attributes.

Example: The learner (ID 1) guessed the meaning of 'scrapbook' by associating 'scrapbook' with 'book' when trying to comprehend the question 'What is a scrapbook?'

R: I don't know the word [Pointing at 'scrapbook']. It is something like a book.

Use Prior Knowledge

Learners activated their prior knowledge of the same or a related topic to facilitate or enhance their understanding of the information presented.

Example: The student (ID 16) utilized prior knowledge of how bats look for food to help process the information related to dolphins. Note that there was no information about bats in the stimulus provided and that the student related the information about dolphins, provided in the stimulus, with the background knowledge about bats.

R: Can you tell me why you chose A ('They make sounds') to this question? [Pointing at the question 'How do dolphins look for food?']
S: Dolphins find food by making sounds, like bats.

Use Knowledge of Punctuation Marks

Punctuation marks were recognized to help process the information presented.

Example: The learner (ID 13) recognized question marks as indicators of questions.

R: Why did you choose A ('To ask a question') to this question? [Pointing at the question 'Why is Beth writing to Pam?']
S: I found . . . No, it should be C ('To say hello').
R: Why did you change your mind?
S: I do not think he was trying to ask questions.
R: Why?
S: There is no question mark.

Test-Taking Strategies

Besides the language learner strategies listed above, we also observed strategies that were used due to the assessment context that otherwise would not be used in real-life situations. We identified a total of 19 test-taking strategies, among which 11 were test-management strategies and eight were test-wiseness strategies.

We observed 71 reported instances of strategy use related to test-management and 114 related to test-wiseness across listening and reading items. The majority of test-management strategy use (62%) and test-wiseness strategy use (85%) was related to the top two most frequently used strategies in each category. Due to space limit, below we only illustrate the top two strategies in each category with excerpts from the interviews.

Eliminate an Option That Is Deemed to Be Incorrect/Unreasonable/Implausible

This was the most frequently used test-management strategy. Learners applied this strategy to help decide which option to choose.

Example: The student (ID 16) eliminated two implausible choices based on her understanding of the stimulus input before marking the answer.

R: Why do you think that Kelly talked to her friend after she made the lemonade?
S: Because the other two options are incorrect. Option A says that she went out but she was already out when making the lemonade. Option C says that she drank some lemonade but in the passage it says her friend drank some lemonade. So I chose B ('Kelly talked to her friends.').

Determine Where the Relevant Information to an Item Can Be Found

This was the second most frequently used test-management strategy. Learners were able to locate the relevant information in the input that was related to a test item.

Example: The learner (ID 13) successfully located the sentence in the stimulus which contained the answer to the question.

R: How did you arrive at the answer for this question? [Pointing at the question 'Why does Jerry wear a suit?']
S: His parents asked him to. I saw this sentence in the story *His parents told him to wear the suit*.

Match Words Between the Options and the Stimulus Input

This was the most frequently used test-wiseness strategy. Without having the knowledge to answer a test item, they simply selected an answer that matched some parts of the stimulus input.

Example: The learner (ID 10) found a common word between her answer and the passage. The learner, however, did not seem to have the necessary understanding of the stimulus input to respond meaningfully to the question.

R: Why did you choose Option B ('Kelly put a sign in front of the table') to this question? [Pointing at the question 'What happened after Kelly put a table outside?']
S: Because this option and the passage both have the word *table*. The other two options do not have the word *table*.

Make a Random Guess

Learners made random guesses in responding to test items. This was the second most frequently used test-wiseness strategy.

Example: The learner (ID 6) did not make any other efforts except for making a random guess.

R: Why did you choose Option A here? [Pointing at the option 'planets']
S: I don't know. I guessed.
R: Do you know this word? [Pointing at the word 'planets']
S: No. I don't know any of the options.

Strategy Use by Proficiency

Based on the total number of correct responses achieved upon the first attempt, the participants were grouped into three performance levels in each modality. Among the participants who took the listening items, three were classified as low, four as medium, and two as high. The number of learners who were classified as low, medium, and high in reading were two, three, and three, respectively. Table 7.4 summarizes the frequencies and normalized frequencies of reported strategies. Normalized frequencies are simply frequencies divided by the size of each proficiency group.

Regarding the relationship between strategy use and proficiency, we observed that among the three groups in both modalities, the high-performing group reported the lowest level of strategy use related to test-wiseness, none for listening and four in total (1.33 per participant) for reading. In contrast, both low- and mid-performing groups reported more frequent use of test-wiseness strategies.

Observations across the modalities also revealed the following two noteworthy differences. First, the high-performing group reported more frequent use of language learner strategies in reading than in listening. For this group, the normalized frequency for language learner strategies is 13 for reading and only three for listening. Second, in reading, the frequency of language learner strategies

TABLE 7.4 Frequency and Normalized Frequency of Reported Strategies

Strategy type	Listening				Reading			
	Low n=3	Mid n=4	High n=2	Total n=9	Low n=2	Mid n=3	High n=3	Total n=8
Language learner strategies	12 (4.00)	35 (8.75)	6 (3.00)	53 (5.89)	3 (1.50)	28 (9.33)	39 (13.00)	70 (8.75)
Test-management strategies	3 (1.00)	22 (5.50)	12 (6.00)	37 (4.11)	2 (1.00)	12 (4.00)	20 (6.67)	34 (4.25)
Test-wiseness strategies	25 (8.33)	43 (10.75)	0 (0.00)	68 (7.56)	16 (8.00)	26 (8.67)	4 (1.33)	46 (5.75)
Total	40 (13.33)	100 (25.00)	18 (9.00)	158 (17.56)	21 (10.50)	66 (22.00)	63 (21.00)	150 (18.75)

Note: The numbers in the parentheses are normalized values.

increased as the proficiency increased. In listening, strategy use was most frequently found in the mid-performing group for language learner strategies.

Discussion

The study reported herein was exploratory in nature and provided preliminary evidence that young L2 learners can capably employ a wide variety of strategies for responding to listening and reading test items. We identified a total of 12 different language learner strategies in the study (see Table 7.3). Some strategies referred to cognitive processes that were mainly applicable at the word level, such as recognizing proper nouns. Our interview results also suggested that the young learners were capable of deploying strategies beyond word or phrase level when responding to test items, such as 'relate bits of information together', 'make inferences', 'relate personal experience', and 'use prior knowledge'. The execution of these cognitive processes is more challenging than applying those that focus on single words. This finding implies that young learners can engage in strategy use at the sentence and discourse levels. Strategic competence has long been recognized as a distinct component in language ability models, such as the communicative competence model (Canale, 1983; Canale & Swain, 1980) and the communicative language use model (Bachman, 1990). Despite the results from a small sample size, this study constitutes an initial step in supporting the inclusion of strategic competence as part of the construct definition for designing assessments for young L2 learners.

By the definition we adopted, both language learner strategies and test-management strategies are considered to be construct-relevant. Language use strategies resemble cognitive processes that language users would normally employ in a real-world nontesting context. Test-management strategies require test takers to use their linguistic knowledge to respond meaningfully to test items, unlike test-wiseness strategies in which learners were not engaged primarily with language. In other words, in order to use test-management strategies effectively, learners need to understand the language provided in the stimuli and/or questions and answer options. The findings from our study indicate that the majority of the strategies used (about 63%) were construct-relevant. This is encouraging for test developers because it suggests that the processes in which learners engaged when responding to the test items were largely relevant to the test construct, which in turn supports interpreting test performance as an appropriate indicator of the construct being measured.

Regarding the relationship between strategy use and performance level, we noticed that there is a general alignment between construct-relevant strategy use and performance level. Low- and mid-performing learners used test-wiseness strategies more frequently than the high-performing group. In contrast, learners in the high-performing groups reported rare use of test-wiseness strategies. The results may indicate that some items were too challenging for some low- and mid-performing learners, and therefore were not able to discriminate among these test takers well. This finding questions the efficiency of using these items as measures of the target construct at lower levels.

Another interesting finding was the noticeable differences in the frequencies of language learner strategies between reading and listening. High-performing students used more language learner strategies in reading than in listening. For listening, the use of language learner strategies peaked at the mid-performing group. We suspect that one possible reason could be that the listening test was too easy for these learners. In this case, language use has become automatic, which makes the conscious use of strategies by learners unnecessary. Interestingly, Purpura (1999) also found that compared to less proficient learners, more proficient learners reported fewer strategies, as they were thought to be automatic.

Relative absence of strategy use by high-performing learners in listening may cause concern for interpreting test results from these learners. The listening items that appeared to be too easy for some test takers might not be able to differentiate high-level learners well. In contrast, the reading test was challenging enough that it required the high-performance group to engage in strategy use when responding. One possible explanation for this finding could be that the learners at this age are more advanced in their listening skills than reading skills. We suspect that this can be attributed to the common tendency for young learners to interact with a second language during early years of learning through oral/aural instead of written channels.

Our findings regarding test difficulty are consistent with the decision to provide two levels of the listening and reading tests in the final makeup of the *TOEFL Primary* tests (see Chapter 3 of this volume). Our findings also suggest that it is critical for test developers to keep in mind the developmental patterns of different skills during early years of language learning when designing assessments for young learners.

Limitations and Concluding Remarks

A few study limitations must be pointed out. Considering the relatively young ages of the participants, we used retrospective interview as the data collection method. One limitation with the interview method is that it might be difficult to verify whether the thought processes elicited during the interview were the ones actually used during the test. Furthermore, data were collected only in one country with a small number of students, which limits the generalizability of the study results. In addition, we noticed that age and proficiency were confounded as older learners tended to be more proficient. The small sample size precluded us from disentangling age from proficiency, and therefore any proficiency-related results should be interpreted with caution.

Despite these limitations, we believe that this study contributes to the understanding of the cognitive processes used by young learners in responding to assessment items. The study also demonstrates how investigations of strategies used by test takers can provide insight for test development and validation. In particular, this study showed that investigating strategy use can help to inform construct definition and gauge whether item difficulty is appropriate for various types of test takers. We hope that further empirical research will be conducted, investigating the generalizability of the current findings on young English language learners' use of strategies in assessment contexts.

Note

1 All interviews were conducted in Chinese, the participants' first language. English was occasionally used either by the students or the researcher to refer to the input and was transcribed with italics. In the excerpts, R refers to the researcher and S refers to the student being interviewed. Gestures are indicated in brackets.

References

Bachman, L. F. (1990). *Fundamental considerations in language testing*. Oxford: Oxford University Press.

Block, E. (1986). The comprehension strategies of second language readers. *TESOL Quarterly*, *20*(3), 463–494.

Canale, M. (1983). From communicative competence to communicative language pedagogy. In J. G. Richards & R. W. Schmidt (Eds.), *Language and communication* (pp. 2–27). London: Longman.

Canale, M., & Swain, M. (1980). Theoretical bases of communicative approach to second language teaching and testing. *Applied Linguistics*, *1*(1), 1–47.

Chang, A. C.-S. (2009). EFL listeners' task-based strategies and their relationship with listening performance. *The Electronic Journal for English as a Second Language, 13*(2), 1–28.

Cho, Y., & So, Y. (2014). *Construct-irrelevant factors influencing young EFL learners' perceptions of test task difficulty* (ETS RM-14-04). Princeton, NJ: Educational Testing Service.

Cohen, A. D. (2006). The coming of age of research on test-taking strategies. *Language Assessment Quarterly, 3*, 307–331.

Cohen, A. D. (2011). *Strategies in learning and using a second language: Research and practice.* Cambridge: Cambridge University Press.

Cohen, A. D. (2012). Test-taking strategies and task design. In G. Fulcher & F. Davidson (Eds.), *The Routledge handbook of language testing* (pp. 262–277). London and New York: Routledge.

Cohen, A. D., & Upton, T. A. (2006). *Strategies in responding to the new TOEFL reading tasks* (TOEFL Monograph Report No. MS-33). Princeton, NJ: Educational Testing Service.

Hosenfeld, C. (1984). Case studies of ninth grade readers. In J. C. Alderson & A. H. Urquhart (Eds.), *Reading in a foreign language* (pp. 231–249). London: Longman.

James, C. J. (1986). Listening and learning: Protocols and processes. In B. Snider (Ed.), *Second language acquisition: Preparing for tomorrow* (pp. 38–48). Lincolnwood, IL: National Textbook Company.

Kern, R. G. (1994). The role of mental translation in second language reading. *Studies in Second Language Acquisition, 16*(4), 441–461.

Murphy, J. M. (1987). The listening strategies of English as a second language college students. *Research in Teaching and Developmental Education, 4*(1), 27–46.

Nevo, N. (1989). Test-taking strategies on a multiple-choice test of reading comprehension. *Language Testing, 6*(2), 199–215.

Nikolov, M. (2006). Test-taking strategies of 12- and 13-year-old Hungarian learners of EFL: Why whales have migraines. *Language Learning, 56*(1), 1–51.

O'Malley, J. M., Chamot, A. U., & Kupper, L. (1989). Listening comprehension strategies in second language acquisition. *Applied Linguistics, 10*(4), 418–437.

Purpura, J. E. (1999). *Learner strategy use and performance on language tests: A structural equation modeling approach.* Cambridge: Cambridge University Press.

Purpura, J. E. (2014). Cognition and language assessment. In A. J. Kunnan (Ed.), *The companion to language assessment* (pp. 1452–1476). Boston, MA: Wiley.

Swain, M., Huang, L., Barkaoui, K., Brooks, L., & Lapkin, S. (2009). *The speaking section of the TOEFL iBT™ (SSTiBT): Test-takers' reported strategic behaviors* (TOEFL iBT Research Report No. iBT-10). Princeton, NJ: Educational Testing Service.

Vandergrift, L. (2003). Orchestrating strategy use: Towards a model of the skilled second language listener. *Language Learning, 53*(3), 463–496.

8
USING THE COMMON EUROPEAN FRAMEWORK OF REFERENCE TO FACILITATE SCORE INTERPRETATIONS FOR YOUNG LEARNERS' ENGLISH LANGUAGE PROFICIENCY ASSESSMENTS

Spiros Papageorgiou and Patricia Baron

The Common European Framework, commonly abbreviated to CEFR (Council of Europe, 2001), is one of several publications of the Council of Europe, such as Van Ek and Trim (1991, 1998) and Wilkins (1976), that have been influential in second or foreign language teaching since the 1970s. In recent years, English as a foreign language (EFL) is being introduced earlier in various national curricula (Butler, 2004), and the learning objectives in EFL instructional programs tend to be more ambitious than before (So et al., 2015). As the CEFR is increasingly being used to set learning objectives not only in educational systems in Europe, but also in Asia and Latin America (Byram & Parmenter, 2012), it seems critical to discuss the use of the CEFR within the context of young learner assessments of English. Such a discussion is the focus of this chapter, with specific reference to two assessments for young learners developed by Educational Testing Service (ETS), namely, the *TOEFL Junior*® tests and *TOEFL*® *Primary*™ tests. We use the term 'young learners' to refer to students between 8 and 15 years old in this chapter because these are the ages primarily tested by these assessments (Cho et al., 2016; So et al., 2015). In this chapter, we first present some important considerations with regard to the use of the CEFR in assessing the language proficiency of young learners. We then discuss how the CEFR has been used to support the inferences that can be made on the basis of the scores of the *TOEFL Junior* and *TOEFL Primary* tests. We conclude this chapter by reflecting upon our own experience and describing possible challenges for developers of young learner assessments who wish to use the CEFR.

Origin, Content, and Impact of the CEFR

The main purpose of the CEFR is to provide a common basis for the elaboration of language syllabuses, examinations, and textbooks by describing in a comprehensive way what language learners have to learn to do in order to use a language effectively for communication (see Council of Europe, 2001). In its nine chapters and four appendices, the CEFR contains rich information about language learning, teaching, and assessment; however, the language proficiency scales[1] it contains are considered its best known part (Little, 2006). The scales describe language activities and aspects of language competence at six main levels: A1 (the lowest), A2, B1, B2, C1, and C2 (the highest), and in some cases 'plus' levels (A2+, B1+, and B2+). The scales contain statements called 'descriptors', which are always phrased positively, as they are intended to motivate learners by describing what they can do when they use the language, rather than what they cannot do. For these reasons, these statements are also referred to as 'can-do' descriptors (Little, 2006, 2007).

The CEFR proficiency scales and performance descriptors were developed based on both quantitative and qualitative methodologies during a large-scale research project reported in North and Schneider (1998) and in more detail in North (2000). An initial pool of 41 proficiency scales with their constituent descriptors was created based on existing ones from around the world, such as the ACTFL Proficiency Guidelines (American Council on the Teaching of Foreign Languages, 2012) in the United States (for a detailed list, see Council of Europe, 2001, pp. 224–225). In the qualitative phase of analysis, the scales were refined through consultations with teachers representing all educational sectors in Switzerland. For quantitative analysis of the refined scales and descriptors, data were collected on teacher ratings. Teachers used the scales to rate the performance of their students and to rate video of selected student performance provided by the project team. Using the many-facet Rasch model (Linacre, 1994), the descriptors were then calibrated and placed at different proficiency levels that subsequently formed the CEFR levels.

The CEFR scales and descriptors have gained popularity because they offer a comprehensive description of the language skills that learners are expected to demonstrate at different levels of language proficiency and the language tasks that learners can accomplish at each level; thus, the CEFR can function as a tool to set teaching and learning objectives and "to facilitate comparisons between different systems of qualifications" (Council of Europe, 2001, p. 21). Such comparability of language qualifications in Europe was difficult to achieve prior to the CEFR because of the plethora of diverse educational systems and traditions. In addition, to help test providers improve the interpretability of test scores in relation to the CEFR levels, the Council of Europe published a manual (Council of Europe, 2009) offering a recommended set of procedures for aligning both test content and test scores with the CEFR levels.

Despite its popularity, the CEFR, however, has been the subject of strong criticism, primarily for its use as a tool to implement policies (McNamara, 2006), especially when policy makers set language proficiency requirements for immigration purposes (Shohamy & McNamara, 2009). Alderson (2007) argues that an unintended consequence of the adoption of the CEFR as a policy tool is that in setting expectations for language proficiency levels, decision makers who lack understanding of language learning may impose unrealistic requirements with respect to achievable levels. Papageorgiou (2016) discusses cases where language requirements are set for similar immigration purposes, but vary noticeably across European countries. He calls for more research taking local contexts into account to identify reasonable standards for language proficiency for specific purposes in order to inform policy making.

According to Fulcher's frequently cited papers on this topic (Fulcher, 2004a, 2004b), another unintended consequence of the use of the CEFR is an oversimplification of the notion of validity. In other words, a test that does not report scores in relation to the CEFR levels might be perceived as insufficiently valid and therefore unacceptable to authorities and institutions, even if the test provider has collected sufficient evidence to support the inferences that are permissible on the basis of test scores. Also related to such misunderstanding is a simplistic view of the comparability of assessments that report scores on similar CEFR levels. The Council of Europe (Council of Europe, 2009, p. 90) warns against viewing assessments as equivalent in terms of difficulty or content coverage simply because their test scores are linked in some way to the same CEFR levels. This is particularly important for the results of assessments intended for young learners that are similar to those we discuss in subsequent sections of this chapter because assessments for young learners differ from most assessments intended for adult learners in terms of test purpose and test content. In the next section, we elaborate on considerations specific to young learners' assessments.

Despite these and other criticisms, it is widely accepted that the CEFR has had a major impact on language assessment and teaching in Europe and beyond. Alderson (2007) points out that its six main levels "have become a common currency in language education" and that "curricula, syllabuses, textbooks, teacher training courses, not only examinations, claim to be related to the CEFR" (p. 660). Applications of the CEFR in these areas are illustrated by several studies presented in three edited volumes (Byram & Parmenter, 2012; Figueras & Noijons, 2009; Martyniuk, 2010) and also North (2014). The CEFR has also had a strong impact on language classrooms through the European Language Portfolio (ELP) project (see www.coe.int/portfolio), which the Council of Europe conceived in parallel with the development of the CEFR (Little, 2005, 2007). Given that the CEFR descriptors do not focus on a specific language or educational context (see further discussion of this point in the next section), the CEFR has gained popularity not only in Europe, but also in other continents, as several case studies in Byram and Parmenter (2012) illustrate.

Considerations in Using the CEFR to Assess Young Learners' Language Proficiency

The CEFR, as its title indicates, is a valuable reference document. It has been used to set learning objectives in various educational contexts and to provide a basis for designing materials for young learners (Hasselgreen, 2005, 2012). Practical application of the CEFR in the classroom is also discussed in the literature (e.g., Kantarcioglu & Papageorgiou, 2012), with special emphasis on self-assessment through the use of the European Language Portfolio and the design of classroom-based assessment tasks. However, researchers also note problems when using the CEFR at various stages of the test development process, in particular for large scale tests, for example, when designing test specifications and test tasks, and when establishing comparability of test content (Alderson et al., 2006; Weir, 2005). Such problems might not be surprising if one considers the fact that the CEFR was intentionally designed to be context-free (in terms of countries, educational context, or language being learned) and underspecified (in terms of the amount of information in the descriptors) so that it could be applied in a wide range of contexts and languages (Milanovic & Weir, 2010). The problems noted above are not necessarily confined to the context of assessing young learners; they are likely to appear in test design irrespective of the age of the test takers.

Researchers who have specifically dealt with the use of the CEFR in the context of younger learner assessments note that the wording of the descriptors and the context of language use in the proficiency scales appear adult-oriented, in particular regarding the assessment of higher language proficiency levels, and nonlinguistic aspects of language competence (Hasselgreen, 2005, 2012; Papageorgiou, 2010). In response to this criticism, North (2014), one of the architects of the CEFR, makes two relevant observations: first, that the lower level descriptors were developed in consultation with learners ages 13–15, and second, that it is critical for young learners to learn a foreign language in relation to future, real-life uses.

The relevant literature points out that, as a generic reference document, the CEFR descriptors should not be perceived as rigid criteria for young learners. Instead, North (2014) and others (Hasselgreen, 2012; Schneider & Lenz, 2000) advocate reformulations of the descriptors to make them more comprehensible and better adapted to the experiences of young learners, while maintaining some of the core functional and linguistic aspects of those CEFR levels that are relevant to young learners. The adaptation of the descriptors is also consistent with the overall philosophy of the CEFR as a reference source. Users of the CEFR are in fact encouraged at the end of each chapter to reflect on the content of the book and apply the relevant information to their own educational contexts (Council of Europe, 2001).

With these considerations in mind, we describe in the next section of this chapter the experience of using the CEFR with the ETS assessments developed for young EFL learners.

Using the CEFR With ETS Assessments for Young Learners

In this section, we discuss the use of the CEFR in the context of young learner English assessments at ETS. Detailed accounts of the relevant work can be found elsewhere for both the *TOEFL Junior*® tests (Baron & Tannenbaum, 2011; Papageorgiou, Morgan, & Becker, 2015; Papageorgiou, Xi, Morgan, & So, 2015; So et al., 2015; Tannenbaum & Baron, 2015) and the *TOEFL Primary* tests (Cho et al., 2016; Baron & Papageorgiou, 2014a, 2014b).

Using the CEFR for the TOEFL Junior Tests

The *TOEFL Junior* tests are available in two testing modes: the paper-based *TOEFL Junior* Standard test and the computer-based *TOEFL Junior* Comprehensive test. The *TOEFL Junior* Standard test consists entirely of selected-response items in three sections: Listening Comprehension, Language Form and Meaning (LFM), and Reading Comprehension. Each section contains 42 items (total 126 items). The duration of the test is one hour and 55 minutes. Section scores are reported on a scale ranging from 200 to 300 points, with five-point intervals. A total score is also reported as the sum of the section scores, ranging from 600 to 900. The *TOEFL Junior* Comprehensive test consists of both selected-response and constructed response items in four sections: the Reading Comprehension and Listening Comprehension sections (each with 36 selected-response items), and the Speaking and Writing sections (each with four constructed-response tasks). The total duration of the test is two hours and 14 minutes. The Reading Comprehension and Listening Comprehension section scores are reported on a scale from 140 to 160. The Speaking and Writing section scores range from 0–16; these scores are linked to the rubrics used to score Speaking or Writing tasks.

The tests are intended to (a) facilitate student placement decisions and (b) monitor student progress in classrooms that use English for content instruction and in English-language programs that prepare students for academic English skills (Gu, Lockwood, & Powers, 2015; Papageorgiou & Cho, 2014). The target language use (TLU) domain (Bachman & Palmer, 2010) of the *TOEFL Junior* test is English-medium instructional environments in secondary education, primarily, but not exclusively, for students aged 11 to 15 (for more details, see So, 2014; So et al., 2015; also see Chapter 4 in this volume). To facilitate the interpretation of test scores in relation to the TLU domain, section and total scores of both modes of the *TOEFL Junior* tests are accompanied by performance descriptors that provide fine-grained information on what test takers are able to do.

In addition to facilitating interpretations of test scores in relation to the TLU domain, the widespread use of the CEFR to set learning objectives around the world coincided with increased interest in the use of the CEFR levels in score interpretation. For this reason, two mapping studies were conducted, first for the *TOEFL Junior* Standard test (Baron & Tannenbaum, 2011) and then for the *TOEFL Junior* Comprehensive test (Tannenbaum & Baron, 2015). The purpose of CEFR mapping studies is to offer recommendations for minimum scores (cut scores) that corresponded to specific CEFR levels (Tannenbaum & Cho, 2014). For the *TOEFL Junior* tests, the CEFR levels targeted by the test development team were levels A2, B1, and B2. A standard-setting methodology appropriate to the test types based on well-established professional standards (American Educational Research Association, American Psychological Association, & National Council on Measurement in Education, 2014; Educational Testing Service, 2014) was implemented. During these studies, diverse groups of panelists with teaching experience representative of the EFL teachers of students in the TLU domain followed specific procedures and examined test performance data under the guidance of two facilitators.

For the test sections containing selected-response items (Listening Comprehension, LFM, and Reading Comprehension), modified Angoff procedures were employed (see Plake & Cizek, 2012 for modified Angoff procedures). The panelists' task in the modified Angoff procedure was to make judgments for each test item with regard to the performance of borderline students (i.e., hypothetical students demonstrating minimally acceptable performance at each of the three CEFR levels). The judgment task was implemented in three rounds. In Round 1, panelists made individual judgments without discussion; Round 2 judgments were made after panelists had the opportunity to review and discuss their individual judgments from Round 1 in relation to other panelists' judgments; and Round 3 judgments were made after panelists reviewed and discussed test performance data with the other panelists. The panelists' individual judgments in Round 3, the final round, were totaled to yield a final cut score for that specific section of the test.

For the test sections containing constructed-response items (Speaking and Writing), a variation of the Performance Profile method (Hambleton, Jaeger, Plake, & Mills, 2000) was followed. This holistic standard-setting method is desirable for test sections with constructed-response items because it allows panelists to review a set of student performance samples. As educators, panelists have expertise making judgments about samples of actual student work in a holistic fashion (Kingston & Tiemann, 2012). The panelists reviewed the test takers' responses (profiles) to a set of 34 speaking and 24 writing tasks and the corresponding scoring rubrics. The test takers' profiles represented the most frequently occurring task-score patterns across the range of total scores in increasing score order. Similar to the procedure followed for selected response items, three rounds of judgments took place, with feedback and discussion between rounds. The recommendation for the speaking and writing cut scores was based on the final round of judgments.

To further explore the relationship between the scores of both modes of the *TOEFL Junior* tests and the CEFR levels, results from a scale alignment study for the Reading and Listening sections of the *TOEFL Junior* Standard test and the *TOEFL Junior* Comprehensive test were considered. These test sections are based on the same test specifications, although with some slight differences in terms of how they are operationalized (So et al., 2015). Therefore, the score scale alignment study was conducted to evaluate empirically score comparability between *TOEFL Junior* Standard Reading and Listening scores and *TOEFL Junior* Comprehensive Reading and Listening scores (Educational Testing Service, 2012; Tannenbaum & Baron, 2015). Approximately 1,000 examinees took both the *TOEFL Junior* Standard test and the *TOEFL Junior* Comprehensive test. The equipercentile equating method (Livingston, 2004) was used to link the Reading and Listening scores; this method aligned scores on the two tests that had the same percentile rank.

The results of the scale alignment study were considered along with the cut score recommendations of the two mapping studies to provide score users with the range of test section scores that correspond to the relevant CEFR levels. These score ranges are presented in Table 8.1. The relevant CEFR levels and descriptors, modified to fit the TLU domain of the test, are included in test taker score reports (So et al., 2015).

In addition to facilitating the interpretation of scores for the different sections, the CEFR has also been employed to facilitate the interpretation of the overall score levels, first for the *TOEFL Junior* Comprehensive test (Papageorgiou, Xi, et al., 2015) and then for *TOEFL Junior* Standard test (Papageorgiou, Morgan, et al., 2015). Content differences between the two tests (i.e., the *TOEFL Junior* Comprehensive test contains both selected-response and constructed-response items, whereas the *TOEFL Junior* Standard test contains only selected-response items) meant that different types of data were considered; nevertheless, the general procedures for the development of the levels and descriptors were the same across the two tests. Due consideration was given to determine the optimal number of overall score levels that could be reported reliably and meaningfully (AERA, APA, & NCME, 2014). The reliability of classifications was evaluated employing a statistical method developed by Livingston and Lewis (1995); interpretability concerns included the levels and descriptors in the speaking and writing scoring rubrics (for the *TOEFL Junior* Comprehensive test) and the difficulty of the items by overall score levels (for the *TOEFL Junior* Standard test).

TABLE 8.1 *TOEFL Junior* Section Scores at Different CEFR Levels

Test	Test section	CEFR levels			
		Below A2	A2	B1	B2
TOEFL Junior Standard test	Listening Comprehension	Under 225	225–245	250–285	290–300
	Language Form and Meaning	Under 210	210–245	250–275	280–300
	Reading Comprehension	Under 210	210–240	245–275	280–300
TOEFL Junior Comprehensive test	Reading Comprehension	140–142	143–150	151–156	157–160
	Listening Comprehension	143–150	143–149	150–156	157–160
	Speaking	1–7	8–10	11–13	14–16
	Writing	1–5	6–9	10–12	13–16

The levels and descriptors of the CEFR were among the sources used to inform the development of the overall score levels and descriptors of both tests. For example, Papageorgiou et al. (2015) examined the average number of reading and listening items targeting a specific CEFR level that were answered correctly by students at each overall score level to facilitate the development of performance descriptors pertaining to the comprehension of written and spoken materials. The targeted CEFR level of the items of one pilot test form, taken by 498 students, was estimated by staff in the ETS Assessment Development group, taking into account the coding of the items during test design and the empirical item difficulty values. The resulting overall score levels and descriptors for both tests are presented in Table 8.2 (*TOEFL Junior* Comprehensive test) and Table 8.3 (*TOEFL Junior* Standard test). For each level, the typical score profile of students at each overall performance level (second column) is also expressed in terms of CEFR levels (third column) to support score interpretations in relation to the CEFR. It should be noted that the typical profile is empirically based on test taker performance on both tests (2,931 test takers for the *TOEFL Junior* Comprehensive test and 3,607 test takers for the *TOEFL Junior* Standard test).

Using the CEFR for the TOEFL® Primary™ *Tests*

The *TOEFL Primary* tests aim to measure the English-language skills of EFL learners who are younger (primarily, but not exclusively, between ages 8 and 11) than those typically taking the *TOEFL Junior* tests. The *TOEFL Primary* tests contain three sections: Reading, Listening, and Speaking. The test consists of

TABLE 8.2 *TOEFL Junior* Comprehensive Overall Performance Levels and Descriptors With CEFR Profile Summary

Level	Typical performance in English-medium schools	Typical CEFR profile
6 Excellent	A typical student at Level 6 consistently demonstrates the skills needed to communicate at a high level in complex interactions and while using complex materials.	B2 for all sections (Reading, Listening, Speaking, and Writing)
5 Advanced	A typical student at Level 5 often demonstrates the skills needed to communicate at a high level in complex interactions and while using complex materials.	B1 or B2 for Reading and Listening; B1 for Speaking and Writing
4 Competent	A typical student at Level 4 demonstrates the skills needed to communicate successfully in some complex situations and in most simple interactions and while using basic materials.	B1 for Reading and Listening; B1 or A2 for Speaking and Writing
3 Achieving	A typical student at Level 3 usually demonstrates the skills needed to communicate successfully in simple interactions and while using basic materials.	A2 or B1 for Listening; A2 for Reading, Speaking, and Writing
2 Developing	A typical student at Level 2 occasionally demonstrates the skills needed to communicate successfully in simple interactions and while using basic materials.	A2 for Reading and Listening; below A2 for Speaking and Writing
1 Beginning	A typical student at Level 1 demonstrates some basic language skills but needs to further develop those skills in order to communicate successfully.	Below A2 for all sections (Listening, Reading, Speaking, and Writing)

multiple-choice questions for the Reading and Listening sections (36 items each) and constructed-response tasks for the Speaking section (eight tasks). The *TOEFL Primary* tests are designed to support teaching and learning by providing meaningful feedback to teachers who use this information to guide their instruction. For this reason, results for each skill area are reported in the form of both numeric scaled scores and band levels (Cho et al., 2016).

Similar to the *TOEFL Junior* tests, a mapping study was conducted to facilitate score interpretation in relation to the CEFR levels (Baron & Papageorgiou, 2014a, 2014b). The purpose of the study was to offer recommendations for minimum scores (cut scores) that corresponded to the CEFR levels targeted by the test development team, that is, CEFR levels A1, A2, and B1 for reading and listening, and, for speaking only, B2 as well. As with the *TOEFL Junior* tests, standard

TABLE 8.3 *TOEFL Junior* Standard Overall Performance Levels and Descriptors With CEFR Profile Summary

Level	Typical performance in English-medium schools	Typical CEFR profile
5 Superior	A typical student at Level 5 consistently demonstrates comprehension of complex written and spoken materials, drawing on knowledge of complex language structures and vocabulary.	B2 for all sections
4 Accomplished	A typical student at Level 4 often demonstrates comprehension of complex written and spoken materials, drawing on knowledge of complex language structures and vocabulary.	B1 for all sections
3 Expanding	A typical student at Level 3 demonstrates comprehension of some complex written and spoken materials and most basic materials, drawing on knowledge of basic language structures and vocabulary.	Mostly B1 for all sections, but occasionally A2.
2 Progressing	A typical student at Level 2 occasionally demonstrates comprehension of basic written and spoken materials, drawing on knowledge of basic language structures and vocabulary.	Mostly A2 for all sections, but occasionally A1 for Reading and Listening.
1 Emerging	A typical student at Level 1 can comprehend some very basic written and spoken texts, drawing on knowledge of basic language structures and vocabulary, but needs to further develop these language skills and comprehension abilities.	Mostly A1 for Listening and Reading; mostly A2 for Language, Form and Meaning.

setting methodology was implemented, and panelists with relevant teaching experience (i.e., EFL teachers of students in the TLU domain) followed specific procedures and examined test performance data under the guidance of two facilitators. A Yes/No modification of the Angoff method and the Performance Profile approach were used, as per the other two mapping studies for the *TOEFL Junior* tests.

The *TOEFL Primary* test-taking population and its design posed two challenges for the mapping study. The first challenge, somewhat similar to the experience with the *TOEFL Junior* tests described above, was that the intended test takers are very young, therefore making the more adult-oriented CEFR descriptors only marginally relevant. For this reason, prior to the mapping study, assessment development staff at ETS modified some of the CEFR descriptors in order to make them more relevant to the experiences of young learners like the *TOEFL Primary* test takers. The modified descriptors were provided to the panelists of the mapping study to help them define just qualified students for the relevant CEFR levels. Two modified descriptors and their original counterparts are presented as an example in Table 8.4. For the Listening descriptor, "common everyday or job related topics" was modified to fit a school context ("common everyday and school-related topics"), and "in a generally familiar accent" was removed to fit the experiences of young learners in EFL environments, who may not have frequent encounters with speakers of English as a first language (L1). In addition, the modified reading descriptor emphasized the need to adapt English text input so that it is more accessible to younger learners.

The second challenge concerned the design of the *TOEFL Primary* tests. The Reading and Listening sections (36 items each) are available for testing students at two levels of proficiency, called Step 1 and Step 2, which share common items and use the same score reporting scale. Step 1, whose scores range from 102 to 109, assesses students with lower levels of language proficiency than Step 2, whose scores range from 104 to 115. Asking panelists to perform judgments on all items of both Step 1 and Step 2 (total 72 items for each test section) would have been impractical and likely to result in fatigue. Instead, a longer test form containing 57 items from field test administration was used for the mapping study for each test section. Apart from addressing practical concerns, a longer test form allowed for a scale representing performance across both Step 1 and Step 2. This was done by employing item response theory (IRT) scaling, which shows where test takers are located on the language ability continuum (Hambleton, Swaminathan, & Rogers, 1991). The panel-recommended cut scores, based on the longer test form, were mapped to the reporting score scale for each

TABLE 8.4 *TOEFL Primary* Modified Descriptors and Original CEFR Descriptors

Language skill and CEFR level	Modified TOEFL Primary descriptors	Original CEFR descriptors
Listening B1	Can understand straightforward factual information about common everyday and *school-related topics*, identifying both general messages and specific details, provided speech is clearly articulated.	Can understand straightforward factual information about common everyday or *job related topics*, identifying both general messages and specific details, provided speech is clearly articulated *in a generally familiar accent*.
Reading B1	Can understand straightforward texts, *controlled for language construction and accessibility*, on familiar topics.	Can read straightforward factual texts on subjects related to his/her field and interest with a satisfactory level of comprehension.

TABLE 8.5 *TOEFL Primary* Score Ranges at Different CEFR Levels

CEFR level	Listening		Reading		Speaking (0–27)
	Step 1 (100–109)	Step 2 (104–115)	Step 1 (100–109)	Step 2 (104–115)	
A1	102–104	104	102–106		10–15
A2	105–109	105–112	107–109	107–113	16–21
B1		113–115		114–115	22–25
B2					26

TOEFL Primary test, Step 1 and Step 2. The score ranges for all three test sections are presented in Table 8.5.

Issues and Challenges in Using the CEFR for Young Learner Assessments

The number of educational systems around the world for which the CEFR levels are used in order to set objectives for students learning a foreign language is growing (Byram & Parmenter, 2012). Therefore, working with the CEFR has been critical in order to support the inferences that can be made on the basis of *TOEFL Junior* and *TOEFL Primary* test scores. The experience, although positive overall, did not come without challenges.

A central challenge we faced was the inevitable conflict between (a) the need to modify the wording of the CEFR descriptors so that they were more relevant to the experience for young learners taking the ETS assessments and (b) the desire to maintain the core meaning of the CEFR descriptors. Maybe, as we have suggested elsewhere (Baron & Papageorgiou, 2014a), one way to better address this conflict is by comparing other test developers' modifications of the CEFR descriptors for tests assessing students of similar ages to those of the *TOEFL Junior* and *TOEFL Primary* tests to locate similarities and differences across the modified descriptors. Another way to address this challenge is to complement the more generic CEFR descriptors with empirically-based descriptors that are specific to the test content, as was the case with the *TOEFL Junior* overall score levels and descriptors (Papageorgiou, Morgan et al., 2015; Papageorgiou, Xi et al., 2015).

A second challenge relates to how score users, teachers, and students may interpret the comparability of assessments for which scores on similar CEFR levels are reported. As we discussed earlier in this chapter, tests should not be viewed as equivalent in terms of difficulty, content coverage, or even construct simply because their test scores are linked in some way to the same CEFR levels. This concern is particularly relevant to the *TOEFL Junior* and *TOEFL Primary* tests. Although both tests are intended for young learners, their content and difficulty differ by design in order to fit the intended TLU domain; therefore, users of the two tests should exercise caution when interpreting scores that are linked to the same CEFR levels.

A third challenge, which has also been pointed out by other researchers (Alderson et al., 2006; Weir, 2005), relates to the limitations of the CEFR as a source for designing test specifications and describing test content. This is hardly surprising, given that the CEFR was never intended to be a test specification document; by design, the CEFR was underspecified to allow it to be applied in a variety of contexts. However, our experience interacting with panelists during mapping studies suggested that score users are sometimes led to believe that some tests are designed based on the CEFR. We believe that although the CEFR is a useful heuristic, as Fulcher and Davidson (2009) point out, it is far from sufficient as the sole source for informing test design. The ETS approach for designing EFL tests for young learners has been very comprehensive, involving expert panels and teachers (Hsieh, 2014), examination of curricula and content standards around the world, and a detailed analysis of the TLU domain and the relevant literature (Cho et al., 2016; So et al., 2015). Although the CEFR levels and descriptors have been useful resources informing these various stages in the test design process, we believe that their primary use remains to communicate information about test scores with regard to what test takers can do when they perform tasks in a foreign language at different proficiency levels.

Conclusion

In this chapter, we discussed the use of the CEFR in the context of young EFL learner assessments and offered a detailed description of how the CEFR has been used to provide an additional framework for supporting inferences that can be made on the basis of scores provided by the *TOEFL Junior* and *TOEFL Primary* tests. This is particularly relevant for educational contexts where the CEFR levels and descriptors are widely used to set learning objectives for young EFL learners (see case studies in Byram & Parmenter, 2012, for example).

We believe that it is critical to conclude by emphasizing a point we made elsewhere in this chapter, that is, the use of the CEFR to facilitate score interpretation should not result in an oversimplification of the notion of validity (Fulcher, 2004a, 2004b). Given the growing use of the CEFR by educational authorities in Europe and beyond, it is reasonable to expect providers of assessments to attempt to link their assessments to the CEFR levels. However, users of these assessments should not misinterpret any type of linking as a sufficient indicator of the overall quality of an assessment or as confirmation of the validity of its scores for their intended use. In fact, the Council of Europe (2009, p. 90) makes it very clear that unless an assessment is of high quality, then linking that particular assessment to the CEFR levels is not appropriate. For this reason, the use of the CEFR for young learner assessments, although important, should remain only part of a wider research program whose aims are twofold: to provide support for claims that can be made about the use of these tests with young EFL learners and bring positive consequences in the EFL contexts where these assessments are used.

Note

1 We use the term "CEFR scales" (plural) to refer to what the CEFR calls "illustrative scales" (of descriptors). Of the dozens such scales describing various language activities and aspects of language competence, a global scale describing overall communicative proficiency is probably the most frequently cited one (Council of Europe, 2001, p. 24).

References

Alderson, J. C. (2007). The CEFR and the need for more research. *The Modern Language Journal, 91*(4), 659–663.

Alderson, J. C., Figueras, N., Kuijper, H., Nold, G., Takala, S., & Tardieu, C. (2006). Analysing tests of reading and listening in relation to the Common European Framework of Reference: The experience of the Dutch CEFR Construct Project. *Language Assessment Quarterly, 3*(1), 3–30.

American Council on the Teaching of Foreign Languages. (2012). ACTFL proficiency guidelines. Available from http://www.actfl.org/sites/default/files/pdfs/public/ACTFLProficiencyGuidelines2012_FINAL.pdf

American Educational Research Association, American Psychological Association, & National Council on Measurement in Education. (2014). *Standards for educational and psychological testing*. Washington, DC: American Educational Research Association.

Bachman, L. F., & Palmer, A. S. (2010). *Language assessment in practice: Developing language assessments and justifying their use in the real world*. Oxford: Oxford University Press.

Baron, P. A., & Papageorgiou, S. (2014a). *Mapping the TOEFL® Primary™ Test onto the Common European Framework of Reference* (ETS Research Memorandum RM-14–05). Princeton, NJ: Educational Testing Service.

Baron, P. A., & Papageorgiou, S. (2014b). *Setting multiple CEFR cut scores for assessments intended for young learners*. Paper presented at the 11th Annual Conference of EALTA, University of Warwick, UK.

Baron, P. A., & Tannenbaum, R. J. (2011). *Mapping the TOEFL® Junior™ Test onto the Common European Framework of Reference* (ETS Research Memorandum RM-11–07). Princeton, NJ: Educational Testing Service.

Butler, Y. G. (2004). What level of English proficiency do elementary school teachers need to attain to teach EFL? Case studies from Korea, Taiwan, and Japan. *TESOL Quarterly, 38*(2), 245–278.

Byram, M., & Parmenter, L. (Eds.). (2012). *The Common European Framework of Reference: The globalisation of language education policy*. Bristol, UK: Multilingual Matters.

Cho, Y., Ginsburgh, M., Moulder, B., Morgan, R., Xi, X., & Hauck, M. (2016). *Designing the TOEFL primary tests* (ETS Research Memorandum RM-16-02). Princeton, NJ: Educational Testing Service.

Council of Europe. (2001). *Common European Framework of Reference for Languages: Learning, teaching, assessment*. Cambridge: Cambridge University Press.

Council of Europe. (2009). Relating language examinations to the Common European Framework of Reference for Languages: Learning, teaching, assessment: A manual. Available from http://www.coe.int/t/dg4/linguistic/manuel1_en.asp

Educational Testing Service. (2012). Mapping the TOEFL® Junior™ Standard Test onto the Common European Framework of Reference: Executive summary. Available from http://www.ets.org/s/toefl_junior/pdf/mapping_toefl_junior.pdf

Educational Testing Service. (2014). *ETS standards for quality and fairness*. Princeton, NJ: Educational Testing Service.

Figueras, N., & Noijons, J. (Eds.). (2009). *Linking to the CEFR levels: Research perspectives*. Arnhem: CITO.

Fulcher, G. (2004a). Are Europe's tests being built on an 'unsafe' framework? Available from http://education.guardian.co.uk/tefl/story/0,5500,1170569,00.html

Fulcher, G. (2004b). Deluded by artifices? The Common European Framework and harmonization. *Language Assessment Quarterly, 1*(4), 253–266.

Fulcher, G., & Davidson, F. (2009). Test architecture, test retrofit. *Language Testing, 26*(1), 123–144.

Gu, L., Lockwood, J., & Powers, D. E. (2015). *Evaluating the TOEFL Junior® Standard test as a measure of progress for young English language learners* (ETS Research Report No. RR-15-22). Princeton, NJ: Educational Testing Service.

Hambleton, R. K., Jaeger, R. M., Plake, B. S., & Mills, C. (2000). Setting performance standards on complex educational assessments. *Applied Psychological Measurement, 24*(4), 355–366.

Hambleton, R. K., Swaminathan, H., & Rogers, H. J. (1991). *Fundamentals of item response theory*. London: Sage Publications.

Hasselgreen, A. (2005). Assessing the language of young learners. *Language Testing, 22*(3), 337–354.

Hasselgreen, A. (2012). Adapting the CEFR for the classroom assessment of young learners' writing. *Canadian Modern Language Review, 69*(4), 415–435.

Hsieh, C. (2014). *Using expert judgments to assess content representativeness of a young learner assessment, TOEFL Primary*. Paper presented at the 36th Language Testing Research Colloquium (LTRC), Amsterdam, The Netherlands.

Kantarcioglu, E., & Papageorgiou, S. (2012). The Common European Framework of Reference. In C. Coombe, P. Davidson, B. O'Sullivan, & C. Stoynoff (Eds.), *The Cambridge guide to language assessment* (pp. 82–88). Cambridge: Cambridge University Press.

Kingston, N. M., & Tiemann, G. C. (2012). Setting performance standards on complex assessments: The body of work method. In G. J. Cizek (Ed.), *Setting performance standards: Foundations, methods, and innovations* (2nd ed., pp. 201–224). New York, NY: Routledge.

Linacre, J. M. (1994). *Many-facet Rasch measurement* (2nd ed.). Chicago: MESA Press.

Little, D. (2005). The Common European Framework of Reference for Languages and the European Language Portfolio: Involving learners and their judgements in the assessment process. *Language Testing, 22*(3), 321–336.

Little, D. (2006). The Common European Framework of Reference for Languages: Content, purpose, origin, reception and impact. *Language Teaching, 39*(3), 167–190.

Little, D. (2007). The Common European Framework of Reference for Languages: Perspectives on the making of supranational language education policy. *The Modern Language Journal, 91*(4), 645–655.

Livingston, S. A. (2004). *Equating test scores (without IRT)*. Princeton, NJ: Educational Testing Service. Available from http://www.ets.org/Media/Research/pdf/LIVINGSTON.pdf

Livingston, S. A., & Lewis, C. (1995). Estimating the consistency and accuracy of classifications based on test scores. *Journal of Educational Measurement, 32*(2), 179–197.

Martyniuk, W. (Ed.). (2010). *Relating language examinations to the Common European Framework of Reference for Languages: Case studies and reflections on the use of the Council of Europe's draft manual*. Cambridge, UK: Cambridge University Press.

McNamara, T. (2006). Validity in language testing: The challenge of Sam Messick's legacy. *Language Assessment Quarterly, 3*(1), 31–51.

Milanovic, M., & Weir, C. J. (2010). Series editors' note. In W. Martyniuk (Ed.), *Relating language examinations to the Common European Framework of Reference for Languages: Case studies and reflections on the use of the council of Europe's draft manual* (pp. viii–xx). Cambridge: Cambridge University Press.

North, B. (2000). *The development of a common framework scale of language proficiency*. New York: Peter Lang.

North, B. (2014). *The CEFR in practice*. Cambridge: Cambridge University Press.

North, B., & Schneider, G. (1998). Scaling descriptors for language proficiency scales. *Language Testing, 15*(2), 217–262.

Papageorgiou, S. (2010). Investigating the decision-making process of standard setting participants. *Language Testing, 27*(2), 261–282.

Papageorgiou, S. (2016). Aligning language assessments to standards and frameworks. In J. Banerjee & D. Tsagari (Eds.), *Handbook of second language* assessment (pp. 327–340). Boston, MA: DeGruyter Mouton.

Papageorgiou, S., & Cho, Y. (2014). An investigation of the use of TOEFL® Junior™ Standard scores for ESL placement decisions in secondary education. *Language Testing, 31*(2), 223–239.

Papageorgiou, S., Morgan, R., & Becker, V. (2015). Enhancing the interpretability of the overall results of an international test of English-language proficiency. *International Journal of Testing, 15*(4), 310–336.

Papageorgiou, S., Xi, X., Morgan, R., & So, Y. (2015). Developing and validating band levels and descriptors for reporting overall examinee performance. *Language Assessment Quarterly, 12*(2), 153–177.

Plake, B. S., & Cizek, G. J. (2012). Variations on a theme: The modified Angoff, extended Angoff, and yes/no standard setting methods. In G. J. Cizek (Ed.), *Setting performance standards: Foundations, methods, and innovations* (2nd ed., pp. 181–199). New York: Routledge.

Schneider, G., & Lenz, P. (2000). European Language Portfolio: Guide for developers. Available from http://www.coe.int/t/dg4/education/elp/elp-reg/Source/Publications/Developers_guide_EN.pdf

Shohamy, E., & McNamara, T. (2009). Language tests for citizenship, immigration, and asylum. *Language Assessment Quarterly, 6*(1), 1–5.

So, Y. (2014). Are teacher perspectives useful? Incorporating EFL teacher feedback in the development of a large-scale international English test. *Language Assessment Quarterly, 11*(3), 283–303.

So, Y., Wolf, M. K., Hauck, M. C., Mollaun, P., Rybinski, P., Tumposky, D., & Wang, L. (2015). *TOEFL Junior® design framework* (TOEFL Junior® Research Report TOEFL JR–02). Princeton, NJ: Educational Testing Service.

Tannenbaum, R. J., & Baron, P. A. (2015). *Mapping scores from the TOEFL Junior Comprehensive® test onto the Common European Framework of Reference* (ETS Research Memorandum RM-15–13). Princeton, NJ: Educational Testing Service.

Tannenbaum, R. J., & Cho, Y. (2014). Criteria for evaluating standard-setting approaches to map English language test scores to frameworks of English language proficiency. *Language Assessment Quarterly*, *11*(3), 233–249.

Van Ek, J. A., & Trim, J. L. M. (1991). *Waystage 1990*. Cambridge: Cambridge University Press.

Van Ek, J. A., & Trim, J. L. M. (1998). *Threshold 1990*. Cambridge: Cambridge University Press.

Weir, C. J. (2005). Limitations of the Common European Framework of Reference for Languages (CEFR) for developing comparable examinations and tests. *Language Testing*, *22*(3), 281–300.

Wilkins, D. A. (1976). *Notional syllabuses*. Oxford: Oxford University Press.

9

MAKING A VALIDITY ARGUMENT FOR USING THE *TOEFL JUNIOR*® STANDARD TEST AS A MEASURE OF PROGRESS FOR YOUNG ENGLISH LANGUAGE LEARNERS

Lin Gu, J. R. Lockwood, and Donald E. Powers

Standardized tests are often designed to provide only a snapshot of test takers' knowledge, skills, or abilities at a single point in time. This is typically the case when test scores are used for selection, admission, or certification purposes, for example. Some tests, however, are expected to meet more demanding functions, one of which is assessing change in knowledge, skills, or ability over time. In fact, many standardized tests claim to be appropriate for the dual purposes of measuring the test takers' abilities in the given construct and monitoring the growth of their abilities over time (e.g., English language proficiency assessments in K-12 schools in the U.S.). The measurement of change over time is an important area in educational research because it offers a means to evaluate the effectiveness of educational efforts, which are intended generally to effect changes in students' attitudes, achievement, and values (Bloom, Hill, Black, & Lipsey, 2008; Carver, 1974; Willett, 1994). Currently, assessing change (or growth) is important in one domain in particular in which millions of young learners are engaged worldwide—English language proficiency.

Regardless of its type or purpose, every test is required to meet a variety of professional standards, including those for the interpretation and use (i.e., validity) of test scores (American Educational Research Association, American Psychological Association, & National Council on Measurement in Education, 2014). Although validity theory has been explicated in a variety of ways, most modern theorists have, in some form, advocated (a) making explicit the claims that are made for a test; (b) developing a validity argument that supports these claims; and (c) evaluating the coherence of the argument, including the plausibility of the assumptions on which it rests and the inferences that follow from it (see, for example, Bachman & Palmer, 2010; Chapelle, Enright, & Jamieson, 2008; Kane, 2006; Messick, 1989).

To argue that a test is capable of measuring change requires evidence that links changes in observed test scores to actual (or at least presumed) changes in the abilities that a test is intended to measure. Because changes in abilities often result from relevant learning experiences, evidence indicating an association between test performance and construct-relevant learning experiences can be used to support a claim that a test is sensitive to change.

Furthermore, establishing a link between test performance and relevant learning experiences also contributes to the overarching goal of construct validation; that is, determining the degree to which a test measures the target construct. For instance, both Messick (1989) and Chapelle et al. (2008) propose that construct interpretation is facilitated to the extent that test performance changes are commensurate with the amount and quality of relevant learning experiences.

This chapter[1] includes an empirical study that employs a longitudinal design to model changes in relation to learning over time. The specific goal of this study was to examine the extent to which a new assessment of young learners' English language ability, the *TOEFL Junior*® Standard test developed by Educational Testing Service (ETS), is capable of reflecting changes in language ability as a function of learning. This property (i.e., sensitivity to changes due to education) is especially crucial for tests designed for learners of young ages because the construct being measured could be in constant development as young learners engage in learning in various contexts, both within and outside of the school environment. To be maximally useful, an assessment developed for young learners should exhibit an ability to reflect growth that accrues from construct-relevant learning. It is therefore also crucial for test developers to provide sufficient validity evidence in support of the claim that such an assessment can be used to monitor growth.

In this chapter, we demonstrate how validity evidence can be gathered based on nonexperimental repeated measures data to examine the claim that the *TOEFL Junior* test can be used to monitor young learners' English language proficiency development. We address issues and challenges that are often encountered in nonexperimental longitudinal studies. It is our hope that this study will contribute both conceptually and methodologically to the literature on assessing English language proficiency for young learners.

The *TOEFL Junior* Standard Test

The *TOEFL Junior* Standard test is a standardized proficiency test designed for adolescent English language learners (primarily between 11 and 15 years old). It measures English language proficiency with respect to the academic and social English language skills needed to meet the demands that young English language learners face in English-medium instructional environments. Test development is based on expectations for middle school students in English-medium secondary schools as informed by a variety of sources. Test tasks are based on both social and academic uses of language in a school context. The test is composed of multiple-choice questions in three sections: listening comprehension (listening), language form and meaning (language), and reading comprehension (reading). For detailed information about the *TOEFL Junior* Standard test, see So et al. (2017) in this volume.

One of the major proposed uses of the *TOEFL Junior* Standard test is to provide objective information about student progress in developing English language skills over time. Language learning usually occurs in two contexts—an instructional context and a communicative context (Batstone, 2002). In an instructional context, learners often develop their language skills from instruction received in a classroom setting where English is taught as subject matter. Formal foreign language training in the home country usually provides such a context. In a communicative context, the objective is to use the target language to perform communicative functions. Study abroad in the target language community is likely to create such communicative contexts for learners. If used repeatedly, the *TOEFL Junior* Standard test is expected to be able to reflect anticipated gains in the target construct that result from learning in various contexts.

Study Objectives

The primary goal of this study was to examine the degree to which the *TOEFL Junior* Standard test could reflect changes in language ability due to learning. The challenge was that there were no direct measures of instructional experiences for the students in our study sample. However, we did know that all students were engaged in instructional programs intended to improve English skills, both in school and perhaps outside of school as well. Therefore, the time interval between test administrations served as a proxy for the amount of English language learning opportunities. The specific research question investigated was to what extent are observed patterns in changes in the test scores consistent with expected changes in language ability as a function of time elapsed between repeated observations. Our analysis thus considers whether larger score gains were exhibited by students with longer intervals between test administrations. The analysis rests on the assumption that, because of true learning, scores should increase as a function of the time interval between administrations. Therefore, a significantly positive relationship between interval and score gains would provide at least circumstantial evidence in support of the claim that the test is capable of reflecting changes in English language ability over time.

Method

Data

As mentioned previously, the study employed a longitudinal data collecton design. This design was made possible by the test developer's communication to test users that the *TOEFL Junior* test could be used to monitor growth in English language learning. As such, a sufficient number of schools and other educational units worldwide have been using the test to monitor student progress, giving rise to longitudinal data on individual students.

Data were retrieved from countries where the test was being administered between early 2012 and mid-2013. Beyond simply encouraging test users to retest students at approximately 6-month intervals, no control was imposed on the frequency of retesting, and indeed, many students took the test only once. Students who took the test multiple times were tested various numbers of times and at variable intervals between test administrations, in most cases according to schedules set by local education agencies or individual schools. Each data record contained a unique student identifier that permitted tracking of students across multiple test administrations.

The original dataset contained 83,595 students who took the test at least once and had complete score reporting data. The majority of these test takers (about 94%) took the test only once. The rest ($N = 4,606$) took the test more than once. Because we are interested in how student test performance changes over time, our analysis focuses only on students who took the test more than once. On the initial administration, these repeat test takers scored only slightly lower (about 0.02–0.03 test standard deviation units) than those who tested only once. This suggests that while repeat test takers were a relatively small fraction of the total examinee population, they were initially not very different in terms of English proficiency. A total of 15 countries and regions were represented in the sample of repeat test takers. About 65% of the examinees were from Korea. Table 9.1 summarizes the distribution of the number of test administrations in the analysis sample. As shown in the table, the vast majority of repeat test takers ($N = 4,205$) took the test exactly twice.

The data had a hierarchical structure. At the highest level, students were nested in countries. Within each country, the grouping structure was more complicated. Students were members of various groups that could influence

TABLE 9.1 Summary of Distribution of Number of Test Administrations in the Repeater Analysis Sample

Number of times test taken	Number of students	Percentage of repeater sample
2	4,205	91.3
3	252	5.5
4	72	1.6
5	75	1.6
6	1	0
7	1	0
All repeaters	4,606	100

their test scores, but we had imperfect information about those groupings. For example, our data did not have links of students to schools, teachers, or other educational programs. We also knew that groups of students were tested together at testing centers, but we did not have test center information in our data, so it was impossible for us to definitively identify groups of students who took the test at the same place at the same time. The grouping structures of the data are relevant to building statistical models that account for potential sources of variances in the test scores. Therefore, we needed to approximate the true grouping structures as accurately as possible given the available data.

The closest proxy we had to schooling experiences for individual students was the "client" in the database. Often, the client corresponded to an instructional provider (e.g., a school district, a school, or a learning center) and so could be thought of as proxy for links of students to schools. The client in many cases was responsible for arranging for the testing of a group of students on certain dates. Therefore, by identifying a group of repeat test takers who were linked to the same client and who took the tests on the exact same dates, we could be reasonably confident that those students were likely to have shared experiences, including similar instruction and similar testing conditions, which could be related to test scores. We refer to such a group of students as a *testing group*. In our analyses, we used testing groups as a grouping variable nested within countries. Students sharing a testing group had, by definition, the same amount of time elapsed between repeat test administrations. Across testing groups, testing schedules (and therefore the time elapsed between administrations) varied, providing the key variation that allowed us to examine the relationship between test scores changes and time between administrations.

Testing groups were intended to serve as a reasonable, but not perfect, proxy for relevant grouping structures. For example, not all clients corresponded to educational entities because individuals could choose to take the exam for reasons unrelated to group educational experiences, such as applying to some educational program that requires demonstrated English proficiency. In our data, 7.8% of the repeat test takers did not appear to be part of any testing group because the specific dates on which they were tested did not match other students in the data. We included these students in the analysis and assigned each one to a unique testing group. We also tested the sensitivity of our findings to the exclusion of these students.

Descriptive Analysis

For our analysis, we used scaled scores for each of the three test sections (language, listening, and reading) as well as the total score based on the three subscores. Scores ranged from 200–300 for each section and from 600–900 for the entire test. Different forms of the test are rigorously equated to ensure that scores from alternate forms are comparable. Results of the sensitivity analyses (see Gu,

158 Lin Gu, J. R. Lockwood, Donald E. Powers

Lockwood, & Powers, 2015 for details on the sensitivity analyses) indicated that our findings were not sensitive to the use of different forms.

We first grouped students by the total number of times they took the test and examined their average scores over the course of the repeated administrations. Figure 9.1 defines groups of students by how many times in total they took the test and then plots the average total scale score (vertical axis) against the average amount of time (in days) between administrations (horizontal axis). We use the term *interval* to refer to the number of calendar days between administrations. Two students who took the test more than five times were excluded from the plot. The figure demonstrates that, on average, students' scores increased over the course of the repeated administrations. The different groups generally show the same increasing trend upon retesting. Trends for the language, listening, and reading subscales (not shown) were similar. Given that more than 90% of the analysis sample took the test only twice, we focused the remainder of our analyses on only the first two test scores from all students in the analysis sample, regardless of how many times they took the test.

Figure 9.2 provides a histogram of interval between the first and second administrations for the analysis sample ($N = 4,606$). The distribution is multimodal, with the largest mode centered around 180 days. According to the *Handbook for the TOEFL Junior Standard Test* (ETS, n.d.), an interval of about

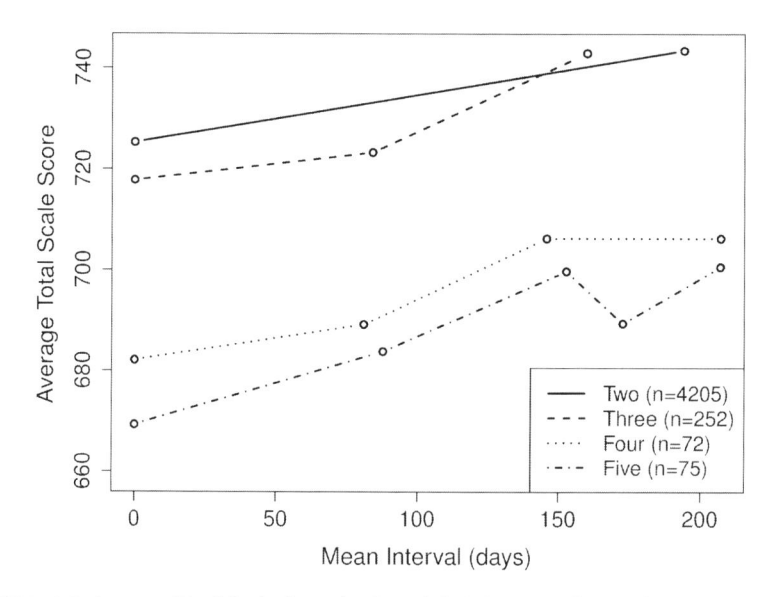

FIGURE 9.1 Average Total Scale Score by Test Administration for Students Who Took the Test Two, Three, Four, or Five Total Times

Note: Scores for repeat administrations are plotted by the average interval (in days) between administrations for each group of students.

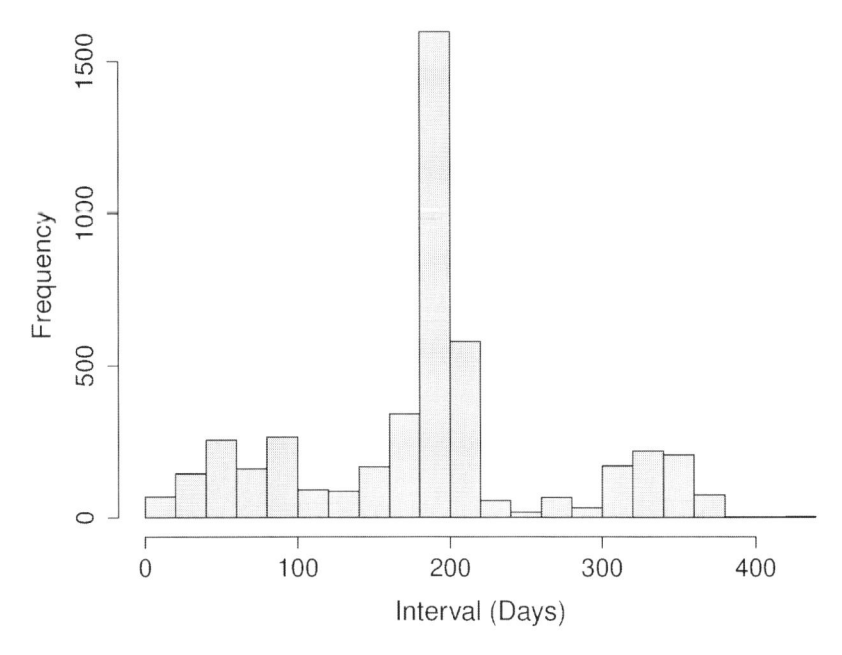

FIGURE 9.2 Histogram of Interval for the Analysis Sample

6 months between repeated test administrations is suggested for students taking a regular English curriculum to show gains in their scores. The largest mode in Figure 9.2 confirms that most students were retested at approximately 6-month intervals, but substantial variation is present around this mode.

Based on the distribution of time interval between testing and retesting, we decided to separate the students into four groups for descriptive purposes. Students in the first group ($N = 619$), the shortest interval group, had less than or equal to 75 days (about 2.5 months) between testing and retesting. Students in the second group ($N = 467$) had an interval between 75 and 150 days (approximately 2.5 to 5 months). Students in the third group ($N = 2,738$) had an interval between 150 and 250 days (approximately 5 to 8.3 months), and the longest interval group ($N = 782$) had more than 250 days between retesting. The cut points for these intervals approximately correspond to points that would separate the different modes evident in Figure 9.2. These groups were used only for the descriptive purposes presented now, and all further analyses we present use the continuous values of interval measured in days between administrations.

Table 9.2 provides the average scores for both test administrations and the average gains for each of the three groups defined by interval between administrations. The table indicates that score gains generally increased as the intervals lengthened for both the subscales and the total score. The longest interval group

TABLE 9.2 Mean First and Second Scores and Mean Gain for Each Outcome by Interval

Outcome	Interval	First	Second	Difference
Language	Interval <= 75	241.1	243.5	2.4
	75 < Interval <= 150	241.5	245.4	3.9
	150 < Interval <= 250	240.1	243.3	3.2
	Interval > 250	242.1	255.3	13.2
Listening	Interval <= 75	245.1	247.6	2.5
	75 < Interval <= 150	247.8	250.5	2.7
	150 < Interval <= 250	246.8	251.1	4.3
	Interval > 250	242.6	253.0	10.4
Reading	Interval <= 75	237.4	240.9	3.5
	75 < Interval <= 150	236.2	242.1	5.9
	150 < Interval <= 250	234.7	242.2	7.5
	Interval > 250	242.7	253.9	11.2
Total	Interval <= 75	723.5	732.0	8.4
	75 < Interval <= 150	725.5	738.0	12.5
	150 < Interval <= 250	721.6	736.6	15.0
	Interval > 250	727.4	762.2	34.8

had the largest score gains, whereas the shortest interval group had the smallest score gains. This was probably due to the fact that longer intervals would allow more opportunties for students to learn compared to shorter intervals.

An alternative display of the relation of average gains to between-test interval is provided in Figure 9.3, where interval is treated as a continuous variable. Figure 9.3 presents estimated smoothed conditional mean of the first and second administration scores as a function of interval. The horizontal axis in each frame of the plot is the interval between testings, and the vertical axis is scaled test score. A separate frame is shown for each section score. The solid curve in each frame is the estimated mean score on the first test administration as a function of interval, whereas the dashed curve is the estimated mean score on the second test administration as a function of interval.

As shown in Figure 9.3, the distance between the dashed and solid curves, representing average score gains, tends to increase as the interval increases. Generally, the effect is modestly evident from the low end of the interval distribution to the middle and very evident at the higher end of the interval distribution, consistent with Table 9.2, in which interval was treated as a categorical variable. The two curves start to diverge at an interval of about 200 days, and this pattern is consistent for all subtests.

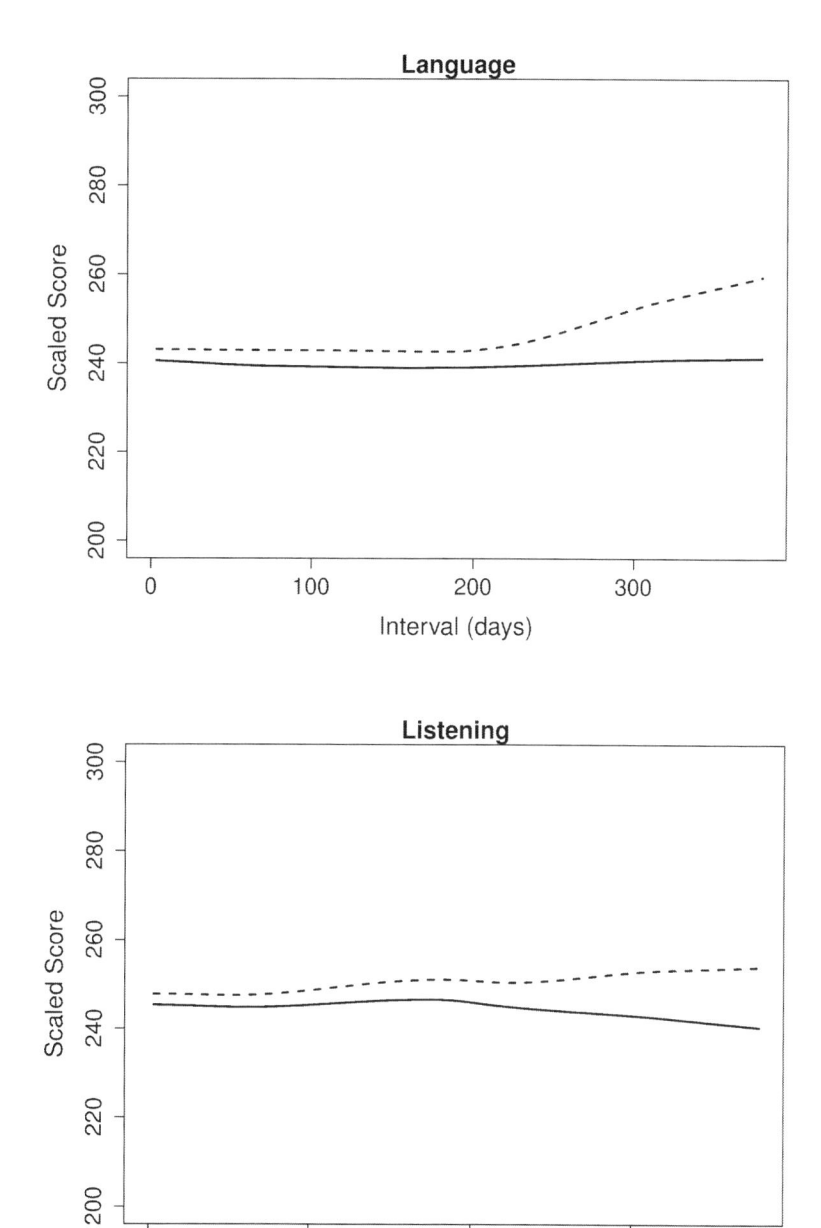

FIGURE 9.3 Smoothed Trends of Initial Score (Solid Line) and Second Administration Score (Dashed Line) as a Function of Interval, Separately for Each Skill Area and the Total

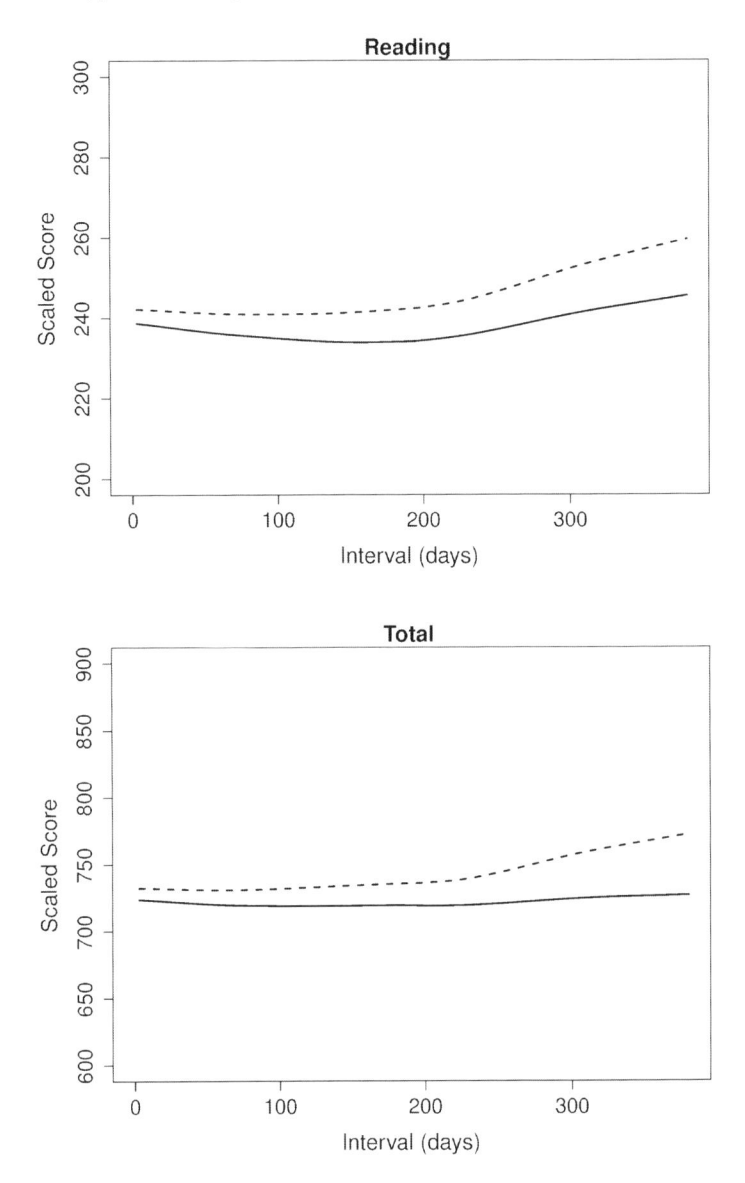

FIGURE 9.3 (Continued)

Multilevel Models (MLM)

The descriptive information is consistent with the hypothesis that the test is sensitive to changes in English ability as a function of interval. We also used multilevel models (MLM; Pinheiro & Bates, 2000; Raudenbush & Bryk, 2002) to estimate the relationship between interval and student gains. The main motivation for conducting MLM analyses was to quantify the relationship between interval and gains in a way that would not be distorted by potential differences in student populations across countries and to obtain a valid test of statistical significance of this relationship. Our MLM is designed to achieve both of these goals. We first present what we call the *base model* and then present what we call the *alternative model*, which we use to address a particular potential source of bias in the base model.

Base Model for Student Gains

Our base model for student gains is

$$(Y_{i2} - Y_{i1}) = \mu_{j(i)} + \beta \, INTERVAL_i + \theta_{g(i)} + \varepsilon_i \quad \text{(Model 1)}$$

where $(Y_{i2} - Y_{i1})$ is the gain score for student i on whatever outcome is being modeled (language, listening, reading, or total scores); $\mu_{j(i)}$ is a dummy variable for the country j in which each student i is nested; $\theta_{g(i)}$ is a random effect for the testing group g for student i assumed to be mean zero, normally distributed, and independent across testing groups g with common variance; and ε_i is a residual error assumed to be mean zero, normally distributed, and independent across students with common variance. INTERVAL refers to the number of calendar days between the first and second administrations. The effect of interest is the coefficient on interval.

All other terms in the model are included only to improve the estimate of the coefficient on interval and to get an appropriate measure of uncertainty for this estimate. We include dummy variables in the model for individual countries to prevent country differences from biasing our estimated relationship between interval and gains. We include random effects in the model for testing groups to account for residual clustering of gains for students sharing educational experiences. Additional details on the justifications for these choices are provided in Gu et al. (2015).

Our model assumes a linear relationship between interval and gains within countries. It is reasonable to question whether a nonlinear relationship would be more appropriate. We tested our model against more complicated alternatives that allowed the relationship to be nonlinear, and the linear specification was preferred by standard model comparison criteria including a likelihood ratio test, the Akaike information criterion, and the Bayesian information criterion (Pinheiro & Bates, 2000). The linear specification is also supported by a graphical analysis. Figure 9.4 provides a scatterplot of total gains versus interval where both quantities are centered by their respective country means. This represents the relationship between total gains and interval within countries, aligning closely to how Model 1 identifies the effect of interval through the use of country dummy variables. The black line is the linear fit, whereas the black dashed curve

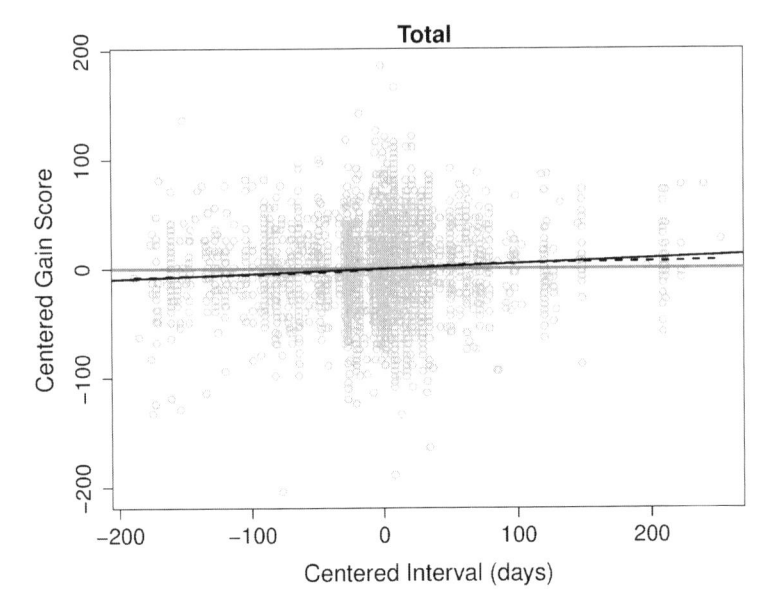

FIGURE 9.4 Scatterplot of Total Score Gain Versus Interval Where Both Are Centered Around Their Respective Country Means

Note: The black solid line is the best linear fit, and the black dashed line is a smooth regression function allowing for nonlinearity. The horizontal gray line at 0 is provided for reference.

is a nonparametric smooth regression flexible enough to capture nonlinearity if it existed. The fact that these two curves nearly coincide supports the assumption that the relationship between gains and interval within country is well approximated by the linear specification of Model 1.

Our model also assumes a common linear relationship across countries. It is reasonable to question whether allowing the slope relating interval to gains varies across countries. We tested such a model against our simpler alternative, and again, our model was preferred by standard model comparison criteria.

Alternative Model for Student Gains

A major threat to validity of the analysis is that the data are purely observational (nonexperimental) in nature. That is, there was no experimental manipulation of the primary independent variable, interval between testing. Furthermore, we had only limited information about how interval was determined. For students with observed testing schedules that did not suggest obvious membership in a group testing situation, we could not discount the possibility that interval was in part determined by initial scores or by other student attributes that may have been related to outcomes. More generally, even for testing groups that had a shared testing schedule, we did not know the basis for the schedule. Although it is reasonable to assume that the interval between tests was often chosen by the educational entity providing instruction, we do not know what information was used in that decision. For example, we do not know whether the decision about when to retest was made prior to any testing or whether it was in part based on students' initial performance. The analyses using gain scores are unaffected by any relationship between interval and unobserved student characteristics that are constant across time and related to scores because the differencing used to calculate gains would negate the impact of those characteristics. On the other hand, if interval is in any way influenced by the observed initial scores of either individual students or groups of students, an analysis based on Model 1 is potentially biased. In this case, a better option would be to augment Model 1 with additional covariates of the initial total scores of both the individual students and their testing groups. The use of total scores as covariates reflects the likelihood that if decisions about when to do follow-up testing are influenced by initial scores, those decisions are most likely to be based on overall performance. The alternative model, Model 2, is

$$(Y_{i2} - Y_{i1}) = \mu_{j(i)} + \beta\ INTERVAL_i + \gamma X_{i1} + \delta \overline{X}_{g(i)1} + \theta_{g(i)} + \varepsilon_i.\quad \text{(Model 2)}$$

Here X_{i1} is the first administration total scale score for student i, and $\overline{X}_{g(i)1}$ is the average first administration total scale score for students in testing group g. All other terms are defined analogously to Model 1.

We fit both Model 1 and Model 2 using the routine *lmer* in R (R Development Core Team, 2007) designed for estimating mixed effects regression models. The two models were fit separately to each of the three subscores and the total score.

Results

Table 9.3 presents estimates of the coefficent on interval for the different outcomes using the base model (Model 1). The coefficients are for interval scaled in days, so that a coefficient of, for example, 0.03 represents an average score gain of 3 points on the *TOEFL Junior* total scaled score range per 100 days of interval, or about 11 points for a year. The estimated coefficient is positive for

TABLE 9.3 Summary of Results of Model 1 of the Effect of Interval on Gains

Outcome	Estimate	SE	t-stat.	p-value
Language gain	0.013	0.005	2.76	0.006
Listening gain	0.010	0.006	1.77	0.076
Reading gain	0.022	0.007	3.23	0.001
Total gain	0.045	0.012	3.69	<0.001

TABLE 9.4 Summary of Results of Model 2 of the Effect of Interval on Gains

Outcome	Estimate	SE	t-stat.	p-value
Language gain	0.012	0.005	2.41	0.016
Listening gain	0.006	0.006	0.95	0.343
Reading gain	0.013	0.007	1.90	0.057
Total gain	0.030	0.012	2.39	0.017

all outcomes and is statisticially significant at the 0.05 level[2] for all outcomes except listening. Because most of our repeat test takers were located in a foreign language environment, we speculate that limited exposure to aural input in English could have hindered listening skill development. The estimated relationship of interval to the total score gain is 0.045 points per day, or about 16.4 points per year. The standard deviation of the total score in the analysis sample in the second administration is about 69 points. Thus, the estimated effect corresponds to an increase of 0.24 standard deviation units over a 1-year interval. This magnitude of change over 1 year is consistent with findings on annual growth on numerous standardized reading exams used in the United States. As reported by Bloom et al. (2008), annual growth over Grades 6–9, which roughly corresponds to the median age of students in our sample of 13 years, tends to be about 0.24 standard deviations per year. We stipulate that because the average interval in our data is much less than a full year, these extrapolations to annual effects rely heavily on our linear model specification and should be interpreted cautiously. We also stipulate that the comparison to similarly-aged English-speaking students in the United States is limited due to the obvious differences between those students and the students in our sample.

Results of the alternative model (Model 2) are summarized in Table 9.4, which is analogous to Table 9.3. The results are similar to those from Model 1, although there is some evidence of the estimated effects being smaller. For the total score, the estimated coefficient on interval is reduced from 0.045 in Model 1 to 0.03 in Model 2, corresponding to a standardized effect size of 0.16 standard deviation units. The reduction in the estimated effects suggests that it is possible that part of the relationship between interval and gains reflects selection of how long to wait to retest based on the initial score. The results shown in Table 9.3 and Table 9.4 are robust to a number of sensitivity analyses involving decisions about the model and analysis sample. The details on each sensitivity analysis are provided in Gu et al.'s report (2015).

Discussion

In this chapter, we presented a validation study to examine the claim that the *TOEFL Junior* Standard test can serve to measure young learners' progress in learning English as a foreign language. We described how we attempted to evaluate the growth by carefully examining the limitations of the data and employing alternative solutions to our analyses. We found that, on average, repeat test takers scored higher on the second administration and that the longer the interval between testing was, the greater the score gain was. The estimated relationship ranged from 0.16 to 0.24 standard deviation units of growth per year depending on the model specification. These values are consistent with annual reading achievement growth rates for similarly aged students in the United States.

We considered the following three plausible explanations for our findings: (a) observed increases were indicative of improved ability in English resulting from learning, (b) increases resulted simply from greater familiarity with the test as a result of having taken it previously (retesting effects), and (c) the relationships were due to inadequacies of our approach of using a nonexperimental proxy for English learning opportunities.

With respect to retesting effects, it seems implausible that the observed pattern of increases was due primarily to test takers having gained familiarity with the test by having taken it previously. Test practice effects are typically observed more often for tests that employ complex directions and item formats (see, for example, Kulik, Kulik, & Bangert, 1984; Powers, 1986). Neither of these qualities is characteristic of the *TOEFL Junior* Standard test. Moreover, because the effects of becoming familiar with a test as a result of having taken it in the past are likely to decrease over time, the longer the interval between retesting is, the less the impact on score increase is likely to be. In our analysis, we found a positive relationship between increase in test score and length of time between retesting, which is inconsistent with score increases being due simply to having taken the test previously.

Two distinct threats arise from our use of a nonexperimental proxy (interval) for English language learning. The first is that because interval was not experimentally assigned, we cannot rule out that the observed relationship between interval and gains is spurious. To the extent that any spurious relationship is driven by students with lower initial scores waiting longer to be retested, Model 2 should be effective in mitigating the bias. However, other forms of spurious relationship are possible, and those would present a source of bias in our findings. The fact that the estimated effects in Model 2 are generally smaller than those in Model 1 leaves open the possibility that such biases might exist. While we can never rule out such scenarios, we can at least be confident that the results of testing both models provided convincing evidence in support of the relationship between interval and gains and that our results are robust to a wide array of sensitivity analyses that were conducted to address potential confounding factors within the limits of the available data.

The second threat arising from our use of interval as the proxy would exist even if interval were randomly assigned and cannot easily be tested given our data. We have assumed that because students in the sample are generally participating in English instruction, interval can be treated as a proxy for English learning opportunities. However, interval serves as a proxy for all maturation processes, not just English learning. We cannot therefore rule out the possibility that gains are due, in addition to language learning, to growth in cognitive or behavioral attributes (e.g., ability to concentrate). Interval may also proxy for test preparation occurring outside the context of the formal test administrations. While we have no direct evidence that the students in our sample were engaging in test preparation, opportunities for that do exist given that the test is part of the *TOEFL*® family of assessments and that some tests in the *TOEFL* family have a high-stakes nature. However, the *TOEFL Junior* Standard test for the students in our sample has only low-to-medium-stakes implications for either individuals or programs, so the possibility that the results are due solely to narrow test practice seems unlikely. The low-to-medium stakes of the test might also explain why our estimate of the annual growth is perhaps smaller than some people might expect. It is likely that in our sample, the test was primarily being used for routine monitoring of student performance in education settings rather than for any high-stakes decisions about individual students, and so it is possible that observed growth may be larger in settings where students were highly motivated to improve performance. In any case, without tying growth in test scores directly to quality and quantity of English and instruction, and demonstrating that more and better instruction produces larger gains, our evidence remains indirect.

However, the simplest explanation for our findings is that observed test score increases are due, at least in part, to real changes in the target ability as a result of English language learning. The magnitude of score increases is related in anticipated ways to the length of interval between retesting, which could be reasonably considered as a proxy for English language learning. We acknowledge the limitation of using this proxy to represent the amount of learning undertaken by participating students over the course of repeated test administrations. In order to fully capture the richness and complexity of learning, future studies should collect test-taker backgound information (e.g., the type of instruction, the type of curricula, language learning inside and outside of classroom, immersion experience, and motivation, etc.) and model these as additional covariates in the analysis. Such information could also allow more accurate accounting of shared experiences of groups of students, which would improve the modeling. What also needs to be acknowledged is that slightly more than half of the study sample came from a single country. This factor may limit the extent to which the study results can be generalized to the entire target test-taking population, that is, young English language learners worldwide.

Despite the aforementioned study limitations, we believe that the current study constitutes an initial step in providing evidence that the *TOEFL Junior* Standard test can reflect changes in language ability that result from learning. The findings therefore provide initial support for the claim that the test can be used to monitor growth for young English language learners. Inarguably, more research is needed to closely examine various contextual factors that may influence young English language learners' growth in their English language proficiency measured by a standardized assessment such as the *TOEFL Junior* test. We hope that analytic techniques employed in our study could be utilized in future research. Finally, the findings also lay open the possibility that score reports can be enhanced by incorporating information on score change in order to provide a historical account for test takers who take the test multiple times.

Notes

1 This chapter is a shortened version of a previously published report: Gu, L., Lockwood, J., & Powers, D. E. (2015). *Evaluating the TOEFL Junior® standard test as a measure of progress for young English language learners* (Research Report No. RR-15–22). Princeton, NJ: Educational Testing Service.
2 Across Tables 3 and 4, we conducted eight hypothesis tests, five of which are significant at level 0.05. To address concerns about multiple testing, we also applied the Benjamini-Hochberg procedure as recommended by the What Works Clearinghouse (2014), using a false discovery rate of 0.05. All five of the originally statistically significant findings are still statistically significant after applying this procedure.

References

American Educational Research Association, American Psychological Association, & National Council on Measurement in Education. (2014). *Standards for educational and psychological testing.* Washington, DC: American Educational Research Association.

Bachman, L. F., & Palmer, A. S. (2010). *Language assessment practice: Developing language assessments and justifying their use in the real world.* Oxford, England: Oxford University Press.

Batstone, R. (2002). Contexts of engagement: A discourse perspective on "intake" and "pushed output". *System, 30,* 1–14.

Bloom, H. S., Hill, C. J., Black, A. R., & Lipsey, M. W. (2008). Performance trajectories and performance gaps as achievement effect-size benchmarks for educational interventions. *MDRC Working Papers on Research Methodology.* Available from http://www.mdrc.org/sites/default/files/full_473.pdf

Carver, R. P. (1974). Two dimensions of tests: Psychometric and edumetric. *American Psychologist, 29,* 512–518.

Chapelle, A. A., Enright, M. K., & Jamieson, J. M. (2008). Test score interpretation and use. In C. A. Chapelle, M. K. Enright, & J. M. Jamieson (Eds.), *Building a validity argument for the test of English as a foreign language* (pp. 1–25). New York, NY: Routledge.

Educational Testing Service. (n.d.). *Handbook for the TOEFL® Junior™ Standard test.* Available from http://www.ets.org/s/toefl_junior/pdf/toefl_junior_student_handbook.pdf

Gu, L., Lockwood, J. R., & Powers, D. E. (2015). Evaluting the TOEFL Junior Standard test as a measure of progress for young English language learners (Research Report ETS RR-15–22). Princeton NJ: Educational Testing Service.

Kane, M. T. (2006). Validation. In R. L. Brennan (Ed.), *Educational measurement* (4th ed., pp. 17–64). Washington, DC: American Council on Education & Praeger.

Kulik, J. A., Kulik, C. C., & Bangert, R. L. (1984). Effects of practice on aptitude and achievement scores. *American Educational Research Journal, 21,* 435–447.

Messick, S. (1989). Validity. In R. L. Linn (Ed.), *Educational measurement* (3rd ed., pp. 13–103). New York, NY: American Council on Education & Macmillan.

Pinheiro, J. C., & Bates, D. M. (2000). *Mixed-effects models in S and S-PLUS.* New York, NY: Springer.

Powers, D. E. (1986). Relations of test item characteristics to test preparation/test practice effects. *Psychological Bulletin, 100,* 67–77.

Raudenbush, S. W., & Bryk, A. S. (2002). *Hierarchical linear models: Applications and data analysis methods* (2nd ed.). Newbury Park, CA: Sage.

R Development Core Team. (2007). *R: A language and environment for statistical computing.* Vienna, Austria: R Foundation for Statistical Computing.

So, Y., Wolf, M. K., Hauck, M. C., Mollaun, P., Rybinski, P., Tumposky, D., & Wang, L. (2017). *TOEFL Junior®* design framework. In M. K. Wolf & Y. G. Butler (Eds.), *English language proficiency assessments for young learners.* New York, NY: Routledge.

What Works Clearinghouse. (2014). *Procedures and standards handbook version 3.0.* Washington, DC: U.S. Department of Education.

Willett, J. B. (1994). Measurement of change. In T. Husen & T. N. Postlethwaite (Eds.), *The international encyclopedia of education* (2nd ed., pp. 671–678). Oxford, UK: Pergamon Press.

10
COMPARING THE PERFORMANCE OF YOUNG ENGLISH LANGUAGE LEARNERS AND NATIVE ENGLISH SPEAKERS ON SPEAKING ASSESSMENT TASKS

Mikyung Kim Wolf, Alexis A. Lopez, Saerhim Oh, and Fred S. Tsutagawa

In the United States, all K-12 public schools are required to identify English learner (EL)[1] students whose limited English language ability may impede their access to content learning delivered in English (Every Student Succeeds Act, 2015). By identifying EL students and measuring their current English language proficiency level, schools endeavor to provide appropriate instruction and services to support their EL students' academic success. The EL identification procedure begins when students are first enrolled in a school district, predominantly in kindergarten. Typically, a home language survey is sent to the parents/guardians of children, asking for the primary language spoken with children at home. If the survey response indicates that the child's home language is something other than English, she or he then takes an English language proficiency (ELP) assessment (Bailey & Kelly, 2013; Wolf et al., 2008).

While initial ELP "screener" assessments are administered to all newcomers in Grades K-12 whose home language is not English, the majority of test takers are in the lower grades. For example, according to a recent report by the California Department of Education on that state's initial ELP screener assessment for the 2014–2015 school year (http://celdt.cde.ca.gov/), kindergartners constituted 64% of the total test takers (186, 269 out of 292,134 students). Initial ELP screener assessments used by schools for EL identification purposes in the United States are mainly standardized assessments measuring listening, reading, speaking, and writing skills (Cook & Linquanti, 2015; Wolf et al., 2008). For students in kindergarten and Grade 1, oral proficiency generally receives more weight than in other grades in the calculation of overall ELP scores. This is attributed largely to the fact that all children, regardless of their home language, begin to formally learn literacy skills only when they start attending school.

Inarguably, administering standardized ELP assessments for young children is a challenging task. Younger primary-grade students, for example, may not be familiar with standardized testing practices. This may lead to insufficient or inadequate elicitation of these students' English language knowledge, skills, and abilities. Thus, making adequate inferences about the ELP of young children who are developing both their first language (L1) and their second language (L2) requires a carefully designed ELP assessment with age-appropriate tasks presented by highly qualified administrators (Lopez, Pooler, & Linquanti, 2016; National Association for the Education of Young Children, 2005; Wolf et al., 2016).

To address this critical need for appropriate ELP assessments for EL identification purposes, Educational Testing Service (ETS) launched a large-scale project in 2011, utilizing effective design principles in the development of technology-enhanced ELP screener assessments for ELs in K–12 schools (the TELP project, for short). The TELP project undertook a series of prototyping studies in which a set of design principles[2] were empirically investigated with prototype tasks integrating various technology-enhanced features (e.g., multimedia, animation, touch-screen interactivity, immediate feedback, and embedded scaffolding functions). One key area of investigation was how to design authentic and interesting tasks to increase young children's engagement and to elicit their speech samples appropriately for the targeted construct in a standardized ELP assessment setting. A second critical area of inquiry was investigating procedures for making adequate decisions about EL identification based on young children's oral proficiency.

This chapter reports on an empirical study that was conducted with a small sample of young EL and non-EL[3] students who participated in one of the prototyping studies undertaken as part of the TELP project. The purpose of the study was two-fold. First, we aimed to examine performance differences between the young EL and non-EL students on speaking tasks. Considering that young children, including native speakers of English in Grades K–2, are still developing their oral proficiency in English, it was critical to understand the performance patterns of the K–2 population in general and to determine what linguistic features distinguish the speaking performances of ELs from those of non-ELs. Second, we attempted to identify important design principles for the creation of speaking tasks for young children in standardized assessment settings.

In this chapter, we first provide a brief description of some of the characteristics of young children that should be considered when designing assessment tasks. Then, we describe the speaking tasks (*retelling* and *describing* tasks) we developed for the project along with the current study design. We report and discuss the major findings of the comparative analyses between the linguistic performances of EL and non-EL students, focusing on the speaking tasks. We conclude with a discussion of the implications of these findings for developing and administering speaking tasks for young children in the context of ELP assessment for EL identification purposes.

Consideration of Young Children's Characteristics in Assessment Task Design

As noted earlier, the majority of test takers for the initial ELP screener assessments in the United States are students in primary grades (K–2, aged 5 to 7), with kindergarten being the greatest. These test takers vary in respect to their level of English language acquisition and their English language developmental pathways. Most kindergartners, who comprise the majority of the target test-taker population, begin their schooling without any formal English language education. Students who arrive as newcomers to the U.S., whether in kindergarten or later on, may also have limited exposure to North American culture. Thus, when developing initial ELP screener assessment tasks for young students, both age-related factors and students' current level of cultural experience and knowledge need to be considered carefully.

With respect to age-related factors, Bailey, Heritage, and Butler (2014) describe the very different developmental, linguistic, and educational (i.e., curricular) challenges faced by students in different age groups. In general, compared with older learners, young children (a) take more time to process input cognitively, (b) have more limitations in available working memory, and (c) are more likely to lose focus and concentration in a testing situation. They also tend to experience testing fatigue more quickly and feel more anxiety and uneasiness in unfamiliar situations.

Prior literature also stresses that many developmental and contextual factors need to be considered when designing assessments for young students (e.g., Bailey et al., 2014; Espinosa, 2010; Hasselgreen, 2005; McKay, 2006; National Association for the Education of Young Children, 2005; Rea-Dickins & Rixon, 1997). Assessment task content should be appropriate in terms of a child's cognitive ability level, so test items must be contextualized, with greater contextualization necessary for younger students. The topics selected for inclusion in test content should also be age-appropriate. To this end, Inbar-Lourie and Shohamy (2009) propose an assessment approach that integrates assessment tasks with learning activities that actually occur in the classrooms of young learners in order to embed meaningful language use and relevant content into assessment. Another factor to consider in test development is young students' short attention span. Hasselgreen (2005) states that devising interesting assessment tasks is particularly important for young learners given their limited attention span.

Considering these characteristics of young students, the prototype tasks created by the TELP project team were designed to be interesting and relevant for the target test-taker population. In order to increase the assessment tasks' potential to engage learners, the tasks were embedded in an immersive environment designed to make test takers feel that they are interacting with the characters from the task stimuli (e.g., interacting with a teacher, peer, or classmates). Some tasks also included animation and immediate feedback. One of the underlying premises of the TELP project was that well-designed tasks increase young students' engagement while completing assessments, thereby eliciting better language samples that support more adequate inferences about the test takers' language abilities.

Because the TELP prototype tasks were designed to distinguish between EL and non-EL students, the project paid special attention to collecting the performances of both native English speakers and ELs. Very little research is available to shed light on the linguistic profiles of young students' English language speaking and writing performance. While Crowhurst (1990) provides a brief qualitative analysis of general performance features of persuasive composition by native English-speaking students between the ages of 10 and 12 (i.e., students in Grades 5–7), detailed lexical, syntactic, and discourse analyses were not performed. More recently, Pérez-Paredes and Sánchez-Tornel (2014) examined the use of general adverbs by nonnative speakers (NNSs) in Grades 5, 6, 9, and 10 in the International Corpus of Crosslinguistic Interlanguage (ICCI), but other linguistic features were not examined. Most noticeably absent are comparative studies of the language produced by nonnative and native English-speaking young students.

In contrast, many studies reporting detailed analyses of lexico-grammatical and discourse features have been conducted to illuminate the linguistic profiles of adult language learners at different proficiency levels and developmental stages (e.g., Biber & Gray, 2013; Friginal, Li, & Weigle, 2014; Jarvis, Grant, Bikowski, & Ferris, 2003; Knoch, Macqueen, & O'Hagan, 2014). This line of research is valuable not only for developing appropriate instructional materials for language learners but also for validating the assessment tasks and scoring rubrics.

As little empirical research is publicly available to compare the linguistic profiles of young EL and non-EL students' speaking performances, the present study was undertaken to begin to fill this important gap in the literature by analyzing the performances of EL and non-EL students on the TELP prototype tasks. In so doing, we aimed to offer useful insights into appropriate performance criteria for identifying young EL students.

Method

We employed a cognitive laboratory (think-aloud) method in order to examine closely a small sample of young students' cognitive processes while completing a sample of tasks. The students participated in one-on-one cognitive labs in which an interviewer administered the assessment, including the retelling and descriptive speaking tasks of interest in this study, and then interviewed the student based on a standardized protocol. Students' verbal reports including their responses to the tasks were the primary source of the data for the study.

Participants

The participants of this study were 64 EL students and 37 non-EL students in Grades K–2 (around 5 to 8 years of age) from three elementary schools in New Jersey. At the time of the study, the students had already been classified as ELs or as non-ELs by their respective schools based on their standardized ELP

TABLE 10.1 The Number of Study Participants

Grade	EL status		Gender		Total
	EL	Non-EL	Girls	Boys	
K	28	20	26	22	48
1	15	7	9	13	22
2	20	9	16	13	29
Total	63	36	51	48	99

assessments. Table 10.1 summarizes the student participants by grade, EL status, and gender.

Prototype Assessment Tasks

The TELP project's prototype tasks were designed with scenario-based assessment features for the purpose of increasing student engagement during the assessment (see Shore, Wolf, O'Reilly, & Sabatini, 2017 in this volume for more details about scenario-based assessments). The tasks were designed to be delivered over a desktop or tablet computer. In the scenario chosen for Grades K–2, the test taker views an animation where a "teacher" first greets her or him at a school. The test taker then proceeds to complete assessment tasks within the context of various school activities such as going to a library, reading books, observing an experiment, listening to a teacher's instructions in an art class, and participating in a small group discussion. Figure 10.1 displays sample screen shots of this school-based scenario where the assessment tasks were embedded.

In this chapter, we present the results from a listening task scenario called "School Day" and three speaking tasks called "Playground," "Mixing Paint," and "Melting Ice." The School Day scenario includes 34 listening comprehension and receptive vocabulary items for Grade K, with an additional 24 items (a total of 58 items) for Grades 1–2. The format for School Day was selected-response/multiple-choice type items. The Playground speaking task was also given to all of the Grade K–2 students. On the other hand, the Mixing Paint task was designed solely for Grade K, whereas the Melting Ice task was designed for Grades 1 and 2 after considering the appropriateness of the content for these specific grade levels. More details about each speaking task are included below.

Retelling: The Playground Task for Grades K–2

This task was designed to measure students' ability to retell a story using the provided pictures. In the task, students followed along in a picture book while listening to a story about a boy who helped some workers build a new playground. Then students were asked to tell the story in their own words, while looking at the four pictures depicting the major events in the story (see Figure 10.2).

FIGURE 10.1 Sample Screenshots of Scenario-based Prototype Tasks for Grades K–2

Source: Copyright 2013 by Educational Testing Service. Reprinted with permission of Educational Testing Service.

FIGURE 10.2 A Screenshot of the Playground Task for Grades K–2

Source: Copyright 2013 by Educational Testing Service. Reprinted with permission of Educational Testing Service.

Describing: The Mixing Paint Task for Grade K and the Melting Ice Task for Grades 1–2

The Mixing Paint and Melting Ice tasks were designed to measure the students' ability to describe a past event based on what they observed. The tasks included an animation in which a teacher explains either the creation of a new color by mixing two colors together (i.e., the Mixing Paint task) or the sequence of what happens when ice melts during an experiment (i.e., the Melting Ice task). For each of these tasks, a set of scaffolding questions (as items) was embedded as a design feature to better elicit young children's responses. That is, instead of asking the students to describe the event in the animation all at once, a set of guiding questions was asked first (i.e., shorter, more focused questions asking what materials the teacher used, what happened first, what happened next, what happened at the end, etc.). The questions were intended to provide scaffolding for young children by directing them to organize the event into a sequence of discrete steps or smaller segments. After these questions, the students were asked to describe the entire event to a classmate who was late for the class. Figure 10.3 displays sample screenshots from the Mixing Paint and Melting Ice tasks.

Linguistic Analysis Coding Scheme

In order to closely examine differences in the linguistic patterns of the spoken performances between the EL and non-EL students, we undertook two approaches: (1) applying an analytic rubric to score student performance at the lexical, syntactic, and discourse levels; and (2) identifying specific types of linguistic errors. It should be noted that although we use the term "errors" following conventions

FIGURE 10.3 Sample Screenshots From the Mixing Paint (Top) and Melting Ice (Bottom) Tasks

Source: Copyright 2013 by Educational Testing Service. Reprinted with permission of Educational Testing Service.

TABLE 10.2 Analytic Scoring Rubric

Categories	Score scale
Lexical	0: no response 1: beginning (limited, inappropriate word choices) 2: developing (some word choice errors) 3: proficient (almost no word choice errors, appropriate and diverse word choices)
Syntactic	0: no response 1: beginning (frequent syntactical errors, often interfere with meaning) 2: developing (some errors, sometimes interfere with meaning) 3: proficient (few errors, do not interfere with meaning)
Discourse	0: no response 1: beginning (frequent problems with cohesive devices, inaccurate use of pronouns and transitional words, limited coherence in response) 2: developing: (some problems with cohesive devices, mostly coherent response) 3: proficient (almost no problems with cohesive devices, coherent response)

for the error analysis techniques that were employed, the results can also be interpreted as indicators of various stages of student language development.

Table 10.2 presents our analytic rubric. The lexical category focused on the appropriateness and variety of the words used. The syntactic category included the accurate usage of syntactic structures and the degree to which syntactic errors may have interfered with the expression of intended meanings. The discourse category focused on appropriate use of such cohesive devices as pronouns and transitional words.

To identify specific types of linguistic errors in the students' performances, we developed a coding scheme using an inductive approach. That is, upon reviewing all the participating students' responses, we identified common error types noted in the sample. We also reviewed past research on the linguistic analysis of writing responses and selected categories that were commonly studied previously (e.g., Ferris, 2006; Friginal, Li, & Weigle, 2014). Table 10.3 provides a list of the error type codes used in this study. Additionally, we included one content-related category called "logic," as errors of this type were found to be prevalent in our preliminary analysis of student responses.

Procedure and Analysis

The students completed the tasks on tablet computers (i.e., iPads). Each student participated in a cognitive lab in which a trained researcher interviewed the student following an interview protocol. Each session lasted approximately 30 minutes. All of the student responses to the prototype tasks and the corresponding interviews were audio recorded and later transcribed.

Student listening items were machine-scored, and the speaking responses were scored on a four-point (0 to 3) holistic scoring rubric as well as an analytic

TABLE 10.3 Error Analysis Categories and Definitions

Categories	Definition
Word choice	Vocabulary-related errors including inaccurate or inappropriate word choices
Plural forms	Errors related to the use of plural nouns
Subject-verb agreement	Subject-verb agreement errors
Verb tenses	Verb tense-related errors including inconsistent use of past tense
Prepositions	Preposition-related errors including inaccurate preposition choice or missing preposition
Articles	Errors related to the use of articles or not using an article when needed
Missing subject	A sentence with a missing subject
Missing verb	A sentence with a missing verb
Missing object	A sentence with a missing object
Pronoun use	Errors related to pronouns as a discourse error (e.g., unclear reference to antecedent)
Transitions	No transition words are used
Content-logic	The retell/description is incomplete or is missing major events; the story/description is not logical partly due to missing events or missing transitional words; telegraphic/fragmented story-telling

rubric (shown in Table 10.2) by a pair of trained raters. The holistic rubric focused on the completeness of the response, appropriateness of the content, and overall linguistic accuracy of the response (see Appendix 10.1 for the holistic rubric).

The raters were four researchers with backgrounds in applied linguistics and ESL/EFL teaching. They also conducted error analyses of the student spoken responses using the established coding scheme (shown in Table 10.3). Inter-rater reliability was examined. Approximately 88% exact agreement was achieved on average across all of the categories. Discrepancies in scores and codings were resolved through discussions among all four researchers to reach consensus scores. The descriptive statistics of the consensus scores and codings were compared between EL and non-EL students, and statistical testing of mean differences of the scores between EL and non-EL students was performed by conducting t-tests and effect size calculations. Effect sizes for the score differences were computed using Cliff's δ for speaking tasks. Cliff's δ was found to be robust for ordinal data (Cliff, 1996; Hess & Kromrey, 2004). Cliff's δ, ranging from -1 to 1, indicates "the degree of overlap between the two distributions of scores" (Hess & Kromrey, 2004, p. 6). The value of 0 means that there is no difference of the scores (or observations) between the two groups, whereas the value of 1 or −1 indicates that all the scores of one group are higher than those in the other group. The significance testing results and effect sizes are reported in the results section wherever appropriate.

Results and Discussion

Performance on the Listening Items

Table 10.4 presents the results of the EL and non-EL students' performances on the School Day items which assessed their basic listening comprehension and vocabulary knowledge. The mean scores between the two groups were very similar, with no statistically significant differences observed ($t = -1.26$, $p = .22$, for Grade K; $t = 1.04$, $p = .31$, for Grades 1–2). The results indicate that the sample EL and non-EL participants in this study performed similarly on the listening assessment that contained receptive vocabulary items. The mean scores of the Grades 1–2 students in both groups also indicate a near ceiling effect showing that the listening items were relatively easy for these participants in the study.

Performance on the Speaking Tasks

For the purpose of illustrating the patterns observed in student performances on the *retelling* and *describing* tasks, we present the results graphically. Figure 10.4 shows the average scores of the kindergarten EL and non-EL students' performances on the Playground and Mixing Paint tasks based on the holistic and analytic rubrics. "Retell" in Figure 10.4 indicates the average holistic scores for the task, whereas the other three categories represent the analytic scores. Overall, as seen in the average holistic and analytic scores, non-EL students performed better than EL students on the Playground task with statistically significant results ($t = -2.74$, $p = .01$, Cliff's $\delta = 0.40$). They also performed better than EL students on the Mixing Paint task. Although no statistically significant difference was observed for the Mixing Paint task, the effect size was moderate ($t = -1.17$, $p = .26$, Cliff's $\delta = 0.32$).

TABLE 10.4 Performance on the School Day Items

Grade	EL					Non-EL				
	n	Min	Max	Mean	SD	n	Min	Max	Mean	SD
K	28	13	34	29.59	4.74	20	26	34	30.89	2.13
1–2	20	52	57	55.00	1.59	11	49	58	54.64	2.98

Note: The highest possible score was 34 for Grade K and 58 for Grades 1–2.

However, considering that the rubric scales ranged from 0 to 3, it is interesting to note that non-EL students also performed at a low level, as seen in the holistic scores of the Playground (*retelling*) task. A common trend also emerged for both EL and non-EL kindergartners in that they generally scored higher in the lexical category but lower for discourse. It also appears that the performance difference between the EL and non-EL groups was more pronounced in the syntactic category than in the lexical and discourse categories for both tasks at this grade level (Cliff's δ = 0.71 and 0.69 for the syntactic category of the Playground and Mixing Paint tasks, respectively).

Similar but less pronounced patterns were observed in the performance of students in Grades 1 and 2 on the Playground and Melting Ice tasks. Figure 10.5 presents the average scores of the EL and non-EL students in Grades 1 and 2

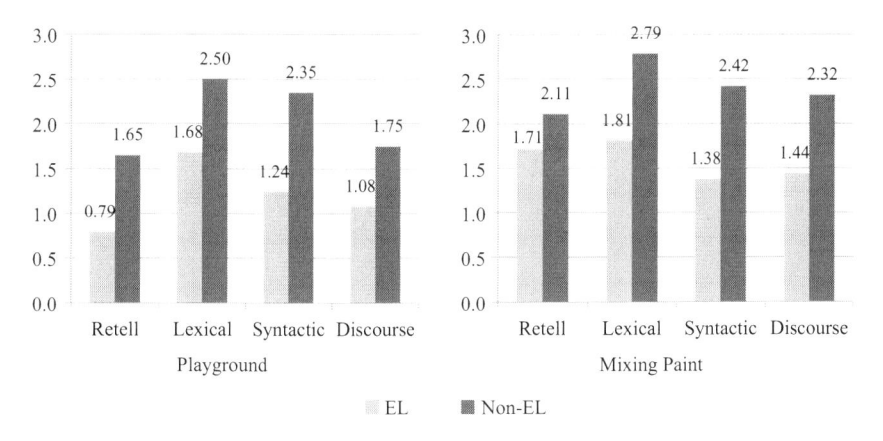

FIGURE 10.4 The Average Scores for the Holistic and Analytic Dimensions of the Playground and Mixing Paint Tasks, Grade K

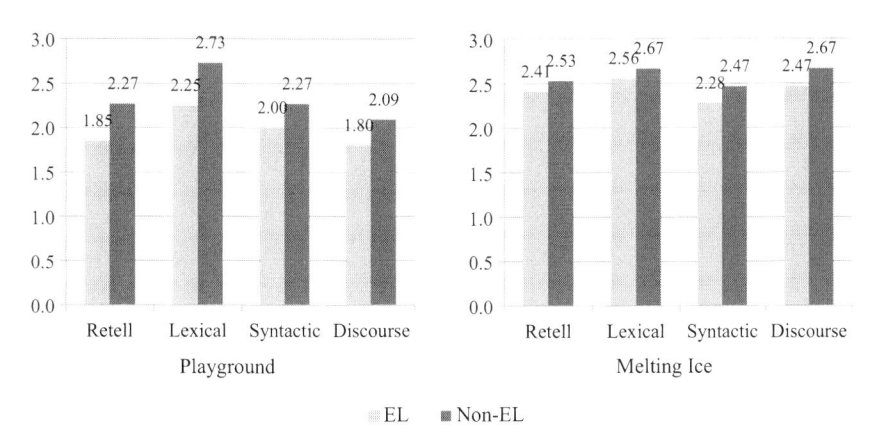

FIGURE 10.5 The Average Scores for the Holistic and Analytic Dimensions of the Playground and Melting Ice Tasks, Grades 1–2

on the two tasks. Generally, the non-EL students performed better than the EL students on both tasks in our sample. However, the performance differences between the EL and non-EL students on the Playground and Melting Ice tasks were trivial, as no significant differences were observed between the groups ($t = -1.40$, $p = .17$, Cliff's $\delta = 0.28$ for the Playground task; $t = -0.54$, $p = .59$, Cliff's $\delta = 0.09$ for the Melting Ice task). A noteworthy observation is that the Playground task seemed difficult for both EL and non-EL students, as shown in the average holistic scores for both groups. This was also true for the kindergarten students (shown in Figure 10.4). Another similar trend was that the students' average scores were lower in the syntactic and discourse categories than in the lexical category on the Playground task.

The students' relatively poorer performance on the Playground task may be explained by two possible factors. First, the language input for the Playground task (i.e., a picture book story) was considerably longer than that for the Mixing Paint and Melting Ice tasks. The story to which the test takers listened had a total of 196 words, whereas the listening inputs for the Mixing Paint and Melting Ice tasks had 56 and 89 words, respectively. Secondly, whereas the input in the Playground task had a series of still images presented in storybook form, the input in the Mixing Paint and Melting Ice tasks included animations. We speculate that the animated inputs might have taken some of the burden off of the students' working memories, allowing them to better process and follow the events. It is also plausible that the animated inputs were more interesting to young students than still images, increasing students' engagement in the tasks.

Common Linguistic Errors

As mentioned earlier, we performed error analysis as a potential way to reveal the language developmental patterns of young children. The results of our analysis indicate that the majority of the students in this study, both EL and non-EL students alike, made similar types of errors when completing each of the four speaking tasks. In this section, we provide sample responses to highlight some of the most common linguistic errors that young students produced. The linguistic errors are classified into three areas: lexical, syntactic, and discourse. To illustrate the level of detail found in the student responses, in Table 10.5 we present sample responses of kindergarten EL and non-EL students who received scores of 2 or 3 (out of 3) on the Playground task. The raters commented that the responses with a score of 3 contained appropriate word choices, relatively good syntactic structures, and coherence in terms of the event sequence and transitions used in describing the events.

To demonstrate the proportion of EL and non-EL students who made linguistic and content-related errors in each task, we present the results in Figure 10.6. The different degrees of shading in Figure 10.6 (also denoted by the number of x's in each box) represent the proportional range of students who

TABLE 10.5 Sample Responses on the Playground Task

Score	Student response, kindergarten	Error analysis notes
3	Non-EL student 1: Luis saw a truck <u>that with</u> workers in the field. Then Luis came over to ask any <u>need</u> help. Then the workers say, "Sure, that was a good idea." Then when, then, the playground was finished. Luis <u>help planted</u> flowers. Then he ran so fast. His friends had a lot of fun playing.	• Syntactic errors: sentence structure (*that with*), verb forms (*need, help planted*)
3	EL student 1: Luis lives across town. He found, he found some workers. He said <u>can, can he help</u>. And they said, "Sure, that's okay. That's awesome." Then Luis helped plant flowers. Then they called their friends and then they had a lot of fun.	• Syntactic errors: word order (*can he help*) • Discourse errors: No antecedents (*they*)
2	Non-EL student 2: Luis saw a truck. He walked over. He asked if he <u>can</u> help and <u>they</u> said. The flowers were all different colors. Luis felt sad. They had fun, lots of fun.	• Syntactic errors: tense, modal (*can*) • Discourse errors: No antecedent (*they*) • Content: Logic, missing events
2	EL student 2: Luis and, and <u>her</u> friends were playing on a playground. And he <u>plant</u> flowers, that <u>flower was their friend colors</u>. And Luis, uh, and <u>Luis tell</u>, um, <u>the girl and the boy</u> he <u>can</u> help to build the playground.	• Lexical errors: word choices (*friend colors, the girl and the boy* for the construction workers/adults) • Syntactic errors: SV agreement (*he plant, Luis tell*), possessive (*her friends*), tense (*can*) • Discourse errors: No antecedent (*their friend*) • Content: Logic, missing events

Note. The underlined texts are the ones that the raters identified as linguistic errors.

made that error in each category for each task. For instance, the darkest shading indicates that more than 50% of the total number of students included that specific category of error in their responses. At a glance, it is notable that errors were prevalent in the responses for both EL and non-EL kindergarten students. The difference in the presence of errors between EL (greater) and non-EL (fewer) student responses is more visible at Grades 1 and 2. It is also notable that the errors in word choice, tense, and content were common to both groups of students irrespective of grade level and task type.

184 Mikyung Kim Wolf et al.

Categories	Playground				Mixing Paint		Melting Ice	
	Gr K		Gr 1-2		Gr K		Gr 1-2	
	EL	Non-EL	EL	Non-EL	EL	Non-EL	EL	Non-EL
Word choice	xx	xx	xx	xx	xx	xx	xx	xx
Plural forms	x	xx	xx			x	x	
Articles	x	x	x	x	x	x	xx	xx
Indirect question	x	xx	x	x				
SV agreement	x	x	x	xx	x	x		
Verb tenses	xx	xxx	xxx	xx	xx	xx	xxx	xx
Possessive	x							
Prepositions	xx	x	xx	x	xx	x	xx	
Pronoun use	xx	xx	x				x	x
Missing subject	x	x	x		xx	xx	x	
Missing verb	xx	x			xx	x	x	
Missing object	x	x	x	x	xx	xx	x	
Conjunctions		x						
Discourse (Pronouns)	xx	xx	xx	xx	xx	xx	xxx	xx
Transitional words	x		x		xx	x	x	
Content - logic	xxx	xx	xxx	xxx	xxx	xx	xx	xx

☐ 0% or NA   x less than 20% of the students
xx 20-49% of the students   xxx more than 50% of the students

FIGURE 10.6 Visual Representation of the Common Error Types in Students' Responses

These results suggest that both EL and non-EL kindergarten students (particularly in the beginning of the school year when data collection took place) were still developing their English language proficiency. As is demonstrated in the sample responses above and with errors produced in regard to content, students were also developing cognitively, making common errors in the logical flow of the retelling or description of the events they had observed. The results provide empirical evidence of the importance of considering young children's linguistic and cognitive developmental stages when designing assessment tasks and scoring rubrics.

Patterns of Errors

In this section, we provide specific examples of error types to postulate young students' language development stages. With respect to the lexical categories in our error analysis, we observed that some errors involved the overuse of "do" to describe a specific action. For example, on the Mixing Paint task, a kindergarten EL student used "do" instead of "made" or "painted," as in "she *did* yellow, second she *do* blue, third she make some green." Other word choice errors appeared to be the simple result of the children choosing words that were more familiar to them rather than more appropriate or accurate terms for the situation or task. For instance, a Grade 1 EL student used the word "girl" instead of "woman" to refer to the construction worker in the Playground task. Another common lexical error seemed to be associated with misinterpretations of the illustrations in the tasks. For example, a few students were using such words as "mom" or "firefighter" to indicate a construction worker. Some students mistook the playground for a garden. Alternatively, the inaccurate word choices might have been a reflection of the students employing the cognitive strategy of substituting words from their known linguistic repertoire to compensate for their lack of vocabulary knowledge.

Regarding syntactic/grammatical errors, the most frequent errors had to do with using verbs, including incorrect forms of a verb, tense, and subject-verb agreement. For example, a kindergarten EL student responded to the Mixing Paint task, "The *teacher play* with the paint." Another example was found in a response on the Melting Ice task from a Grade 1 non-EL student: "The teacher did, the teacher had the science experiment and he took the um spoon and he got a ice cube then he put it on a plate. Next he, next he was waiting for it to melt and then it *start* to melt at the end." Other common syntactic errors were found in the use of articles, prepositions, or pronouns. For example, a kindergarten non-EL student used the article "a" before plural nouns: "*A builders*. Them come with a truck. *And a flowers*. She and him plant the flowers and him going to help them. And it was all finished."

Another interesting finding was students' tendency to omit a subject, verb, or object in their responses. Some errors in these categories appeared to stem from their lack of grammatical knowledge, whereas others seemed related to cognitive ability levels. For example, a kindergarten EL student responded to the Playground task: "Luis live across a field. And he saw a truck and the workers. And will bring a playground. Luis so happy. Luis came over if he can help and them say great. And the flowers all different colors, and the playground was done." In this example, the omission of the verb from the underlined segments is related to the student's linguistic knowledge. On the other hand, the following response from a kindergarten non-EL student on the Mixing Paint task is an example of a conversational style, speaking to the interviewer: "Put yellow on a plate, put blue on a plate, put blue on a plate and then she dipped the brush in the yellow then painted it and it turned green." In this example, the student omitted the subject in her sentence, apparently assuming that the interviewer understood who the agent was. A good portion of the students in this study sample made similar omissions. The interviewers from the cognitive labs reported that many students were in fact retelling/describing the events to the interviewers like a conversation, as the students were not accustomed to recording their responses onto a computer or iPad for assessment purposes.

Even though all of the student responses were relatively short, we were able to identify some discourse-related features and errors. One of the most common discourse errors was the use of unclear references, such as using pronouns without clear antecedents. For example, when asked to retell the story in the Playground task, a kindergarten EL student used the pronoun "they" without including the noun (antecedent) that the pronoun referred to. The student's response was: "Louise helped plant flowers. Then *they* called their friends and then *they* had a lot of fun." Similarly, a Grade 1 non-EL student used the pronoun "they" to retell what the teacher did in the Melting Ice task without including its antecedent: "First, the teacher picked up a ice cube with the spoon. Second, the teacher put it put, take up the spoon from the ice cube bowl. He put it on the plate and *they* waited a few minutes and, and the ice cube melted on the plate." This kind of pronoun use was prevalent in both EL and non-EL students' responses. This trend might be characteristic of how children might tell a story with the assumption that their listeners would understand what/who they were referring to.

Another common discourse error was failing to use transitional devices to recount a story about sequential events in a more coherent fashion. One example was found in the response from a Grade 1 EL student: "Teacher put ice cube. Teacher wait minute." Similarly, a non-EL kindergarten student gave the following response: "He put yellow on the paper. She put blue on the paper, she mixed the colors and made green." The lack of transitional words in these examples makes their responses sound fragmented. As indicated by the fact that the analytic scores for the discourse dimension were consistently the lowest in comparison to the other two dimensions, students (particularly those in kindergarten) appeared to demonstrate emerging discourse abilities for the *retelling* and *describing* tasks.

Conclusion

Despite the limitations of the data analyzed in terms of sample size and task type, the study presented in this chapter offers a few important implications for the development and use of ELP assessments designed to identify young EL students. First, the significance of examining the performance of both EL and non-EL students on the assessment tasks was clearly evident from our study, as both groups were shown to be still developing in their language ability. This was particularly true of the young students who were developing both their L1 and L2 simultaneously. The study provided empirical evidence that both EL and non-EL students in kindergarten, and even Grades 1 and 2, produced linguistic errors and demonstrated an insufficient command of discourse devices to retell a story or describe events coherently. These results suggest that students at these age/grade levels are still developing their language competencies. Thus, when designing scoring rubrics and rater training materials, careful thought and attention is needed to ensure that raters have reasonable and realistic expectations regarding student speaking performance for this age group.

Second, the results of the study shed light on possible ways in which task types can be developmentally inappropriate for the target test-taker population. The Playground task, which asked kindergarten students to retell a story, was found to be challenging for our sample of students who had just begun their formal schooling. Considering that initial ELP screener assessments are typically administered at the beginning of the school year, tasks that are likely to be learned only through schooling (e.g., retelling a story based on a book) may not be appropriate for this specific purpose. While target language use domains and assessment purposes are presently the major factors influencing assessment task design, characteristics of the targeted test takers are inevitably important considerations as well, especially for young learners with all of their unique developmental needs.

In addition to implications for assessment design, the study results offer interesting insights into the stages of second language development. There is emerging consensus among recent second language acquisition (SLA) theories that, because of individual differences and contextual factors, the development of multifaceted language competencies does not take place in a linear fashion (e.g., Larsen-Freeman, 2011; van Lier & Walqui, 2012; also see Chapter 2 of this volume for an overview of current SLA theories). However, the data collected from this study and subsequent error analysis of student responses has yielded promising results that may enable the categorization of ELP developmental patterns for both young EL and non-EL students.

Several limitations of the study should be noted. First, the results were based on a small sample size. This chapter was also limited to discussing the performance differences between young EL and non-EL students in general. Other issues, such as test administration, score uses, and validation of assessment uses for young students, were beyond the scope of this chapter. However, we hope that the present study adds important empirical evidence to the existing language acquisition and assessment research concerning young children's ELP. Much more empirical research is needed to advance our understanding of how to appropriately assess young students' English language proficiency and describe their varying stages of language acquisition.

APPENDIX 10.1

Holistic Rubric for Spoken Responses

Score	Level	Description
3	High	The test taker successfully achieves the task. The response: • is appropriate to the task • is mostly accurate • does not require listener effort to comprehend
2	Mid	The test taker partially achieves the task. The response: • addresses the task with some lapses in completeness or appropriateness • contains errors in accuracy • requires listener effort to comprehend
1	Basic	The test taker attempts to complete the task. The response: • is inaccurate, incomplete, or inappropriate for the task • has frequent errors in grammar and/or word choice • requires significant listener effort to comprehend
0		No response or response is not in English

Notes

1 Although ESL students has been the term most used in the literature, we use *English learner* (EL) students in this chapter to refer to students whose first or home language is not English, needing ESL service in U.S. K–12 schools. The term EL is prevalently used in official documents of the U.S. government currently.
2 Some key design principles for the TELP project include the evidence-centered design, balance of discrete and integrated language knowledge and skills, balance of foundational and higher-order language skills, enrichment of context and input to elicit meaningful

language use, and provision of different levels of scaffolding items. For more details, see Wolf et al. (2014).

3 Non-EL students refers to students who were already identified as fully English-proficient students by school.

References

Bailey, A. L., Heritage, M., & Butler, F. A. (2014). Developmental considerations and curricular contexts in the assessment of young language learners. In A. J. Kunnan (Ed.), *The companion to language assessment* (pp. 1–17). Boston, MA: Wiley.

Bailey, A. L., & Kelly, K. R. (2013). Home language survey practices in the initial identification of English learners in the United States. *Educational Policy*, *27*, 770–804.

Biber, D., & Gray, B. (2013). *Discourse characteristics of writing and speaking task types on the TOEFL iBT® Test: A lexico-grammatical analysis* (TOEFL iBT Research Report No. TOEFL iBT-19). Princeton, NJ: Educational Testing Service.

Cliff, N. (1996). Answering ordinal questions with ordinal data using ordinal statistics. *Multivariate Behavioral Research*, *31*, 331–350.

Cook, H. G., & Linquanti, R. (2015). *Strengthening policies and practices for the initial classification of English learners: Insights from a national working session*. Washington, DC: Council of Chief State School Officers.

Crowhurst, M. (1990). Teaching and learning the writing of persuasive/argumentative discourse. *Canadian Journal of Education*, *15*(4), 348–359.

Espinosa, L. M. (2010). Assessment of young English language learners. In E. E. García & E. C. Frede (Eds.), *Young English language learners: Current research and emerging directions for practice and policy* (pp. 119–142). New York, NY: Teachers College Press.

Every Student Succeeds Act. (2015). *Pub. L. 114–354*. Washington, DC: U.S. Department of Education.

Ferris, D. (2006). Does error feedback help student writers? New evidence on the short- and long-term effects of written error correction. In K. Hyland & F. Hyland (Eds.), *Feedback in second language writing: Contexts and issues* (pp. 81–104). Cambridge, UK: Cambridge University Press.

Friginal, E., Li, M., & Weigle, S. (2014). Revisiting multiple profiles of learner compositions: A comparison of highly rated NS and NNS essays. *Journal of Second Language Writing*, *23*, 1–16.

Hasselgreen, A. (2005). Assessing the language of young learners. *Language Testing*, *22*(3), 337–354.

Hess, M. R., & Kromrey, J. D. (2004, April). *Robust confidence intervals for effect sizes: A comparative study of Cohen's d and Cliff's delta under non-normality and heterogeneous variances*. Paper presented at the annual meeting of the American Educational Research Association, San Diego, CA.

Inbar-Lourie, O., & Shohamy, E. (2009). Assessing young language learners: What is the construct? In M. Nikolov (Ed.), *The age factor and early language learning* (pp. 83–96). Berlin, Germany: Mouton de Gruyter.

Jarvis, S., Grant, L., Bikowski, D., & Ferris, D. (2003). Exploring multiple profiles of highly rated learner compositions. *Journal of Second Language Writing*, *12*(4), 377–403.

Knoch, U., Macqueen, S., & O'Hagan, S. (2014). *An investigation of the effect of task type on the discourse produced by students at various score levels in the TOEFL iBT writing test*

(TOEFL iBT Research Report No. TOEFL iBT-23 & RR-14–43). Princeton, NJ: Educational Testing Service.

Larsen-Freeman, D. (2011). A complexity theory approach to second language development/ acquisition. In D. Atkinson (Ed.), *Alternative approaches to second language acquisition* (pp. 48–72). New York, NY: Routledge.

Lopez, A., Pooler, E., & Linquanti, R. (2016). *Key issues and opportunities in the initial identification and classification of English learners* (ETS Research Report No. RR-16–09). Princeton, NJ: Educational Testing Service.

McKay, P. (2006). *Assessing young language learners.* Cambridge, UK: Cambridge University Press.

National Association for the Education of Young Children. (2005). *Screening and assessment of young English-language learners.* Washington, DC: Author. Available from https://www.naeyc.org/files/naeyc/file/positions/ELL_Supplement_Shorter_Version.pdf

Pérez-Paredes, P., & Sánchez-Tornel, M. (2014). Adverb use and language proficiency in young learners' writing. *International Journal of Corpus Linguistics, 19*(2), 178–200.

Rea-Dickins, P., & Rixon, S. (1997). The assessment of young learners of English as a foreign language. In C. Clapham & D. Corson (Eds.), *The encyclopedia of language and education, Vol. 7: Language testing and assessment* (pp. 151–161). Dordrecht, The Netherlands: Kluwer Academic Publishers.

Shore, J. R., Wolf, M. K., O'Reilly, T., & Sabatini, J. (2017). Measuring 21st century reading comprehension through scenario-based assessments. In M. K. Wolf & Y. G. Butler (Eds.), *English language proficiency assessments for young learners.* New York, NY: Routledge.

van Lier, L., & Walqui, A. (2012, January). Language and the Common Core State Standards. Paper presented at the Understanding Language Conference. Stanford, CA. Retrieved from http://ell.stanford.edu/papers

Wolf, M. K., Everson, P., Lopez, A., Hauck, M., Pooler, E., & Wang, J. (2014). *Building a framework for a next-generation English language proficiency assessment system* (ETS Research Report No. RR-14–34). Princeton, NJ: Educational Testing Service.

Wolf, M. K., Guzman-Orth, D. A., Lopez, A., Castellano, K., Himelfarb, I., & Tsutagawa, F. S. (2016). Integrating scaffolding strategies into technology-enhanced assessments of English learners: Task types and measurement models. *Educational Assessment, 21*(3), 157–175.

Wolf, M. K., Kao, J., Griffin, N., Herman, J. L., Bachman, P., Chang, S. M., & Farnsworth, T. (2008). *Issues in assessing English language learners: English language proficiency measures and accommodation uses—practice review* (CRESST Technical Report No. 732). Los Angeles, CA: University of California, National Center for Research on Evaluation, Standards, and Student Testing (CRESST).

SECTION 4

Future Assessments and Innovations for Young Learners

11
CONSIDERING YOUNG LEARNERS' CHARACTERISTICS IN DEVELOPING A DIAGNOSTIC ASSESSMENT INTERVENTION

Eunice Eunhee Jang, Megan Vincett, Edith H. van der Boom, Clarissa Lau, and Yehbeen Yang

Assessment is more important than ever in today's K–12 classrooms that are becoming linguistically and culturally diverse at an unprecedented rate. For many students, the instructional language is neither what they hear and speak at home nor the language with which they feel most competent and comfortable. Students learn English as a foreign language as part of curriculum requirements or because they seek admission to higher educational programs in English-speaking countries. These language learners, typically aged 6 to 18, are expected to develop social and academic language proficiency to meet both language and academic demands in schoolwork. Therefore, assessing and supporting their language learning needs have become critical pedagogical concerns among teachers, test developers, and educators.

While assessment serves various pedagogical and programming purposes in K–12 school contexts, its formative and diagnostic use has been recognized as critical for differentiated instruction for individual students. In particular, cognitive diagnostic assessment (CDA) is one of a few innovative assessment approaches that have drawn much attention from the fields of language assessment and educational measurement in the past decade (Jang, 2009; Lee & Sawaki, 2009). Yet, little is known about how diagnostic feedback generated from the CDA has positive interventional effects on individual students, in particular young learners given their developmental nature of cognitive, metacognitive, and affective characteristics that dynamically influence their language development. Drawing upon empirical classroom research with 11- to 12-year-old students in Grades 5 and 6 in Ontario elementary schools, this chapter examines how struggling young readers (identified from CDA-based profiling) respond to one-to-one diagnostic assessment interventions and concludes by offering considerations for designing innovative young learner assessment.

Learner Variables Associated With Effects of Cognitive Diagnostic Assessment Feedback

Cognitive diagnostic assessment (CDA) is intended to provide individual students with diagnostic feedback customized to their strengths and weaknesses in cognitive processing skills associated with successful performance outcomes. CDA is driven by a growing interest in learning-oriented assessment approaches (Carless, 2007) to meeting pedagogical needs to support learners with detailed diagnostic feedback. Based on multidimensional item response theory (IRT) latent class modeling, CDA provides diagnostic profiles of individual students' mastery status of user-specified skills in detail (see Leighton & Gierl, 2007 for more information about cognitive diagnosis models). Furthermore, diagnostic feedback provided for young learners should include both what they can demonstrate and what they need to improve in order to promote positive experiences with assessment and learning.

While diagnostic feedback is intended to support differentiated instruction and guide students' self-regulated learning, few studies examined how young students respond to feedback and what factors mediate students' responses to feedback. Jang, Dunlop, Park, and van der Boom (2015) filled this gap by investigating how young students' ability to plan for future learning based on CDA-based diagnostic feedback they received is associated with their goal orientations and perceived abilities. Our discussion in this chapter is based on a subsequent study that further examined how struggling young readers identified from diagnostic profiles respond to eight-week individual interventions intended to direct their attention to cognitive, metacognitive, and affective states while engaging in reading comprehension tasks. For the remainder of this section, we share our conceptualization of learners as dynamic systems followed by brief discussions of learner variables believed to influence the effect of diagnostic feedback interventions.

Learners as Dynamic Systems

In designing assessment for young learners, we consider learners as dynamic systems within which the interplay between intrapersonal variables and environmental elements mutually influence their cognitive growth necessary for developing bi- and multi-lingual competence (van Dijk & van Geert, 2014). The resulting growth is unlikely to be linear over time and uniform across multiple dynamic systems (i.e., learners). Such person-oriented approaches to assessment over variables-oriented measurement direct our attention to the idiosyncratic nature of learning process and outcomes (Bergman, Magnusson, & El-Khouri, 2003). For example, the traditional notion of measurement error is treated as residuals from a model fit to be minimized and excluded from interpretation and use of assessment information. However, these fit deviations may reflect the uniqueness of individual learners, which need to be recognized as key ingredients in interpreting and using assessment. This person-oriented interactionist view, that is, the individual as an organic whole, is reflected in differentiated instructional approaches which use a repertoire of strategies to address the unique needs of students based on the assessment of their current proficiency level (*readiness*), relevance of learning to students' experience (*interest*), and preferred ways of learning (*learning preference*) (Tomlinson et al., 2003). Assessment that supports such approaches needs to see individual students' unique strengths and areas for improvement as the driving force of development by focusing on tracking and scaffolding learning progressions, which drives our diagnostic assessment interventions reported in this chapter.

Mediation in diagnostic assessment interventions is viewed as essential for raising students' metacognitive awareness of their learning process by prompting their goal setting, monitoring, and reflecting on their own learning progress. The criticality of 'mediation' has been well conceptualized and widely studied by dynamic assessment researchers (see Poehner, Zhang, & Lu, 2017 in this volume). As learning is not only acquiring necessary knowledge but also developing skills embedded within cultural and social processes (Shepard, 2005), interactions between a student and a teacher as well as between students influence the learning process. While mediation can play both explicit and implicit roles in student learning, its primary role in our diagnostic assessment interventions is to guide a learner to progress from externally mediated learning to self-regulated. This progression is often influenced by noncognitive characteristics such as interest, motivation, and emotion regulation, whose characteristics are summarized in Figure 11.1.

Cognitive Skills in Language Development

Language development for school-aged learners (both L1 and L2 learners) involves cognitive skills required for processing knowledge involving vocabulary, grammar, discourse, and language functions in specific communicative contexts (Jang, 2014; McKay, 2006). Children start to develop vocabulary capacity by increasing the breadth and depth of vocabulary knowledge (Schoonen & Verhallen, 2008). Vocabulary expansion occurs by recognizing the most frequent 2,000 words found in spoken and written text (Coxhead, 2006). They continue to expand their knowledge by learning academic vocabulary common across content areas, later specializing in vocabulary specific to content areas in secondary school. Gradually, students identify grammatical features that distinguish among different text genres and develop discourse knowledge by identifying particular structures of spoken and written text used in socially acceptable and effective manners.

As their cognition matures, learners can interpret and use nonverbal cues and tones across various social contexts (Schleppegrell & O'Hallaron, 2011). In order to assess and scaffold their cognitive potential, assessment tasks need to elicit specific language functions associated with core linguistic and cognitive language skills of interest. This is the key argument for cognitive validity, that is, the extent

Metacognition

- Develop metalinguistic awareness of linguistic forms and use.
- Self-regulate learning by setting goals, planning, monitoring, and evaluating at various points.
- Facilitate cognitive processing.
- Develop self-awareness about approaches to learning and demonstrate high self-efficacy and intrinsic interest in tasks.
- Create optimal learning environments by seeking advice.
- Regulate emotions in social interactions during language learning.
- Cope with test anxiety by self-talking or giving themselves positive appraisals.

Emotion

- Emotions that learners experience in academic settings vary widely depending on whether they are task-related, self-related, or performance-related.
- Task-related emotions are directly associated with the task.
- Self-related emotions are feelings, thoughts, or experiences that are related specifically to individuals' belief in themselves within a specific context.
- Performance-related emotions are associated with students' progress towards their goal, as well as their performance in achieving the required task.
- The most frequently observed academic emotions are task-related, and test anxiety has been a major focus in language testing.

Cognition

- Begin to acquire the most frequent 2,000 words of English that occur regularly in academic text, which accounts for up to 75% of the words used in spoken and written text.
- Develop oral language skills rapidly through social interactions.
- Begin to develop early literacy skills.
- Begin to understand different genres used in text.
- Have limited cognitive memory and attention span, resulting in limited ability to automatize information processing.
- Learn general academic vocabulary.
- Use abstract ideas expressed with grammatical nominalization and an abstract lexicon beyond their personal experience.
- Engage in lexically dense and syntactically complex texts.

Interest

- Develop situational interest triggered by learning environment.
- Maintain situational interest through focused attention and persistence given meaningful learning tasks.
- Develop individual interest that generates curiosity for learning.
- May have difficulty keeping interest when language demands are too high or topics are not interesting.
- Show less interest in literacy possibly due to the density of and complexity of the reading in school, called the "fourth grade slump."
- Develop different orientations to learning as a response to environmental influence.
- Develop inflated or deflated perception about own ability.

FIGURE 11.1 Young Learner Characteristics

to which assessment tasks allow for a range of cognitive repertoire relevant to the context of real-life learning (Field, 2011). For example, assessment tasks that are cognitively-rich encourage students to draw upon their background knowledge in comprehending multimodal text and prompt them to create mental imagery to synthesize comprehended information. The extent of background knowledge varying among students of different ages may constrain the repertoire of skills required for processing linguistic knowledge.

Metacognition

Metacognition involves the ability to self-regulate one's own learning by setting goals, planning, monitoring, and evaluating conscious and strategic efforts to solve tasks. Research consistently supports the significant and positive role that metacognitive strategy use plays in developing language proficiency (e.g., Purpura, 1997). There is converging evidence that it is not the number or kind of strategies but the efficacy of metacognitive control that has significant influence on task performance. It is through metacognitive control that cognitive strategies are selected, executed, and regulated. Effectiveness depends on the knowledge learners have about themselves and their learning styles, which explains why struggling readers show low self-efficacy when faced with assessment tasks beyond their level (Locke & Latham, 1990). Continuous failure impairs their ability to strategically self-regulate their learning and to set appropriate goals to successfully complete tasks. These learner beliefs influence the extent of metacognitive control students have, and in turn, their cognitive processing and emotional regulation (Pekrun, Goetz, Titz, & Perry, 2002).

While the driving force behind learning goals and motivation should be internal, students' ability to take advantage of external sources is a part of effective metacognitive strategy use. Self-assessment can provide an opportunity for learners to engage in the assessment process. It is being recognized as a tool to promote students' metacognitive awareness of and confidence about their learning process and strategy use, with a better sense of control over their learning pace and actions taken towards learning. Further, students' self-assessment ability is shown to be correlated with their overall ability levels (Jang, 2014; Zimmerman, 1990). Higher-proficiency learners show higher metacognitive ability, which enables them to more accurately assess their performance. However, as students proceed to higher grades in school, their self-assessed ability may show more variability. Students with high language proficiency in higher grades develop the ability to differentiate their perceived ability in finer detail, resulting in harsher self-assessment. On the other hand, less proficient language learners appear to have a less differentiated perception of their own ability, resulting in an overestimation of their own ability (Butler & Lee, 2010; Jang et al., 2015). In order for students to develop the ability to self-assess their performance with accuracy as they progress in learning, teachers need to provide careful guidance.

Interest

The notion of interest is a motivational variable relevant to young learner assessment. While older students' language learning is more likely to be driven by external goals, such as going to university or securing a scholarship, younger learners are more likely to be affected by the 'interestingness' of their learning activities and assessment tasks. Research on the role of interest on young children's reading performance has shown that readers' interest influences their discourse processing, cognitive attention, recognition, and recall of expository texts (Hidi, 1990). Interest not only enhances the recall of comprehended text information but also leads readers to deeper textual processing beyond its surface meaning (Schiefele & Krapp, 1996). Noting that interest may be triggered not only by text features, but also by visual and auditory stimuli, Hidi (1990) proposed the term situational interest to refer to all externally triggered interest beyond text-based interest. She distinguishes situational interest from individual interest in that the former concerns a reaction triggered by immediate environmental stimuli, whereas the latter refers to a relatively stable trait reflecting long-term value, knowledge, and feelings.

Text topics and themes are shown to influence children's comprehension, inferencing, and cognitive attention and, thus, can be used as a means for mediating interest (Hidi, 2001). Specifically, textual features that include novelty, surprise, intensity, concreteness, and visual imagery are shown to trigger situational interest (Hidi & Baird, 1988). Green, Hamnett, and Green (2001) describe user-friendly features of reading comprehension tests based on interviews with young children: novelty of stimuli, topic familiarity, text with humor and pictures, and nontraditional question types.

Additionally, interest can be generated through the provision of choice (Evans & Boucher, 2015). Although educational settings might be difficult environments to promote relevance and meaning for all students, incorporating personalization is one way through which student meaning and relevance can be supported. Many studies suggest positive outcomes when students are provided with choice within educational settings (Casey, 2008; Lenters, 2006; Williams, Wallace, & Sung, 2016). Choice alone does not generate student interest, but must be relevant and meaningful, competence enhancing, and provided in just the right amount. Furthermore, learners can adaptively generate interest in initially uninteresting tasks when they are asked to self-regulate their own learning. For example, when students are asked to think about why they value a task, they approach it with increased strategies to make uninteresting tasks more interesting (Sansone & Smith, 2000). This has important implications for assessment and learning because it recognizes the learner's active role in generating interest in addition to responding to external input. Metacognitive control that mediates interest may have a great influence on cognitive performance.

Academic Emotions

Academic emotions, that is, emotional experiences taking place in academic settings, may carry influence on cognitive and metacognitive engagement in academic tasks (Pekrun et al., 2002). Such academic emotions vary widely depending on whether they are task-related, self-related, or performance-related. Task-related emotions are directly associated with the task, whereas self-related emotions are feelings, thoughts, or experiences that are related specifically to individuals' belief in themselves within a specific context. Positive emotions such as enjoyment, hope, and pride encourage students to approach tasks with flexible strategy use and metacognitive control. Negative emotions such as anger, anxiety, and shame are cognitively demanding by reducing cognitive resources. Interest in a task elicits enjoyment, which can be expressed as excitement or relaxation depending on whether the task is challenging or routine (Pekrun et al., 2002). When a task is valued negatively but still manageable, it prompts anger, whereas a task with less controllability tends to prompt frustration. If task difficulty is set too low, cognitive stimulation will be minimal, likely resulting in boredom, which can also occur when it is too challenging and devalued.

Performance-related emotions are associated with students' progress towards goals, as well as their performance in accomplishing required tasks. Deactivating emotions such as boredom and hopelessness likely impair motivation and strategy use, inducing performance goal approaches. Among deactivating emotions, test anxiety has been a major focus for research in the field of language assessment to date. It tends to be associated with performance-avoidance goals, which is the tendency to avoid a task due to fear of performance failure. Both task- and performance-related emotions have significant implications for designing and implementing assessments for young learners.

Study Background

The main data sources discussed in this chapter come from the second-phase field research of a large-scale research project (Jang, Dunlop, Wagner, Kim, & Gu, 2013) that examined developmental patterns of reading skills among various student groups. The field research involved four classroom teachers with 105 Grade 5 and 6 students aged 11 to 12 from two schools (Schools A and B) in Ontario to examine students' responses to and use of diagnostic profiles. We developed diagnostic profiles for the field-research students by applying cognitive diagnosis modeling to students' performance in 32 multiple-choice reading comprehension test items with five reading passages. The diagnostic profiles consisted of four different parts: 1) students' mastery status of six reading comprehension skills presented in graphs; 2) their self-assessment of their own reading skills in comparison with their skill mastery status; 3) their goal-orientations (based on their responses to a goal orientation questionnaire completed along with the reading comprehension diagnostic test); and 4) plans for subsequent learning based on diagnostic feedback. Appendix 11.1 illustrates the first two parts in a bar graph and shows the student's written response to the diagnostic feedback. Appendix 11.2 presents the other two parts related to goal orientations and future plans. The diagnostic profile report ends with a learning contract signed by the student and his teacher. Jang et al. (2015) provide the methodological details for profiling individual students in School A. The same profiling approach was applied for students in School B. Table 11.1 presents consolidated learner profiles.

Fourteen students participated in one-to-one diagnostic assessment interventions over eight sessions lasting approximately 30 to 40 minutes after school. These students came from an inner-city school where over 50% of the students in Grade 6 spoke languages other than English at home. As shown in Table 11.1, they (shaded cells) were selected because of their learning needs. The eight-week interventions included the following activities as shown in Table 11.2.

TABLE 11.1 Consolidated Diagnostic Profiles of Students in School B

Self-assessment discrepancy class[1]	Reading skill mastery class[2]	Goal orientation class[3]						
		001	011	101	111	010	110	100
Overestimate	111111							
	000000	QV6C154	QV6C27	QV6N20	QV6C01			
	010000	QV6C13 QV6C14 QV6C23 QV6N03 QV6R20		QC6C06	QV6N02 QV6N04 QV6N08 QV6N10			
	100000							
	110000	QV6C03	QV6C07					
	010010	QV6N17 QV6R12			QV6C22			
	010100	QV6N21					QV6C18	
	011000			QV6R01				
	111000		QV6C24					

Note. [1]Self-assessment discrepancy classes are based on discrepancy scores between skill mastery estimates from CDA and self-assessment.

[2]Reading skill mastery classes show reading skill mastery patterns from cognitive diagnosis modeling (1 means mastery and 0 means nonmastery) in the order of Explicit comprehension, Implicit comprehension, Inferencing, Processing grammatical knowledge, Processing vocabulary knowledge, and Summarizing.

[3]Goal orientation classes show students' dominant goal orientations in the order of Performance-prove, Performance-avoid, and Mastery (see Dweck, 1986).

[4]Shaded student IDs show individuals selected for subsequent diagnostic assessment interventions in one of two field research schools.

TABLE 11.2 Diagnostic Assessment Intervention Activities

Session 1	2	3	4	5	6	7	8
• Reflect on diagnostic profiles • Set learning goals • Choose a passage for task 1 • Read silently • Complete reading task 1	• Report parent discussions • Think-aloud task 1	• Review learning goals • Review task 1 performance • Choose a passage for task 2 • Read silently • Complete task 2	• Report parent discussions • Think aloud task 2	• Review learning goals • Review task 2 performance • Choose a passage for task 3 • Read silently • Complete task 3	• Report parent discussions • Think aloud task 3	• Review learning goals • Review task 3 performance • Choose a passage for task 4 • Think aloud task 4	• Report parent discussions • Plan future learning • Reflect on learning during interventions

The researcher as a mediator facilitated the activities through mediation by prompting questions and providing scaffolding feedback.

In the following section, we highlight key findings from the interventions critical for young learner assessment. Student names mentioned are pseudonyms.

Key Findings

Students Built on Strengths to Improve Weaknesses

Assessment that repeatedly highlights what students cannot do is of little use for them especially if they struggle academically. Assessment needs to guide students to take an action for improvement and experience one small success at a time through conscious effort. One method through which opportunities for incremental success were incorporated into the intervention was by having students work on specific goals within each session. In this way, students were able to break apart the larger task of reading, while engaging in many opportunities for reflection on skill development.

Most students participating in the intervention required improvement in the following skills: explicit text comprehension, making connections, grammar knowledge, vocabulary knowledge, and summarizing (see Table 11.1 for intervention students' consolidated profiles). All made improvements in comprehending implicitly stated text information. Unlike inferential comprehension that requires higher-order thinking, implicit textual comprehension demands relatively obvious textual information processing where answers to questions are stated in the text or students make connections between text segments by paying attention to syntactic markers (Applegate, Quinn, & Applegate, 2002). In the first intervention session, students were encouraged to reflect on their strength in implicit textual comprehension and set their learning goals by deciding which skill to work on during interventions (see Table 11.2 for activity descriptions). In doing so, students were encouraged to consider cognitive strategies for comprehending a passage of their choice. Providing students with the opportunity to see progress acted to build self-efficacy. A small yet visible indication of improvement acted as a motivator to enhance reading abilities.

Explicit Feedback on Strategy Use Facilitated Improvement in Reading

Throughout the interventions, students were asked to write down specific strategies they thought would improve skills of their choice. Although they gradually increased the number of strategies, they still failed to demonstrate effective strategy use. Most of the students chose to work on explicit textual comprehension and were guided to utilize various strategies including rereading, looking back at the text, and reading for details. The most effectively used strategy was referencing the text to answer questions, which is supported by research suggesting that looking back in the text increases comprehension (Israel & Duffy, 2014; Leslie & Caldwell, 2006). The look-back strategy was used as an aid in answering questions for constructing coherent textual meaning (Palinscar, Magnusson, Pesko, & Hamlin, 2005). Most of the students tended to answer comprehension questions from memory, failing to recall explicit textual information. Over the sessions, they were encouraged to look back after reading, locating explicitly stated textual information.

Another successful strategy was to slow down and pay attention to details in the text. While reading aloud, some students showed difficulty with chunking text and recalling details in the text after reading. For these students, the intervention focused on slowing down and directing attention to details by chunking the text into smaller meaning units. For example, when one of the participating students, Anthony, was asked about how he would achieve his learning goals, he stated, "I'm gonna read the two chapters of my book slowly so I can notice more things. And I'm going to think about the important parts of a story." Additionally, when another student, Alex, was encouraged to slow down during reading, he was able to reduce disfluency rates (e.g., repetitive reading text segments), an effective strategy in targeting his difficulty with chunking and recall.

However, this strategy may sound counter-intuitive considering current instructional emphasis on top-down processing skills for making connections between text and personal experience. In addition, it may be hampered by the *seductive details* effect, known to interfere with the recall of main ideas when the text includes too many interesting but irrelevant adjuncts (Harp & Mayer, 1998). Seductive details tend to be novel, active, concrete, personally involving, and so memorable as to disrupt the identification of main ideas (Garner, Brown, Sanders, & Menke, 1992). While such details are shown to increase students' situational interest, careful guidance is necessary when they are encouraged to read for details through slow reading and chunking into smaller segments. Instructing students to identify main ideas by putting together details, for example, can be an effective strategy for preventing the seductive details effect.

Providing explicit feedback about strategy use, such as looking back in the text, reading for details, and chunking text into meaningful units, can be an effective way to increase young readers' comprehension. Assessments that do not allow such strategy use may underestimate students' potential reading ability (Israel & Duffy, 2014). Young learner assessment should be cognitively rich, stimulating strategy use and eliciting cognitive processes in order to ensure cognitive validity.

Mediated Feedback Facilitated Students' Improvement in Inferential and Summarizing Skills

Inferential comprehension involves higher-order thinking, requiring a reader to integrate textual information with prior knowledge to summarize, predict, or reconstruct it. For young readers, their background knowledge is limited.

Therefore, they need to make connections by not only activating existing prior knowledge but also creating new background knowledge. This prior knowledge is the building block of higher-order thinking used for mental representations during reading.

Over the interventions, struggling readers tended to show overreliance on top-down processing through exclusive reference to personal experience without attention to its textual base. These students needed feedback to facilitate a shift from simply accessing rigid and partial background knowledge, to mobilizing knowledge from multiple conceptual and experiential sources for textual comprehension. One of the students, Andrea, showed the most flexibility with schema mobilization during her think-aloud session, as shown in the following (note that the italic parts are from the text students read):

Andrea: *With his icy breath on everything.* So, like, um, his icy breath is like, it like turns to like ice and stuff. *Then up comes the sun; down fall the showers.* So it's, like, the sun is rising and sometimes it's like raining and stuff. *Welcome to spring and her yellow flowers!* I imagine the flowers blooming. *So sing the birds on the budding tree.* Birds singing on, like, the trees that are almost growing.

The following quotes from Alex during his interaction with the researcher illustrate how his summarizing improves through mediation during the intervention.

[At the beginning of the intervention session]

Alex: *Persia flew on a golden throne carried by four eagles. . . . As the hungry eagles tried to fly up to the food, they carried the throne up with them.* Ummm . . . It's . . . the . . . He like put this fishing net I think and then he put the meat on it and then after that he sat on this chair and then after that the eagles were flying him higher because they were attached to this line so they were flying higher though they sat, they were trying to get the meat but it was useless.

[Toward the end of the intervention session]

Alex: *More isn't necessarily better—at least when it comes to wings. . . .* So he had a lot of wings I think when he took some away or something and then he flew it and it went further because light, when it was lighter it flew further but when it is heavier it didn't go as far.

The quote illustrates that whereas the earlier summary consists of details from the text, the later summary also conveyed prediction and critical reasoning. Mediation through questioning and scaffolding allowed students to develop summarizing skills by identifying and building relations among concepts in the text, connecting these to prior knowledge, and recognizing comprehension gaps.

Students Developed Metacognitive Control Through Self-Questioning

Among various self-regulatory strategies, we observed changes in students' questioning, shifting from asking no questions, to questioning when prompted, then self-questioning. Self-questioning appeared to support students' active engagement as an effective strategy for improving inferential comprehension. Traditionally, questions emanate from the teacher or text and the role of the student is to answer them. However, when readers are guided to self-question various aspects of the text, they show improvement in reading comprehension (Beck, McKeown, Hamilton, & Kucan, 1998). The self-questioning strategy can help students engage in elaborative activities such as summarizing the text, recognizing comprehension gaps, and critically judging their own learning.

Students in the intervention represented various stages related to their level of active engagement and independence in the reading process. During early intervention sessions, students neither sought help nor initiated questions when encountering unknown words. Later, they began to ask for definitions and clarifications; however, their questioning was limited to help-seeking behavior rather than self-questioning, as shown in the following excerpts:

Alex: What does editorial mean?

Mediator 3: Editorial is a piece of writing that a person from the newspaper writes and they are in charge of the whole paper. So they are the one who checks everyone's writing. They are the main person to be in charge of writing the paper. So they always write a piece for the paper.

Alex: Okay.

Mediator 3: But in this case it was a magazine. Good question. I like when you ask questions.

Mediator 3: Okay, so you read the sentence again, and, did you try to guess what the word meant from the sentence?

Tony: Not really.

Mediator 3: No? You did get this part though, Samuel was tapping on her desk? Right? Because that was in the sentence?

Tony: I didn't get it, what was he doing in paragraph 3, why is Janet startled? Why is he beside the, why is he beside the . . .
Mediator 3: She has been concentrating on her book. What do you think *startled* might mean? Even based on the answers that are given. (Pause) Any guesses?
Tony: Why she's scared?

Across the intervention sessions, students became more strategic and aware of their own understanding and generated more questions while acknowledging what they failed to understand in the text.

Giving Students Choices Triggered Student Situational Interest

As discussed, certain textual features have been theorized to trigger students' situational interest, and such interest is associated with more positive student outcomes (Hidi & Baird, 1988). During the intervention, when asked to provide reasoning behind their text selections, students' responses fell into approximately seven categories: interest with some expansion, preference of a particular literary device, prediction of text content of interest, interest without expansion, perceived difficulty based on surface structure, lack of clear reasoning behind text choice, and lack of any reasoning ("I don't know"). Later on, the level of interest demonstrated by students appeared to be related to students' perceived task difficulty during the interventions. Students with higher interest were more responsive to the interventions than students who showed less interest. For example, Indy selected reading passages based on individual interest in the topic and text genre.

Mediator 1: Take a couple of minutes to think which one you'd like to work on.
Indy: Ok. [pauses, paper shuffles] Can I do Moon Trees?
Mediator 1: Absolutely. Why do you want to do Moon Trees? I saw you picked it up.
Indy: Coz, yeah 'coz Moon Trees um ah it was about the first ahm I read, I just read the first like summaries for everyone, yeah. And then after that I saw that Moon Trees was about ahm space and like the first ah the first person to go to the Moon. And ah space to go to space you need um ah ah science. Yeah.
Mediator 3: Science? Yeah.
Indy: Yeah. And yeah I like science.

Some students chose reading passages based on such features as topic familiarity, titles, and pictures, indicating that their interest was situational rather than individual. The majority of students, however, chose reading passages but failed to elaborate on the reasoning underlying their choices. Some chose reading passages that appeared easier to avoid challenges, for example, Nadine said, "It sounds interesting," but failed to explain why she chose The Secret when prompted. Anthony and Jacob used avoidance strategies instead by saying, "Because it was shorter. Mm 'coz it might not have a lot of questions" (Anthony) and "Ah, Trailblazer, it wasn't that interesting, it was just like, um, there's too much dialogue, I don't like it when there's too much dialogue" (Jacob).

Lastly, some students had difficulty expressing why they chose passages, simply stating, "I don't know." They required mediation to provide reason behind their choices. When prompted, students often explained that they had chosen passages because topics appeared familiar. For example, Alex initially could not explain why he chose Popcorn Under Pressure. When prompted, he said, "Maybe it is because [pause] popcorn under pressure and I already know a little bit about popcorn under pressure."

Emotional Responses to Feedback Were Indicative of Cognitive and Metacognitive Ability

Understanding students' emotional states during learning and assessment can shed light on their level of cognitive and metacognitive engagement. We analyzed students' written responses to open-ended questions ("What do you think of your achievement of this skill? Please share your thoughts by writing here.") included in their diagnostic profile reports (see Appendix 11.1). Pekrun et al.'s (2002) academic emotion framework was used to identify emotional states, interest and motivation, and the quality of future plans. Further quantitative analysis examined the relationship between those variables and skill mastery levels determined by cognitive diagnosis modeling (see Appendix 11.1). More frequently expressed emotions included surprise, joy, contentment, disappointment, and shock. Among these emotions, contentment showed a positive relationship with the quality of students' future learning plans, determined on the basis of relevance to diagnostic feedback. Overall, high skill masters tended to plan their learning according to their diagnostic profiles. When we examined the relationship between students' emotional states and their overall skill mastery levels, those with more positive emotional responses showed higher skill mastery levels for most of the skills except two basic comprehension skills ($r = .32, p < .05$). Out of six reading skills, only inferencing was positively correlated with positive emotional states when we examined students' perceived ability ($r = .38^*$, $p < .05$). In other words, students who rated their inferencing skill highly tended to show more positive emotions towards their diagnostic profiles.

The study results support the need to take into account young learners' emotional engagement during learning and assessment. Fine-tuning assessments in order to induce positive emotional experiences will help them to focus on tasks and learning. Through enhanced metacognitive control, students need to be aware of negative emotions and develop strategies to regulate them so that cognitive resources are devoted to learning tasks.

In sum, comprehensive metacognitive control is believed to serve as the driving force for cognitive growth and sustained interest in learning. To facilitate students' cognitive skill development, mediation through diagnostic feedback needs to dynamically modify scaffolding to foster students' self-regulatory behavior. It is worth noting that the dynamic between the mediator and each student may vary greatly as a result of adaptive scaffolding; however, the mediation was observed to shift in focus from externally to self-regulated learning behavior for most students over the intervention sessions. Such shifts in mediation were evidenced by a decrease in the amount of explicit prompting and an increase in independent elaborations with less prompting in later sessions.

Future Development

The purpose of the diagnostic assessment intervention was to provide mediated scaffolding for individual students whose diagnostic profiles had indicated the most needs by facilitating their metacognitive control over their reading strategy use. Based on what we learned from this field research, we offer some considerations for future assessment design for young learners.

One of the most important considerations is that students need to be engaged in the entire assessment process, especially in reviewing and using feedback from assessment for future learning. In order to foster self-regulated learning, students should be provided with diagnostic feedback on progress made towards goals they have set out for themselves. When students work towards goals that are both personally challenging and meaningful, they can be motivated to become self-regulated learners (Hattie & Timperley, 2007).

Future young learner assessment should consider ongoing and adaptive mediation tailored to individual students' cognitive, metacognitive, and affective progress. In learning-oriented assessment, mediation should not be standardized for all students across learning contexts. Instead, the focus and intensity of mediation should be adjusted according to students' responses to mediated assessment. Efforts should be made to facilitate transition from externally-driven to self-generated mediation. Young learner assessment should prompt students to generate their own questions instead of responding to questions and to make choices based on their interests and preferences during assessment.

We call for further research on the role of assessment on students' self-regulation. Research on learners' self-regulated strategy use should consider the effectiveness of strategies, not just strategy frequencies. Although a higher frequency of strategy use might imply the improvement of skills, the goal is to work towards consistent and effective strategy use. The frequency of strategies alone does not differentiate among students with different proficiency levels. Student metacognitive control contributes to predicting language proficiency levels. We suggest future assessment provide students with opportunities to generate their own questions in addition to answering questions. Evaluating the quality of self-generated questions may provide useful information about not only comprehension level from literal to higher-order thinking, but also metacognitive control.

Research on interest and emotions offers insights into developing innovative young learner assessment. Assessment tasks and materials can foster students' situational interest. This is especially important for young learners because their interest in learning tends to be contextual and temporal. Text topics and themes trigger children's interest, which in turn contributes to inferencing and cognitive attention. With technological advances, young learner assessment tasks can incorporate digital environments, such as gamified tasks, interactive media, or hypertexts. When these interactive digital stimuli are provided with student choices, they can generate interest through personalization of assessment tasks. Currently, the potential of neurophysiological methods, such as eye-tracking, is actively being researched to understand processes involving choice behavior and cognitive attention. Physiological trace data while students perform a task in real time will help assessment provide adaptive scaffolding to support students' sustained interest.

Lastly, students' emotional experiences can have a great influence on their cognitive and metacognitive engagement in assessment tasks. Both task-related and performance-oriented emotions may facilitate or impair students' motivation and strategy use. Young learner assessment can benefit from facial expression analysis based on less intrusive methods that do not depend on self-reports. Corpus-based computer systems are being developed to automatically analyze and recognize facial motions and expressions from visual data (Fasel & Luettin, 2003). Data mining and machine learning approaches used to analyze synchronous data will allow us to assess young learners' cognitive growth through a dynamic interplay with other traits in digital environments.

APPENDIX 11.1

Skill Mastery Profile Report and Student Response

I can use my knowledge of grammar when I read text

In general, with the mastery of this skill students are able to:

- Understand writing that may be long and complicated
- Focus on different types of tense (e.g. past, present, future) to understand the order of an event better
- Read long sentences without much difficulty
- Use punctuation to understand what is happening in a passage

What do you think of your achievement of this skill? Please share your thoughts by writing them below.

I did well because whenever I dont understand something I re-read the sentence or paragraph.

APPENDIX 11.2

Goal Orientations and Future Plan Parts in the Skill Profile Report

PLANNING YOUR GOALS

Now let's plan your next steps. In doing so, we encourage you to think of your approach to learning. This is really important information as it will help you to become a better learner. For example, some people like to learn just because they enjoy learning new things while other people like to learn so that they can show others that they can do it. Or some people don't like to learn because they think it is too hard for them.

In one of the surveys you filled out in December, you indicated that you **learn mostly because you enjoy learning things.**

Do you agree? Tell us more about your learning approach. What makes you want to learn?

Yes I agree because I enjoy learning new facts and concepts.

Now let's plan! When you know what your goals are and work towards meeting them, you become a better learner!

What skills do you want to work on in the next few weeks?

I think I want to work on summarizing because I need to learn how to find the major key points.

Thank you very much for sharing your thoughts with us. We strongly encourage you to share them with your parents and work closely with your teacher.

I am committed to achieving the learning goals I set out above.

I am committed to supporting you in achieving your learning goals.

References

Applegate, M. D., Quinn, K. B., & Applegate, A. J. (2002). Levels of thinking required by comprehension questions in informal reading inventories. *The Reading Teacher, 56*(2), 174–180.

Beck, I. J., McKeown, M. G., Hamilton, R. L., & Kucan, L. (1998). Getting at the meaning: How to help students unpack difficult text. *American Educator, 22*, 66–71.

Bergman, L. R., Magnusson, D., & El Khouri, B. M. (2003). *Studying individual development in an interindividual context: A person-oriented approach.* Mahwah, NJ: Lawrence Erlbaum Associates, Inc.

Butler, Y. G., & Lee, J. (2010). The effects of self-assessment among young learners of English. *Language Testing, 27*(1), 5–31.

Carless, D. (2007). Learning-oriented assessment: Conceptual bases and practical implications. *Innovations in Education and Teaching International, 44*(1), 57–66.

Casey, H. K. (2008). Engaging the disengaged: Using learning clubs to motivate struggling adolescent readers and writers. *Journal of Adolescent & Adult Literacy, 52*(4), 284–294.

Coxhead, A. (2006). *Essentials of teaching academic vocabulary.* Boston: Houghton Mifflin.

Dweck, C. S. (1986). Motivational processes affecting learning. *American Psychologist, 41*(10), 1040–1048.

Evans, M., & Boucher, A. R. (2015). Optimizing the power of choice: Supporting student autonomy to foster motivation and engagement in learning. *Mind, Brain, and Education, 9*(2), 87–91.

Fasel, B., & Luettin, J. (2003). Automatic facial expression analysis: A survey. *Pattern Recognition, 36*, 259–275.

Field, J. (2011). Cognitive validity. In L. Taylor (Ed.), *Examining speaking: Research and practice in assessing second language speaking* (pp. 65–111). Cambridge, UK: Cambridge University.

Garner, R., Brown, R., Sanders, S., & Menke, D. (1992). "Seductive details" and learning from text. In K. A. Renninger, S. Hidi, & A. Krapp (Eds.), *The role of interest in learning and development* (pp. 239–254). Hillsdale, NJ: Erlbaum.

Green, C., Hamnett, L., & Green, S. (2001). Children put the national tests to the test. *Education 3–13, 29*(3), 39–42.

Harp, S. F., & Mayer, R. E. (1998). How seductive details do their damage: A theory of cognitive interest in science learning. *Journal of Educational Psychology, 90*, 414–434.

Hattie, J., & Timperley, H. (2007). The power of feedback. *Review of Educational Research, 77*, 81–112.

Hidi, S. (1990). Interest and its contribution as a mental resource for learning. *Review of Educational Research, 60*(4), 549–571.

Hidi, S. (2001). Interest, reading, and learning: Theoretical and practical considerations. *Educational Psychology Review, 13*(3), 191–209.

Hidi, S., & Baird, W. (1988). Strategies for increasing text-based interest and students' recall of expository texts. *Reading Research Quarterly, 23*(4), 465–483.

Israel, S. E., & Duffy, G. G. (2014). *Handbook of research on reading comprehension.* New York: Routledge.

Jang, E. E. (2009). Cognitive diagnostic assessment of L2 reading comprehension ability: Validity arguments for Fusion Model application to LanguEdge assessment. *Language Testing, 26*(1), 31–73.

Jang, E. E. (2014). *Focus on assessment.* Oxford: Oxford University Press.

Jang, E. E., Dunlop, M., Park, G., & van der Boom, E. H. (2015). How do young students with different profiles of reading skill mastery, perceived ability, and goal orientation respond to holistic diagnostic feedback? *Language Testing, 32*(3), 359–383.

Jang, E. E., Dunlop, M., Wagner, M., Kim, Y. H., & Gu, Z. (2013). Elementary school ELLs' reading skill profiles using cognitive diagnosis modeling: Roles of length of residence and home language environment. *Language Learning, 63*(3), 400–436.

Lee, Y. W., & Sawaki, Y. (2009). Cognitive diagnostic approaches to language assessment: An overview. *Language Assessment Quarterly, 6*(3), 172–189.

Leighton, J. P., & Gierl, M. J. (Eds.). (2007). *Cognitive diagnostic assessment for education: Theory and applications.* Cambridge, MA: Cambridge University Press.

Lenters, K. (2006). Resistance, struggle, and the adolescent reader. *Journal of Adolescent & Adult Literacy, 50*(2), 136–146.

Leslie, L., & Caldwell, J. S. (2006). *Qualitative reading inventory-4* (4th ed.). Boston: Allyn & Bacon.

Locke, E. A., & Latham, G. P. (1990). *A theory of goal setting and task performance.* Englewood Cliffs, NJ: Prentice Hall.

McKay, P. (2006). *Assessing young language learners.* Cambridge: Cambridge University Press.

Palinscar, A. S., Magnusson, S. J., Pesko, S., & Hamlin, M. (2005). Attending to the nature of the subject matter in text comprehension. In S. G. Paris & S. A. Stahl (Eds.), *Children's reading comprehension and assessment* (pp. 257–278). Mahwah, NJ: Erlbaum.

Pekrun, R., Goetz, T., Titz, W., & Perry, R. P. (2002). Academic emotions in students' self- regulated learning and achievement: A program of quantitative and qualitative research. *Educational Psychologist, 37*, 91–106.

Poehner, M. E., Zhang, Y., & Lu, X. (2017). Computer-mediated scaffolding assessments. In M. K. Wolf & Y. G. Butler (Eds.), *English language proficiency assessments for young learners* (pp. 214–233). New York, NY: Routledge.

Purpura, J. E. (1997). An analysis of the relationships between test takers' cognitive and metacognitive strategy use and second language test performance. *Language Learning, 47*, 289–325.

Sansone, C., & Smith, J. L. (2000). The "how" of goal pursuit: Interest and self-regulation. *Psychological Inquiry, 11*(4), 306–309.

Schiefele, U., & Krapp, A. (1996). Topic interest and free recall of expository text. *Learning and Individual Differences, 8*, 141–160.

Schleppegrell, M. J., & O'Hallaron, C. L. (2011). Testing academic language in L2 secondary settings. *Annual Review of Applied Linguistics, 31*, 3–18.

Schoonen, R., & Verhallen, M., (2008). The assessment of deep word knowledge in young first and second language learners. *Language Testing, 25*, 211–236.

Shepard, L. A. (2005). Linking formative assessment to scaffolding. *Educational Leadership, 63*(3), 66–70.

Tomlinson, C. A., Brighton, C., Hertberg, H., Callahan, C. M., Moon, T. R., Brimijoin, K., . . . Reynolds, T. (2003). Differentiating instruction in response to student readiness, interest, and learning profile in academically diverse classrooms: A review of literature. *Journal for the Education of the Gifted, 27*(2/3), 119–145.

van Dijk, M., & van Geert, P. (2014). The nature and meaning of intraindividual variability in development in the early life span. In M. Diehl, K. Hooker, & M. Sliwinski (Eds.), *The handbook of intraindividual variability across the life span* (pp. 37–58). New York: Taylor & Francis.

Williams, J. D., Wallace, T. L., & Sung, H. C. (2016). Providing choice in middle grade classrooms: An exploratory study of enactment variability and student reflection. *Journal of Early Adolescence, 36*(4), 527–550.

Zimmerman, B. J. (1990). Self-regulated learning and academic achievement. *Educational Psychologist, 25*(1), 3–17.

12
COMPUTERIZED DYNAMIC ASSESSMENTS FOR YOUNG LANGUAGE LEARNERS

Matthew E. Poehner, Jie Zhang, and Xiaofei Lu

The field of second language acquisition (SLA) has long contested how learners' emerging control over features of the L2 may best be supported through teacher feedback and correction (e.g., Aljaafreh & Lantolf, 1994; Nassaji & Swain, 2000). While most SLA scholars recognize a need for both meaning-centered, communicative activities for practicing language use as well as instruction that focuses on particular language forms, opinions diverge as to whether learner struggles and errors may most appropriately be addressed through relatively implicit teacher moves, such as recasts, or through more explicit feedback that might include overt correction and metalinguistic explanations (see Erlam, Ellis, & Batstone, 2013; Lantolf, Kisselev, & Kurtz, 2015). This debate concerns theoretical understandings of the quality of knowledge learners acquire during L2 development, specifically whether this knowledge is explicit or implicit in nature, as well as which form(s) of knowledge might be advantageous for promoting learners' spontaneous and appropriate use of the target language (for discussion, see VanPatten & Williams, 2014). In addition to competing conceptual explanations among researchers, this debate also holds consequences for language teachers looking to research for recommendations to guide their practice.

Within the tradition of L2 research informed by L. S. Vygotsky's (1987) Sociocultural Theory of Mind (SCT), the notion of scaffolding has been proposed as a way of organizing interactions to provide support that is responsive to learner needs and adapted moment-to-moment during interaction according to learner responsiveness. While scaffolding has a long history in both the general education and L2 research literatures and has become part of the professional terminology of teachers in many countries, the concept has only relatively recently come to the attention of language testing specialists. Among the drivers of this change has been the emergence of a framework known as Dynamic Assessment (DA), in which various forms of support, often provided through one-to-one interaction, are included in the assessment procedure for the purpose of determining the extent of support learners require to improve their performance (Poehner, 2008). The principle here, derived from Vygotsky's formulation of the Zone of Proximal Development (ZPD), is that observation of learner independent performance of tasks reveals the development of abilities that have already occurred, whereas learner responsiveness during joint functioning with a teacher or other expert is indicative of abilities that have begun to form, but have not yet completed their development. DA thus advocates that to understand the full range of learner abilities—including both those that have already developed and those that are only emerging—joint engagement is required.

Our aim in this chapter is to consider how DA, especially in a computerized form, may be applied to understand the abilities and needs of school-aged (K–8) learners of English as an additional language. As DA is relatively new in the field of language assessment, and computer-based applications of DA have only just begun to be explored, we are unaware of any empirical studies applying this framework to contexts involving young English language learners. Nonetheless, our experience employing DA principles in one-to-one, small group, and computerized contexts with learners of different languages and at various proficiency levels and ages compels us to view computerized DA (C-DA) as offering much to researchers and practitioners in English language education. To this end, our discussion includes an explication of the theoretical principles behind C-DA as well as presentation of examples from two recent projects conducted with L2 learners.

The first study involved learners of L2 Spanish in a U.S. elementary school. Our reason for sharing this work is to illustrate the process of mediation with young L2 learners. While the target language in this case is Spanish rather than English, our interest is in the activity of engaging with learners and offering increasingly explicit forms of support in order to determine the level at which learners identify and overcome mistakes. The logic of this principle drives DA procedures and does not vary depending on the language studied.

The second study involves the application of C-DA to listening and reading comprehension assessments of university-level learners of L2 Chinese. Of interest here is that this project is, to our knowledge, the first to exclusively employ computers to deliver mediation to L2 learners. Outcomes from this project thus far have been sufficiently promising that we believe it represents a new and important direction for assessing L2 learners, including school-aged learners of English. Before we discuss the theoretical background behind DA and the particular considerations associated with C-DA, we present examples from the elementary school L2 Spanish project so that readers may glimpse a DA procedure firsthand.

Scaffolding Young L2 Learners During Classroom Activity

The following interaction is taken from a larger project (Poehner, 2015) in which a U.S. elementary school fourth-grade classroom teacher followed principles of DA to scaffold, or *mediate*, her students' engagement in daily activities focused on L2 Spanish instruction. The teacher, Anne (a pseudonym), was given considerable latitude in designing her lessons and the particular features of Spanish language and culture upon which she focused. In the lesson from which this lesson was drawn, Anne and her students were studying a unit on Argentina that included historical and cultural information while also targeting beginning level vocabulary and grammar. Anne had arranged for an Argentinian guest to visit the class and to take their questions about the country. In order for the students to use Spanish as much as possible during the visit, Anne was working with the class to help them formulate questions in the target language. The activity also provided an opportunity for students to practice the use of Spanish interrogatives.

Early in the lesson, Anne reminded the class of frequent interrogative pronouns and adjectives in Spanish and then solicited example questions from students. One of the children, Tyler (a pseudonym), volunteered. We enter the exchange as Anne recognizes him and he shares a sentence he has drafted.

1. *Anne:* Okay. Shh. Okay, Tyler?
2. *Tyler:* ¿Qué es tu favorito equipo de fútbol?
   What is your favorite soccer team?
3. *Anne:* [Pause]
4. *Tyler:* [Silence]
5. *Anne:* ¿Qué es tu favorito equipo de fútbol?
   What is your favorite soccer team
6. *Tyler:* Fútbol equipo. . .
   Soccer team. . .
7. *Anne:* ¿favorito equipo?
   Favorite team?
8. *Tyler:* si, favorito equipo.
   Yes, favorite team
9. *Anne:* ¿Qué es tu "favorito equipo" o "equipo favorito"?
10. *Tyler:* equipo favorito.
11. *Anne:* uh-huh. ¿Por qué? Why?
12. *Tyler:* umm
13. *Anne:* ¿Qué es tu equipo favorito? Tyler porque es equipo favorito y no es favorito equipo?
    What is your favorite team? Tyler why is it favorite team [noun first] and not favorite team [adjective first]?
14. *Tyler:* [Silence]

15. *Anne:* Como dijo. . . . porque the adjective a lot of times will come after
as I said. . . . because
the noun. Umm hmm. Okay, ¿Otros voluntarios?
Other volunteers?

It is worth noting from the outset that Tyler selects the interrogative form *qué* rather than *cuál*, which is what one would normally use for the kind of question he is posing. The source of confusion here is that *qué* is an interrogative pronoun typically rendered in English as 'what' and *cuál* is rendered as 'which.' In the present context, *cuál* is actually the appropriate pronoun in Spanish because it involves selecting from among a set of options (i.e., which team) rather than seeking a definition (e.g., what is a sports team?). Of course, in English, Tyler's L1, 'what' is often used in such instances, particularly when speaking. Anne chooses not to address this issue and in fact repeats *qué* herself in lines 5, 9, and 13. It may be simply that she chose instead to focus her attention on the noun-adjective construction in the sentence and did not mention the use of *qué* so as to not further confuse Tyler. That issue aside, the interaction showcases how the teacher attempted to implement the logic of graduated prompting in DA. That is, rather than overtly correcting Tyler's erroneous placement of *favorito*, which in Spanish would normally follow rather than precede the noun it is modifying, Anne opted to work through a series of prompts wherein each became more explicit than the last. Specifically, in line 3 we see that Anne pauses in response to Tyler's error. This move creates a space in which the learner might consider his response and attempt to identify and even correct any mistake. When this does not lead to a response from Tyler, Anne repeats his construction with a questioning intonation, signaling that there is at least some doubt that this is acceptable and that he must reconsider it. In line 6 Tyler responds by offering a revised statement. While he has indeed altered the original word order, he has mistakenly focused on the noun *equipo de fútbol* rather than the placement of the adjective *favorito*. His change to the incorrect *fútbol equipo*, following English syntax, nonetheless, indicates his awareness that English and Spanish have their own word order patterns.

Anne's next move becomes more explicit as she repeats only the portion of his original utterance that was problematic (i.e., *favorito equipo*). In doing so, she redirects his attention to the actual error without in fact providing any feedback as to the nature of the problem. Interestingly, this too proves insufficient for Tyler to correct as he instead confirms that *favorito equipo* was indeed what he had produced. At this point, Anne might have provided an additional prompt such as a reminder about nouns and adjectives in Spanish or perhaps another example he could see as a model for adjective placement. In line 9 she offers him a choice between two constructions (with the adjective preceding and following the noun, respectively). Tyler's selection of the correct *equipo favorito* of course does not imply that he understands his mistake; he may simply have chosen that form because he understood that Anne had not accepted his original response. For this reason, it is important that Anne prompted him to explain his choice. Tyler is unable to comply, and ultimately it is Anne herself who concludes the exchange by reminding him that this pattern (noun followed by adjective) occurs frequently in Spanish. She offers no additional explanation but chooses to move on at that point to other students' questions.

As a purely teaching-focused episode, it would have perhaps been helpful to Tyler and his classmates if Anne had offered more details about this kind of syntactic construction and provided additional examples for them to practice. However, viewed as an assessment of Tyler's understanding of this feature of the target language, Anne was able to ascertain that he likely will require additional instruction. Her diagnosis would certainly have been different if, for instance, Tyler had recognized and corrected his mistake early in the interaction. The point is that the process of scaffolding, in this case, providing increasingly explicit forms of what Vygotsky called mediation allows for insights into learner abilities according to the level of support they require to correct their performance. In the exchange we considered, this process of mediation began with Anne's initial pause, followed by a repetition of Tyler's utterance, then a repetition of only the part containing an error, offering a choice between alternating forms, and finally asking him to explain his response. In the next section, we explain in detail Vygotsky's argument that the level of support learners require is inversely proportional to their proximity to successful independent functioning.

Theoretical Background and Approaches to Dynamic Assessment

As mentioned earlier, Vygotsky's (1978, 1987) proposal of the ZPD provides the theoretical basis for DA. Holzman (2008) explains that many find an almost intuitive appeal to the concept of the ZPD and that this helps to explicate both its popularity with researchers and teachers as well as the differing interpretations of it that have taken root. She continues that the ZPD has been understood in terms of a set of latent capacities that individuals possess, a set of techniques for measuring such capacities, a dialogic framework for teaching and learning, or simply a justification for trying to help learners when they encounter difficulties. Indeed, the notion of scaffolding itself, originally proposed by Wood, Bruner, and Ross (1976) and strongly influenced by Vygotsky's writings on the ZPD, has similarly been subject to numerous interpretations and applications, with the result that the term can evoke very different assumptions and practices (see Walqui, 2006).

Placed within the broader context of SCT, the ZPD captures concretely Vygotsky's thesis of the centrality of mediation for the development and functioning of the human mind. Various forms of culturally available mediation, including notably language but also counting systems, images, and concepts, characterize human psychological functioning in contexts of working alone (e.g., a learner completing assessment or instructional tasks independently) as well as collaboration with others (e.g., that same learner completing the tasks through interaction with a teacher or with peers).

In both cases, learner psychological activity is mediated; in the former setting, the learner relies upon mediation she or he has already fully appropriated or *internalized*; in the latter scenario, the learner relies on this internalized mediation, but also may benefit from interaction as a valuable resource. Vygotsky (1978) conceived of these two different ways of functioning as indicative of an individual's Zone of Actual Development and Zone of Proximal Development, respectively, and emphasized that these capture two different dimensions of abilities. While actual development pertains to abilities that have already fully formed, proximal development concerns what appears to be on the horizon of an individual's psychological functioning. These abilities have begun to form, but are not yet fully developed. This is an essential point to keep in mind, as the ZPD should not be taken to mean anything that an individual can do when others are present. For example, a young child could follow a teacher's explicit directions to put specific marks on a page and so might appear to solve advanced problems in physics, but this does not mean that the relevant conceptual understandings are in the process of emerging for the child. It is for this reason that graduated support, as in the elementary school L2 Spanish example, is necessary for determining whether abilities are in fact developing for an individual and how near or far the individual is from independent functioning. An individual who requires only very implicit support is close to independent functioning (i.e., operating fully within their Zone of Actual Development) whereas an individual who needs more extensive, explicit prompting has further to go.

Vygotsky (1998) wrote of the importance of the ZPD for both assessment and teaching. With regard to assessment, it should be clear that the provision of mediation during activity helps to reveal abilities that are emerging. In terms of teaching, Vygotsky argued that it is precisely those same abilities that should be the focus of intervention. Put another way, instruction that targets abilities that have already formed (an individual's Zone of Actual Development) will have little or no impact on development, and instruction aimed at abilities that are so advanced that the learner has not yet begun to develop them will similarly be of limited value. The principle of aligning mediation to learner needs drives both efforts to diagnose a learner's ZPD as well as instruction to promote further development. As Lantolf and Poehner (2014) explain, Vygotsky conceived of assessment and teaching as interrelated features of the same process. A full assessment of learner abilities requires a specialized form of teaching (the provision of graduated mediation) just as teaching that is optimally aligned with learner needs requires sustained tracking of their emerging abilities.

The various procedures that have been developed in the general education and psychology research literatures and that are collectively referred to as Dynamic Assessment each represent efforts to formalize an approach to diagnosing learners' emerging abilities through the integration of mediation in the assessment. In their review of DA research, Haywood and Lidz (2007) suggest that these approaches may be grouped along a continuum, with some opting for interventions in learner thinking that are both extensive and intensive and others tending more toward probing thinking in order to gauge learner responsiveness. Deeper intervention would seem to realize Vygotsky's understanding of the relevance of the ZPD for instruction. In the L2 field, Poehner and Infante (2015) have recently suggested the term Mediated Development to refer to interactions that differ from DA's commitment to diagnosis in favor of actively guiding learners toward new ways of thinking. The probing end of the spectrum orients to the goal of determining the level of prompting that a learner needs before correctly responding to test items.

Both poles of this continuum implicate teaching and assessment, but they differ with regard to which is given the priority. Between the poles exists a range of DA procedures. Space does not permit a review of them in the present chapter, but we refer readers to Haywood and Lidz (2007) and Poehner (2008) for detailed discussions. What is most relevant for our purposes is that some approaches to DA conceive of mediation through open-ended, dialogic interaction between teachers and learners, where both are free to explore problems as they arise and there is considerable latitude given to how teachers may respond to learner difficulties. Such approaches to DA, which Lantolf and Poehner (2004) have termed *interactionist*, are most frequently found in classroom settings. Other approaches to DA, which Lantolf and Poehner refer to as *interventionist*, tend more strongly toward the probing end of the continuum and generally use mediation in a standardized format. Here, mediation is scripted as sets of prompts or feedback that is administered in precisely the same manner to all learners who experience difficulties during the assessment. We suggest that neither of these ways of conceiving DA is 'correct,' but rather that both offer advantages relative to different purposes and contexts. As we explain in the next section, both interactionist and interventionist DA informed our work as we designed a computerized model of L2 DA.

Toward Programmed Scaffolding: Computerized Dynamic Assessment (C-DA)

Since its introduction to the L2 field, DA has mostly been implemented in instructional contexts and has typically favored an interactionist approach (see, for instance, Poehner & Rea-Dickins, 2013). This trend reflects perhaps perceptions of DA's immediate relevance to teacher efforts to better understand and respond to learner needs during classroom activities. From the perspective of research, this work permitted the elaboration of concepts and principles in DA that have been drawn upon as researchers have more recently turned their attention to uses of DA in more formal testing situations.

Here, we describe what we consider to be an especially important avenue for future assessment practice with L2 learners, including young learners of English: computerized DA. Our initial exploration of delivering mediation in DA through a computerized system focused on listening and reading abilities among university learners of L2 Chinese, French, and Russian.[1] The assessments are delivered online through a web-based interface written in PHP and HTML. Both the listening and reading tests in the three languages are comprised of multiple-choice format questions. The precise number of questions varies among the tests as the administration time for each test is designed to be no more than one hour, with most students during the piloting phase requiring approximately 40 minutes for completion. Three rounds of piloting were included in the design of C-DA tests. The first focused on refining the test instruments themselves and was done in a paper-and-pencil format. The second pilot involved administering the tests in a one-to-one DA format in order to determine the challenges that each question presented to learners and the forms of mediation that appeared most helpful. For the third pilot, the computerized tests were used and a set of four prompts, based on analysis of the one-to-one DA interactions, were scripted to accompany each test item. These prompts are included as part of the test program so that they automatically appear, one at a time, when a learner answers a test question incorrectly. All piloting was conducted with university level intermediate learners of Chinese, French, and Russian. Additional details of the larger project have been discussed elsewhere (Poehner & Lantolf, 2013; Poehner, Zhang, & Lu, 2015).

Our present discussion draws examples from the Chinese tests to illustrate the logic behind the tests, conceptualizations of performance, and procedures for scoring and reporting outcomes, all of which needs to be taken into consideration when developing such assessments. Following this, we share lessons gleaned from this experience that will be informative for future work aimed at following principles of C-DA to assess young learners of English.

Designing Test Instruments and Built-in Scaffolding

The C-DA tests were intended to determine learner control over grammatical features as well as knowledge of vocabulary and culture required for listening and reading comprehension at a level roughly equivalent to third-semester undergraduate university study (the level of basic language study required by many U.S. universities). In addition to potential relevance to placing students in a program of L2 study, the tests were also planned to be relevant to language instructors who might administer them at the start and conclusion of a semester as a means of charting learner progress. With these aims in mind, multiple-choice listening and reading tests were written inspired from practice items for the Chinese Proficiency Test (HSK), China's national standardized test designed for nonnative speakers of Chinese. In total, 23 multiple-choice items were prepared for the listening test and 24 for the reading test. Each item targets one or two of the following language constructs: phonetics (for the listening test), vocabulary, grammar (with a tense/potential form sub construct), pragmatics, contextual inference, and information seeking. The tests were then piloted with students enrolled in second- and third-year Chinese courses, item analyses conducted, and revisions to the tests carried out before moving to the next stage of the project.

At this point, efforts shifted from development of the test instruments themselves to an administration procedure that integrated DA principles. To this end, both the listening and reading tests were administered in a one-to-one format with roughly six students. A member of the research team was present as students individually completed the tests, and that person asked students to verbalize reasons for their responses. Equally important, the team member engaged in a process of graduated prompting and interaction with learners when they responded to test items incorrectly. The interactions paralleled the exchange between Anne and Tyler in the Spanish example discussed earlier in that prompts were offered to learners as needed and became increasingly explicit if learners continued to struggle. This process was followed for every item on both tests with each learner. The interactions were video recorded, analyzed by the research team, and used as a basis for scripting inventories of prompts for each test item. This approach in itself was regarded by the research team as an important advance over previous uses of C-DA because the mediation was conceived not merely according to testers' assumptions of how items might challenge learners but was informed by interaction with learners and learner verbalizations.

The basic logic of moving from implicit to explicit characterizes the inventories for all test items, and certain moves, such as directing learner attention to a particular construction or offering a choice between two forms, are very common. However, variability also exists as the prompts needed to target the specific construct underlying the test item in question. Test takers are permitted a total of four attempts for each item as the number of choices associated with each item was increased from four in the original version to five. In this way, the tests maximize learner opportunities to receive prompts. After the student has chosen the correct answer or after all four prompts are used, an explanation of the correct answer is offered to ensure that all learners have the opportunity to fully understand the problem, including those who picked the correct answer but only partially understood the question. Appendix 12.1 illustrates the mediation process that accompanies the sample item from the Chinese reading test that is reproduced in Figure 12.1. Readers may refer to Appendix 12.1 as they read the description of the mediation process in what follows.

The passage in Figure 12.1 comprises a first-person narrative in which the author, noting friends' frequent complaints despite their life getting better, voices disagreement by recounting personal experience concerning money 'wasted' on medication to overcome asthma.

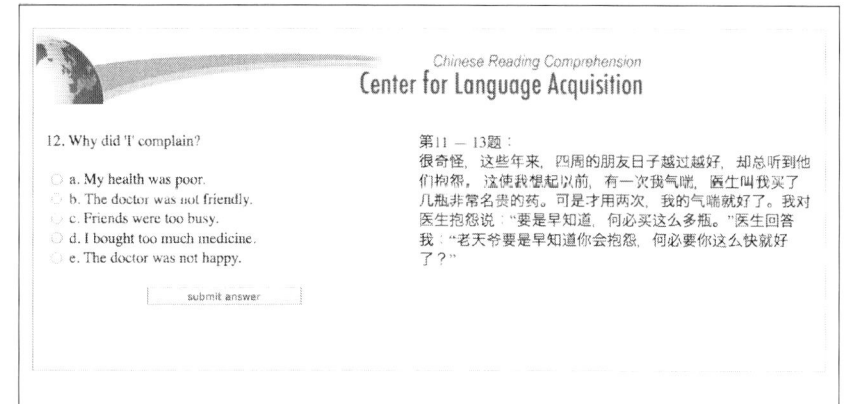

> 12. Why did 'I' complain?
>
> ○ a. My health was poor.
> ○ b. The doctor was not friendly.
> ○ c. Friends were too busy.
> ○ d. I bought too much medicine.
> ○ e. The doctor was not happy.
>
> [submit answer]
>
> 第11 — 13题：
> 很奇怪，这些年来，四周的朋友日子越过越好，却总听到他们抱怨，这使我想起以前，有一次我气喘，医生叫我买了几瓶非常名贵的药。可是才用两次，我的气喘就好了。我对医生抱怨说："要是早知道，何必买这么多瓶。"医生回答我："老天爷要是早知道你会抱怨，何必要你这么快就好了？"
>
> **Translation of the Chinese text:**
>
> *Strangely, the life of my friends has been getting better and better over the years, but they keep complaining. This reminds me of what once happened to me. I had asthma one time, and my doctor prescribed several bottles of expensive medicine. But I was cured after only two doses. I complained to my doctor, "Had I known this earlier, why would I have bought so many bottles?" My doctor replied, "Had God known you would complain, why would He have had you recover so soon?"*

FIGURE 12.1 Sample Reading Text and Item From Chinese C-DA Test

Source: Screenshot taken from http://calper.la.psu.edu/dynamic_assessment/exams/.

If a student's initial response is incorrect, the first prompt is given: "*That's not the correct answer. Read the highlighted part again.* The segment of the text is highlighted in green shown on the right column of the computer screen: 可是才用两次，我的气喘就好了。我对医生抱怨说："要是早知道，何必买这么多瓶。" (But I was cured after only two doses. I complained to my doctor, "Had I known this earlier, why would I have bought so many bottles?"). If a student's second attempt is also incorrect, the second prompt narrows the search space and point students to the key language constructs: "*That's still not the correct answer. Did you notice the highlighted part* 可是才用两次，我的气喘就好了。 *What does it mean?*" Again, the text mentioned in this prompt is projected on the right side of the computer screen highlighted in orange. If this also fails to provoke a correct response, the third prompt provides more explicit support by explaining the key elements in the segment: "*Let's try it one more time.* 可是才用两次，我的气喘就好了 *means 'I only took the medication twice and then I recovered from asthma.' What does this sentence tell you?*" The relevant bit of text this time is highlighted in red. The last and most explicit form of mediation reveals the correct answer along with the option to view an explanation for the answer: "*The correct answer was 'd'. Click to view an explanation.*" The explanation reads: "*Because the author recovered by taking the medication only twice, he complained about having bought too many bottles of medicine.*"

Scoring and Profiling Learner Abilities

Upon completion of the test, students immediately receive an automatically generated report that includes a set of scores and a learning profile. A sample learner profile and group profile is provided in Appendix 12.2. The decision to add a profile along with the scores was a response to the complexity of trying to capture both abilities that have already developed and those that are still emerging. In total, four scores are included for each learner: an *actual score*, a *mediated score*, a *transfer score*, and a *learning potential score*. Each is described in detail below. The accompanying learner profile groups test items according to the dimension of L2 comprehension targeted and so in this way reveals how much support (i.e., how many prompts) the learner requires in different language areas (vocabulary, grammar, phonetics, pragmatics, contextual inference, and so forth). As mentioned, in addition to reports of individual learner performance, the program also generates reports for groups or classes of learners that may be accessed by teachers and other stakeholders.

To understand the scoring procedures, recall that mediation in our C-DA tests, as in DA research more generally (e.g., Poehner, 2007, 2008), conceives of learner responsiveness as an indication of their development. Students needing minimal, implicit meditation are closer to independent functioning and will likely require less instructional investment to reach that point than will learners requiring extensive, explicit mediation during the tests. To reflect these differences, weighted scores are generated by the C-DA tests. The maximum points for each item is four, and each prompt used results in a one-point deduction from the maximum points. In other words, a student who uses the first prompt to arrive at the correct answer to an item receives three points for that item; a student who uses two prompts receives two points for the item, and so on. This weighted score reflecting the number of mediating prompts used is referred to as the learner's *mediated score*. In the test report, the *actual score*, i.e., the sum of the scores for the items answered correctly without mediation, reflects the student's independent performance, whereas the *mediated score*, i.e., the sum of the weighted scores for all items, reflects the student's assisted performance and the amount of mediation they required during the test.

While *actual* and *mediated scores* reflect, respectively, students' unassisted performance (their actual development) and their assisted performance (how near they are to independent function), a third score that was introduced aimed to quantify the difference between these test scores relative to the maximum score possible on the test. This score, referred to as *learning potential score* (LPS), was conceived by Kozulin and Garb (2002) in their use of DA with children and adult immigrant learners in Israel. They propose LPS as calculated according to the following formula:

$$2 * (\text{Mediated Score} - \text{Actual Score}) / \text{Maximum Score}$$

According to Kozulin and Garb, the advantage afforded by LPS is that it allows one to track relative gains after mediation experienced by individual learners. Indeed, a recent study of pilot administrations of the C-DA tests has revealed that students with the same *actual score* sometimes end up with different *mediated scores* or surprisingly different *LPSs* (Poehner et al., 2015). This suggests that learners benefit differentially from mediation during the tests, a finding that in fact aligns with Vygotsky's (1987) writings on the ZPD. Although we have adopted Kozulin and Garb's (2002) formula and believe that LPS offers insights into learner development, we wish to note that our use of the term 'learning potential' does not connote any fixed or innate capacity but rather may be properly understood as the receptiveness to mediation a learner exhibited during the testing procedure, which in SCT is indicative of the amount of continued instruction likely to be required to promote development.

The final score reported by the C-DA tests is *transfer*. This builds upon the principle in SCT and other learning theories that true development involves flexible application of concepts and principles to situations and problems that differ from those previously encountered by learners. Given that the availability of prompts as well as the explanations accompanying every test item are intended to support learning during the procedure itself, the C-DA tests also evaluate whether and how well a learner can apply new knowledge gained from mediation to solve new problems later in the test. To this end, we included a number of transfer items at the end of each test. A transfer item targets a similar language construct tested by one or more earlier items but presents it in a different and more complex context. The test reports a *transfer score* that reflects learner performance on those transfer items. The *transfer score* allows us to see whether mediation provided for previous items led to improved understanding and performance in new contexts, which provides additional information about how much the student has benefited from the mediation. For more discussion on transfer items, readers are referred to Lantolf and Poehner (2014).

Taken together the *actual*, *mediated*, *transfer*, and *learning potential scores* offer a detailed picture of where each student stands and how students differ from one other. In the C-DA tests, these scores are supplemented by a breakdown of learner performance—including the number of prompts they required—according to items that targeted particular constructs or dimensions of comprehension. Learner profiles visually present a performance both by language construct and by test item. By considering profiles alongside the scores, it is possible to see whether, for example, learners who have identical mediated scores or actual scores might also exhibit differences (strengths or weaknesses) with regard to particular language dimensions (e.g., grammar, phonology, and lexical knowledge). This information may be of considerable value to planning future instruction.

Discussion and Looking Ahead for the Application of Computerized DA for Young Language Learners

As explained, the use of DA to understand the needs of L2 learners and to support their development is relatively new, and the integration of DA principles into a computerized testing environment has only just begun. Nonetheless, these initial efforts have been sufficiently encouraging that we believe C-DA holds considerable promise as a part of broader education practices to help school-aged English learners to succeed. Drawing from the empirical studies we have discussed, we conclude this chapter by pointing to three areas that future research will need to examine if C-DA's relevance to English learner education is to be realized.

Among the most important issues in L2 C-DA, in our view, is that outcomes of the procedure are shared with stakeholders in a manner that is both comprehensible and actionable. Any insights into learner abilities gained through C-DA are of no value if, for instance, teachers and learners are unable to determine how to act upon the information provided. We offer, as a hypothetical example, a C-DA procedure designed to assess English learners' comprehension of academic writing such as that found in their textbooks. Such a project would certainly begin by defining the overall construct as well as the particular component features that would be targeted by various test items. In this regard, the procedure of developing a C-DA would not differ from other assessments. As with other assessments, reporting of learner performance could include a global score on the test as a whole as well as scores for various subsections. However, C-DA also has a commitment to representing learner abilities that are in the process of forming, that is, their ZPD, as well as any development that might have occurred during the test's mediation process. In the C-DA project described in this chapter, the actual score, reflecting learners' current abilities, was supplemented by a weighted score to capture the degree of mediation they required during the assessment as well as a transfer score for their performance as they attempted items written at a higher level of difficulty. There may well be more effective means of communicating these diagnostic insights to stakeholders, such as through qualitative descriptions of an individual's performance on particular sections of the test.

We suggest that at a minimum a set of scores, such as the ones we have considered, is important for fully representing learner abilities. As we hope the reader can appreciate, Vygotskian theory compels us to argue that learner independent performance cannot, by itself, adequately predict their immediate potential development. Put another way, examining whether English learners can complete particular tasks on their own may reveal abilities that have fully formed, but it tells us little about abilities that are still developing. This is where their responsiveness to mediation is crucial. Similarly, transfer scores emphasize the potential for the mediation provided during C-DA to not merely probe learner development but to promote it. Including transfer items in a C-DA procedure and reporting learner scores for those items captures whether movement has already begun to occur in learner abilities and how much instructional investment might be required following the test.

Interconnected with the presentation of C-DA outcomes is the question of what teachers of English learners might do with that information. One possibility would be to consider grouping learners not according to their current abilities but according to their ZPD, as indicated by their responsiveness to mediation during the assessment. The logic here is that if learners have similar ZPDs, then instruction could be tailored to the abilities that are currently emerging for a group of learners. Such tailored instruction would, according to SCT, be optimal for guiding learner development. This is a matter for empirical investigation, and in fact one study is currently underway by two of the authors (Zhang & Lu, 2015). This project uses learner performance on the Chinese C-DA tests to create groups within classes of learners so that teachers may better align their efforts to learner emerging abilities. For this project, learners are first categorized as high, intermediate, or low scorers according to their performance on the tests. Different assignments are then given to students to target particular areas of difficulty, as indicated by their learning profile from the test. Students also receive support that is tailored to their learning needs according to DA principles both during in-class activities as well as take-home work. The results of this work remain to be seen, but it may carry considerable import for guiding the day-to-day instructional practices of teachers as they work to meet the needs of L2 learners.

Finally, there is the matter of the precise form of mediation designed for use in C-DA. While a system of graduated prompting proved both feasible and useful in the L2 Chinese project, which targeted adolescent and adult learners, future designs of C-DA, especially those intended for use with younger learners, could explore more interactive ways of providing mediation. Indeed, school-aged learners of English may well represent a higher degree of variation in their abilities than is the case for adult learners of a foreign language. Given the potentially wide-ranging backgrounds of English learners, greater flexibility in what is targeted by the computer-based mediation would likely yield more nuanced and accurate diagnoses of their abilities. One approach that may be viable is to offer more expanded menus of prompts that are grouped to provide different kinds of support for different tasks. In this way, some English learners might receive lexical support with a task, whereas others could avail of assistance with complex grammatical structures. Multiple menus of graduated prompts for the same assessment task could allow assessors and learners to further tailor mediation to specific difficulties that individuals experience. In fact, depending upon learners' awareness of their own abilities and challenges, one might also consider the design of clickable and expandable options that would allow learners themselves to select the menu of prompts they believe will be most helpful to them as they work through a given task.

In addition to engineering greater flexibility within the mediation process in C-DA, there are other considerations in designing appropriate mediation for school-aged English learners. One issue is that it is likely not feasible to provide mediation in the L1 of each learner. Consequently, mediation in English introduces further complexity as a lack of responsiveness on the part of learners might indicate that the mediation was not explicit enough but could equally signal that the language in which the mediation was offered was simply too difficult. Similarly, lengthy written prompts, feedback, and explanations may prove less helpful with young learners or learners with limited reading abilities in English. Auditory provision of prompts along with pictorial representations and other images might prove far more useful—and potentially engaging—to young learners. It is our hope that these questions as well as others will be taken up by researchers in an effort to better understand how C-DA might be undertaken with learners of English in U.S. schools.

APPENDIX 12.1

Screen Shots of the Mediation Process for Sample Test Item

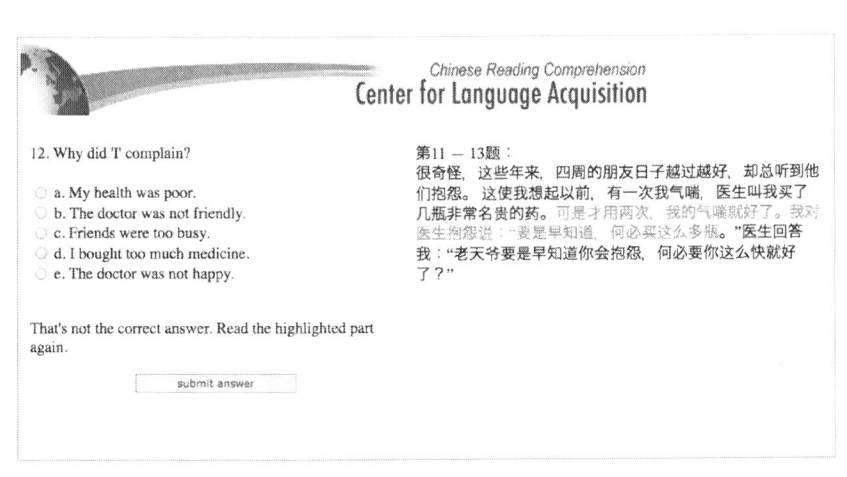

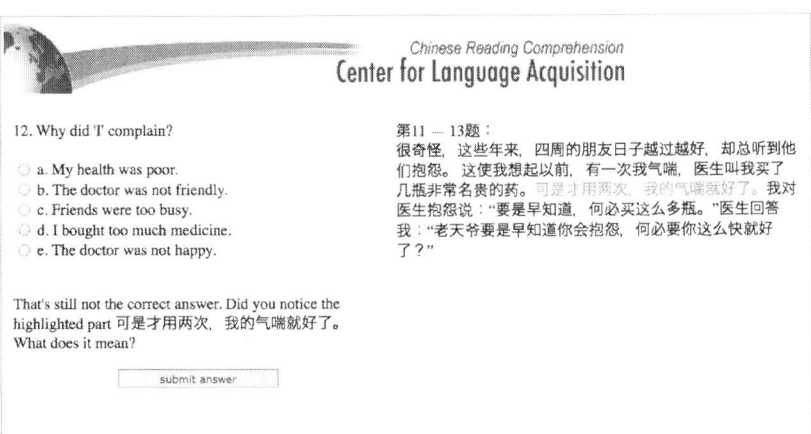

Chinese Reading Comprehension
Center for Language Acquisition

12. Why did 'T' complain?

○ a. My health was poor.
○ b. The doctor was not friendly.
○ c. Friends were too busy.
○ d. I bought too much medicine.
○ e. The doctor was not happy.

第11 — 13题：
很奇怪，这些年来，四周的朋友日子越过越好，却总听到他们抱怨。这使我想起以前，有一次我气喘，医生叫我买了几瓶非常名贵的药。可是才用两次，我的气喘就好了。我对医生抱怨说："要是早知道，何必买这么多瓶。"医生回答我："老天爷要是早知道你会抱怨，何必要你这么快就好了？"

That's not the correct answer. Read the highlighted part again.

[submit answer]

Chinese Reading Comprehension
Center for Language Acquisition

12. Why did 'T' complain?

○ a. My health was poor.
○ b. The doctor was not friendly.
○ c. Friends were too busy.
○ d. I bought too much medicine.
○ e. The doctor was not happy.

第11 — 13题：
很奇怪，这些年来，四周的朋友日子越过越好，却总听到他们抱怨。这使我想起以前，有一次我气喘，医生叫我买了几瓶非常名贵的药。可是才用两次，我的气喘就好了。我对医生抱怨说："要是早知道，何必买这么多瓶。"医生回答我："老天爷要是早知道你会抱怨，何必要你这么快就好了？"

That's still not the correct answer. Did you notice the highlighted part 可是才用两次，我的气喘就好了。What does it mean?

[submit answer]

230 Matthew E. Poehner, Jie Zhang, Xiaofei Lu

Chinese Reading Comprehension
Center for Language Acquisition

12. Why did 'I' complain?

○ a. My health was poor.
○ b. The doctor was not friendly.
○ c. Friends were too busy.
○ d. I bought too much medicine.
○ e. The doctor was not happy.

第11 — 13题：
很奇怪，这些年来，四周的朋友日子越过越好，却总听到他们抱怨。这使我想起以前，有一次我气喘，医生叫我买了几瓶非常名贵的药。可是才用两次，我的气喘就好了。我对医生抱怨说："要是早知道，何必买这么多瓶。"医生回答我："老天爷要是早知道你会抱怨，何必要你这么快就好了？"

Let's try it one more time. 可是才用两次，我的气喘就好了 means 'I only took the medication twice and then I recovered from asthma.' What does this sentence tell you?

[submit answer]

Chinese Reading Comprehension
Center for Language Acquisition

12. Why did 'I' complain?

a. My health was poor.
b. The doctor was not friendly.
c. Friends were too busy.
⦿ d. I bought too much medicine.
e. The doctor was not happy.

第11 — 13题：
很奇怪，这些年来，四周的朋友日子越过越好，却总听到他们抱怨。这使我想起以前，有一次我气喘，医生叫我买了几瓶非常名贵的药。可是才用两次，我的气喘就好了。我对医生抱怨说："要是早知道，何必买这么多瓶。"医生回答我："老天爷要是早知道你会抱怨，何必要你这么快就好了？"

The correct answer was 'd.' [Click to View an Explanation]

[next item]

Taken from http://calper.la.psu.edu/dynamic_assessment/exams/.

APPENDIX 12.2

Screen Shots of the C-DA Chinese Reading Test

Date Taken: March-16-2014
Total Number of Questions: 24
MEDIATED SCORE: 63 / 96
ACTUAL SCORE: 24 / 96
(TOTAL TIME: 0:24:04 (1444 seconds))
Requested explanations for the following items: 1 3

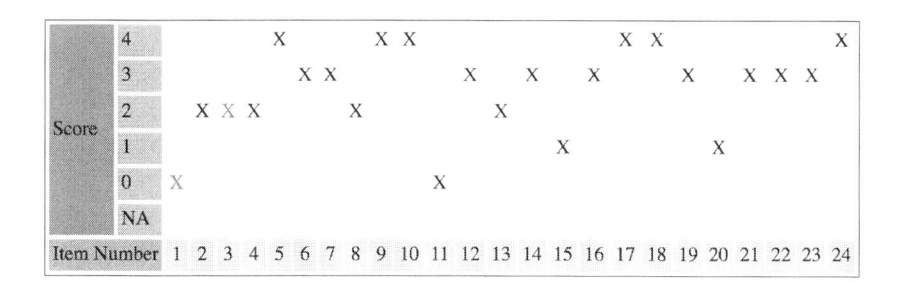

Score																								
4				X		X X							X X				X							X
3					X X			X		X	X			X				X		X X X				
2	X X X				X				X															
1										X					X									
0	X							X																
NA																								
Item Number	1	2	3	4	5	6	7	8	9	10	11	12	13	14	15	16	17	18	19	20	21	22	23	24

Score																								
4		X		X		X X			X	X		X				X			X					
3			X X		X			X	X X		X X				X		X	X			X			
2	X X			X					X			X	X X			X								
1						X		X												X				
0	X			X														X						
Construct				Vocabulary											Structure		Genre				Discourse			
Item Number	1	2	3	5	6	7	8	9	11	14	15	17	18	19	20	21	22	23	24	2	9	22	23	24	3	4	7	8	10	11	12	13	16	17	20	21

A. Screen shots of a learner profile generated by the C-DA Chinese reading test

B. Screen shots of a group profile generated by the C-DA Chinese reading test

Taken from http://calper.la.psu.edu/dynamic_assessment/exams/results.php

Acknowledgements

We would like to thank Kristin Davin for her work with the Spanish data discussed in this chapter.

Note

1 The listening and reading tests in each of the three languages can be accessed for free at http://calper.la.psu.edu/daexams_request.php.

References

Aljaafreh, A., & Lantolf, J. P. (1994). Negative feedback as regulation and second language learning in the Zone of Proximal Development. *The Modern Language Journal*, 78, 465–483.

Erlam, R., Ellis, R., & Batstone, R. (2013). Oral corrective feedback on L2 writing: Two approaches compared. *System*, 41(2), 257–268.

Haywood, H. C., & Lidz, C. S. (2007). *Dynamic assessment in practice: Clinical and educational applications.* Cambridge: Cambridge University Press.

Holzman, L. (2008). *Vygotsky at work and play.* New York, NY: Routledge.

Kozulin, A., & Garb, E. (2002). Dynamic assessment of EFL text comprehension of at-risk students. *School Psychology International*, 23(1), 112–127.

Lantolf, J. P., Kisselev, O., & Kurtz, L. (2015). *Explaining the zone of proximal development: Why levels of mediation matter.* Paper presented at the Second Language Research Forum, Atlanta, GA.

Lantolf, J. P., & Poehner, M. E. (2004). Dynamic assessment: Bringing the past into the future. *Journal of Applied Linguistics*, 1(1), 49–74.

Lantolf, J. P., & Poehner, M. E. (2014). *Sociocultural theory and the pedagogical imperative in L2 education: Vygotskian praxis and the research/practice divide.* London: Routledge.

Nassaji, H., & Swain, M. (2000). A Vygotskian perspective on corrective feedback in L2: The effect of random versus negotiated help on the learning of English articles. *Language Awareness*, *9*(1), 34–51.

Poehner, M. E. (2007). Beyond the test: L2 dynamic assessment and the transcendence of mediated learning. *The Modern Language Journal*, *91*(3), 323–340.

Poehner, M. E. (2008). *Dynamic assessment: A Vygotskian approach to understanding and promoting second language development*. Berlin: Springer.

Poehner, M. E. (2015). *A casebook of dynamic assessment in foreign language education*. University Park, PA: Center for Advanced Language Proficiency Education and Research, The Pennsylvania State University.

Poehner, M. E., & Infante, P. (2015). Mediated development: Inter-psychological activity for L2 education. *Language and Sociocultural Theory*, *2*(2), 161–183.

Poehner, M. E., & Lantolf, J. P. (2013). Bringing the ZPD into the equation: Capturing L2 development during computerized dynamic assessment. *Language Teaching Research*, *17*(3), 323–342.

Poehner, M. E., & Rea-Dickins, P. (Eds.). (2013). *Addressing issues of access and fairness in education through dynamic assessment*. London: Routledge.

Poehner, M. E., Zhang, J., & Lu, X. (2015). Computerized Dynamic Assessment (C-DA): Diagnosing L2 development according to learner responsiveness to mediation. *Language Testing*, *32*(3), 337–357.

VanPatten, B., & Williams, J. (Eds.). (2014). *Theories in second language acquisition: An introduction* (2nd ed.). London: Routledge.

Vygotsky, L. S. (1978). *Mind in society: The development of higher psychological processes*. Cambridge, MA: Harvard University Press.

Vygotsky, L. S. (1987). *The collected works of L. S. Vygotsky, Vol. 1: Problems of general psychology, including the volume thinking and speech*. R. W. Rieber & A. S. Carton (Eds.). New York, NY: Plenum.

Vygotsky, L. S. (1998). The problem of age. In R. W. Rieber (Ed.), *The collected works of L. S. Vygotsky, Vol. 5: Child Psychology* (pp. 187–205). New York, NY: Plenum.

Walqui, A. (2006). Scaffolding instruction for English language learners: A conceptual framework. *The International Journal of Bilingual Education and Bilingualism*, *9* (2), 159–180.

Wood, D., Bruner, J. S, & Ross, G. (1976). The role of tutoring in problem solving. *Journal of Child Psychology and Psychiatry*, *17*, 89–100.

Zhang, J., & Lu, X. (2015). *Computerized dynamic assessment: Measuring learning potentials and supporting L2 Chinese development in classrooms*. Paper presented at the 27th North American Conference on Chinese Linguistics, Los Angeles, CA.

13
MEASURING 21ST-CENTURY READING COMPREHENSION THROUGH SCENARIO-BASED ASSESSMENTS

Jane R. Shore, Mikyung Kim Wolf, Tenaha O'Reilly, and John P. Sabatini

In the United States, educational thought leaders have called for higher expectations (Gordon Commission, 2013), more rigorous college and career readiness standards for K–12 education (National Governors Association Center for Best Practices & Council of Chief State School Officers, 2010), and new constructs such as 21st-century skills, including collaborative problem solving in digital environments (Leu, Kinzer, Coiro, Castek, & Henry, 2013; Partnership for 21st Century Skills, 2004, 2008). They have also challenged assessment developers to address how best to provide information that is useful for instruction for various learners (Gordon Commission, 2013; Purpura & Turner, 2014; Watkins & Lindahl, 2010). Expanding the scope and variety of constructs (e.g., including elements like collaborative learning and digital literacy) will ensure measurement keeps pace with how people function and interact in various everyday reading activities.

This chapter describes a new assessment design approach called scenario-based assessment (SBA) and explains how it can be used to measure the reading ability of school-aged children in the current context of high standards. SBA combines a cluster of techniques for delivering a set of tasks and items that provide a platform for measuring the kinds of demanding reading skills, while simultaneously affording the potential to increase the instructional relevance of the assessment.

SBAs in reading typically include a range of principles and techniques that distinguish them from other types of assessments: (1) they provide an authentic purpose for reading, (2) they place reading in context for completing a set of interrelated activities that may move from more guided to independent performance, (3) items tend to require the integration and evaluation of a wide range of diverse sources and, (4) in many cases, items provide scaffolds (e.g., a graphic organizer for an analysis of text structures) and guidelines (e.g., tips for summary writing) to help better understand and model the target performance in the assessment (O'Reilly & Sabatini, 2013). Some SBAs also include items that model the social aspects of literacy and learning, such as engaging with peers or a teacher to clarify understanding in reading, reviewing, and evaluating peer writing. Using these principles, SBAs may broaden the range of interactions, perspectives, and information a test taker is exposed to on a topic. Ultimately, the key aims of scenario-based reading assessments are to *measure* 21st-century reading ability while simultaneously *supporting* reading development and instructional usefulness.

In this chapter, we delineate two types of SBAs in reading, the Global, Integrated Scenario-Based Assessment (GISA) and English Learner Formative Assessment (ELFA). These two assessments were part of two separate research projects housed in Educational Testing Service (ETS). GISA was developed with a primary focus on benchmark or summative applications, across kindergarten through 12th grade in U.S. schools. ELFA, on the other hand, was developed as a classroom-based, formative assessment of reading comprehension at the middle-school grade level. The GISA framework and design relied on computer delivery and principles from cognitive science, whereas ELFA was paper-based for its easier integration in daily instruction. Employing the SBA approach to developing reading assessments, both projects also aimed to build their SBAs to be feasible and practical, while maintaining adequate psychometric properties. Consequently, we also briefly describe some empirical evidence collected to date in support of these aims. We conclude this chapter with some considerations in designing SBA assessments based on the lessons we have learned from GISA and ELFA.

The Global, Integrated Scenario-Based Assessment

GISA Framework

The GISA (ETS, 2015) was developed under a federal research project called the Reading for Understanding (RfU) Initiative. The RfU initiative was funded with the overarching goal of improving reading comprehension though intervention and assessment research for K–12 students (Institute of Education Sciences, 2010). In the RfU project, the development of GISA began with the construction of a reading assessment framework designed to explain the purpose(s) of the assessment system, the constructs measured, the theoretical underpinnings, and the general design principles derived from a synthesis of the cognitive science literature. Consistent with evidence-centered design (Mislevy & Haertel, 2006), a series of framework papers was created to increase the transparency of the design *before* the assessments were created (O'Reilly & Sabatini, 2013, Sabatini & O'Reilly, 2013, Sabatini, O'Reilly, & Deane, 2013). With this documentation, potential users of the measures can make more informed decisions about whether to adopt the new assessments. The documentation also provides a partial road map for identifying and evaluating key claims underlying GISA's design.

To date, three installments of the reading framework have been developed for GISA. The first installment provides a set of general cognitive principles that guide the overall assessment design (Sabatini & O'Reilly, 2013). Some of these principles include the rationale for measuring the foundational components of reading, digital literacy, and purposeful reading.

The second installment provides a definition of the reading processes, the constructs to be measured, a position on reading development, and an overview of two types of assessments—component and higher-order skill measures (Sabatini et al., 2013). For the 21st-century reading construct, the reading process is described as a set of purpose-driven activities, where one's goals serve as a standard for evaluating the quality and relevance of text sources (Linderholm, Virtue, Tzeng, & van den Broek, 2004; McCrudden, Magliano, & Schraw, 2011; van den Broek, Lorch, Linderholm, & Gustafson, 2001). In modern reading environments, students are also expected to access and develop the language needed to comprehend a wide variety of texts (Bailey, 2007; Lesaux & Kieffer, 2010), build understanding within and across multiple sources (Britt & Rouet, 2012), engage in disciplinary reading (Goldman, 2012; Lee & Spratley, 2010; Shanahan, Shanahan, & Misischia, 2011), and evaluate (Graesser et al., 2007; Metzger, 2007) and integrate information in digital literacy environments (Coiro, 2009).

The third installment of the framework describes performance moderators and characteristics of SBA as applied to GISA. Performance moderators are factors that impact reading, but are not considered a direct part of the construct (for more information on performance moderators and their role in assessment, see O'Reilly & Sabatini, 2013). These include background knowledge (Shapiro, 2004), metacognition and self-regulation (Hacker, Dunlosky, & Graesser, 2009), motivation (Guthrie & Davis, 2003), and reading strategies (McNamara, 2007).

The decision to include measures of performance moderators in the GISA design was twofold. First, the developers wanted to improve the interpretation of reading scores. For instance, if a student scores high on a reading test, does the score reflect high reading ability or high background knowledge? By having measures of performance moderators in the assessment, inferences about student performance can be enhanced. To further the example above, if the student has a lot of background knowledge on the topic, then they might not need to read the text deeply to answer the questions correctly. In this case, the reading test score might be questioned as it may reflect more about the students' background knowledge than their actual ability to read and comprehend text. Similarly, one might question the validity of a reading score if other performance moderator information was collected on the test that suggested the student was not motivated to try their best.

Second, GISA was designed to model and encourage good reading practices through the test itself. One might hypothesize that having students complete items that required metacognitive, self-regulatory, and other strategic reading behaviors may help promote their use in other academic contexts and could encourage more strategic reading. In this way, the use of the assessment itself serves as a tool *for* and *as* learning (Bennett & Gitomer, 2009).

Although GISA was designed to primarily measure higher-order reading skills (e.g., synthesis, evaluation, and application), the reading framework also describes the need for measures of foundational reading skills. This is accomplished in a separate assessment battery called the Reading Inventory of Scholastic Evaluation (RISE). RISE consists of six computer-administered subtests that assess reading skills (e.g., decoding and morphology) identified in the literature as foundational to higher-order comprehension. Together, GISA and RISE are intended to provide a comprehensive picture of reading ability. As we describe later in the chapter, GISA and RISE can be used together to help determine whether a student has difficulties in higher-order reading comprehension or foundational reading skills (for more on foundational skills and the RISE battery, see Sabatini, Bruce, Steinberg, & Weeks, 2015).

SBA Approach to GISA

GISA measures higher-order reading comprehension by using SBA techniques to deliver a set of sequenced and thematically interrelated items. In GISA, students are presented with a purpose for reading a collection of related sources (e.g., to decide if a community garden is a good idea for their neighborhood). Sources include traditional forms of print such as a news article, and more modern digital forms of communication such as web pages, e-mails, or simulated students' responses.

However, these higher-order skills are difficult, and a variety of students have not mastered them. For example, providing a test that asks students to write an essay that requires them to integrate a variety of perspectives from a range of sources is likely to reveal that many students cannot even begin to do this task. One might question the value of such unsupported assessment because the test does not provide any information on what parts of the complex task lower ability students can or cannot do. To this end, many of the tasks and activities within the GISA forms are sequenced both to *model* skilled performance and to *gather evidence* on what parts of a more complex task students can or cannot do. This sequencing is, in part, possible because the assessment is computer delivered and the order of items and tasks can be controlled.

For instance, before students read any texts, their level of background knowledge is measured to help determine what they already know about a topic.

As mentioned previously, this performance moderator can be used to contextualize the reading score (e.g., did students already know the topic; thus, the reading score is potentially compromised). However, the GISA assessments are also structured to *build up* students' understanding over the course of the assessment. For example, the first text in a GISA assessment typically describes the general issue (e.g., whether or not to create a community garden), subsequent texts then dig deeper into the issue (e.g., pros and cons of creating a community garden), and the final section requires the student to complete more complex tasks (e.g., integrate the information, make a decision, and communicate your understanding in a flyer). This way, the assessment design probes into progressively deeper, more complex literacy skills over time, while sampling what students can and cannot do along the way. This is not to say that all GISA tasks are supported with modeling and scaffolding. Such an approach could result in the complexity of the tasks always being reduced, and higher-order thinking would, in effect, not be assessed. However, when appropriate, the goal is to also model and elicit information on what parts of a complex task students can or cannot do. Thus, the assessment is designed to both *measure* and *support* complex thinking.

To illustrate these issues, a short sequence from the community garden assessment intended for fifth and sixth graders is described. To measure independent performance, students are asked to write a summary about an article. Even though GISA is a reading assessment, the tasks are designed to measure integrated skills. In this example, a summary-writing task was designed to focus students' attention on constructing a more global representation of the text. To model desired performance, guidelines for writing a summary are provided. These guidelines contain suggestions such as to include only the main ideas, avoid adding one's own opinions, to paraphrase, etc.

Writing a summary is a difficult task; so even with the guidelines, many student's responses provide minimal evidence of their capabilities. However, this does not necessarily mean that students do not have some of the component skills needed to create summaries. Therefore, in addition to providing guidelines, other techniques are used to elicit desired evidence of partial skills. For instance, GISA assessments also include simulated peer and teacher interactions that facilitate the elicitation of test takers' skills within the assessment. Continuing with the community garden example, after the test takers write their summaries of the article, simulated peers show their written examples of text summaries. The peer summaries contain violations of the provided guidelines and the test taker is asked to *identify* the particular guideline that was not followed. In a subsequent task, the test taker is provided with the same peer summary, but is now told which guideline was violated, and asked to highlight *where* the violation occurred. In the following task, the violation is highlighted and the test taker is asked to *fix* the error. Thus, in this four-part sequence, information is collected on whether a student can write a summary independently, identify if a given summary contains a violation, locate the violation, and correct the error.

Such sequencing and scaffolding techniques are not only useful for gathering more information about what students can or cannot do, but also help to model strategic reading behaviors (strategy use, metacognition, and self-regulation). Again, technology and computer delivery is critical to these aims by allowing the test designer to control the sequence and flow of the tasks.

To date, the RfU team has developed over 20 GISA forms that are appropriate for students in kindergarten through 12th grade. Some forms contain the same structure and item types, but the content addresses different topics. The parallel structure can be useful in intervention evaluation designs, as well as in instructional programs. For instance, assessments with a parallel structure[1] can be used to evaluate the effectiveness of a reading intervention or alternatively, to measure changes in reading ability over time. While many of the skills measured in the assessments overlap, each assessment may emphasize some skill sets more than others (e.g., summary writing or disciplinary reading or error detection and repair). With a range of skill foci, educators can choose the particular assessment that best fits their needs—a system level feature anticipated in the framework (Sabatini et al., 2013).[2]

Empirical Validity Evidence for GISA

During the development stage of GISA, evidence was collected to evaluate key claims that would support valid inferences about GISA use and scores. In a recently published study, O'Reilly, Weeks, Sabatini, Halderman, and Steinberg (2014) discuss the use of GISA forms as an outcome measure in a large-scale reading intervention evaluation. The intervention designers and evaluation team chose to use GISA because its theoretical foundation aligned well to the disciplinary-focused reading constructs that their intervention targeted. The report documents how the items, scores, and scales were evaluated to ensure that they met the research aims for this application of the tests.

In terms of the psychometric quality of the assessments, data have been collected on over 250,000 administrations across 28 states, sampled from urban, suburban, and rural populations including both public and denominational schools. This work has shown that despite the novel interface and skills tested, the prototype forms are reliable ($\alpha = .80$ or higher), and the range of scores shows wide variability. In other words, SBA seems to have adequate internal properties and is feasible to implement on computers in real school settings.

Moving beyond the basic psychometric properties of the test, other data indicate that certain features of the scenario could be useful for understanding more about students' reading abilities. For instance, O'Reilly and Sabatini (2015) found evidence to support the usefulness of the scenario-based sequencing technique. In the summary example mentioned earlier, items were sequenced to reveal what parts of the more complex task students could or could not handle. Data analyses revealed that, although the majority of students had difficulty writing a summary without support, many of them were able to complete the tasks that measure important summary writing subskills (O'Reilly & Sabatini, 2015). For high-scoring students, the subsequent "diagnostic" tasks serve as confirmation that their independent summary writing was undergirded by a solid understanding of the skills that enter into writing a strong summary of the article provided. On the other hand, for low-scoring students, there was evidence to suggest the test takers could do some of the subskills that fed into summarization skills (e.g., locate an error in a peer summary). Similarly, in the same study, when students were given support such as scaffolding, they were able to demonstrate evidence of complex thinking in a range of task types dealing with some components of argumentation (O'Reilly et al., 2015). While more research is needed to uncover the potential value of using SBA, there is preliminary evidence to suggest that it can both help elicit complex thinking and help identify what parts of a more complex task students can or cannot do.

While we are still exploring evidence to support the validity arguments for GISA, it is important to note the added value of the RISE components battery, which is a computer-delivered non-scenario based assessment. The RISE may be used in conjunction with GISA. If a student scores low on GISA, the reading components measured by the RISE may be helpful in identifying foundational skill weaknesses that are impacting higher level comprehension.[3]

Higher-order comprehension skills as defined here are complex and require thinking, manipulating, synthesizing, analyzing, evaluating, and applying concepts, facts, and information. While these skills may be complex, they draw upon foundational reading skills such as accurate and efficient decoding, word recognition, and fluent text reading skills. Although more research is needed, we hypothesize that including assessments that measure foundational and higher-order comprehension may be particularly useful for teachers to identify students' underlying reading difficulties while simultaneously engaging them in the kinds of complex reading tasks they are likely to encounter in classroom settings.

Using an SBA for English Learners: English Learner Formative Assessment (ELFA)

Now we turn to a second SBA example, ELFA. We also discuss English learner (EL)-specific design features of ELFA (e.g., activating background knowledge, scaffolding, and including tasks for both foundational and higher-order reading skills) that integrate specific SBA design features.

ELFA Constructs

K–12 reading curricula place great importance on higher-order reading skills such as a close reading of complex texts, citing evidence from the texts to support a main idea, analyzing a text structure, or evaluating an argument (Bunch, Kibler, & Pimentel, 2012). Yet teachers of ELs in middle schools also need to constantly assess and monitor the progress of students' foundational reading skills (e.g., vocabulary knowledge and sentence-level understanding) as EL students' English language proficiency profiles vary greatly.

Addressing the need to engage EL students in rigorous reading tasks as well as to provide teachers with a classroom-based assessment tool for formative purposes, the ELFA assessment design framework (Wolf, Shore, & Blood, 2014) was developed to delineate ELFA constructs and task design features of the performance indicators and moderators. ELFA focuses on the measurement of ELs' basic and higher-order reading skills. The overall construct of ELFA is reading comprehension of persuasive texts at the middle-school level. It encompasses an array of skills that are based on an analysis of K–12 academic standards (e.g., Common Core State Standards), academic language characteristics (Bailey, 2007; Schleppegrell, 2004), and subskills found to be differentially influential in EL reading comprehension (August, Francis, Hsu, & Snow, 2006; Gottardo & Mueller, 2009; Lesaux & Kieffer, 2010; Proctor, Carlo, August, & Snow, 2005; Wong, Fillmore, & Snow, 2000). Figure 13.1 summarizes the constructs and skills covered in the ELFA assessment.

Design of ELFA Assessment Structure

The current version of ELFA includes nine assessment forms, three forms in each difficulty category (*Developing*, *Intermediate*, and *Experienced*). The intent of developing multiple forms was to provide a system of ongoing classroom

Subconstructs	Subskills
Foundational reading skills	• Academic lexical ability • Interpreting grammatical structures
Literal comprehension skills	• Comprehending details • Comprehending main ideas / arguments
Higher-order comprehension skills	• Drawing inferences and conclusions • Working with argument structure • Making connections within and between texts • Evaluating arguments

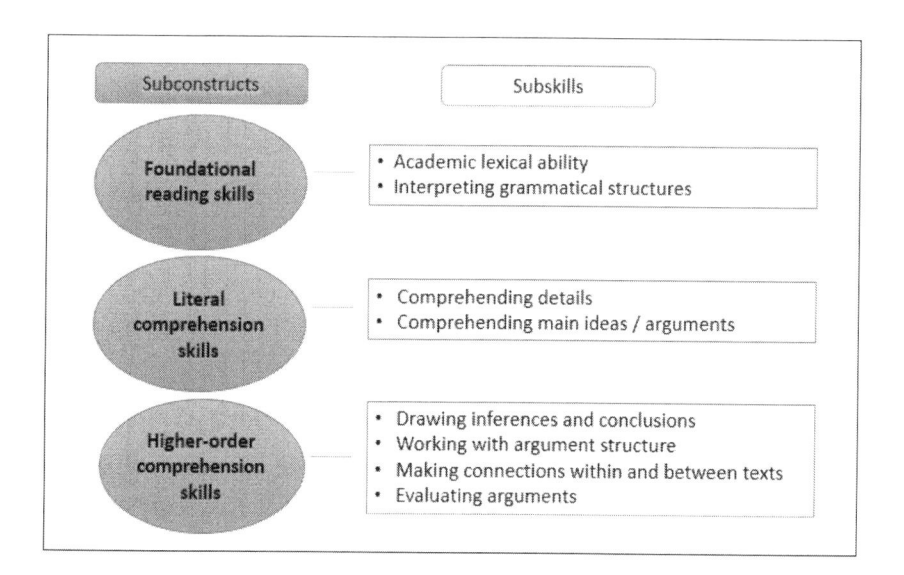

FIGURE 13.1 ELFA Subconstructs and Subskills

Source: Adapted from Wolf and Shore (2014). Copyright 2014 by Educational Testing Service.

assessment. The reading passages for each form were purposefully developed for the three levels of English reading proficiency. They vary in linguistic complexity, academic orientation, topic, and argument structure (for more information see Wolf et al., 2014). ELFA developers utilized readability software called e-rater and TextEvaluator to measure dimensions of the linguistic complexity of the passages (Sheehan, 2012; Sheehan, Kostin, & Napolitano, 2012). These tools provided developers with a profile of the linguistic complexity of each reading passage (e.g., the total number of words, lexical density, number of academic words, complexity of sentence structures, and grade-level difficulty indices). All reading passages were also rated by ESL teachers at the middle-school level for appropriateness of topic, interest, relevance, and language complexity for their students, and feedback was provided on which were most relevant, engaging, and appropriate for each level.

In designing ELFA assessment forms, aside from the construct, two major design factors were taken into consideration. First, the assessment needed to be easily integrated into daily instruction for formative purposes. Second, it needed to provide opportunities for ELs to collaborate with peers while engaging in the assessment tasks. To support these two design characteristics, each form of the ELFA assessment was made up of two parts, Parts 1 and 2, both based upon two reading passages. The two reading passages are referenced in both parts and present opposing viewpoints from two authors regarding one topic. Part 1 of each assessment form is designed to be completed with a peer and to provide scaffolding activities to help ELs unpack a given passage and sequentially utilize basic to high-order reading comprehension skills. Teachers are also encouraged to observe, take notes, and participate in student discussions during Part 1 tasks. Because Part 1 is completed in pairs and with teachers' engagement, it does not provide individual students' reading ability. Hence, Part 2 was added to each assessment form in order to measure students' individual reading ability. In Part 2, students completed the tasks independently.

Scenario-Based Task Design in ELFA

SBA features were applied in developing Part 1 tasks, which include both selected-response and constructed-response tasks. The warm-up activities and main tasks follow a sequence of authentic reading activities (Wolf et al., 2014). All activities were designed to engage students in a realistic reading context by providing a purpose for reading, an authentic sequence of reading activities that move from general to specific while progressing to more challenging skills that require students to synthesize information, evaluate reasoning, and gather supporting evidence to support an argument.

Similar to GISA, ELFA's Part 1 begins with a scenario to establish a purpose for reading, like the one shown in Figure 13.2. For example, an authentic reading situation is provided for students in the beginning of each assessment (e.g.,

Directions:

> In this activity you are going to read an article from an education magazine. The author of the article is **Sofia Fletcher**. Ms. Fletcher wants to persuade you. She wants you to agree with her. Your job is to read the article and answer questions. Later, you will read a letter from a reader named **Jason Choi**. Mr. Choi disagrees with Sofia Fletcher. In the end, you have to decide who you agree with.

FIGURE 13.2 ELFA Example Item Directions

Source: Adapted from *English Learner Formative Assessment (ELFA), Form 6* by Educational Testing Service. Copyright 2013 by Educational Testing Service.

to prepare for a class discussion, to find specific information, to agree/disagree with the author, and to evaluate the adequacy of arguments and evidence).

As students progress to higher-order reading tasks in Part 1, they also encounter scaffolding tasks that focus on foundational skills. In this way, the SBA-based ELFA forms evaluate not only a student's higher-order reading skills, but also foundational reading skills, identifying subskill challenges that could impede higher-order reading comprehension. The tasks are also designed to provide formative information that identifies which reading subskills might require more instructional attention.

ELFA uses the SBA approach to embed scaffolded tasks in an authentic and meaningful sequence. ELFA scaffolding and sequencing are designed to support: (1) a reading process that would engage readers to accomplish a given reading purpose (Linderholm et al., 2004); (2) tasks that would help EL students unpack the passage to build comprehension (Beck, McKeown, & Kucan, 2002; Francis, Rivera, Lesaux, Kieffer, & Rivera, 2006; Taboada, 2009); (3) tasks that reinforce students' close reading of the text (Silverman & Hines, 2009; Stahl & Fairbanks, 1986); and (4) tasks that would foster students' use of reading strategies (DeLuca, 2010; Taboada, 2009). A guiding principle for designing the sequence of assessment tasks is to mirror actual stages in the negotiation of textual meaning that a typical EL middle-school student might experience. Figure 13.3 displays a high-level description of the Part 1 task sequencing.

This sequence is incorporated into the scenario for each assessment form. One of the intents in this sequence is that students build comprehension of texts as they move through the purposefully-ordered tasks. To serve the role of scaffolding (particularly important for EL students to complete the given tasks), the tasks are designed with the following principles. First, the tasks are completed based on students' comprehension of the text, not on their test-taking strategies. Second, the tasks provide explicit strategies that the EL students can use to help them complete the tasks successfully. Third, in some cases, the task questions can provide essential information that a student needs in order to begin. By designing the tasks with scaffolding in mind, it is anticipated that teachers can also use the tasks selectively depending on their students' abilities and learning goals.

244 Jane R. Shore et al.

To illustrate a portion of the sequence, three sample tasks are provided below. Figure 13.4 presents the first activity that students see in Part 1, a warm-up activity to activate students' background knowledge and increase their interest in a given reading topic.

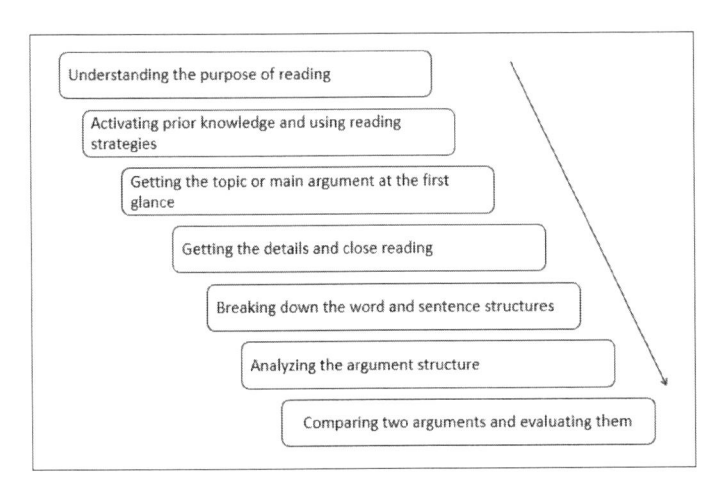

```
Understanding the purpose of reading
    Activating prior knowledge and using reading strategies
        Getting the topic or main argument at the first glance
            Getting the details and close reading
                Breaking down the word and sentence structures
                    Analyzing the argument structure
                        Comparing two arguments and evaluating them
```

FIGURE 13.3 Task Sequencing in ELFA

Source: Adapted from Wolf and Shore (2014). Copyright 2014 by Educational Testing Service.

Before you read...

Look at the article by Sofia Fletcher. Look at the title, the images, and the first sentence of each paragraph.

Where should cell phones be allowed? Where should they *not* be allowed? What is your opinion? Discuss with your partner and make two lists.

Places where cell phones should be allowed:

- _____
- _____
- _____
- _____

Places where cell phones should not be allowed:

- _____
- _____
- _____

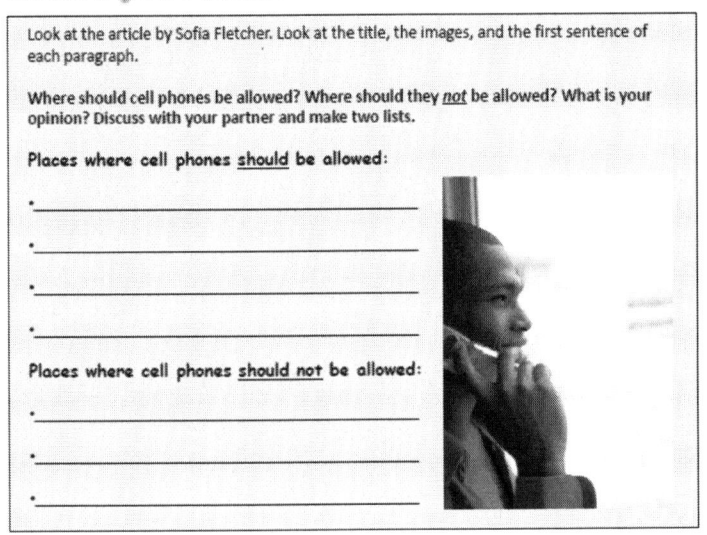

FIGURE 13.4 Task Sample: Warm-up

Source: Adapted from *English Learner Formative Assessment (ELFA), Form 6* by Educational Testing Service. Copyright 2013 by Educational Testing Service.

Scenario-Based Assessments 245

Directions: Read each sentence in the ANSWER CHOICES. One of the sentences is the **main idea** of the article. Three of the sentences are **other ideas** in the article. Two sentences are **not in the article**. Write letters in the blanks in the table below to show where each sentence belongs.

ANSWER CHOICES
A. Cell phones with internet access can be expensive.
B. Cell phones should be allowed in schools, but with clear and strict rules.
C. 63 percent of all students send text messages every day.
D. Cell phone trucks are a new service that can be found near some schools in New York City.
E. Students, teachers and parents have different thoughts about cell phones in schools.
F. Cell phones became very popular in the 1990s because of advertising.

Main Idea	Other Ideas	Not In The Article
② ___	③ ___ ④ ___ ⑤ ___	⑥ ___ ⑦ ___

FIGURE 13.5 Task Sample: Getting a Main Idea

Source: Adapted from *English Learner Formative Assessment (ELFA), Form 6* by Educational Testing Service. Copyright 2013 by Educational Testing Service.

Then, students read the first passage, and Part 1 main tasks begin by asking students to identify the main idea of the passage they read. Subsequent tasks involve close reading of the passage and sorting the details and a main idea, as shown in Figure 13.5.

This task is followed by a few foundational skill tasks for teachers to determine whether students' difficulties in identifying a main idea and details were attributed to lexical and syntactic knowledge in certain sentences. Toward the end of Part 1, the tasks assess the students' higher-order reading skills, where they have to identify reasons and details by comparing and integrating information across multiple sources (see Figure 13.6).

ELFA also includes teacher resource materials to accompany the ELFA assessment forms. The main materials are the ELFA Teachers' Guide (Shore, Wolf, & Blood, 2013) and the ELFA Observation and Teacher Probes. These documents describe how teachers can use the scenario-based ELFA assessment tasks for formative purposes as part of their instruction. As ELFA was designed for classroom use, inherent in the design framework is the collection of additional evidence. This evidence is collected not only through the assessment items themselves, but also through teachers' observation and probing questions during Part 1 of ELFA.

Directions: Let's compare Sofia Fletcher's opinions about using cell phones in school with Jason Choi's opinions.
- In the table below, first circle "Yes" or "No" to show the author's opinion.
- Next, use the ANSWER CHOICES to fill in the blanks in the table with reasons and details that the authors use to support their opinions. Two answer choices will not be used!

ANSWER CHOICES
A. In emergencies parents don't need to use cell phones to contact their children at school.
B. Some researchers think that cell phones can harm students' health.
C. Banning cell phones is unrealistic because they are a part of modern life.
D. Some teachers now use cell phones as learning tools.
E. Smartphones allow users to play games, watch videos, and listen to music.
F. Cell phones don't improve learning and don't offer anything new.

Sofia Fletcher Vs. Jason Choi	
(41) Does Sofia Fletcher think cell phones should be banned from schools? (circle one answer.) Yes No	What reasons and details does she give? (choose two from the ANSWER CHOICES) **(42)** _____ **(43)** _____
(44) Does Jason Choi think cell phones should be banned from schools? (circle one answer.) Yes No	What reasons and details does he give? (choose two from the ANSWER CHOICES) **(45)** _____ **(46)** _____

FIGURE 13.6 Task Sample: Comparing and Integrating Multiple Sources of Information

Source: Adapted from *English Learner Formative Assessment (ELFA), Form 6* by Educational Testing Service. Copyright 2013 by Educational Testing Service.

Collecting Validity Evidence for ELFA

A number of pilot and field studies were conducted during the development process to explore the item properties, usability, and applications of ELFA in classroom settings. First, pilot studies were conducted for all nine forms, focusing primarily on task and item qualities, both quantitatively and qualitatively. Analyses were done on the forms to determine the internal consistency of the items, confirm item difficulty level, and demonstrate discrimination among items and between levels. At the form level, internal consistency reliability estimates were moderate, ranging from .73 to .84. Overall, however, the reliability estimates were found to be at an acceptable level for classroom-based assessments. The correlation coefficients between Part 1 and Part 2 scores ranged from .67 to .78 across the forms. These moderate correlations were not surprising as Part 1 was completed collaboratively with Part 2 being done individually. In addition, Part 1 and Part 2 item types were somewhat different despite the fact that they measured different aspects of the same construct. Part 1, the formative assessment done collaboratively, had several constructed-response items, and Part 2, the independently completed test, consisted of only selected-response items.

Usability studies were also conducted using a collective case-study approach (Shore, Wolf, & Heritage, 2016). As formative assessment, by definition, centers on the teacher's practice and process of collecting evidence of learning to inform instructional next steps, a usability study to investigate teachers' use of ELFA is an essential step in ELFA's validation work. The results of this collective case study indicated that ELFA was seen as adding unique value to classroom tools available for EL students. In particular, the scenario-based design approach to meaningfully sequence the crucial reading skill tasks, as well as scaffolding tasks to ultimately engage ELs in grade-level higher-order reading tasks, was perceived positively by the teachers who participated in the usability studies. Further, the results suggested that teachers enhanced their understanding about formative assessment by way of implementing assessments that were specifically designed for formative purposes like ELFA (Shore et al., 2016).

Essential Considerations in Developing Scenario-Based Reading Assessments

In this chapter, we described how SBA design features could be applied in creating new reading assessments for school-aged children. We focused on illustrating concrete examples of scenario-based tasks using two research and development projects, GISA and ELFA. We described how tasks were designed to measure higher-order reading skills expected of school-aged children. We also briefly discussed ongoing research to evaluate the validity of claims stemming from the construct frameworks and intended uses of the tests.

Students, especially those who may struggle to read subject-area texts, are best served with sensitive, engaging measurement tools that can inform instruction (Francis et al., 2006; Turner & Purpura, 2016). Whether outcome-based or formative, classroom-based, the value of reading comprehension measurement is enhanced when it can be used to identify learner challenges, take into account students' knowledge, and inform decisions with regard to student learning. Drawing from the prototype development and empirical research we conducted, we now summarize a few key elements to consider in designing scenario-based reading assessments for both native English-speaking and EL students. These may be broken down to describe how SBAs have addressed three key issues: (1) measuring 21st-century reading abilities in complex and evolving literacy environments, (2) supporting the learning of essential reading skills while engaging in assessment, and (3) ensuring that results are instructionally meaningful.

As described in this chapter, increased attention on ensuring assessments attend to complex and evolving reading skills has inspired innovation. Both assessments described in this chapter attempt to address the primary goal of reading assessment innovation by the use of SBAs. First, GISA uses specific scenarios to measure a variety of integrated and complex higher-order reading skills aligned with the 21st-century skills, such as multiple text comprehension, disciplinary literacy, digital literacy, and perspective taking. It also captures information on performance moderators, such as background knowledge, to help interpret test scores, and in the case of reading strategies, to help encourage good habits of mind. While higher-order reading skills are assessed, tasks and activities are sequenced and modeled to help gather information on whether students can complete tasks that contribute to the understanding of more complex skills. In these ways, GISA integrates components of reading comprehension in authentic and meaningful ways.

ELFA takes a different approach to SBA, but also aims to measure the multilayered processes of reading comprehension, specifically those involving the reading abilities of EL students. It uses scenarios for tasks that work from foundational to higher-order skills progressively, using collaborative and individual forms, to assess and describe EL reading profiles. Using SBA techniques, both approaches are offered to meet the challenge of measuring multifaceted reading processes.

Both GISA and ELFA also support the idea of engaging in a learning activity while completing a measurement task. That is, both GISA and ELFA assessment tasks are designed to be learning experiences themselves. GISA forms work through scenarios, engaging learning in strategic reading behaviors, and mirroring activities that support reading, like reflection and peer interaction, through tasks themselves. ELFA is also designed to echo an authentic learning experience in reading, moving learners through the stages reflected in the reading process. Collaborative and individual forms, along with Teacher Probes that guide teachers to extract individualized information on learning, further underlie ELFA's SBA approach as a learning activity as well as a way to gather measurement information. As further illustration, teachers in the ELFA case study reported that using ELFA was like a form of professional development on instructional approaches to formative assessment and reading components, indicating that this type of SBA could be easily integrated into instruction (Shore et al., 2016).

Finally, a goal in assessments such as GISA and ELFA is to ensure that the results are instructionally meaningful. In this respect, GISA not only measures higher-order reading skills, but also the subskills that feed into it, and performance moderators like background knowledge to help contextualize the reading score. This combination of information is aimed at providing instructional relevance, ensuring that information about an individual's skill level can be parsed and analyzed to ensure that information is truly relevant to individual reading challenges, at a granular level. ELFA is framed in the same way, to provide evidence that is meaningful to instruction. In this case, ELFA's collaborative form involves teacher interaction and instructional engagement guided by Teacher Probes, making the form itself a prompt to collect instructionally relevant information. In these ways, both GISA and ELFA intend to get to the essence of reading challenges, ensuring these challenges exposed by reading tasks can inform specific pedagogical decisions.

In the effort to bring purpose and engagement to assessment designs to foster both learning and teaching in 21st-century environments, SBAs represent a promising set of techniques that broaden the construct of reading to accommodate different needs. However, continued empirical studies to support the benefits of SBAs for both teachers and learners are necessary.

Acknowledgements

The research reported here was supported by the Institute of Education Sciences, U.S. Department of Education, through grants R305F100005, R305G04065, and R305A100724 to Educational Testing Service as part of the Reading for Understanding Research Initiative and the English Learners Formative Assessment research grant programs. The opinions expressed are those of the authors and do not represent views of the Institute or the U.S. Department of Education. We would like to thank members of ETS's Cognitively Based Assessment *of, for,* and *as* Learning team (CBAL) for their collaboration on these two projects.

Notes

1 Comparability of test forms requires that the forms are on the same scale or equated.
2 For more information on GISA, including some released screen shots of the assessment, please visit the ETS website at: http://www.ets.org/research/topics/reading_for_understanding/.
3 For more information on RISE, please see: http://rise.serpmedia.org.

References

August, D., Francis, D., Hsu, H.-Y. A., & Snow, C. (2006). Assessing reading comprehension in bilinguals. *Instructional Research on English Learners. Special Issue of Elementary School Journal, 107*(2), 221–239.
Bailey, A. L. (2007). *The language demands of school: Putting academic English to the test.* New Haven, CT: Yale University Press.
Beck, I. L., McKeown, M. G., & Kucan, L. (2002). *Bringing words to life.* New York, NY: Guilford Press.
Bennett, R. E., & Gitomer, D. H. (2009). Transforming K–12 assessment: Integrating accountability testing, formative assessment and professional support. In C.

Wyatt-Smith & J. J. Cumming (Eds.), *Educational assessment in the 21st century* (pp. 43–62). New York, NY: Springer.

Britt, A., & Rouet, J. (2012). Learning with multiple documents: Component skills and their acquisition. In M. J. Lawson & J. R. Kirby (Eds.), *The quality of learning: Dispositions, instruction, and mental structures* (pp. 276–314). Cambridge, UK: Cambridge University Press.

Bunch, G. C., Kibler, A., & Pimentel, S. (2012). *Realizing opportunities for English learners in the Common Core English Language Arts and disciplinary Literacy Standards*. Commissioned paper by the Understanding Language Initiative. Stanford, CA: Stanford University. Available from http://ell.stanford.edu/papers/practice

Coiro, J. (2009). Rethinking reading assessment in a digital age: How is reading comprehension different and where do we turn now? *Educational Leadership, 66*, 59–63.

DeLuca, E. (2010). Unlocking academic vocabulary. *The Science Teacher, 77*, 27–37.

Educational Testing Service. (2013). *English Learner Formative Assessment (ELFA), Form 6*. Princeton, NJ: Author.

Educational Testing Service. (2015). *Reading for understanding*. Available from http://www.ets.org/research/topics/reading_for_understanding/

Francis, D. J., Rivera, M., Lesaux, N., Kieffer, M., & Rivera, H. (2006). *Practical guidelines for the education of English language learners: Research-based recommendations for instruction and academic interventions*. Portsmouth, NH: Research Corporation, Center on Instruction. Available from https://www2.ed.gov/about/inits/ed/lep-partnership/interventions.pdf

Goldman, S. (2012). Adolescent literacy: Learning and understanding content. *Future of Children, 22*, 89–116.

Gordon Commission. (2013). *To assess, to teach, to learn: A vision for the future of assessment*. Princeton, NJ: Author. Available from http://www.gordoncommission.org/rsc/pdfs/gordon_commission_technical_report.pdf

Gottardo, A., & Mueller, J. (2009). Are first and second language factors related in predicting L2 reading comprehension? A study of Spanish-speaking children acquiring English as a second language from first to second grade. *Journal of Educational Psychology, 101*, 330–344.

Graesser, A. C., Wiley, J., Goldman, S., O'Reilly, T., Jeon, M., & McDaniel, B. (2007). SEEK web tutor: Fostering a critical stance while exploring the causes of volcanic eruption. *Metacognition and Learning, 2*, 89–105.

Guthrie, J., & Davis, M. (2003). Motivating struggling readers in middle school through an engagement model of classroom performance. *Reading and Writing Quarterly, 19*, 59–85.

Hacker, D. J., Dunlosky, J., & Graesser, A. C. (2009). *Handbook of metacognition in education*. Mahwah, NJ: Erlbaum.

Institute of Education Sciences. (2010). *Reading for understanding initiative*. Washington, DC: U.S. Department of Education. Available from http://ies.ed.gov/ncer/projects/program.asp?ProgID=62

Lee, C. D., & Spratley, A. (2010). *Reading in the disciplines: The challenges of adolescent literacy*. New York, NY: Carnegie Corporation.

Lesaux, N. K., & Kieffer, M. J. (2010). Exploring sources of reading comprehension difficulties among language minority learners and their classmates in early adolescence. *American Educational Research Journal, 47*, 596–632.

Leu, D., Kinzer, C., Coiro, J., Castek, J., & Henry, L. (2013). New literacies: A dual-level theory of the changing nature of literacy, instruction, and assessment. In D. E. Alvermann, N. J. Unrau, & R. B. Ruddell (Eds.), *Theoretical models and processes of reading* (6th ed., pp. 1150–1181). Newark, DE: International Reading Association.

Linderholm, T., Virtue, S., Tzeng, Y., & van den Broek, P. (2004). Fluctuations in the availability of information during reading: Capturing cognitive processes using the landscape model. *Discourse Processes, 37,* 165–186.

McCrudden, M. T., Magliano, J. P., & Schraw, G. (Eds.). (2011). *Text relevance and learning from text.* Greenwich, CT: Information Age Publishing.

McNamara, D. S. (2007). *Reading comprehension strategies: Theories, interventions, and technologies.* Mahwah, NJ: Erlbaum.

Metzger, M. J. (2007). Making sense of credibility on the Web: Models for evaluating online information and recommendations for future research. *Journal of the American Society for Information Science and Technology, 58,* 2078–2091.

Mislevy, R. J., & Haertel, G. (2006). Implications for evidence-centered design for educational assessment. *Educational Measurement: Issues and Practice, 25,* 6–20.

National Governors Association Center for Best Practices & Council of Chief State School Officers. (2010). Common Core State Standards for English language arts and literacy in history/social studies, science, and technical subjects. Available from http://www.corestandards.org/assets/CCSSI_ELA%20Standards.pdf

O'Reilly, T., & Sabatini, J. (2013). *Reading for understanding: How performance moderators and scenarios impact assessment design* (ETS RR-13–31). Princeton, NJ: ETS.

O'Reilly, T., & Sabatini, J. (2015, July). *Effect of local and global reading skills on argumentation skill.* Paper presented at the Society for Text and Discourse conference, Minneapolis, MN.

O'Reilly, T., Sabatini, J., Halderman, L., Bruce, K., Weeks, J., & Steinberg, J. (2015, March). *Building theoretical and developmentally sensitive reading assessments for students in 3rd through 12th grade: Implications for intervention, and potential changes in reading proficiency.* Paper presented at Society for Research on Educational Effectiveness conference, Washington, DC.

O'Reilly, T., Weeks, J., Sabatini, J., Halderman, L., & Steinberg, J. (2014). Designing reading comprehension assessments for reading interventions: How a theoretically motivated assessment can serve as an outcome measure. *Educational Psychology Review, 26,* 403–424.

Partnership for 21st Century Skills. (2004). *Learning for the 21st century: A report and mile guide for 21st century skills.* Washington, DC: Author. Available from http://www.p21.org/storage/documents/P21_Report.pdf

Partnership for 21st Century Skills. (2008). *21st Century skills and English map.* Washington, DC: Author. Available from http://www.p21.org/storage/documents/21st_century_skills_english_map.pdf

Proctor, C. P., Carlo, M. S., August, D., & Snow, C. E. (2005). Native Spanish-speaking children reading in English: Toward a model of comprehension. *Journal of Educational Psychology, 97,* 246–256.

Purpura, J. E., & Turner, C. E. (2014, Fall). *A learning-oriented assessment approach to understanding the complexities of classroom-based language assessment.* New York, NY: Teachers College, Columbia University. Available from http://www.tc.columbia.edu/tccrisls/

Sabatini, J., Bruce, K., Steinberg, J., & Weeks, J. (2015). *SARA reading components tests, RISE forms: Test design and technical adequacy* (2nd ed.). ETS RR. Princeton, NJ: ETS.

Sabatini, J., & O'Reilly, T. (2013). Rationale for a new generation of reading comprehension assessments. In B. Miller, L. Cutting, & P. McCardle (Eds.), *Unraveling reading comprehension: Behavioral, neurobiological, and genetic components* (pp. 100–111). Baltimore, MD: Brookes Publishing.

Sabatini, J., O'Reilly, T., & Deane, P. (2013). *Preliminary reading literacy assessment framework: Foundation and rationale for assessment and system design* (ETS RR-13–30). Princeton, NJ: ETS.

Schleppegrell, M. J. (2004). *The language of schooling: A functional linguistics perspective.* Mahwah, NJ: Erlbaum.

Shanahan, C., Shanahan, T., & Misischia, C. (2011). Analysis of expert readers in three disciplines: History, mathematics, and chemistry. *Journal of Literacy Research, 43,* 393–429.

Shapiro, A. M. (2004). How including prior knowledge as a subject variable may change outcomes of learning research. *American Educational Research Journal, 41,* 159–189.

Sheehan, K. M. (2012). *A cognitively-based text analysis system designed to help test developers ensure that admissions assessments incorporate suitably complex text.* Riyadh, Saudi Arabia: National Center for Assessment in Higher Education.

Sheehan, K. M., Kostin, I., & Napolitano, N. (2012, April). *SourceRater: An automated approach for generating text complexity classifications aligned with the Common Core Standards.* Paper presented at the National Council on Measurement in Education, Vancouver, BC.

Shore, J., Wolf, M. K., & Blood, I. (2013). *English Learner Formative Assessment (ELFA) teacher's guide.* Princeton, NJ: ETS. Available at https://www.ets.org/s/research/pdf/elfa_teachers_guide.pdf

Shore, J., Wolf, M. K., & Heritage, M. (2016). Formative assessment tools as teacher professional development: A case study in the use of the English Learner Formative Assessment system. *Journal of Educational Research & Innovation, 5*(2), 1–19.

Silverman, R., & Hines, S. (2009). The effects of multimedia-enhanced instruction on the vocabulary of English-language learners and non-English language learners in prekindergarten through second grade. *Journal of Educational Psychology, 101,* 305–314.

Stahl, S., & Fairbanks, M. M. (1986). The effects of vocabulary instruction: A model-based meta-analysis. *Review of Educational Research, 56,* 72–110.

Taboada, A. (2009). English language learners, vocabulary, and reading comprehension: What we know and what we need to know. *Yearbook of the College Reading Association, 30,* 307–322.

Turner, C. E., & Purpura, J. E. (2016). Learning-oriented assessment in the classroom. In D. Tsagari & J. Banerjee (Eds.), *Handbook of second language assessment* (pp. 255–274). Berlin, Germany/Boston, MA: DeGruyter Mouton.

van den Broek, P., Lorch, R. F., Jr., Linderholm, T., & Gustafson, M. (2001). The effects of readers' goals on inference generation and memory for texts. *Memory & Cognition, 29,* 1081–1087.

Watkins, N., & Lindahl, K. (2010). Targeting content area literacy instruction to meet the needs of adolescent English language learners. *Middle School Journal, 4,* 23–33.

Wolf, M. K., & Shore, J. R. (2014, March). *Formative assessment as a means to improve teaching and learning for English learners.* Paper presented at the ETS Research Forum, Washington, DC.

Wolf, M. K., Shore, J. R., & Blood, I. (2014). *English Learner Formative Assessment (ELFA): A design framework.* Princeton, NJ: ETS. Available from https://www.ets.org/s/research/pdf/elfa_design_framework.pdf

Wong Fillmore, L., & Snow, C. (2000). *What teachers need to know about language.* Washington, DC: Center for Applied Linguistics.

SECTION 5
Conclusion

14
CHALLENGES AND FUTURE DIRECTIONS FOR YOUNG LEARNERS' ENGLISH LANGUAGE ASSESSMENTS AND VALIDITY RESEARCH

Yuko Goto Butler

The assessment of English as a second or foreign language (ESL/EFL) for young learners (who are defined as children ages 5–13 in this volume) is situated in the midst of many contextual and theoretical changes. Such changes have influenced how we conceptualize second/foreign language (L2/FL) assessment for young learners as well as how such assessments are developed and validated. Given the growing demand for assessing young learners' ESL/EFL, more research is needed on how best to develop and use assessments for young learners. More validation work targeting these learners is also necessary. The wealth of published research on L2/FL assessment for adult learners can certainly inform this work, but assessing young learners poses unique challenges unaddressed by the literature on adults.

The aim of this chapter is to discuss the challenges of both developing assessments for young learners and building validity arguments for test development and score use, focusing on large-scale standardized tests[1] such as the *TOEFL Junior*® tests, the *TOEFL*® *Primary*™ tests, and U.S. K–12 English language proficiency assessments developed by Educational Testing Service (ETS). I organize my discussion around validation using an argument-based approach—specifically, Kane's interpretation/use argument (Kane, 2013a, Kane, Crooks, & Cohen, 1999) and Chapelle, Enright, and Jamieson's framework (2008), the latter of which expanded the validity inferences from Kane's work and was widely used for validating ETS's *TOEFL iBT*® test.[2] The argument-based approach to validation is advantageous compared to others, such as Cronbach's (1988) and Messick's (1989). This approach conceptualizes validation as the evaluation of a set of explicit claims linking inferential steps to support score interpretation and use, and thus it provides researchers and test developers with a framework for specifying and presenting the kinds of empirical evidence needed to evaluate the adequacy of the claims. It thereby facilitates the validation process.

The chapter comprises three main sections. In the first section, I address four major contextual and theoretical changes that seem to be influencing our general conceptualizations of assessment for young learners: (a) changes in the target population, (b) changes in the way young learners use language, (c) changes in how L2/FL development is conceptualized (theory of second language acquisition/development), and, finally, (d) changes in how the purpose of assessment in educational settings is conceptualized. In the second section I discuss how these contextual and theoretical changes create new challenges for developing and validating assessments for young learners, particularly standardized tests. In the final section, I suggest some unresolved issues as future directions for research.

Changing Environments of Young Learners' Language Learning and Assessment

Changes in the Target Population

Partially due to globalization, the target population of English proficiency assessments has been radically changing and diversifying, and this in turn influences many aspects of assessment contents, procedures, and use. Assessing younger children inevitably makes us pay closer attention to the role of cognitive and social/affective development in children's language use and task completion. Task content and procedures in assessment need to be age-sensitive and aligned with children's life experiences. What makes the matter complicated for the development of standardized English proficiency assessments is that there are tremendous individual differences in cognitive and social/affective development as well as in life experiences among young learners within the "same" chronological age group.

We can safely assume that variations in children's background characteristics, the type and amount of contact they have with the target language, and their learning goals would yield substantial differences in learning outcomes (e.g., general proficiency in English). But these variations may also influence the nature of language abilities that assessments are meant to capture. Previous studies have suggested that we cannot rule out the possibility that learners develop different structures for language abilities as a function of their different characteristics (e.g., proficiency level in Shin, 2005; L1 background in Stricker & Rock, 2008) as well as their different instructional and learning contexts (e.g., study-abroad vs. home-country contexts in Gu, 2014). Children in an oral-focused English program may have a skewed proficiency profile (e.g., much stronger in oral domains than in written domains). Although we have little research-based data on children's ESL/EFL learning and assessment, it seems that a one-size-fits-all approach to conceptualizing target language abilities would be particularly problematic for young learners because of their developmental diversity within the defined age range as well as the wide variety of learning environments they inhabit.

Changes in the Way We Use Language

Largely owing to advances in technology, the way we use language is drastically changing. We engage in various kinds of communication through technology in increasingly multimodal ways—to such an extent that the traditional classification of the four language skill domains may not reflect one's actual daily language use. Literacy is no longer limited to a written domain; multimodal literacy has gained a stronger presence (Mills, 2010).

Technology also influences children's language use in the target domain (*Target Language Use* domain, Bachman & Palmer, 2010). A growing number of children engage in computer-mediated language tasks in English, including watching videos, chatting with friends online, and playing online games. Assessment tasks need to reflect such changes in children's language use. For example, listening tasks may need to involve not only aural but also visual activities.

Technology is changing not only the way children use language but also how they learn language and their attitudes toward learning. Prensky (2001) suggested that children growing up with technology and with computer games in particular have different cognitive styles compared with older generations. Their unique characteristics include that (a) they process information much faster than previous generations, (b) they feel more comfortable with parallel processing than linear processing, (c) they prefer accessing information randomly rather than in a step-by-step fashion, and (d) they approach graphics before texts (i.e., they develop sophisticated visual sensitivities) (see Prensky, 2001, for the full list of characteristics). Although we need more empirical research to better understand characteristics of information processing and learning styles among children growing up with technology, their unique characteristics in and styles of cognitive processing should be taken into consideration when designing and evaluating assessment tasks and procedures (for concrete examples of technology applications for young learners, see Bailey, 2017; Poehner, Zhang, & Lu, 2017; Shore, Wolf, O'Reilly, & Sabatini, 2017, all in this volume).

Changes in Conceptualization of L2/FL Development

Earlier works on second language acquisition (SLA) were largely based on cognitive approaches; however, more recently, other approaches have been used (also see Bailey, 2017 in this volume). Cognitive approaches primarily view language abilities as residing in individuals; such approaches seek universal developmental stages irrespective of the contexts in which learning takes place. Standardized testing has been largely based on these ideas. More social-oriented approaches challenge such premises and stress the importance of context in one's L2 development; they also question the assumption of universal and linear development of L2 (Atkinson, 2011).

In the last couple of decades, child development researchers have shown growing interest in the *process* of learning and have discovered that there is substantial variability in task performance not only across individuals but also within an individual: namely, intraindividual variability, such as variability over time, variability across similar tasks at a single point in developmental time, and variability in a single task across contexts at a single point in developmental time (Alibali & Sidney, 2015). Instead of treating such variability as noise, researchers are shedding new light on the role of variability in human development, including language development. For example, in dynamic systems theory (DST), variability—a state of instability—indicates a transition from one system to a new system and thus predicts a change in knowledge structure (Lewis, 2000). According to the cognitive evolution perspective, variation, along with selection, is the driving force for making adaptive change over time. When children face a new task, they develop a repertoire of strategies and try them out until they eventually discover the most effective strategies and abandon older or less effective ones (Siegler, 2006). Thus, paying attention to children's variability affords greater understanding of how they develop knowledge and skills than we can gain by simply looking at the accuracy of their performance alone (Alibali & Sidney, 2015). Although researchers have just begun to tackle the seemingly idiosyncratic nature of variability, it has been suggested that identifying patterns of variability at both group and individual levels may help us better uncover mechanisms of human development (van Dijk & van Geert, 2015). These new ways of conceptualizing variability challenge the traditional approach to standardized testing, where variability has been treated as a source of measurement error and thus something that should be minimized. Namely, we probably need to think about how to account for such variability as part of constructs that should be measured rather than treating it as construct-irrelevant factors (see Gu & So, 2017 in this volume for an example of such an approach).

Changes in How We View the Purpose of Assessments

Growing interest in process-oriented views of learning also influences the way we see the role of assessment in education. The traditional measurement-based view of assessment is concerned with how best to elicit meaningful information from an individual learner in order to make accurate and consistent inferences about his/her "true" ability at a given point in time, primarily for a summative purpose (an *assessment of learning* orientation). However, assessment professionals and educators have paid increasing attention to the role of assessment as a support for their learning and to making direct connections between assessment and students' learning (an *assessment for learning* orientation, Black & Wiliam, 1998). Considering that young learners are in the midst of developing various cognitive, metacognitive, social, and affective skills and knowledge, the notion of assessment for learning is particularly relevant to them.

The assessment for learning approach may require different conceptualizations for validity and reliability than those held by the traditional assessment of learning approach. According to Brookhart (2003), *validity* in the context of the assessment for learning approach refers to the extent to which the assessment content and procedures match instruction. The assessment thus is embedded in a particular context; the context is relevant to validity concerns. *Reliability* for the assessment for learning approach can be understood as the degree of sufficiency of "information about the gap between students' work and 'ideal' work (as defined in students' and teachers' learning objectives)" (Brookhart, 2003, p. 9) rather than the degree of consistency in placing students on a predetermined continuum of mastery learning.

These two assessment orientations stand on different philosophical grounds, and researchers, even those who advocate for assessment for learning, disagree about whether the two orientations can potentially have complementary roles or be compatible with each other within a given assessment system (Green, 2014). Some researchers reject the idea of such compatibility and advocate for more dynamic, process-focused, and socially oriented approaches to assessment (e.g., dynamic assessment in Poehner, Zhang, & Lu, 2017, this volume). Even if we accept that the spirit of assessment for learning can be incorporated into the standardized testing format, actually achieving this blend poses many theoretical and practical challenges.

Challenges in Building Validity Arguments for Large-Scale Standardized English Language Proficiency (ELP) Assessments for Young Learners

The changes outlined above influence the way we develop assessments and interpret and use those assessment results with young learners; they raise a number of unique challenges when validating assessments for their intended uses. In discussing validation of ELP assessments for young learners, as mentioned before, I focus on the *argument-based approach* to validation, more specifically Kane's *interpretation/use argument* (2013a) and Chapelle et al.'s (2008) validity argument, which was built upon Kane's approach. The argument-based approach to validation was intended to make the validation work "simpler" while maintaining "the breadth and rigor" of previous validation models (Kane, 2013b, p. 451). In the following sections, I first briefly describe Kane's and Chapelle et al.'s interpretative arguments, and then I discuss current challenges that we face in validating standardized ELP assessments for young learners. I base the organization of my discussion on Chapelle et al.'s argument approach because it provides an expanded chain of validity inferences pertinent to the validation of language assessments. As mentioned above, Chappelle et al.'s framework was widely used as a basis for validating *TOEFL iBT*, a large-scale standardized ELP assessment.

Kane's and Chapelle et al.'s Interpretative Arguments

The argument-based approach to validation aims to "develop a measurement procedure that supports the proposed interpretations and uses of test scores and an interpretative argument that is plausible, given the measurement procedure and the proposed interpretations and uses" (Kane, 2013a, p. 45). Both Kane and Chappelle et al. (2008) identify a series of inferences bridging multiple steps that lead to a specific score interpretation and use. As shown in Table 14.1, in Kane's earlier work (Kane et al., 1999), his argument consisted of three types of inferences (evaluation, generalization, and extrapolation) that link four inferential steps supporting interpretation and use (observation, observed score, expected score, and target score). Chapelle et al. referred to Kane's approach as a *three-bridge argument*. Each inference is credited by a *warrant* (a general rule for inference) and *assumptions* that underlie the warrant. The assumptions in turn need to be backed up through theoretical and empirical evidence (*backing*). (Note, however, that in more recent publications, Kane [2013a] clarified that the three inferences should be regarded as examples but not as the fixed inferences.)

Seeing the lack of a link to theoretical constructs in the three-bridge argument, Chapelle et al. (2008) added three components (target domain, construct, and test use, shaded in Table 14.1), which resulted in three additional types of inferences (domain description, explanation, and utilization, indicated in italics

TABLE 14.1 Kane et al.'s (1999) and Chapelle et al.'s (2008) Interpretative Arguments

Kane et al. (1999)		*Chapelle et al. (2008)*	
Components	Inferences	Components	Inferences
		Target Domain	
			Domain Description
Observation		Observation	
	Evaluation		Evaluation
Observed Score		Observed Score	
	Generalization		Generalization
Expected Score		Expected Score	
			Explanation
	Extrapolation	Construct	
			Extrapolation
Target Score		Target Score	
			Utilization
		Test Use	

Note: The table was created based on Kane et al. (1999) and Chapelle et al. (2008).

in Table 14.1); there are six types of inferences altogether. In the following subsections, based on Chapelle et al. (2008), I lay out the warrant that supports each inference and assumptions that underlie the warrant as well as major backings reported in this volume at each inference phase. I then discuss challenges associated with validating score interpretation/use for young learners in light of the major changes that I outlined in the previous section.

Challenges at Inference Phases

Domain Description

The domain description inference warrants that young learners' performance in a given test represents their relevant knowledge, skills, and abilities in their target domain—namely, their English use in classrooms and other learning contexts. Assumptions underlying this warrant include that (a) assessment tasks that represent the target domain are identifiable, (b) critical knowledge and skills that students are expected to learn in the target domain are identifiable, and (c) assessment tasks that represent the target domain can be simulated (Chapelle et al., 2008). As backings for these assumptions, in the case of the *TOEFL Primary* and *TOEFL Junior* tests, for example, researchers examined curriculum, standards, and textbooks used in select target countries and regions. Teachers of the target young learners were asked to judge the appropriateness of the assessment tasks (see Cho et al., 2017; Hauck, Pooler, Wolf, Lopez, & Anderson, 2017; So et al., 2017, all in this volume). Although these are quite legitimate approaches for the test development stage, now that the tests have been developed, further domain analyses and task modeling may be necessary.

Due to the diversity of the target population, defining the target domain itself can be a challenge; accordingly, it is difficult to identify the target language use and abilities that children are expected to learn in the target domain. This is particularly the case with the *TOEFL Primary* tests, where potential test takers are so diverse in terms of their characteristics, learning goals, the quality and the amount of learning, and their learning contexts. Early English educational policies are constantly changing as well. Given all of these challenges, researchers should continuously conduct domain analyses.

Moreover, we have only a limited understanding of L2/FL tasks for young learners. Research on tasks in SLA has primarily focused on adult learners, and we still do not know much about the interaction between linguistic abilities and nonlinguistic abilities (e.g., cognitive abilities) in completing tasks among young learners. As Jang, Vincett, van der Boom, Lau, and Yang (2017 in this volume) argued, the role of metacognitive and affective elements (e.g., interests and emotions) in children's task performance are hardly understood despite their potential significant influence.

Researchers have just begun to explore the role of interlocutors in children's interaction, but we do know that young learners interact differently during tasks depending on the dyads' characteristics (e.g., Butler & Zeng, 2011; Oliver, 2002). In language-focused programs (as opposed to more content-focused classrooms or English-medium contexts), one can assume that the target domain is language classrooms. However, partially due to our limited understanding of task designs for young learners, pedagogical language tasks used in classrooms are not necessarily communicative (Littlewood, 2007). Thus, they may not be good candidates for assessment tasks representing children's target abilities, despite children's familiarity with the task formats and procedures. In addition, selected-response test formats that are commonly used in standardized language tests are inevitably limited in assessing communicative language abilities. In order to handle specific test formats, children need to be socialized into test-taking practices; such tasks often deviate from the real-world experiences of children.

Research indicates that children are sensitive to pragmatic oddness in testing contexts; for example, some children may be confused if they are asked to describe events in pictures if the listener/teacher also sees the picture or already knows the events in the pictures (Carpenter, Fujii, & Kataoka, 1995). The meaning of "authentic"[3] or "real-world" language use—a major characteristic of tasks—is often not clear when applied to young learners. For example, fantasy (e.g., having a conversation with an animal) can be their reality, and indeed fantasy plays an important role in children's cognitive development (Vygotsky, 1978) and motivation for engaging in tasks (Butler, 2015). However, how best to incorporate fantasy elements in assessment tasks remains an open question. The meaning of fantasy differs depending on children's age (Vygotsky, 1978) and possibly their culture or the amount of exposure to fantasy (e.g., playing computer games), but the precise functions of fantasy in children's cognitive and affective development are not yet well understood. Clearly, much more research needs to be conducted in order to identify the types of assessment tasks that provide young learners with opportunities to exhibit their abilities in a pedagogically sound and age-appropriate fashion.

Evaluation

The warrant for the evaluation inference is that observations made on a young learner's performance in assessment tasks are evaluated to provide observed scores that reflect the child's targeted abilities in the domain. Assumptions for this warrant include: (a) rubrics, ratings, and scales used for the evaluation and task administration conditions are all appropriate for providing evidence of test takers' target abilities; and (b) scores have appropriate psychometric properties in order to make norm-referenced decisions (Chapelle et al., 2008). For example, based on a series of statistical analyses (both classical test theory [CTT] and item response theory [IRT] analyses) and experts' judgments in prototype and field studies, ETS's test development teams made a number of decisions and modifications on test items, scores, and administrations, including offering two levels of test (easy and difficult versions) in the *TOEFL Primary* tests (see Cho et al., 2017; So et al., 2017; Zu, Moulder, & Morgan, 2017, all in this volume).

Even though these evaluation procedures are standard, due to our insufficient understanding of young learners' L2/FL development, we need to understand that we still face challenges for developing rubrics and setting assessment criteria that are developmentally sound and statistically rigorous (e.g., How many bands should represent young learners' language developmental patterns, and how well will those bands discriminate students at different proficiency levels? How much difference in difficulty level between adjacent levels should there be, and should each band have an equal score interval?). Recent reconceptualizations and emergent empirical findings of L2/FL development, such as nonlinear developmental trajectories (e.g., children's heavy reliance on memorized chunks, especially at an early stage of learning) and high instabilities of performance, can make the validation work more complicated. Ideally, each band should be meaningful in light of children's L2/FL development *and* pedagogical sequence, but this is an extremely challenging goal given significant individual differences and program variations. Growing diversity and the size of the target population may also require test developers to modify descriptors and to reconsider statistical properties. Substantial individual differences may also make it difficult to standardize administration procedures, such as setting appropriate time limits for tasks.

Generalization

The warrant for the generalization inference is that observed scores (scores that test takers receive) consistently estimate expected scores that test takers would receive in compatible test forms. The underlying assumptions for this warrant include having a sufficient number of test items/tasks, appropriate configuration of tasks, appropriate scaling and equating procedures, and well-defined specifications of tasks and rating for designing parallel test forms (Chapelle et al., 2008). Reliability studies have been conducted as a backing effort (e.g., Papageorgiou, Xi, Morgan, & So, 2015; So, 2014, for the *TOEFL Junior* Comprehensive test).

As exemplified in the case of the *TOEFL Primary* tests (see Cho et al., 2017; Zu et al., 2017 in this volume), one of the major challenges for test developers is that tests for young learners cannot have many items due to young learners' relatively limited attention span, and yet the tests should maintain acceptably high reliability. In addition to this constraint, substantial differences in proficiency levels among the target test takers led to the decision to split the *TOEFL Primary* tests into two difficulty steps because measuring a wide range of proficiency levels with a limited number of items was a challenge. Growing diversity of the target test-taking population also requires careful sampling and resampling for successive validation work. From the traditional psychometric point of view, the unstable nature of young learners' performance itself is a potential challenge to securing high reliability.

Explanation

The warrant for the explanation inference is that expected scores are attributable to defined constructs. Assumptions for this warrant include (a) knowledge and processing skills necessary for task completion vary in accordance with theory; (b) task characteristics systematically influence task difficulty; (c) scores in the test in question have theoretically expected relations with other measures; (d) the internal structure of test scores is consistent with theory; and finally (e) test performance varies in relation to relevant students' learning experiences (Chapelle et al., 2008). See Gu (2015) and Gu, Lockwood, and Powers (2017 in this volume) as backing examples of these assumptions.

The major challenge for this inference phase stems from a lack of a theory of language proficiency for young L2/FL learners. There are many unanswered questions here. For example, are theories such as Bachman and Palmer's (2010) model of language knowledge applicable to children without any modifications? Do young learners develop different components of language knowledge in tandem, or should we weight certain components more than others? We have insufficient understanding of the relationship between task characteristics and task difficulty among young learners. Much more work needs to be conducted to specify underlying abilities and knowledge needed to complete tasks in relation to the task characteristics, as well as to identify cognitive and noncognitive factors (or other construct-irrelevant factors) that are responsible for task difficulty for young learners. It is also hard to conduct meaningful concurrent correlation studies due to the lack of reliable and compatible construct-driven measures for young learners. Finally, it is very difficult to systematically and accurately capture the target students' learning experiences (both the amount and quality of learning). This yields a challenge to provide evidence that test scores vary systematically and reliably according to students' learning. In investigations, the length of learning is often used as an indicator of one's learning experience. However, as Gu et al. (2017 in this volume) acknowledged, length of learning is only an approximation, given the substantial diversity of learning experiences among young learners (e.g., instructional/learning hours per a given time vary greatly, not to mention the types and quality of instruction/learning that young learners have).

Extrapolation

The extrapolation inference is based on the warrant that the constructs assessed by the test in question account for the quality of performance in the target context. The assumption behind this warrant is that learners' performance in the test has a positive relationship with criteria of language performance used in the target contexts. Criterion-related information is often based on stakeholders' (e.g., teachers') judgment. For example, Papageorgiou and Cho (2014), in a study conducted in an ESL context in the United States, found that ESL students' test scores in the *TOEFL Junior* Standard test was highly correlated with the placement levels assigned by their ESL teachers.

Depending on target contexts, however, criteria of language performance may not be clearly identified or may vary substantially, such as in the case of the *TOEFL Primary* tests, which target general EFL contexts. Even in English-medium contexts (e.g., the *TOEFL Junior* tests and U.S. K-12 EL English language proficiency assessments), where the target criteria for students' performance are more clearly defined, we still have limited understanding of learners' abilities, mental processing, and strategies that they use to perform well in tasks in real classrooms and other social contexts. We need more basic information for *cognitive validity* (e.g., Field, 2011): information on learners' mental processes when engaging in tasks in testing and/or nontesting conditions, obtained through verbal reports or other means (e.g., eye-tracking and event-related potentials [ERPs]). Jang et al. (2017 in this volume) and Gu and So (2017 in this volume) have undertaken such efforts. It is also important to keep in mind that stakeholders' judgments may not be reliable, depending on the target context. For example, because English education for elementary school children is a new policy mandate in many parts of the world, teachers may not have sufficient professional experience to make reliable judgments on criteria. So (2014), who described how EFL teachers' voices were meaningfully incorporated into the process of developing the *TOEFL Junior* tests, also addressed how difficult this process was due to teachers' "heterogeneity in characteristics such as county, years of teaching experience, and types of schools, to name a few" (p. 301). Insight from learners themselves is important as well, but it may be difficult, if not impossible, for young learners to make criterion-related judgments even with substantial guidance, depending on their age and experiences.

Utilization

The utilization inference is based on the warrant that estimates of test takers' quality of performance (as measured by the test results) in a target domain is useful for decision making, such as monitoring their learning and placement. The underlying assumption for this warrant is that the meaning of test scores is clearly interpretable for test users and that one can expect to have a positive impact on young learners' L2/FL learning (Chapelle et al., 2008). Efforts have been made to make score interpretation material accessible to test users and to develop instructional material and workshops for teachers. In EFL contexts, researchers (e.g., Gu et al., 2017 in this volume; Papageorgiou & Cho, 2014) have just begun to understand and evaluate score-based decision-making procedures and their consequences among stakeholders of young learners (e.g., teachers, parents, program administrators, and policy makers).

It has been suggested that we need to critically review decision-making practices among test users in general (Kane, 2013a). When it comes to tests for young learners, because young learners are vulnerable to test-taking experiences as well as to successive decisions that are usually imposed on them by adults, it is critically important to listen to them; however, collecting their perspectives and opinions may not be easy depending on their age and experience with tests. Moreover, because they are beginning or in the midst of L2/FL learning while developing other knowledge and skills (or developing their first language, in some cases), it is difficult to predict long-term effects of tests, not to mention to make value judgments on them (i.e., positive or negative washback effects).

Unintended misuse of tests may be commonplace. Students who are outside of the age range that a test specifies or outside of the designated target learning context may take the test. For example, despite the test developers' intentions, a group of Japanese colleges decided to use the *TOEFL Junior* Comprehensive test scores for high school seniors (students outside of the defined age range) who did not learn English in English-medium instructional settings (a nontarget learning context) for admissions decisions—a very high-stakes purpose (Global edu, 2015). It is important to understand why such decisions are made and by whom, in addition to understanding the consequence of these decisions, in order to come up with better strategies to communicate with test users. If instructional materials or workshops are provided to teachers, care needs to be taken not to make a direct connection between the content of the material/workshops and that of the test, so that the materials and workshops will not be used for test-taking preparation purposes. It is a challenge to offer pedagogically useful assistance to teachers without imposing a particular view on how they should instruct young learners to develop target abilities L2/FL.

Finally, an increasingly common practice is to link learners' test scores in language proficiency tests with the Common European Framework of Reference (CEFR, Council of Europe, 2001), perhaps because doing so is appealing to test users; however, CEFR was not designed specifically for young learners. Using CEFR with young learners, therefore, requires not only modifications in the wording of descriptors (as seen in Papageorgiou & Baron, 2017 in this volume) but also an examination of the age appropriateness of descriptors (i.e., contextualizing the descriptors in test-taking children's lives while considering their cognitive and social developmental levels).

Future Directions and Conclusions

Empirical validation research for large-scale standardized tests for young learners is in its infancy. Based on the challenges to validity arguments articulated above, I next discuss three major issues for future validation research: namely, to better understand young learners' L2/FL language proficiency, use, and development; to better conceptualize the role of learning in standardized tests; and to better understand the use of, and consequences for, tests.

To Better Understand Young Learners' Second/Foreign Language Proficiency, Use, and Development

We need a better understanding of young learners' L2/FL proficiency and use—their knowledge, processes, and strategies—as well as their development. More information on how children from a wide range of contexts (both inside and outside of school/academic contexts) use language is indispensable. Corpus building on classroom language use and analyses based on such data would be very informative. Systematic longitudinal investigations of young L2/FL learners' language use and development remain limited; projects such as the Dynamic Language Learning Progressions project (Bailey & Heritage, 2014)—a longitudinal project monitoring academic English development among English-learning students in the United States—are very promising. Similar investigations of language use in other contexts are needed in order to understand the trajectory (more likely multiple trajectories by different student groups) of their L2/FL development.

As children develop their cognitive and other nonlinguistic abilities, we can expect that the role of these nonlinguistic factors in their task performance would change as well. As mentioned already, rigorous cognitive validity work from various contexts is necessary (e.g., Field, 2011). What kinds of cognitive and metacognitive knowledge and skills are required when young learners engage in tasks in their L2/FL? How do the roles of knowledge and skills vary according to task characteristics and children's development of L2/FL? As Jang et al. (2017 in this volume) suggested, we need more information about the role of social and affective factors such as motivation, interest, and anxiety in task performance.

As technology plays increasingly greater roles in young learners' lives, we need to know more about how they interact with technology and how they learn and use language through technology. Technology is a means for communication (language use) as well as a means for learning languages and other subject matter content (e.g., math and science). Young learners' use of language through technology may be different from their language use in physical settings (e.g., interactions in physical classrooms) and may require additional or different skills and strategies when using language online. We cannot simply assume that the "same" tasks delivered in computer and noncomputer formats would assess the same sets of abilities. As language-related activities are increasingly carried out in a multimodal fashion, we may need to redefine our constructs of language abilities. For example, listening ability may no longer be limited to processing aural information but also entail processing visual information. Similarly, reading ability involves processing not only print information but also various types of nonprint visual and aural information. Technology opens up new opportunities to assess young learners in innovative ways. For example, computer game-based assessment may make it possible to leverage big data and provide children with instant feedback while they engage in learning through games. It is important to keep in mind, however, that computer-mediated assessment tasks should represent children's actual language use on computers as well as their cognitive styles and interests. Finally, we need to identify individual differences in the experience of and attitudes toward technology and how these experiences and attitudes influence young learners' computer-mediated task performance. We may assume that modern-day children growing up in the technology era have positive attitudes toward computers and computer-mediated learning, but there is some evidence showing that this may not always be the case (Lebens, Graff, & Mayer, 2009).

To Better Conceptualize the Role of Learning in Standardized Tests

A strong emphasis on assessment for learning in young learners' education has influenced the way we approach the development and use of large-scale standardized tests. As mentioned already, researchers disagree about whether the notion of assessment for learning is really compatible with standardized testing (Green, 2014); however, there is no doubt that supporting learning should be an important purpose of any assessment for young learners, and that efforts should be made to incorporate some elements of fostering learning even in standardized tests. Because assessment for learning and assessment of learning stand on different theoretical and philosophical grounds, incorporating the elements of assisting one's learning into standardized testing will require substantial theoretical reformulations as well as innovations to address practical challenges.

What does "learning" entail? Does it refer to outcome (the traditional view) or process, or does it even include potential? Should learning still be conceptualized as a cognitive phenomenon (as in the traditional view) or should it be viewed as a more socially oriented phenomenon (e.g., learning is social as well as cognitive)? If standardized tests go beyond the traditional view of learning, should our conceptualizations of validity and reliability be changed? If so, how would these changes influence the argument-based approach to validation? A number of elements for assisting test takers' learning have been incorporated into standardized tests, including providing learning-oriented feedback (e.g., positive can-do statements in descriptors and score-interpretation assistance for teachers), offering children opportunities to learn new words while taking tests, incorporating self-assessment components, and so forth. These are very encouraging efforts, but it is not totally clear what roles these elements play in the interpretative validation arguments. The argument-based approach, at least the validity inferences that have been identified, does not seem to provide researchers with an appropriate framework for learning-oriented assessment. We need a clear conceptualization of the role of learning in standardized testing.

To Better Understand the Use and Consequences of Tests for Young Learners

The last major issue for future research concerns the use of tests for young learners and the consequences of such tests—specifically, their influence on learning and teaching (washback effects) and any larger effects on educational systems and societies (impact). Effects of a test can be caused by factors related to the test itself as well as other factors embedded in particular contexts where the test was implemented (Messick, 1996). As a given test can be used among various types of students for various purposes—such as placement, program evaluation, monitoring learners' progress, motivating learners (parents and teachers may ask children to take tests to motivate them), and admissions—research from diverse contexts is needed.

Previous research on washback effects—largely conducted on adults—highlights the substantial roles that teachers play in both positive and negative washback (Cheng, Sun, & Ma, 2015). Because the ultimate goal of any educational assessment/test is to support student learning, we should better understand how teachers use their students' test results to help the students facilitate their own learning; contextualized classroom-based research is called for. Given the large individual differences among the test-taking population, attention should be paid to varying consequences across individuals or groups of students who share similar characteristics.

Due to the association of English with global power, one may argue that young learners' English proficiency largely reflects their access to high-quality English education, which in turn is highly correlated with their socioeconomic status. For example, Chik and Besser (2011) described a situation in Hong Kong where a commercial-based English proficiency test was used to empower young learners who could afford to take it (thereby increasing their likelihood of being admitted into better secondary schools, even though the test did not have an official status in Hong Kong's educational system), while the test "systematically disadvantages other groups" (p. 88). Researchers should be mindful that the potential long-term effects of tests on learners vary according to their degree of access to English-learning resources. Given the growing importance of English proficiency among young learners, tests designed to be "low stakes" can easily be (mis)used for high-stakes decisions. Thus, we probably need to assume that English proficiency tests for young learners are potentially all high-stakes affairs.

Finally, we may need to move beyond our traditional approaches to understanding the "consequences," "washback," or "impact" of tests/test score interpretations. Empirical research on washback conducted so far has largely concentrated on examining flows in only one direction: from tests to individuals or societies. However, the needs and expectations of stakeholders and societies seem to have a substantial influence on test development processes and validation. Kane (2013a) asserts that "interpretations and uses can change over time in response to new needs and new understandings leading to changes in the evidence needed for validation" (p. 1). It would be nice to have a two-way flow of information to better understand mutually influential relationships between tests and individuals/societies.

In conclusion, because we are in the midst of many changes in environments and theories of young learners' L2/FL learning and assessment, we face a number of challenges developing and validating assessments. We need much more research—both theoretical and empirical—on assessment for young learners. Because a growing number of young learners are taking ELP standardized tests and because the potential consequences of test taking on their learning and lives can be substantial, the responsibilities of test developers, researchers, teachers, and other stakeholders are greater than ever.

Notes

1 In this chapter, the terms *assessment* and *test* are used interchangeably.
2 The *TOEFL iBT* test is a standardized proficiency test of English for academic purposes at the university level, and thus is intended for older learners.
3 Following a definition accepted in the task-based language teaching research, *authenticity* here refers to the extent to which situations or interactional patterns in the given task correspond to those found in the real world (Ellis, 2003).

References

Alibali, M. W., & Sidney, P. G. (2015). The role of intraindividual variability in learning and cognitive development. In M. Diehl, K. Hooker, & M. J. Sliwinski (Eds.), *Handbook of intraindividual variability across the life span* (pp. 84–102). New York: Routledge.

Atkinson, D. (Ed.). (2011). *Alternative approaches to second language acquisition*. London: Routledge.

Bachman, L., & Palmer, A. (2010). *Language assessment in practice: Developing language assessments and justifying their use in the real world*. Oxford, UK: Oxford University Press.

Bailey, A. L. (2017). Issues to consider in the assessment of young learners' English language proficiency. In M. K. Wolf & Y. G. Butler (Eds.), *English language proficiency assessments for young learners* (pp. 25–40). New York, NY: Routledge.

Bailey, A. L., & Heritage, M. (2014). The role of language learning progressions in improved instruction and assessment of English language learners. *TESOL Quarterly*, *48*(3), 480–506.

Black, P. J., & Wiliam, D. (1998). Assessment and classroom learning. *Assessment in Education: Principles Policy and Practice*, *5*, 7–73.

Brookhart, S. M. (2003). Developing measurement theory for classroom assessment purposes and uses. *Educational Measurement: Issues and Practice*, *22*(4), 5–12.

Butler, Y. G. (2015). The use of computer games as foreign language learning tasks for digital natives. *System*, *54*, 91–102.

Butler, Y. G., & Zeng, W. (2011). The roles that teachers play in paired-assessments for young learners. In D. Tsagari & I. Csepes (Eds.), *Classroom-based language assessment* (pp. 77–92). Frankfurt: Peter Lang.

Carpenter, K., Fujii, N., & Kataoka, H. (1995). An oral interview procedure for assessing second language abilities in children. *Language Testing*, *12*(2), 158–181.

Chapelle, C. A., Enright, M. E., & Jamieson, J. M. (2008). Test score interpretation and use. In C. A. Chapelle, M. K. Enright, & J. M. Jamieson (Eds.), *Building a validity argument for the test of English as a foreign language* (pp. 1–25). New York: Routledge.

Cheng, L., Sun, Y., & Ma, J. (2015). Review of washback research literature within Kane's argument based validation framework. *Language Teaching*, *48*(4), 436–470.

Chik, A., & Besser, S. (2011). International language test taking among young learners: A Hong Kong case study. *Language Assessment Quarterly*, *8*(1), 73–91.

Cho, Y., Ginsburgh, M., Morgan, R., Moulder, B., Xi, X., & Hauck, M. C. (2017). Designing TOEFL® Primary™ tests. In M. K. Wolf & Y. G. Butler (Eds.), *English language proficiency assessments for young learners* (pp. 41–58). New York, NY: Routledge.

Council of Europe. (2001). *Common European Framework of Reference for languages: Learning, teaching, assessment*. Cambridge: Cambridge University Press.

Cronbach, L. J. (1988). Five perspectives on validity argument. In H. Wainer & H. Braun (Eds.), *Test validity* (pp. 3–17). Hillsdale, NJ: Lawrence Erlbaum.

Ellis, R. (2003). *Task-based language learning and teaching*. Oxford: Oxford University Press.

Field, J. (2011). Cognitive validity. In L. Taylor (Ed.), *Examining speaking* (pp. 65–111). Cambridge, UK: Cambridge University Press.

Global edu. (2015, October 5). TOEFL Junior—Tsukuba-nado 6 daigaku-ga nyushi-de saiyou [Six universities such as Tsukuba University will accept TOEFL Junior scores for admission]. Available from http://globaledu.jp/%E3%80%8Ctoefl-junior-13056.html

Green, A. (2014). *Exploring language assessment and testing: Language in action*. London: Routledge.

Gu, L. (2014). At the interface between language testing and second language acquisition: Language ability and context of learning. *Language Testing*, *31*(1), 111–133.

Gu, L. (2015). Language ability of young English language learners: Definition, configuration, and implications. *Language Testing*, *32*(1), 21–38.

Gu, L., Lockwood, J. R., & Powers, D. (2017). Making a validity argument for using the TOEFL Junior® Standard test as a measure of progress for young English language learners. In M. K. Wolf & Y. G. Butler (Eds.), *English language proficiency assessments for young learners* (pp. 153–170). New York, NY: Routledge.

Gu, L., & So, Y. (2017). Strategies used by young English learners in an assessment context. In M. K. Wolf & Y. G. Butler (Eds.), *English language proficiency assessments for young learners* (pp. 118–135). New York, NY: Routledge.

Hauck, M. C., Pooler, E., Wolf, M. K., Lopez, A., & Anderson, D. (2017). Designing task types for English language proficiency assessments for K-12 English learners in the U.S. In M. K. Wolf & Y. G. Butler (Eds.), *English language proficiency assessments for young learners* (pp. 79–95). New York, NY: Routledge.

Jang, E. E., Vincett, M., van der Boom, E., Lau, C., & Yang, Y. (2017). Considering young learners' characteristics in developing a diagnostic assessment intervention. In M. K. Wolf & Y. G. Butler (Eds.), *English language proficiency assessments for young learners* (pp. 193–213). New York, NY: Routledge.

Kane, M. T. (2013a). Validating the interpretation and uses of test scores. *Journal of Educational Measurement*, *50*(1), 1–73.

Kane, M. T. (2013b). The argument-based approach to validation. *School Psychology Review*, *42*(4), 448–457.

Kane, M. T., Crooks, T., & Cohen, A. (1999). Validating measures of performance. *Educational Measurement: Issues and Practice*, *18*(2), 5–17.

Lebens, M., Graff, M., & Mayer, P. (2009). Access, attitudes and the digital divide: Children's attitudes towards computers in a technology-rich environment. *Educational Media International, 46*(3), 255–266.

Lewis, M. D. (2000). The promise of dynamic systems approaches for an integrated account of human development. *Child Development, 71*, 36–43.

Littlewood, W. (2007). Communicative and task-based language teaching in East Asian classrooms. *Language Teaching, 40*, 243–249.

Messick, S. (1989). Validity. In R. L. Linn (Ed.), *Educational measurement* (3rd ed., pp. 13–103). New York: Macmillan.

Messick, S. (1996). Validity and washback in language testing. *Language Testing, 13*, 243–256.

Mills, K. A. (2010). A review of the "digital turn" in the new literacy studies. *Review of Educational Research, 80*(2), 246–271.

Oliver, R. (2002). The patterns of negotiation for meaning in children interactions. *The Modern Language Journal, 81*(1), 97–111.

Papageorgiou, S., & Baron, P. (2017). Using the Common European Framework of Reference to facilitate score interpretations for young learners' English language proficiency assessments. In M. K. Wolf & Y. G. Butler (Eds.), *English language proficiency assessments for young learners* (pp. 136–152). New York, NY: Routledge.

Papageorgiou, S., & Cho, Y. (2014). An investigation of the use of TOEFL® Junior™ Standard scores for ESL placement decisions in secondary education. *Language Testing, 31*(2), 223–239.

Papageorgiou, S., Xi, X., Morgan, R., & So, Y. (2015). Developing and validating band levels and descriptors for reporting overall examinee performance. *Language Assessment Quarterly, 12*, 153–177.

Poehner, M. E., Zhang, J., & Lu, X. (2017). Computerized dynamic assessments for young language learners. In M. K. Wolf & Y. G. Butler (Eds.), *English language proficiency assessments for young learners* (pp. 214–233). New York, NY: Routledge.

Prensky, M. (2001). *Digital game-based learning*. New York: McGraw-Hill.

Shin, S.-K. (2005). Did they take the same test? Examinee language proficiency and the structure of language tests. *Language Testing, 22*(1), 31–57.

Shore, J. R., Wolf, M. K., O'Reilly, T., & Sabatini, J. P. (2017). Measuring 21st century reading comprehension through scenario-based assessments. In M. K. Wolf & Y. G. Butler (Eds.), *English language proficiency assessments for young learners* (pp. 234–252). New York, NY: Routledge.

Siegler, R. S. (2006). Microgenetic analyses of learning. In D. Kuhn & R. S. Siegler (Eds.), *Handbook of child psychology, Vol. 2: Cognition, perception and language* (6th ed., pp. 464–510). Hoboken, NJ: Wiley.

So, Y. (2014). Are teacher perspectives useful? Incorporating EFL teacher feedback in the development of a large-scale international English test. *Language Assessment Quarterly, 11*, 283–303.

So, Y., Wolf, M. K., Hauck, M. C., Mollaun, P., Rybinski, P., Tumposky, D., & Wang, L. (2017). TOEFL Junior® design framework. In M. K. Wolf & Y. G. Butler (Eds.), *English language proficiency assessments for young learners* (pp. 59–78). New York, NY: Routledge.

Stricker, L. J., & Rock, D. A. (2008). Factor structure of the TOEFL Internet-Based Test across subgroups. *TOEFL iBT Research Report No. 07*. Princeton, NJ: Educational Testing Service.

van Dijk, M., & van Geert, P. (2015). The nature and meaning of intraindividual variability in development in the early life span. In M. Diehl, K. Hooker, & M. J. Sliwinski (Eds.), *Handbook of intraindividual variability across the life span* (pp. 37–58). New York: Routledge.

Vygotsky, L. S. (1978). *Mind and society*. Cambridge, MA: Harvard University Press.

Zu, J., Moulder, B., & Morgan, R. (2017). A field test study for the *TOEFL® Primary*™ Reading and Listening tests. In M. K. Wolf & Y. G. Butler (Eds.), *English language proficiency assessments for young learners* (pp. 99–117). New York, NY: Routledge.

SUBJECT INDEX

21st-century skills 234, 248

academic English 62, 63, 140, 267; *see also* academic language
academic language 62, 63, 66, 85, 193, 241; *see also* academic English
administration procedures/settings 11, 222, 263
affective 5, 8, 15, 120, 193, 194, 208, 256, 258, 261, 262, 267; affective factors 8–9
affordances 32
alternative assessment(s) 27, 31, 34
American Council on the Teaching of Foreign Languages (ACTFL) Proficiency Guidelines 137
argument-based approach 255, 259, 260, 268
assessment for learning 9, 29, 258–9, 268
assessment of learning 9, 30, 258–9, 268
attention spans 8, 11, 50, 100, 173, 196, 263

band level 74, 101, 110–12; *see also* score level
basic interpersonal communication skills (BICS) 62
behaviorist models of learning 31
biserial correlation 105, 107

can-do descriptors 137
classical item analysis 14, 105, 107, 116, 262; classical test theory 262
cognitive academic language proficiency (CALP) 62

cognitive development 5, 7–8, 91, 184, 262
cognitive process 120, 132, 133, 134, 174, 194, 196, 197, 203, 257
cognitive strategy 185, 197, 202; metacognitive strategies 197
cognitive validity 195, 203, 265, 267
college and career readiness (CCR) standards 81, 234
Common Core State Standards (CCSS) 81, 241
communicative competence model 132
communicative language ability model 7
communicative language use model 132
Complex Adaptive Systems (CAS) theory 13, 31–2
conceptual assessment framework 83, 84, 85
construct 5, 7, 10, 13, 27, 28, 34, 42, 44, 45, 46–7, 65–8, 84–6, 93, 120, 133, 154, 222, 225, 234–6, 240–1, 260, 267
construct-irrelevant 14, 92, 118, 121, 124, 132, 133, 154
construct-relevant 11, 12, 49, 121, 124, 264; construct-irrelevant 121
construct validation 99, 154
constructed-response item 51, 53, 73, 141, 247
content coverage 25, 27, 138, 147
Council of Europe 31, 41, 71, 136, 137, 138, 148
cut scores 10, 74, 110, 141, 142, 146

design feature 53, 120, 177, 240–1, 247
diagnostic assessment 15, 193–5, 200, 208
diagnostic feedback 16, 193, 194, 199, 207–8
domain analysis 83–5
domain description 56–7, 260, 261
domain modeling 83, 84
dynamic assessment (DA) 28–9, 195, 214, 218–20; computerized dynamic assessment 215, 221
Dynamic Language Learning Progressions (DLLP) Project 32, 267
dynamic system 32, 194, 258; dynamic systems theory 32, 258

effect size 166, 179, 180
Elementary and Secondary Educational Act 80
EL identification 171, 172
ELP standards 6, 14, 61, 80–5, 87, 88, 90, 93
emotion 9, 16, 195, 196, 199, 207, 209, 213; academic emotions 196, 199, 207
enabling skills 65, 67, 68
English as a foreign language (EFL) contexts 6, 29, 34, 149, 265
English as a second language (ESL) contexts 3, 4, 5, 6, 10, 13, 15, 265
English language development (ELD) assessments 62
English language learning contexts 5, 60
English language proficiency 3, 4, 5, 25 34, 42, 60, 79, 99, 110, 119, 136, 153, 154, 169, 171, 187, 255, 259
English language proficiency (ELP) construct 13, 33, 39, 84, 87, 93
English Language Proficiency Assessment for the 21st Century (ELPA21) 13, 80, 81, 82, 85, 86, 87, 88, 89, 90, 91
English Language Proficiency Assessments for California (ELPAC) 13, 80, 81, 82, 86, 88, 89, 90, 91, 92
English learner (EL) students, K–12 79
English Learner Formative Assessment (ELFA) 235, 240–9
English-medium 6, 34, 60, 61, 62, 63, 68, 69, 70, 140, 144, 154, 262, 265, 266
equating 73, 100, 111, 112, 263; equipercentile equating method 142; pre-equating 100
error analysis 178, 179, 182–4, 187
European Language Portfolio 31, 45, 138, 139
evaluation 255, 260, 262–3, 269

Every Student Succeeds Act (ESSA) 80
evidence-centered design 73, 79, 80, 82–3, 235
expected score 260, 263, 264
explanation 260, 264
extrapolation 260, 264

federal accountability 80, 91
field test 54, 55, 85, 99–111, 116, 146
formative assessment 9, 16, 29–30, 32, 92, 235, 247–8
formulaic chunks 5, 44
foundational reading skills 237, 240, 241, 243

games 27, 34, 35, 257, 262, 268; game-based assessment 35, 267
generalization 260, 263
Global, Integrated Scenario-Based Assessment (GISA) 235
growth 10, 15, 27, 153, 154, 155, 166–9, 194, 208, 209

higher-order reading comprehension 237; higher-order comprehension skills 240, higher-order reading skills 240

individual difference 187, 256, 263, 268, 269
informal assessments 27
initial ELP screener assessment 171, 173, 187
integrated language skills 86, 87
internal structure 99, 264
interpretation/use argument 255, 259, 261
interval 155, 158–60
item parameters 49, 54, 106, 107, 113
item response theory (IRT) 54, 100, 101, 104, 105, 107, 115, 146, 194, 262
item specifications 84
item/task design 11

language demands 62–3, 81, 82, 85, 86, 196; of academic contexts 62
Language Form and Meaning 67, 68, 140, 143, 155
language functions 30, 31, 45, 62, 64, 85, 195
language learner strategies 120, 121, 124, 125, 126, 130, 131, 132, 133
language progression 28, 32
learning objectives 14, 136, 137, 139, 141, 148, 259

learning-oriented assessment 194, 208, 212, 268
lexile 56–8
linguistic analysis 177–8
linguistic errors 177–8, 182–3, 186
literacy 6, 26, 79, 91, 92, 171, 196, 234, 235, 236, 238, 248, 257
longitudinal 15, 154, 155, 156, 267

mapping study/studies 141, 142, 144, 145, 148, 162
mediation 16, 195, 202, 204, 207, 208, 215, 218–28; mediated score(s) 224, 225; mediation process 16, 222, 226, 228, 229
metacognition 16, 196, 197, 236, 239
metacognitive control 197, 198, 199, 205, 207, 208, 209
model of language knowledge 65, 69, 264
modified Angoff procedure 141
motivation 8–9, 11, 26–7, 59, 163, 168, 195, 197–9, 207, 209, 236, 262, 267
multilevel models (MLM) 162–3
multiple choice 50, 51, 54, 55, 100, 125, 144, 154, 175, 199, 221

No Child Left Behind (NCLB) 80
non-EL student(s) 15, 172, 174, 177, 179, 180–3, 185–8
nonexperimental repeated measures 154
nonparametric smooth regression 164

observation(s) 5, 10, 27, 29, 30, 32, 44, 131, 139, 171, 180, 182, 215, 245, 260, 262
observed score(s) 260, 262, 263
organizational knowledge 65

paired-assessment 29, 34
parallel forms 99
performance descriptors 45, 56, 71, 72, 73–5, 110, 111, 137, 141, 143
performance moderator 236, 237, 248
pilot testing 48, 50, 52, 91, 99, 100, 101
portfolio assessment 10, 30–1
pragmatic knowledge 69, 88, 125, 129, 132, 203–5
proficiency levels 3, 11, 14, 41, 43, 88, 89, 110, 112, 113, 118, 120, 121, 137, 139, 174, 208, 215, 263
proficiency scale(s) 56, 137, 139
prototype 48, 75, 85, 119, 121–2, 172–6, 178, 239, 247, 262
prototyping 48, 89, 99, 100, 118, 119, 172

Rasch model 137
raw scores 72–3, 105, 106–7, 111–15
Reading Inventory of Scholastic Evaluation (RISE) 237
reading process(es) 205, 236, 243, 248
reliability 49, 50, 55, 74, 110, 111, 115–16, 142, 179, 247, 259, 263, 268
rubric(s) 15, 72, 73, 75–6, 120, 140, 142, 174, 177–9, 181, 184, 186, 188, 262, 263

scaffolding 13, 33, 53, 86, 89–92, 172, 177, 188, 195, 202, 204, 208, 209, 214, 216–18, 220–1, 238–40, 242–3, 247
scale score(s) 71, 101, 110, 111–12, 115, 158, 165
scaling 10, 14, 111, 116, 146, 263
scenario-based assessment (SBA) 16, 175, 234–49
score band 55–6
score level 71, 72, 73, 74–5, 142–3, 147; see also band level
score report 9, 10, 12, 55, 56, 59, 71–2, 142, 169
second language acquisition 13, 25–6, 187, 214, 256, 257
self-assessment 10, 27, 30, 35, 139, 197, 199–200, 268
self-efficacy 196, 197, 202
self-regulated 16, 194–5, 208; self-regulation 208, 236, 239
sensitivity analysis/analyses 157–8, 166–7
social cultural theory (SCT) 29–30
social interactionist theory/theories 13, 28–9
social language 62–3
socio-emotional development 26–7
speaking task(s) 49, 53, 70, 75, 90, 120, 172, 174–5, 179, 180, 182
standard error of measurement 111, 115
standard setting 10, 14, 71, 85, 93, 101, 110, 141
standardized assessment(s) 4, 10, 15–16, 27, 33–5, 84, 90–1, 169, 171–2
standardized test(s) 30, 100, 111, 153, 172, 221, 255–9, 266, 268, 270
stealth assessment 35
strategic competence 7, 120, 132
strategic reading 237, 239, 248
strategies: test-management strategies 120–1, 125–6, 130, 133; test-taking strategies 119–21, 130–1, 243; test-wiseness strategies 120–1, 124–6, 130–1
systemic functional linguistic theory 13

Subject Index

target domain 257, 260–2, 265
target language use 6, 29, 261
target language use (TLU) domain(s) 6, 10, 59, 76, 187, 257; the characteristics of 61
target language use tasks 65–6, 70
target score 260
task-based language teaching (TBLT) 270
task content 173, 256
task design(s) 11, 13–14, 31, 48, 53, 87, 89, 173, 187, 241–2, 262
task type(s) 12–13, 15, 19, 33, 46, 48–50, 52–3, 79, 83–6, 120, 183, 186–7, 240
technology 13, 16, 33–6, 49, 93, 172, 239, 257, 267–8
test blueprints 84, 113
test characteristic curves 113, 114
test practice effects 167
test structure 51–2, 54, 101
TOEFL iBT 56, 75, 104, 118–20, 255, 259, 270
TOEFL Junior 13–15, 59–76, 118, 136, 140–5, 153–5, 261, 263

TOEFL Primary 13–14, 41–2, 45–6, 48, 50–2, 54–8, 99–101, 107–8, 110–13, 115–19, 121–2, 133, 136, 140–8, 261, 263
transfer 6, 16, 28, 224–7

U.S. K–12 English language proficiency (ELP) assessments 4, 13, 14, 79, 80–9, 91, 92, 93
utilization 260, 265

validity argument(s) 14–16, 25, 41, 56–7, 100, 153, 240, 255, 259, 266
validity evidence 12, 14, 59, 76, 97, 99, 116, 154, 239, 246
verbal reports 120, 123, 174, 265

warrant 260–5
working memory 7–8, 26, 173

zone of proximal development (ZPD) 16, 28, 215, 219; zone of actual development 219